Economics for Nonprofit Managers and Social Entrepreneurs

To Julius Margolis, Richard Nelson, Robert Solow, Stephen Spurr and
Michael Lavelle, S.J., our early mentors who inspired us to learn economics
and teach it to others

Our book may be a public good, but I hope they realize they have to pay for it!

Economics for Nonprofit Managers and Social Entrepreneurs

Dennis R. Young

National Center on Nonprofit Enterprise
Georgia State University
Jack, Joseph and Morton Mandel School of Applied Social Sciences, Case Western Reserve University, USA

Richard Steinberg

Indiana University – Purdue University Indianapolis (IUPUI), USA

Rosemarie Emanuele

Ursuline College, Pepper Pike, Ohio, USA

Walter O. Simmons

Boler College of Business, John Carroll University, USA

Edward Elgar PUBLISHING

Cheltenham, UK • Northampton, MA, USA

Published by
Edward Elgar Publishing Limited
The Lypiatts
15 Lansdown Road
Cheltenham
Glos GL50 2JA
UK

Edward Elgar Publishing, Inc.
William Pratt House
9 Dewey Court
Northampton
Massachusetts 01060
USA

A catalogue record for this book
is available from the British Library

Library of Congress Control Number: 2018967799

Printed on elemental chlorine free (ECF)
recycled paper containing 30% Post-Consumer Waste

ISBN 978 1 78643 675 7 (cased)
ISBN 978 1 78643 677 1 (paperback)
ISBN 978 1 78643 676 4 (eBook)

Typeset by Servis Filmsetting Ltd, Stockport, Cheshire
Printed and Bound in the USA

Contents in brief

Full contents

Tables

About the authors

Dennis R. Young is Professor Emeritus at Georgia State University and Visiting Professor in the Jack, Joseph, and Morton Mandel School of Applied Social Sciences at Case Western Reserve University. He is current and founding editor of the journal *Nonprofit Policy Forum* and founding editor of *Nonprofit Management and Leadership*. His awards include an honorary doctorate from the University of Liege in 2010 and the Award for Distinguished Achievement and Leadership in Nonprofit and Voluntary Action Research from ARNOVA in 2004. His recent books include *Financing Nonprofits and Other Social Enterprises: A Benefits Approach* (Edward Elgar Publishing, 2017) and *The Social Enterprise Zoo* (with Elizabeth A.M. Searing and Cassady V. Brewer, Edward Elgar Publishing, 2016).

Richard Steinberg is Professor of Economics and Philanthropic Studies at IUPUI and its Lilly Family School of Philanthropy. He is the coeditor of *The Nonprofit Sector: A Research Handbook* (Yale University Press, 2006, 2nd ed.) with Walter W. Powell and has served as Co-President of ARNOVA (Association for Research on Nonprofit Organizations and Voluntary Action). His research concerns public policy towards nonprofit organizations and donations, the determinants of giving and volunteering, the managerial economics of nonprofits, and the three-failures theory of the role of nonprofit organizations in a mixed economy. He is an enthusiastic actor in community theater, building social capital through his appearances as Friar Laurence in *Romeo and Juliet*, Father Finnegan in *Harold and Maude*, Jonathan Brewster in *Arsenic and Old Lace*, and Mr. Dussel in *The Diary of Anne Frank*.

Rosemarie Emanuele earned her Ph.D. in Economics from Boston College in 1992. Her dissertation, *The Demand for Volunteer Labor Under Impure Altruism: An Inquiry into Demand-Side Behavior by Nonprofit Organizations* was funded in part by the Indiana University Center on Philanthropy. Her research on the nonprofit sector focuses on the labor market, especially volunteer labor. In addition to teaching Math and Economics to undergraduate students, she has taught in the nonprofit management programs of Case Western Reserve University and John Carroll University, and the MBA program of Ursuline College. She is currently a Professor in the departments of Business and Mathematics at Ursuline College.

Walter O. Simmons is Professor of Economics and the Associate Dean for Graduate and International Programs in the Boler College of Business, John Carroll University, in Cleveland, Ohio. Professor Simmons developed and teaches the Economics of the Nonprofit Sector class to graduate students at his institution. He was a Visiting Professor of Economics at Regent's University, London, and St. Georges University, Grenada. He has received many distinguished awards, including the "Excellence in Education" award from *Ohio Magazine*, for outstanding performance as educator and teacher in Ohio.

Foreword

Patrick Rooney

Since the original edition of this book was published more than twenty years ago, the nonprofit sector, philanthropy, and indeed the study of economics, have changed in a number of important ways, making a compelling case for a substantially new and revised version. All of the chapters in this book reflect these changes to some degree. For example, the text is now laced with applications to social enterprise and entrepreneurship in addition to traditional nonprofit management and philanthropy. Moreover, several new chapters – on decision making under risk, game theory and behavioral and experimental economics – address the changes more fully. At the same time, many of the fundamental issues facing nonprofit management and philanthropy have not changed very much, so that the underlying concepts introduced in the original edition and retained in this revised version, remain as salient as ever.

One of the most important trends over the past 20 years has been an ever greater blurring of the nonprofit, business and governmental sectors to the point that terminology used in one sector is now applied across the sectors. For example, fund-raisers and nonprofit leaders have "borrowed" the phrase Return on Investment (ROI) from the business community to convey that grants and gifts to their charity would yield an ROI – although they really mean a societal rather than narrowly financial ROI. In the present era of social entrepreneurs, impact investing, program-related investments (PRIs), and so on, ROI has simultaneously taken on both a more precise and more vague meaning.

Recently, I had a conversation with two people interested in Social Impact Equity Investing. They explained that the expected ROI for these investments is in the 4 percent to 20 percent per year range, whereas for the Social Impact Loans (including PRIs), the expected ROI might be in the 1 percent to 2 percent range. These compare favorably (or not) to "Social Impact Grants," which generate a complete loss of the financial investment from the traditional for-profit ROI perspective; however, grant makers and grantees hope that the grants create substantial social ROI through the good works enabled by the grant. This book will be useful to social entrepreneurs, philanthropies and others involved in such discussions as it clearly differentiates between private and social costs and benefits and provides ways to understand social returns of philanthropy, nonprofits and social enterprises.

Another important trend is the growth in sheer size and impact of the non-profit sector and philanthropy. Total philanthropic giving has more than doubled since 1995 – even after adjusting for inflation (see *Giving USA 2017*). The growth in jobs in the nonprofit sector makes it one of the larg-est employment segments in our entire economy. As nonprofits have grown larger and more numerous, so have business corporations and governmental agencies. Moreover, the economy is now inherently more global and interac-tive both in its transactions and in the intentions of its component organi-zations, which makes decision making in the nonprofit, philanthropic, and social enterprise sectors both more complicated and riskier. Accordingly, this revised version of the book updates the chapter on "the place of the social sector in the economy" and adds chapters on "market power," "economic decision making under risk," and "games of collaboration and competition."

Of course, the advent of the Internet and social media have disrupted the philanthropic sector in ways that would make Joseph Schumpeter smile – even if in disbelief. Individual donors and major foundations are all demand-ing more "metrics," more "value added" and more "impact." This has made philanthropy a more competitive marketplace but one that can offer tre-mendous first mover advantages to those clever enough to understand the research in economics, and can "think at the margin" and conduct proper cost–benefit analyses (CBA) as this book prescribes.

Many things have not changed over the past two decades, including the dif-ferentiating force of the nondistribution constraint, the fundamental laws of supply and demand, the challenges of free riders and public goods, and the actual and/or perceived pressures for charities to report low fund-raising and overhead costs. This book does a fantastic job of distilling these concepts for charities, nonprofits and social enterprises, applying them in a manner that is especially meaningful and relevant to nonprofit leaders and social entrepreneurs.

As a faculty member, I have taught the Economics of the Philanthropic Sector regularly for the past twenty years and have always used this book as one of the required readings. I have found it to provide elegant and simple approaches without being too technical or too simplistic for both the person not versed in economics and for faculty members, who are well versed in economics and the nonprofit sector, but who need a tool to help their students understand both the theoretical constructs and the applications of economics to philanthropy, nonprofit organizations and social ventures. For example, the book helps us to think at the margin in decision making in ways that may not be obvious. Are volunteers free? Charities don't pay them wages, but somebody on staff must manage the process and the volunteers, and the volunteers need training and often incur incidental costs to the charity. How do we assess the opportunity cost to the organization? For the volunteers themselves, is their value the opportunity cost of their time or the value of the work being done by the volunteer? Volunteers donate their time for many different reasons, including altruism, skill acquisition, career networking, and expanding one's dating options, as well as others. Do we think about the opportunity cost of the volunteer differently depending on their motivations?

Another important subject for philanthropy and nonprofit management is the optimization of fund-raising efforts for any given charity. Given the charity ratings, media coverage of charities with high fund-raising costs, and web access to IRS 990s, nonprofits may be inclined to keep their average fund-raising costs low. I use the book to stress that organizations need to think about fund-raising costs and benefits on the margin – not only in an overall manner but in allocating investments in fund-raising between various fund-raising strategies and tactics.

I look forward to using this new and revised edition in the future!

 REFERENCES

Lilly Family School of Philanthropy, *Giving USA 2017*. Published by Giving USA Foundation.

Patrick Rooney
Executive Associate Dean for Academic Programs
Professor of Economics and Philanthropic Studies
Indiana University Lilly Family School of Philanthropy
December 2018

Foreword to the 1995 edition

Burton A. Weisbrod

Dennis Young and Richard Steinberg have produced the first introductory textbook intended primarily for students of nonprofit management. These organizations constitute a rapidly expanding sector of the economy, and economics has much to contribute to our understanding of the factors that shape their decisions.

Nonprofit organizations combine attributes of the private sector and government in fascinating ways. Both students and managers of nonprofit organizations need to understand the elements of the economist's "tool kit," and Young and Steinberg have provided a fine introduction to microeconomics as it applies to the nonprofit sector in a mixed economy. Amending the conventional analysis to accommodate the special characteristics of the nonprofit marketplace, they have done much more, however, than simply demonstrate that traditional economic analysis can be extended to nonprofit organizations.

By showing that nonprofit organizations typically face competition not only from other nonprofits but from private firms and sometimes governments, Young and Steinberg challenge the reader to think about differing organizational goals ("objective functions") and how they affect the outcome of the competitive process. Are nonprofits more altruistic than other organizations? Are nonprofit managers really different from their private enterprise and government counterparts – that is, less motivated to maximize their own incomes? By highlighting the "nondistribution constraint," which restricts what a nonprofit organization may do to achieve its goals – for example, paying out to managers any profit they generate – Young and Steinberg compel the reader to think about regulatory problems and the limits to competition in industries where consumers are poorly informed.

They also show how subjects examined in conventional texts can be understood through illustrations from the nonprofit world. Thus, for example, when they turn to labor markets, they focus on volunteer labor. While volunteer labor is not even counted in official labor-force statistics, and is generally unimportant for private firms, it is a significant factor in the nonprofit world, and Young and Steinberg show how even volunteers respond to economic forces despite their lack of pay. Similarly, when they discuss how revenues affect a nonprofit organization's decisions, they focus on charitable donations, demonstrating for the reader how supply and demand operate even in unconventional markets, the reasons why people donate, and how a nonprofit organization is able to affect the amount of donations it receives.

The concept of "market failure," applied to activities such as basic medical research and aid to the poor – which private firms cannot be counted on to provide at efficient levels because they benefit persons other than those who pay for them – is fundamentally important in economics. In most textbooks, such activities are said to justify a role for government. Young and Steinberg show, however, how nonprofit organizations are also active in the provision of such goods and services. In the process, they justify the need for nonprofit organizations in a predominately private-enterprise economy, and they highlight the questions of what society should expect from nonprofits relative to government.

These discussions make it clear that nonprofits are both like and unlike private firms and public-sector entities. No organization can avoid making decisions about precisely what goods and services to provide, how to allocate resources to produce them, to whom they should be made available, and how to finance these activities. Economics can help us understand how the ways in which organizations deal with these matters determine which organizations will survive, whether nonprofit organizations will displace private firms from certain markets or industries in the long run or, instead, be driven out by them, and whether taxes and subsidies have the same kinds of effects on nonprofit organizations as they do on private firms.

In chapter after chapter, problems faced by nonprofit managers are analyzed with the tools of introductory microeconomics. Young and Steinberg illustrate their lessons with lively examples involving such varied nonprofits as universities, museums, day-care centers, and Meals on Wheels programs, while touching on such practical questions as whether to raise funds through direct mail or phone solicitation and whether public subsidies to nonprofits distort these decisions. As a result, readers of this well-written introduction to economics are rewarded by learning the fundamentals of economics as they apply to decisions faced by nonprofit managers in output and input markets and to the relationships of nonprofits with private firms and governments.

Preface

This new and revised version of what was originally entitled *Economics for Nonprofit Managers* is long overdue. Since the original publication in 1995, the field of nonprofit management education has expanded enormously in both size and scope. Hardly a U.S. university is without some form of nonprofit management education program, and within the field of public administration in particular, the study of nonprofits has become *de rigueur*. Moreover, nonprofit management study has spread throughout the world, with university programs found on every continent. In addition, the framework for studying nonprofit management has expanded to new kinds of social purpose organizations – various types of "social enterprises" including social businesses and social cooperatives – which, like traditional nonprofits, combine the pursuit of social mission with success in the economic marketplace. Thus, in addition to nonprofit managers, we now speak of "social entrepreneurs" responsible for establishing, growing and maintaining these enterprises.

Following these developments, and while maintaining the core text, we have decided to widen the purview of this book to accommodate the broader contemporary field of social purpose organizations. In some ways, this makes things easier for us because economics is grounded in the study of the marketplace and the new forms of social enterprise and social entrepreneurial management are more explicitly grounded in the market environment and more focused on market success. However, these new forms present a somewhat different challenge. While traditional nonprofits need to acquire greater awareness and sophistication about operating in a market setting, the new social enterprises may instead require a greater appreciation for their differences from traditional for-profit businesses. For nonprofits, progress towards mission is impossible without economic success, but for social enterprises that seek profits as well as mission impact, success must be measured in terms of economic and social benefits broader than simply financial surplus.

As was the case when we published the original edition, economics is not yet a strong suit in the graduate education of nonprofit managers. In some university programs, economics still remains absent from the curriculum despite its critical importance to understanding how to make decisions when resources are scarce, as they always are. In programs of public administration, economics is commonly taught in a traditional way without any special focus on the nonprofit sector or social enterprise, and with general emphasis on public sector issues and decisions. In schools of business, economics is also taught in traditional ways, but with more attention to business sector decision making. As in the original edition, the special contribution of this book is its explicit focus on nonprofit organizations and social enterprises, an orientation not found in other texts.

Why is this important? Aren't the basic concepts, principles and tools of microeconomic analysis generic and the same for all sectors? The answer to that is certainly 'yes' but the application of these ideas in the domain of nonprofit organizations and social enterprises can be subtly or even substantially different. In this book we apply the basic concepts – thinking at the margin, opportunity cost, market failure, externalities and public goods, costs and benefits, and so on – to the peculiar and particular challenges that nonprofits and social enterprises commonly face: raising charitable funds, pricing services to account for social as well as revenue goals, allocating volunteer resources, collaborating as well as competing with peer organizations, operating programs with alternative social and profitmaking objectives, balancing the welfare of different societal groups and constituencies, and so on. These applications are not only specifically responsive to the needs of nonprofit managers and social entrepreneurs, but they add nuance to the perspectives of managers in other parts of the economy as well. For example, managers of traditional corporations and small businesses are increasingly aware of the importance of community relations and social image to the success of their products and services, hence they too are finding it essential to consider social goals in their strategic decisions. And as government has become more dependent on private organizations, especially nonprofits, to deliver public services under contract or through various systems of regulation and subsidy, public officials too must become more knowledgeable about the economics of these organizations, how they make their decisions, and how they can remain viable. It is our hope, therefore, that this text can make a significant contribution to the education of organizational managers across the economy, not just within a narrowly defined category of nonprofits and social enterprises. As for traditional nonprofits themselves, it has become clear over the past few decades that success depends more and more on sophisticated market strategies to navigate an increasingly competitive economic environment in which growing numbers of nonprofits compete among themselves for scarce charitable dollars and volunteer resources, and often compete with businesses for market share in their service markets. Our hope is that this

xxii • Economics for nonprofit managers and social entrepreneurs

new edition helps the leaders of these organizations think through those strategies.

Similarly, we hope that this text continues to contribute to the teaching of economics in general by demystifying the discipline and demonstrating its very pragmatic value. Traditionally economics has been taught in graduate schools by building on the relatively abstract mathematical foundations of classical microeconomic theory. Our perspective here, as in the original book, is that the important ideas of economic analysis are intuitive, demonstrable and can be applied in practice without requiring a strong background in mathematics and economic theory. Moreover, the strict assumptions underlying classical economic theory must be reconciled with real-world settings where they can be evaluated for their limitations as well as their analytical power. For example, to what degree does the assumption of human rationality allow us to gain new insights into economic behavior and in what circumstances must this assumption be leavened? One addition to this new version is a chapter on the growing fields of behavioral and experimental economics where economists are actively evaluating the predictive power of their models and incorporating additional ideas about human behavior that can usefully round out the orthodoxies of classical economic theory. Furthermore, throughout the text, we indicate where classical notions such as profit-maximizing intent, strict competition, or self-interest, must be supplemented or replaced in order to reflect the nature of economic decisions outside of the conventional business environment. We also offer greater appreciation in this book of the growing complexity of the environments in which nonprofits and social enterprises now operate, where the deterministic models of classical economic theory may not suffice for situations where organizations face significant risk and uncertainty, or where the outcomes of their decisions are affected by the behavior of other organizations with which they closely interact. Two additional chapters have thus been included here to bring in concepts from statistical decision theory and from game theory which can help account for the fact that nonprofits and social enterprises are rarely lone actors in a deterministic world as they address the social and economic needs of their constituencies and stakeholders.

After many years of prodding each other to undertake a revised edition, Dennis R. Young and Richard Steinberg made the wise choice to get some help. Rosemarie Emanuele of Ursuline College and Walter O. Simmons of John Carroll University had been using the original edition in their courses for years and needed an updated version for their own classes. No real substitutes for this text have emerged over the past two decades although the changes that have taken place since the last edition have increased the urgency. So we are all very pleased that the new team, with a new publisher – Edward Elgar – was finally able to make the commitment to produce this updated volume. As for the original edition, the book builds on our continuing work with students in our classes over the years, at Case Western Reserve University, Indiana University, Georgia State University, John Carroll University and Ursuline College. We thank these students for their interest, patience, and enthusiasm, and for helping to validate for us the importance of promulgating a better understanding of economic principles to improve decision making in the nonprofit and social enterprise sectors of the economy. As before, our intent is not to make economists out of nonprofit managers and social entrepreneurs, but to help them become more conversant in this discipline so as to employ its potent ideas for the benefit of more efficient and effective nonprofit organizations and social enterprises and the important social missions they address.

A companion website containing a Methodological Appendix along with the Review Concepts and Exercises for each chapter is available at: https://www.e-elgar.com/textbooks/young

Dennis R. Young
Richard Steinberg
Rosemarie Emanuele
Walter O. Simmons
December 2018

Acknowledgments

We wish to thank several colleagues familiar with the original edition of this book who provided suggestions for this new and revised version. These include John Barlow, Joe Cordes, Andreas Ortmann and Elizabeth Searing. Rosemarie Emanuele expresses her thanks to Ursuline College for the time granted her to work on this book.

We also thank students in our classes at Georgia State University, Case Western Reserve University, IUPUI, Ursuline College and John Carroll University who learned from the original edition and provided us with feedback and ideas for this new version.

Cartoons

The cartoons in this book are original, and a collaborative effort of authors Rosemarie Emanuele and Dennis Young.

1

Why should nonprofit managers and social entrepreneurs study economics?

Maybe I should have studied economics in school!

1.1 Introduction

Almost any important decision in life involves the deployment of valuable resources. For nonprofit managers and social entrepreneurs this is especially evident as they work to address an unlimited universe of social needs and aspirations with limited means at their disposal. So many homeless people, so limited a budget to shelter and nourish them. So much to teach our children within the time, budget and personnel available. So many people who are ill or injured; how to use limited resources to reduce the number afflicted and treat those who are? So much beauty in the world; so few resources to expose art to appreciative audiences and to encourage artistic expression. So wondrous a natural world we live in; so desperate are we to preserve it for future generations. So much we don't know; so little time and money available to expand our knowledge.

Economics provides no easy answers to such pressing concerns, but this discipline does offer productive ways to think about them, so that decision makers can make the best of it. Economics is not just for economists but for everyone charged with making responsible decisions, especially those affecting other people. This has long been recognized in business schools and schools of public administration, which educate our business and public-sector leaders. However, it has been accepted more grudgingly in the curricula devoted to the development of leaders and managers of nonprofit organizations and other forms of social enterprise. Such resistance makes little sense, given the pivotal nature of the subsectors of our society that nonprofit organizations and social enterprises serve – for example, health care, education, the arts, social services, community development, environmental conservation, international relief and development, religion, policy advocacy – and the existential issues that they address – poverty and inequality, climate change, social justice, and so on. While the "social sector," as Peter Drucker used to call it, is a relatively small part of national and global economies by conventional standards (e.g., proportions of GDP, employment, etc.; see Chapter 2) it is in many respects the critical sector that holds us all together.

Before probing further into the nature of economics itself, consider some of the important resource-related management and policy issues in a few major "industries" that are part of the social sector.

Health care

Health care is a huge, cross-sectoral, complex service industry that includes government institutions (e.g., V.A. hospitals; Medicare and Medicaid), businesses (for-profit hospitals, clinics and nursing homes; medical suppliers, pharmaceutical companies, insurance companies, etc.), as well as numerous and varied nonprofit organizations (hospitals, clinics, nursing homes, and major hospital systems such as the Cleveland Clinic and the Mayo Clinic). Recent controversies have swirled around the Affordable Care Act of 2010 (so-called Obamacare), which was motivated largely by the fact that many citizens of the U.S. did not have health insurance.

A core principle of the ACA is that everyone must purchase insurance because, otherwise, the system must weigh the high costs of insuring only unhealthy people against insolvency. Another important factor in the design of Obamacare was a desire to control the costs of health care, which have been escalating for decades at a rate faster than general inflation in the economy. While the ACA has succeeded in expanding access to health insurance for millions of people, it remains mired in controversy along partisan political lines, with some central economic questions at the heart of the issue. For example:

- What are the implications of revoking the penalties for those who do not purchase insurance?
- How much must government subsidize insurance premiums through Medicaid and other means, so that they remain affordable to all groups of people, regardless of income or pre-existing medical conditions?
- How can we guarantee that all consumers have a choice of insurers and insurance plans?

While these are fundamentally policy questions that must be addressed by government, many additional operational economic questions confront decision makers within nonprofit institutions of the health care system. Consider just a small handful of illustrative vignettes:

- A small nonprofit hospital wishes to provide home health care services. Should it do so on its own or in partnership with other hospitals?
- A nonprofit mental health agency is considering raising money by selling employee benefit plans to local businesses, but it could lose money if donors react adversely or not enough businesses sign up. Should it go ahead with this initiative?
- Blood for transfusions is in short supply, but paying donors leads to problems with blood quality. Should a blood center confine its solicitation efforts to volunteer donors?
- A community health center has discretionary funds that it can use to educate residents about nutrition and exercise or it can expand its urgent care nursing staff. What course of action will best advance its mission to improve health in its community?

Education

As in health care, the education subsector engages organizations in all sectors of the economy, including nonprofit organizations (e.g., private colleges and universities), for-profit firms (e.g., day-care centers, job-training institutes) and government (public schools and universities). Many basic and disruptive changes have occurred in the economic character of education in recent years. In primary education, charter schools now provide parents with publicly funded alternatives to traditional public schools. In higher education, emphasis has shifted from reliance on full-time faculty members to greater employment of adjunct professors, substitution of online for on-site courses, and the creation of "Massive Open Online Courses" (MOOCs) that promise broader access to higher education through the Internet. Like health care, rising cost is also an important issue in higher education, with tuitions climbing faster than prices in the economy at large over the past few decades.

Nonprofit organizations and social entrepreneurs in education face a wide variety of resource-related decisions. Consider the following illustrative situations:

- A private college wishes to raise money to build a new wing on its library. Should it use direct mail fund-raising, personal solicitations, or some combination of both? How much money should the college invest in these fund-raising efforts?
- A nonprofit research institute, pressed for funds, is considering a performance compensation system under which its staff would receive salary bonuses tied to the level of research contracts they bring in. Should it go ahead with this proposal?
- A private school must decide between a cost-of-living increase for all its teachers versus selective bonuses for teachers based on their performance evaluations. How should it decide?
- A private university must set its level of tuition as well as its student aid policy. How does it ensure that it will attract a robust, highly qualified and diverse entering class?

The arts

Nonprofit organizations are an important part of the arts and cultural sector, encompassing a broad spectrum of fine arts institutions including museums, theaters, dance companies, and orchestras. In recent decades, many of these institutions have experienced intense fiscal stress, especially during the deep recession of 2008–2009. Some, such as the New York City Opera Company, have even closed their doors.

Arts institutions have some special characteristics underlying their economic distress. First, they are subject to what economist William Baumol called "cost disease" (Baumol, 2012). Cost disease is the rapid increase in labor costs that results when an organization cannot improve its productivity as fast as productivity increases in the economy at large. Symphonies cannot perform as well with fewer musicians, nor can Shakespeare's plays appear with fewer actors. This limits the ability of orchestras and theaters to respond to rising labor costs through workforce reductions. Second, many nonprofit arts institutions have large fixed costs, for example, their buildings (concert halls, museums), collections, and permanent ensembles of performers. These fixed costs must be paid for, regardless of the number of performances or the size of audiences, putting arts organizations at risk. Of course, arts organizations have many different strategies they can consider for coping with such issues, including some productivity improvements using technology (such as live broadcasts through movie theaters), additional products (such as recordings and gift shop sales), nonmarket funding (e.g., through philanthropy) and reduction of fixed costs (e.g., by renting versus owning their facilities, or relying more on itinerant versus resident artists). These are the kinds of economic decisions that keep nonprofit arts managers up at night. Nonprofit arts organizations face a wide variety of economic challenges such as these:

- A museum sells art reproductions in its gift shop. What is the best price and quality level for these sales?
- An orchestra requires major repairs to its concert hall. Should it dip into its endowment to finance these repairs, or try to secure funds some other way?
- A community theater in a working-class neighborhood runs an operating deficit at current ticket prices. How can it remain fiscally healthy while accommodating local residents with limited ability to pay?
- An early music ensemble that performs in local churches enjoys growing demand for its concerts. Should it buy or rent its own concert venue?
- The opera company in a nonprofit performing arts center in a large city cannot pay its rent. Should the center evict the opera and seek an alternative tenant?
- A local donor offers a large personal collection of paintings to a museum. Under what circumstances should the museum accept the gift?
- A modern-dance company must renew its contract with its resident dance troupe. What is the right mix of salaried resident artists versus itinerant or pick-up performers and how much should it pay its resident-ensemble members?

Social services

Nonprofit organizations have long been central to the provision of social services to vulnerable populations, in the U.S. and indeed worldwide (e.g., through relief and development NGOs), although the economic issues for social service nonprofits have changed over the years. Prior to the 1960s in the U.S., social services were largely reliant on philanthropic funding and volunteering, with federated fund-raising institutions such as United Way playing a major role in providing operating support. With the War on Poverty and Great Society programs of the 1960s, government became a major funder, often relying on nonprofits to provide foster care, child day care, job training, mental health counseling, community development and other services through grants, contracts, vouchers, and other subsidies (Smith and Lipsky, 1993). In the 1990s, "welfare reform" during the Clinton administration changed the emphasis of federal support from delivery of social-welfare services to re-integration of poor people into the labor market, leading to greater participation of for-profit businesses in areas such as employment training. In the early 2000s, under the George W. Bush administration, faith-based nonprofits (churches) were encouraged to join traditional social service organizations in the government-financed delivery of community services. Since then, fiscal pressures and conservative politics have led to reductions in government support for social services, renewed emphasis on private giving, and new health care funding (including expansion of the Medicaid program and the ACA). This occurred in an environment of increasing competition within the nonprofit social service sector and between nonprofits and for-profits for purchase-of-service contracts (Smith, 2012).

The increased importance, volatility, and competitiveness of government funding for social services has had important impacts on the economic structure and health of nonprofit social service agencies. Some major nonprofit social service organizations closed their doors, including Hull House in Chicago and FEGS (Federation and Employment Guidance Services) in New York, partly because of their inordinately heavy reliance on government funding (Cohen, 2012; Young and Casey, 2017). Other organizations such as Good Shepherd Services in New York and the Centers for Families and Children in Cleveland have grown large through multiple mergers of smaller and more specialized nonprofit social service agencies. These agglomerations reflect what economists call "economies of scale and scope." Conglomerate social service agencies have the capacity to administer complex government-funding programs and deliver coordinated services more efficiently than multiple narrowly focused organizations.

Given this rich and turbulent history, it is not surprising that nonprofit social service organizations face challenging economic problems. Consider the following illustrative vignettes:

- A community agency for the elderly runs a day-care program and a Meals on Wheels program. How large should each program be, and how should it allocate its limited staff and budget between the two programs?
- A small social service organization that offers counseling for troubled children is encouraged by local funders to merge with a larger local, comprehensive social services provider. What are the economic benefits and costs of this consolidation?
- Most of the staff members of a large youth-serving nonprofit organization are volunteers. As the organization expands, should it adjust the mixture of volunteers and paid staff in its workforce?
- A mental health organization that serves homeless people faces major cuts in government funding. Should it cut back its services or invest in a new fund-raising initiative?
- A nonprofit day-care center for children faces new competition from a local franchisee of a national for-profit chain. How should it respond in terms of its pricing, quality of services, and wage structure?
- A local united fund wishes to attract a well-known youth agency into its system. What terms should it offer for sharing the proceeds of its combined campaign with this new member? Under what terms should the agency agree to join?
- An international relief agency receives a grant to assist war refugees who are scattered among several countries. How can it target the expenditure of those funds to have the greatest impact?

Other subsectors

Although health care, education, the arts, and social services constitute a large part of the nonprofit sector, there are many other areas in which nonprofit organizations are active and important. U.S. nonprofits are classified by the National Taxonomy of Exempt Entities (NTEE) into 26 major subsectors, and we have yet to discuss foundations, advocacy, environmental, and religious organizations, among others (McKeever, Dietz, and Fyffe, 2016). Managers and leaders in all these fields face decisions like these:

- An environmental advocacy group is mounting a campaign to clean up hazardous waste in its community. Should it hire a paid public relations staff member or continue to rely exclusively on volunteer efforts?
- A religiously-affiliated college, sensitive to the preferences of its donors, must offer all health care services, including contraception, required by the ACA in its student health center. How can it determine if the losses from antagonized donors if it maintains its health service on campus outweigh the costs of contracting this service out to an independent provider?

- A community foundation administers a system of "donor-advised funds" (DAFs) through which local donors can make gifts to the foundation and then advise the foundation on how to allocate those funds to selected charities. DAFs offer a convenient and inexpensive way for major donors to oversee their philanthropies without having to administer their own foundations. What minimum level of donation should the community foundation require for establishing such a fund?
- A women's rights organization seeks legislation to support paid maternity leave and family care giving. How can it determine if additional funds should be allocated to hiring a professional lobbyist versus recruiting more volunteers?

Social enterprises

Nonprofit organizations have long been involved in commercial activities that support their missions both indirectly (by generating profits to subsidize mission-related services) and directly by offering mission-related commercial services. For example, museums, hospitals, and universities operate retail stores, and social service organizations run thrift shops that cross-subsidize their mission-related activities. If these stores employ the right kind of volunteers (recovering addicts, rehabilitated convicts, or others needing special help in employability), the organization's mission is directly advanced. Often, nonprofits have special expertise or excess capacity that provide competitive advantages in particular commercial markets. For example, botanical gardens can market their grounds for weddings and other special occasions, and universities can organize educational travel programs with faculty as expert tour guides. Over the past decade and more, the concept of social enterprise has expanded beyond the bounds of the nonprofit sector per se to the realm of "social businesses" (Young, Searing, and Brewer, 2016). In the U.S., new hybrid legal forms such as the Low-profit Limited Liability company (L3C) and the Benefit Corporation have emerged. In other countries, social enterprises take the form of social cooperatives and hybrid forms such as the United Kingdom's Community Interest Company (CIC). Not surprisingly, economic decision making is integral to the success of social enterprises, nonprofit or otherwise. Here are some illustrative vignettes in which social entrepreneurs face important economic choices:

- A social justice nonprofit seeks to enhance the prospects of ex-felons in the labor force. Should it employ such individuals directly by running a business such as a landscaping company, or should it invest in advocacy programs to reduce legal barriers to employment of individuals with prison records in the general labor force?

- A for-profit coffee company considers itself a social business that seeks to promote fair trade so that farmers in agricultural economies can improve their standards of living. How should it determine the prices at which it buys their beans and sells coffee in the markets of developed countries?
- A for-profit social business seeks to promote literacy by buying or receiving donated used books, selling some of them and distributing others free of charge to schools in low-income neighborhoods. How can it best decide how much to sell and how much to give away?
- A community foundation is approached by a social business asking for a loan in the form of a "program-related investment" (PRI). PRIs combine social investments with financial returns to the lender. How do PRIs compare to the alternatives of making a grant or to increasing the foundation's regular financial portfolio? Should the foundation respond favorably to this request?

1.2   Economic decision making

What do these various illustrations of decisions faced by managers and leaders of nonprofit organizations and social enterprises, across the various subsectors, have in common? In a word, they are all decisions about the *effective use of scarce resources* to carry out organizational goals. In every case, leaders must choose among courses of action because resources are not sufficient to pursue all desirable possibilities, or because making one choice eliminates others. If the relief agency spends its grant money on refugees in one group of countries, it cannot do so in others. If the youth agency joins the united fund, it must forego some funds it would otherwise raise on its own. In all cases, actions and decisions require *trade-offs* between one set of possibilities and another. The relief agency trades-off benefits to one group of refugees versus another. The youth agency trades the benefits of united fund-raising against the additional funds it might have raised itself. The orchestra weighs the benefits of a refurbished concert hall against lost returns on its endowment and hence against financing other projects or greater security for the future. And the environmental advocacy group considers the public relations and motivational benefits of engaging volunteers in its cleanup campaign versus the efficiency of a professional public relations staff.

Having to regularly address these kinds of choices is the main reason managers and leaders in nonprofit organizations and social enterprises should study economics. No less than in business or government, nonprofit and social enterprise leaders must make decisions in situations where valuable resources are scarce and difficult choices require trade-offs. The discipline of economics helps decision makers to logically think through choices in circumstances of scarcity. Arguably, the study of economics is even more important in the nonprofit and social enterprise worlds than in the traditional business world because many of the choices are so complicated. Social decisions involve unpriced resources such as volunteer time or free care for the needy. This makes the values of alternatives more difficult to measure and the making of choices less clear. In addition, the objectives of social decision making are often less clear and more complicated than simple profit maximization. The basic principles of economics provide the framework for thinking through nonprofit and social enterprise decisions in such nuanced circumstances.

Operational decision making is not the only reason nonprofit managers, leaders, and social entrepreneurs should study economics. These leaders operate in complex, often harsh public policy environments that are also driven by the scarcity of resources. Leaders must understand this environment to ensure that their organizations respond effectively to it, or indeed, in cases such as advocacy organizations, determine how to change it. Consider, for example, a few of the ways in which nonprofit organizations and social enterprises in the U.S. are affected by public policy and governmental decision making:

- IRS determination of whether a commercial activity is related or unrelated to a nonprofit organization's mission affects whether the profits will be taxed and hence the degree to which the organization may decide to undertake the activity.
- Postal subsidies to nonprofit organizations affect the degree to which these organizations can mount public appeals, and the choices they make between mail-based and other forms of solicitation.
- Policies specifying how donated property may be valued and deducted from personal income taxes affect whether such properties are donated to nonprofits or disposed of by their owners in other ways.
- Income tax rates affect how much disposable income individuals and corporations have, the impact of a donor sacrifice of pre-tax income on charitable output, and hence the incidence and size of donations.
- Interpretation of antitrust laws affects whether nonprofits decide to collaborate or compete with one another and how they will determine their pricing and service policies.
- Social entrepreneurs can choose alternative organizational forms for their social ventures, including for-profit (proprietorship, partnership, C-corporation, limited liability company, worker-managed firm), nonprofit (corporation, trust, unincorporated), mutual benefit (consumer cooperative), and hybrid (low-profit limited liability companies (L3Cs),

benefit corporations, cross-sectoral subsidiaries) forms. There are also alternative tax designations for nonprofits that focus on policy advocacy and lobbying, or pursue other missions not formally considered charitable, each with differences in associated tax benefits. Social entrepreneurs must choose forms most effective for their particular missions.

Such policies affect all nonprofit organizations and social enterprises. Moreover, organizations operating in particular fields of service – for example, environmental conservation, affordable housing, the fine arts, or higher education – will be familiar with a host of other policies that affect their decision making, for example, tax credits for pollution control, housing subsidies, grants for artists, or student loans. All these policies reflect societal trade-offs in the use of scarce resources. Without an appreciation of the choices and trade-offs involved in these policies, sector leaders can neither react effectively to public policies already in place, nor develop intelligent alternatives to those policies they seek to change.

Implicit in these examples is another important concept intrinsic to economics, and why decision makers should study this subject: *incentives*. Government policies, by altering financial incentives, influence the behavior of nonprofit organizations and social enterprises and their various constituencies. Tax rates influence how much people give to charity, service subsidies such as scholarships or low-cost loans affect how much consumers demand and how much organizations are willing to supply, and subsidies on inputs such as postal rates influence how much nonprofit organizations use particular resources such as the postal service. Thus, if nonprofit leaders and social entrepreneurs are to understand, effectively utilize, and intelligently influence the formulation of policies affecting their organizations or constituents, they must understand the effects of incentives. In a very large measure, this is what economics is about – *the study of incentives and how these incentives influence the behavior of individuals and organizations involved in choices about the use of scarce resources.*

1.3   Economics as a science

Economics as a discipline is a way of thinking that applies widely to many facets of human activity, though this may not be universally appreciated. Some equate economics with the management of businesses, while others see economics as a social science, like sociology or political science. Still others, such as the Nobel Prize Committee in Economics, which awarded the 1994 Nobel Prize in Economics to the Mathematician John Nash, may see the field as a branch of applied mathematics. President Reagan is said to have quipped that "an economist is someone who sees something happen in practice and wonders if it will work in theory." Indeed, economics is a field that has many different faces, and is applied in many different contexts.

Economics has been used to study such divergent topics as the decision to purchase a home, to marry, and even to commit a crime or to end one's own life. The word "decision" appears in each of these applications. Economics is a field that helps illuminate how people make decisions such as whether to work for pay or volunteer, whether a firm should buy or rent its central office, whether a nonprofit organization should expand its volunteer staff, or whether a social enterprise should include unrelated commercial activities in its business plan. The discipline of economics, while commonly associated with for-profit businesses and the private marketplace, is equally relevant to the management of nonprofit organizations, social enterprises, as well as to government and other institutions and groupings of individuals.

Still, the discipline of economics has its roots in the study of decisions made by for-profit firms operating in markets as they seek to maximize their profits. It was not always so obvious that the same theories and approaches can be used to study the workings of nonprofit organizations, social enterprises, and the public sector. In the remainder of this chapter we take a quick tour of the conceptual framework of economics. We first define economics as a field of study and characterize its nature as a science. Because economics is about valuing goods and services, we discuss the concept of value more deeply. Then we consider the various institutional mechanisms through which society allocates valuable resources. We go on to consider the two main branches of economics – micro and macro, and then give attention to the essential ideas that economists use to guide their thinking. Traditionally, economists assume that people behave "rationally," but the behavioral revolution in economics moves us to consider predictable irrationality as well. We take a moment to examine the traditional assumption and how it both enhances and limits our ability to understand the world through the lens of economics. We then proceed to discuss the idea of economic efficiency – the principal criterion by which economists judge the merit of alternative actions. Finally, we note the limits to this criterion and juxtapose it against various notions of equity or fairness.

Let's start with a more formal definition of economics:

Economics is the study of how decision makers (individuals, organizations, industries, sectors, countries, society) generate, accumulate, allocate, distribute, and consume resources and create value.

Integral to this definition is the notion of creating economic value. By utilizing resources in the most desirable way, by making the best choices or trade-offs, people increase the value of the goods and services at their disposal. This idea pervades the chapters of this text as we determine how value is created in markets and through policies that alter the outcomes of decision making in various ways. Such notions as "gains from trade," consumer and producer "surpluses," and "Pareto efficiency" all reflect the basic idea of economic value.

As with every scientific discipline to some degree, economics is limited in its capacity to describe, explain and predict the phenomena it studies. There are too many uncontrolled variables to account for, and measurements are often too difficult to consistently permit accurate descriptions and forecasts. Although recent progress has been made in experimental economics (see Chapter 12), segments of society cannot easily be put into a laboratory to allow precise testing and experimentation. However, economics is a science that it is based on testable theory and utilizes the scientific method to describe and analyze social phenomena. It relies largely on careful, often quantifiable, formulation of theory and hypotheses, and testing of those hypotheses where possible against objectively collected data and observations.

We can speak of economics as a science on at least three levels – as a behavioral science, as a decision science and as a moral science.

As a *behavioral science* economics helps us to describe and understand how people and institutions behave. Such understanding is an obvious prerequisite to formulating policies and strategies (incentives) for influencing such behavior in desired ways. For example, the "theory of the firm" describes how organizations set prices and make decisions about how much to produce. It thus suggests how those decisions might be influenced by such factors as taxes or changes in technology. In the nonprofit world, economics can help us understand the behavior of donors, service consumers, paid workers and volunteers, and suppliers of other input resources such as equipment or real estate. We can also analyze the behavior of nonprofit organizations, how they respond to changes in government policy, market competition, donor behavior, and internal incentives.

The assumption that traditional microeconomics makes, that people and institutions behave "rationally," is both a strength and a weakness of traditional economic theory. The assumption provides a unifying structure for developing sophisticated models of institutions and markets, but the results are subject to the caveat that human capacity and proclivity to behave rationally is limited. We suffer from *cognitive illusions* that are hard to un-think in the same way that optical illusions are hard to un-see, and this can lead to illogical decisions (Ariely, 2008). It is important to know the sources of cognitive illusions. Then we would know whether the assumption of rationality is a harmless simplification and when we need to abandon traditional models. This sort of boundary patrol is a major focus of behavioral economics.

Rationality means that people will make logical and consistent choices and that they will consider all relevant alternatives. Fully rational creatures are labeled *homo economicus* or economic man in the literature, although sometimes the term is reserved for those who are both fully rational and concerned only with their own well-being. For clarity, we use the term as including both selfish and altruistic individuals in this text. Herbert Simon, a Nobel Prize winner in economics, was one of the first to offer structured alternatives to *homo economicus* with his theory of "bounded rationality" (Simon, 1956). Recognizing cognitive limits in formulating and processing information and the opportunity costs of trying to solve complex problems, he proposed that people use simpler rules of thumb (heuristics) to "satisfice" rather than "optimize."

Since then, psychologist and Nobel laureate in economics Daniel Kahneman, together with his frequent coauthor Amos Tversky, developed the theory of predictably irrational behavior based on cognitive limitations and illusions. They summarize diverse research findings using the metaphor of two cognitive processing systems in the brain. System I is fast, effortless, and intuitive and operates through heuristics and the ability to tell a good story. System II is slow, effortful, and logical, and for those reasons, system I makes most decisions. Even when the problem is passed on to system II, system I's judgment is influential and biases logical thinking.

Ariely (2008) provides an amusing example of a cognitive illusion. He says (at 11 minutes and five seconds into the video):

> Imagine I give you a choice: Do you want to go for a weekend to Rome, all expenses paid – hotel, transportation, food, a continental breakfast, everything – or a weekend in Paris? Now, weekend in Paris, weekend in Rome – these are different things. They have different food, different culture, different art. Imagine I added a choice to the set that nobody wanted. Imagine I said, "A weekend in Rome, a weekend in Paris, or having your car stolen? It's a funny idea, because why would having your car stolen, in this set, influence anything?

The requirement that the presence of an inferior alternative should not affect the choice between two reasonable options is called "independence from irrelevant alternatives," and is obviously part of rational behavior. But Ariely goes on to summarize numerous studies finding that people violate this assumption in predictable circumstances.

Because our brains seem to be hard-wired to make logical errors, economist Richard Thaler (another winner of the Nobel prize in economics) has, together with political scientist Cass Sunstein, investigated ways to help humans make better decisions in their 2009 book, *Nudge*. They define a "choice architecture" as the way a decision problem is presented to the decision maker. This includes the number of choices presented, the way choices are described, and the presence or absence of a default option. Synthesizing many studies, they conclude that a well-designed choice architecture helps people make better decisions in the face of cognitive limitations and illusions. Nudge economics can help social entrepreneurs and nonprofit managers, particularly with their social-marketing missions.

As a *decision science*, economics describes actual behavior (through behavioral economics) and recommends algorithms for calculating "optimal" behavior. The basic optimizing approach requires three things: a careful and complete description of personal or organizational objectives, a list of relevant decision variables whose value can be chosen by the decision maker, and a complete specification of the time, resource, and other constraints that limit one's success in achieving those objectives. Optimal decision rules have been developed for individual decision makers, but economics also analyzes collective decision making. For instance, by providing a precise definition of benefits and costs, economics helps us decide whether an organization should, say, undertake a new educational program or a new fund-raising campaign.

Economics is also, perhaps paradoxically in view of its grounding in business and markets, a *moral science*. Indeed, Adam Smith, regarded as the founder of modern economic thinking, was as concerned by moral questions as he was with efficiency (Smith, 1759/2016). Economists divide the field into normative economics (concerned with defining "the good economy" in terms of theories of justice and ethics) and positive economics (concerned with descriptions of behavior and how the economy works). Both issues are confronted in collective decision making. Positive economics is involved in rigorously defining the total costs and benefits of a collective decision, but normative economics is required to judge whether the gains of some individuals outweigh the losses to other people. We discuss how to build distributional justice and other fairness concerns into the cost–benefit calculation in Chapter 14. There are many other interesting normative questions arising from the study of social entrepreneurs and nonprofit managers. As private agents for the public good, should nonprofit organizations treat distributional justice concerns differently than government agencies? Additional normative issues have not yet been adequately studied (such as valuing autonomy, human dignity, and other basic human rights), so we leave these issues for future texts.

For leaders of nonprofit organizations and social enterprises, all three aspects of economic science are important. We need to understand how institutions and constituents (consumers, donors, volunteers, clients, and suppliers) behave, for these are all economic actors who influence the work and performance of our organizations. We need to know how to make decisions involving hard choices with important resource implications, else our organizations will not be efficient and effective or even sustainable. And we need to understand what kinds of actions are in the public interest and which are not, for that is ultimately what justifies the existence of most nonprofit organizations and social enterprises.

1.4   Scarcity and value

Underlying the scientific uses of economics – as a behavioral, decision, or moral science – is the singular concept *scarcity* as the source of value. In essence, economists attribute value to a unit of a good, service or resource, to the degree that it is in short supply relative to people's desire for more of it. That is, economists focus on the "incremental" value of scarce resources – how much more of something is desired relative to what is already available. Thus, ocean water at the shore, sand in the desert, or ice in Antarctica have no incremental economic value because they are so plentiful relative to local needs for these resources. While water is essential for the ecology and people desire a healthy ecological system, ocean water has no (incremental) value because more salt water at the shore does not contribute to this purpose. And, while sand has its industrial purposes, it is so plentiful in some deserts that it has no value unless it can be restricted and sold to external buyers. Ice in Antarctica has no intrinsic value to expeditionary groups and other local occupants since it is so abundant there, although loss of polar ice is an indicator of global warming, reduction of which clearly does have economic value to residents of the planet as a whole. On the other hand, fresh water in California, or clean air in Los Angeles, are most certainly of economic value. Alternatively, a very rare painting would have value only if people wanted it. (You may have saved only one picture that you drew in the 3rd grade, but it would have no economic value if even your mother didn't want it!)

In the world of nonprofits and social enterprises, managers and leaders deal with many kinds of valuable, scarce resources. The services they produce are often not sufficient to serve all who need them, the time that volunteers can devote to organizational activities is limited, the art work or historical archives they tend is unique and of intense interest to scholars and connoisseurs, and there is never enough money, staff or time to accomplish all of an organization's goals and objectives. These are all resources in the social economy that have value because they are scarce and people want more of them.

While the concept of value, based on incremental scarcity, is clear, the *measurement of value* is often very tricky and difficult. In principle, economists define the measure of economic value as follows:

> We measure the (incremental) economic value of a good, service or resource by what people are intrinsically willing to pay for another unit of it.

The word "intrinsic" is an important modifier here. It highlights the fact that people often do not have the necessary information they need to determine how much something is worth to them, or they do not have the incentive to reveal that value to anyone else. (We will discuss both these problems extensively in subsequent chapters.) But if they did, their expressed willingness to pay would properly represent the economic value of the good or service at issue.

It is one thing to identify willingness to pay as the indicator of value and another thing to measure it in practice. How does one determine what people are really willing to pay for something? Economists often rely on the efficient operation of markets to create observable prices for goods and services. Under proper circumstances, these prices can be accurate measures of the incremental economic value of these resources. However, there are many instances where markets for valued resources do not exist, or where they function poorly. In such cases, prices do not accurately reflect incremental economic value. Thus, in general, we must distinguish between economic value as characterized by willingness to pay, and the price at which a good or service may be selling. For example, the value of a glass of water to a severely dehydrated long-distance runner, as measured by his or her willingness to pay, is likely to be substantially higher than the price at which the water is generally available. As we will study later, people's willingness to pay is just one factor influencing the price at which a good or service may be offered for sale.

Willingness to pay makes sense when assessing the value to a given decision maker of alternative purchases. Nonprofit managers, social entrepreneurs, and individual consumers face budget constraints, so a high willingness to pay indicates that the decision maker is willing to give up a lot to obtain a good or service. In the traditional economist's view, this is the measure of value, and actual purchasing behavior rather than testimony is the real test. But across people, willingness to pay differs for an additional reason – they have different amounts of money to spend. When a wealthy person says they are willing to pay $1000, this does not mean that the purchased service is more valuable than when a poor person is willing to pay $900. More sophisticated economists have developed adjusted willingness-to-pay measures that reflect social judgments as to what constitutes an equal sacrifice or other notions of fairness and distributive justice. We discuss some of these alternatives briefly in Chapter 14.

1.5 How does society allocate valuable economic resources?

We have already noted that markets are a key mechanism for allocating scarce resources among competing uses. But markets are just one mechanism that society uses to allocate valuable resources. How do markets do this and what are the other mechanisms?

- *Markets* are decentralized institutions in which independent producers (sellers) and consumers (buyers) voluntarily *exchange* their resources, goods, and services for money.
- *Barter* is a money-free system of direct exchange. Organizations frequently use barter internally to allocate resources across departments while generally using markets for external exchange. Nonprofits sometimes barter among themselves, trading specialized goods and services not easily found in the open market, or where cash budgets are limited. Barter is also used, sometimes, in the underground economy to evade taxes and regulations.
- *Governments* use their monopoly over the legitimate coercive powers of the state to allocate goods, services, and other resources. The tools of government include direct production and distribution, market exchange, taxation, price and quantity controls, and regulatory policies, procedures, and rules developed through the *political process* and administered by a bureaucracy that is answerable to an electorate.
- *Tradition* is a set of culturally-specific rules used to allocate resources in particular contexts. Tradition assigns parents the responsibility to provide for their children and places taboos against trading particular goods in markets. In some cultures and time periods, tradition sets the rules of inheritance, restricts participation of women in formal labor markets, and assigns trades and professions dynastically.

- *Gifts* are regarded by some as unilateral transfers, as *quids* without *quos*. Others view gifts as bilateral exchanges, in which givers receive a good feeling or "warm glow" in exchange for their gift, making gift-giving similar to a conventional market activity.
- *Theft* is involuntary exchange brought about by actual and threatened violence.

While markets are a dominant mode for allocating resources in western industrialized countries such as the U.S., they are by no means the only mode. Even in the U.S., one of the most strongly market-oriented western countries, the for-profit sector's share of gross domestic product (the value of all traded goods and services in the economy) was only 75.4 percent in 2014 with government (12.1 percent), the nonprofit sector (5.4 percent), and households (7.1 percent) accounting for the rest (McKeever, Dietz, and Fyffe, 2016). Markets in these countries are perhaps freer than elsewhere but are by no means completely free as government taxes and regulates the use and exchange of resources, restricts property rights through zoning and other laws, and directly produces such goods as roads and public schools. Tradition, gifts, barter, and theft also play their parts in western industrialized democracies.

Prices determine who gets to consume goods and services in market economies. But in mixed economies like those in most modern industrialized countries, it is well to appreciate the numerous other mechanisms that society utilizes to allocate valuable resources. These include taxation; rules, policies and direct orders used within organizations; planning within organizations and systems of organizations; rationing through waiting and queuing up for goods and services; lotteries; ethical norms, rules and traditions used by families and ethnic and religious groups; and coercion and brute force. For our purposes, it is relevant to focus on certain mechanisms that are important in the nonprofit sector and social enterprises. These include: persuasion, social pressure, and other forms of solicitation to induce people to give resources and volunteer time; and individually motivated initiative (voluntary giving of time and money). This is not to say that prices are unimportant as an allocation mechanism in the nonprofit sector; indeed, prices govern many if not most of the input and product markets in which nonprofit organizations are involved (for example, see Weisbrod, 1988; Hammack and Young, 1993; Powell and Steinberg, 2006). However, allocations of charitable resources such as donated funds and gifts-in-kind, volunteer time, and the provision of charitable services, are not primarily governed by market prices.

The limited role that prices play, and the variety of other mechanisms in place for allocating resources in nonprofit organizations and social enterprises, point to the challenges of applying economic analysis to this part of the economy. In those areas of the economy that are solely market-driven, prices serve to allocate resources towards their most valued uses. What, if anything, ensures that proper allocations will be made outside the sphere of the market? Will the decentralized choices of individual donors and volunteers efficiently support the most pressing social needs, or is voluntary coordination, say, through United Ways or state intervention required? Economic concepts arising from the analysis of markets require careful adaptation and extension to make them useful for understanding the nonmarket segments of the economy, and that is why the crowded market of economics textbooks needs a volume like this one.

1.6   What are the major branches of economics?

The study of economics is normally divided into two major parts. *Microeconomics* is concerned with the study of economic processes at the level of individuals, organizations, industries and markets. It is concerned with such topics as:

- the decision-making behavior of consumers, organizations, industries, and other groups;
- prices, quantities, qualities, costs, revenues, benefits, and taxes associated with particular goods and services;
- the effect of government interventions (taxes, price controls, quotas, regulation) in particular markets;
- external benefits and costs, collective goods, imperfect competition, information problems, and other causes of "market failure" that can justify intervention or supplementation by nonmarket institutions; and
- the *social efficiency* of resource use, alternative institutional arrangements, and the allocation of outputs.

In this book, we are almost exclusively concerned with microeconomics. The other main branch of economics, which we will mention briefly, is *macroeconomics*. Macroeconomics addresses how the economy works as a whole and is concerned with *aggregate phenomena* such as:

- gross domestic product and income;
- the money supply;
- inflation, unemployment, and business cycles;
- aggregate demand and supply for all goods and services at once;

- aggregate savings, investment and economic growth; and
- the balance of payments among nations.

This is not to say that nonprofit leaders and social entrepreneurs can safely remain uneducated in macroeconomics. The overall health of the economy determines the availability of resources (from sales, donations, volunteering, social capital funds, and investment returns) and the need for services (particularly in the human services subsector), leading to frequent mismatches (Steinberg, 2018). Social entrepreneurs and nonprofit managers must plan for economic uncertainty and forecast recessions. Moreover, nonprofits and social enterprises are subject to the same (sometimes more severe) inflationary pressures as other organizations in society, and they must pay attention to interest rates and other macroeconomic variables that affect their own economic health.

In the next chapter, we will see how the nonprofit sector and social enterprises fit into the economy as a whole. We will examine the size of the sector relative to the economy as a whole, and its impact on employment. We also look at subsectors where nonprofits and social enterprises compete with for-profits and government agencies, and at flows of resources across the sectors. This is the one chapter in which we stray into macroeconomic territory.

1.7 How do economists think?

Economists have a particular way of looking at the world. They make simplifying assumptions to keep their methods and theories manageable. When their assumptions are close to the truth or otherwise does not affect results, they produce insights by clearing away the brush and getting a clear view of the trees if not the forest. When their assumptions are off-base in a particular situation, economists modify the assumptions and take another look at empirical results (recall the caveats introduced by behavioral economics). Here are some of the key ideas and assumptions that economists use.

As already noted, *economists start by assuming that people are "rational."* This assumption, combined with other starting assumptions, means:

- People know what their alternatives are and have good information about these alternatives. When people do not have good information, they compare the costs and benefits of obtaining more information and rationally decide how much information to obtain before deciding on an alternative. For example, economists would assume that donors are aware of different charities they may give to and will seek out more detailed information on these alternatives to the extent that they feel such information will be worth the satisfaction they receive from making more informed decisions. Some will economize on the information they look for, trusting a community foundation or United Way to decide who receives donations.

- People understand their preferences and when fully informed, can specify which alternative is best. In particular, they are able to rank alternatives in a transitive way so that one is the best option: if a donor prefers charity A to charity B and charity B to charity C, then he or she will prefer charity A over charity C. Behavioral economics has uncovered cases where these assumptions are violated, but for choices made by the same person every day, this is a harmless simplification.

- People optimize; they select their most-preferred alternative among those available to them. Thus, if choices A, B, and C are available to the donor who prefers charity A over the others, then economists assume that the donor will choose to give to charity A.

- There is no conflict between stated preferences and preferences revealed through behavior. A person stating that they want to lose weight while eating their seventh piece of chocolate cake is not *homo economicus*. Obviously, behavioral economists find exceptions to this assumption.

- People act out of self-interest, broadly defined. Thus, economists assume that donors give because of their individual preferences to give. The personal reward to giving is not necessarily a material benefit but may arise from the joy of fulfilling a perceived obligation, reputational benefits, relief of guilt, and many other psychological and cultural factors. Andreoni (1990) labeled preferences for *the act of giving* (as opposed to *the consequences of giving*) as "warm glow," although the concept goes back at least as far as Kenneth Arrow (1972).

Economists usually take individual preferences as given, leaving to other disciplines the question of why people prefer particular things and how preferences change over time. This simplification is one reason why economists can maintain a sharp, focused analytical edge in their reasoning, but also limits the applicability of economic analyses. In cases where this limitation is particularly important, economists have begun to collaborate with psychologists, sociologists, and marketing scholars to develop more complex models that are still simple enough to provide tractable insights.

Normative economics presumes that, all else equal, social efficiency is desirable. Much confusion results from the word "efficiency," because it suggests that economists are concerned only with productivity and not the quality of life. In economics, efficiency is a much broader concept that encompasses both. We take preferences as given and look for the best way to use scarce resources to satisfy these preferences. More formally, we follow the nineteenth-century Italian economist Vilfredo Pareto, who sought to rank alternative states of the economy. An economic state is a list of all the people in the economy, all the goods and services produced in the economy, and the amount of each good that affects each individual. Pareto had no use for dream states of the economy and restricted attention to economic states that are feasible – achievable with a given set of resources and technology. He made the relatively uncontroversial ethical judgment that one economic state is superior to another when there is unanimous preference for that state. Nowadays we say that an economic state A is *Pareto-preferred* to another economic state B if nobody in the economy prefers B to A and at least one person prefers A to B. Whenever there is disagreement over the ranking of A versus B, we say the states are *Pareto noncomparable*. So, the Pareto criterion cannot be used to rank every economic state against every other economic state but can rank particular pairs of alternatives. Pareto then defined social efficiency in the following way:

> *An economic state is efficient (or "Pareto optimal") if it is feasible and there are no feasible Pareto-preferred economic states.*
>
> *Inefficiency exists if feasible changes (in production methods, the quantity of each good or service, or the distribution of each good to each person) can make at least one person better off (as judged by their preferences) and no one worse off.*

This is quite a mouthful but cannot be accurately simplified. It is complicated because we are making only a minimal value judgment, and so we do not have a complete ranking. There are many efficient economic states, and more controversial value judgments must be made about the proper distribution of income to pick one as best.

Consider the following example, which illustrates the subtleties of efficiency. Suppose that a charity has been given three vouchers by a local company, each of which pays for a day of housekeeping services for impaired elderly residents of the community. If there are only two eligible clients in that community, then each of the following allocations is efficient: three vouchers to the first client and none to the second; two vouchers to the first and one to the second; one voucher to the first and two to the second; and no vouchers to the first and three to the second. It would be inefficient to distribute only two of the vouchers and throw out the third, because the alternative of giving that third voucher to either client would make somebody better off and nobody worse off.

Now suppose that initially the first client is given two vouchers and the second is given only one. The caseworker discovers that a mistake was made, demands that the first client return one voucher, and gives this voucher to the other client. Is this change inefficient because we have made one person worse off? No, we are simply moving from one efficient allocation to another. The Pareto criterion defines *in*efficiency. An economy is said to be efficient if it is not inefficient. Neither the initial allocation nor the redistributed allocation was inefficient, but the Pareto criterion is mute on the question of which allocation is better.

The Pareto criterion is like the preliminary round in a tournament – it eliminates some allocations from further consideration but does not select an overall winner. Because Pareto defined social efficiency so precisely, subsequent mathematical economists were able to produce operational tests for determining whether an economic state is efficient. While we leave the math to more advanced texts, we offer an intuitive treatment here. An economic state is efficient if three tests are met: productive efficiency, allocative efficiency, and trading efficiency.

- *Productive efficiency* means that goods or services of a given quality and quantity are produced at the least cost; or that the highest possible quality or quantity is attained for a given expenditure of valuable resources. Productive efficiency implies that the best combination of inputs and production methods (technology) is used.
- *Allocative efficiency* means that the right mixture of goods and services is produced, taking account of preferences and costs. Cost–benefit analysis (see Chapter 14), ideally, is about calculating whether a given project is allocatively efficient.
- *Trading efficiency* means that no pair of consumers wants to swap what they bought for what the other person bought.

If there is productive inefficiency, the economy can produce more of one good without cutting production of other goods. This is inefficient because with more production of one good, we could make somebody better off and with no reduction in production of other goods, we would not make anyone worse off. If there is allocative inefficiency so the wrong mixture of goods is produced (for example, a mixture with too much fossil fuel and not enough clean air) then we could make some people better off without harming others by adjusting the mixture and using some of the gains to those made better off to compensate those made worse off by the change. Finally, if there is trading inefficiency, letting that pair of consumers trade voluntarily will help them and hurt no one.

To choose among alternative efficient allocations, we need some other criterion, and this distributional question hinges on political and ethical notions of fairness or "equity." Unlike efficiency, which pretty much everyone can agree is good, there is considerable dispute over how to think about equity. Economists, in collaboration with philosophers and other social scientists, think about equity systematically within the following categories:

- *Horizontal equity*: The degree to which individuals or organizations in the same category (e.g., income class, age, family, or organization size) are treated the same.

Thus, we ask whether differences in property tax rates across communities are fair, or whether students in some public schools receive the same education as students in other public schools. We question the horizontal equity of various arrangements in the nonprofit and social enterprise world. For example, we ask donors to contribute what their peers have given to fairly share the burden of funding charitable services. We complain that the poor in suburbs are better supported by local charities than the poor in inner cities.

- *Vertical equity*: The degree to which there is an equitable distribution of rewards or burdens between ordered classes of individuals. The criterion is usually applied to fairness across the distributions of income or wealth.

There is no consensus on what constitutes vertical equity (Blum and Kalven, 1952, is still relevant), with some objecting to recent U.S. tax reforms because they chiefly benefit the wealthy and others dismissing the argument as an appeal for class warfare. Economists, together with philosophers, have contributed to the debate on both sides, using ideas like the "diminishing marginal utility of money" or "risk aversion of individuals in Rawls' original state" to justify varying levels of tax progressivity. Arguments fall into two broad categories – ability-to-pay arguments (the rich have greater ability to pay) and the benefits principle (the rich receive more benefits from government). Purely normative arguments are accompanied by positive economics, analyzing the side effects of redistribution through the tax and welfare system on growth, employment, earnings, savings, and risk-taking. In the nonprofit and social enterprise world, the vertical equity criterion motivates adoption of sliding-scale fees and need-based eligibility requirements. Vertical equity plays a role in development organizations, guiding selection of sites and choice of interventions. Fair trade certification is designed to promote payment of "working wages" to employees of consumer cooperatives in underdeveloped areas of the world. Membership organizations use vertical equity arguments to design dues structures, with lower rates for students and retirees and sometimes rates that depend on a member's income level (Steinberg, 2006).

What, exactly, is it that should be fair? Again, opinions differ, with some wanting everyone to have a fair chance, others wanting fair rules for playing the economics game, and others wanting a fair outcome. Attention may focus on:

- *Equity of endowments*: The degree to which people start at the same place in life (i.e., equal opportunity). This is a consideration, for example, in determining public policy on inheritance taxes which in turn influences how people plan their estates and bequests to charity. It is an issue of vertical equity (how people in different wealth categories are differentially treated by tax policy) and also horizontal equity (whether all children get to start life with comparable advantages).
- *Equity of process*: The degree to which the rules of the game are fair or the same for all participants. This is an issue, for example, in the controversy over unrelated business income tax on commercial activities of nonprofits. Should the rules be the same for businesses and nonprofits in similar circumstances (horizontal equity), and should small businesses and nonprofits be treated differently from large ones (vertical equity)?
- *Equity of outcomes*: The degree to which differential resources are provided to different groups so that they can achieve fair final outcomes. This applies to such provisions as special tax exemptions for the blind, affirmative action policies, and day care for children of working parents. It is a matter of horizontal equity (are all individuals within the target group treated the same?) and vertical equity (do the special benefits to the target group suffice to compensate for inequalities in health or job opportunities or special costs borne by the target group?).

Policy and management issues that confront nonprofit leaders, social entrepreneurs and public officials often require grappling with trade-offs between efficiency and equity:

- Laws mandating access to public facilities by people with disabilities may be enormously costly and resources devoted to their implementation might be more efficiently allocated in other ways. Handicapped spaces go unused while non-handicapped users search distant locales for a space. However, these laws do help assure equal treatment for physically challenged individuals.
- Inheritance taxes and progressive income taxes reduce efficiency by undermining incentives to work, save, and take risks, but they can be

used to address market failures and arguably make the distribution of income more just.

- Subsidy of nonprofit postal rates may be an inefficient way to allocate public resources because they may bias nonprofit organizations towards using more costly means of communication, but they may help nonprofits carry out work to aid the most unfortunate members of society.

These issues are much more complex than a few sentences can indicate. However, by properly defining and clearly articulating program or policy goals, the conflicts between efficiency and equity can be understood and sometimes reconciled. For example, if access for people with disabilities can be shown to produce general benefits for society then it may be efficient as well as equitable to implement such programs. In other cases, such as choosing between investments in programs for children versus the elderly, or drug abuse treatment versus preventative education programs, economic efficiency will not be adequate as a sole decision criterion because priorities need to be assigned to one group versus another. Nonetheless, the efficiency-equity framework encourages clear thinking and focuses attention on inefficiency-minimizing approaches to improve equity.

SUMMARY

The study of economics is important for managers and leaders of non-profit organizations and social enterprises in several ways. At the *appreciative level*, nonprofit leaders and social entrepreneurs must have a sense of where nonprofit organizations and social enterprises fit into the rest of the economy, how big a part of that economy they occupy, how they interact with other kinds of economic units, how their own organizations behave, and how they are affected by changes in the economy as a whole. At the *policy level*, nonprofit managers and leaders and social entrepreneurs must understand how their organizations are affected by changes in public policy, and they must be able to analyze the impacts of policies they seek to change or to implement in order to accomplish their goals. Finally, at the *managerial level*, leaders continually make decisions that have important resource implications. Economics provides the conceptual principles and methods that make the consequences of alternative decisions explicit and logically consistent, and so can lead to better choices. In the following chapters, we will tour some of the basic ideas of economic analysis, to inform the thinking of nonprofit managers and leaders and social entrepreneurs at all three levels. The intent is not to make economists out of those who read these pages – that would take years of study and probably some brainwashing! Rather, the purpose is to put readers in a position to understand and utilize the work of economists more effectively and, even more importantly, to encourage them to apply the powerful concepts of economic thinking in daily and long-term decision making.

SELECTED REFERENCES AND CITATIONS

Andreoni, J. (1990). Impure Altruism and Donations to Public Goods: A Theory of Warm-Glow Giving. *Economic Journal, 100,* 464–477.

Ariely, D. (2008). Are We in Control of Our Own Decisions? Retrieved from https://www.ted.com/talks/dan_ariely_asks_are_we_in_control_of_our_own_decisions?language=en#t-25215 (accessed December 12, 2017).

Arrow, K.J. (1972). Gifts and Exchanges. *Philosophy and Public Affairs, 1(4),* 343–362.

Baumol, W.J. (2012). *The Cost Disease,* New Haven: Yale University Press.

Blum, W.J. and Kalven Jr., H. (1952). The Uneasy Case for Progressive Taxation. *The University of Chicago Law Review, 19(3),* 417–520.

Cohen, R. (2012). Death of Hull House: A Nonprofit Coroner's Inquest. *Nonprofit Quarterly,* August. Retrieved from https://nonprofitquarterly.org/2012/08/02/hull-house-death-nonprofit-coroners-inquest/ (accessed November 16, 2018).

Eggert, J. (1997). *What is Economics?* (4th ed.). Mountain View, CA: Mayfield Publishing Company.

Hammack, D.C. and Young, D.R. (Eds.) (1993). *Nonprofit Organizations in a Market Economy.* San Francisco: Jossey-Bass.

Heilbrun, J. and Gray, C.M. (2001). *The Economics of Arts and Culture* (2nd ed.). New York: Cambridge University Press.

Kahneman, D. (2011). *Thinking, Fast and Slow.* New York: Farrar, Straus and Giroux.

Levi, M. (1985). *Thinking Economically.* New York: Basic Books.

McKeever, B.S., Dietz, N.E., and Fyffe, S.D. (2016). *The Nonprofit Almanac* (9th ed.). Lanham, MD: Rowman & Littlefield.

Powell, W.W. and Steinberg, R. (Eds.) (2006). *The Nonprofit Sector: A Research Handbook* (2nd ed.). New Haven, CT: Yale University Press.

Rhoads, S.E. (1999). *The Economist's View of the World.* New York: Cambridge University Press.

Simon, H.A. (1956). Rational Choice and the Structure of the Environment. *Psychological Review, 63(2),* 129–138.

Smith, A. (2016). *The Theory of Moral Sentiments.* Los Angeles: Enhanced Media Publishing (Original edition published in 1759).

Smith, S.R. (2012). Social Services. In Salamon, L.M. (Ed.), *The State of Nonprofit America* (2nd ed., pp. 192–228). Washington, DC: Brookings Institution Press.

Smith, S.R. and Lipsky, M. (1993). *Nonprofits for Hire.* Cambridge, MA: Harvard University Press.

Steinberg, R. (2006). Membership Income. In Young, D.R. (Ed.), *Financing Nonprofits: Putting Theory into Practice* (pp. 121–156). Lanham, MD: Altamira Press and the National Center for Nonprofit Enterprise.

Steinberg, R. (2018). Nonprofit Organizations and the Macroeconomy. In Seaman, B.A. and Young, D.R. (Eds.), *Handbook of Research on Nonprofit Economics and Management* (2nd ed.) (pp. 442–460). Cheltenham, UK and Northampton, MA, USA: Edward Elgar Publishing.

Thaler, R.H. and Sunstein, C.R. (2009). *Nudge.* New York: Penguin Books.

Weisbrod, B.A. (1988). *The Nonprofit Economy.* Cambridge, MA: Harvard University Press.

Young, D.R. and Casey, J. (2017). Supplementary, Complementary, or Adversarial? Non-Profit-

Government Relations. In Boris, E.T. and Steuerle, C.E. (Eds.), *Nonprofits and Government: Collaboration and Conflict* (3rd ed., pp. 37–70). Lanham, MD: Rowman & Littlefield.

Young, D.R., Searing, E.A., and Brewer, C.V. (Eds.) (2016). *The Social Enterprise Zoo*. Cheltenham, UK and Northampton, MA, USA: Edward Elgar Publishing.

🎓 REVIEW CONCEPTS

Allocative Efficiency: When the right mixture of goods and services is produced, taking account of the preferences and costs of all economic actors.

Bounded Rationality: The recognition that people have cognitive limits in formulating and processing information and recognizing opportunity costs in trying to solve complex problems.

Cost Disease: The rapid increase in labor costs that results when an organization cannot improve its productivity as fast as productivity increases in the economy at large.

Economics: The study of how decision makers (individuals, organizations, industries, sectors, countries, society) generate, accumulate, allocate, distribute, and consume resources and create value.

Economies of Scale: Reductions in the unit cost of a good or service as a result of expanding the scale of production (see Chapter 4).

Economies of Scope: Reductions in the unit cost of a good or service as a result of co-producing that good or service jointly with other goods or services (see Chapter 9).

Equity of Endowments: The degree to which people start at the same place in life.

Equity of Outcomes: The degree to which differential resources are provided to different groups so that they can achieve fair final outcomes.

Equity of Process: The degree to which the rules of the game are fair or the same for all participants.

Gifts: Unilateral transfers of economic value between economic actors, a donor and a recipient, for which there is no explicit *quid pro quo*.

Homo Economicus: A stereotype of economic actors as fully rational decision makers.

Horizontal Equity: The degree to which individuals or organizations in the same category (e.g., income class, age, family, or organization size) are treated the same.

Incentives: Economic rewards or penalties meant to influence the economic behavior of organizations or individuals.

Incremental Value: The additional value of consuming or producing one more unit of an economic good; synonymous with "marginal" value.

Macroeconomics: The study of how the economy works as a whole.

Market: A decentralized institution in which independent producers (sellers) and consumers (buyers) voluntarily *exchange* their resources, goods, and services for money.

Microeconomics: The study of economic processes at the level of individuals, organizations, industries and markets.

Normative Economics: The study of how economic actors should make decisions to achieve social efficiency and other social goals such as equity.

Positive Economics: The study of how economic actors and institutions actually make economic decisions and how the economy actually works.

Productive Efficiency: When goods or services of a given quality and quantity are produced at the least cost, or when the highest possible quality or quantity is attained for a given expenditure of valuable resources.

Rational: Economic decision making where people make logical and consistent choices and consider all relevant alternatives.

Satisfice: The use of simpler rules of thumb (or heuristics) to make decisions or solve problems, rather than search for the best possible (optimal) alternatives.

Social Business: A profitmaking business which seeks to maximize a combination of profits and social impact.

Social Efficiency: A feasible state of an economy in which there are no possible changes (in production methods, the quantity of each good or service, or the distribution of each good to each person) that can make at least one person better off without making someone else worse off. Synonymous with Pareto-optimality.

Trading Efficiency: When no pair of consumers wants to swap what they bought for what the other person bought.

Vertical Equity: The degree to which there is a fair distribution of rewards or burdens between ordered classes of individuals (such as classes of individuals categorized by income or wealth).

Warm Glow: Good feeling received in exchange for giving a gift.

Willingness to Pay: The amount of money a consumer is willing to pay in order to purchase an additional unit of a good or service.

EXERCISES

1. Can you think of three trade-offs that must be made in a nonprofit organization or a social enterprise for which you have worked or volunteered? Did that organization address these trade-offs in a systematic fashion? Do you think management decisions would have been different if ideas from economics were applied in these cases?

2. Critically analyze the following imaginary quote: "Because volunteers are not paid by the organizations that employ them, economics is irrelevant to the questions of volunteer recruitment and allocation." (William Acrimony, *The 3.5 Minute Nonprofit Manager*)

3. Critically analyze the following imaginary quote: "If a donor has unsatisfied consumption needs, he is acting irrationally by disregarding his self-interest." (Aynt Rand, *The Bubblehead*)

4. Imagine a world where the entire economy consists of two nonprofit fraternities – Alpha Alpha and Kappa Chino, each containing three "brothers." There is only one good in this economy – beer, and needless to say, every brother likes more beer better than less beer. Beer is not produced, but magically appears under their pillows each night, brought by the beer fairy (who is a teetotaler and not part of the economy). The beer fairy places the same number of six-packs under each brother's pillow within a fraternity but may give different amounts to each fraternity. An economy is a complete listing of the quantities of each good consumed by each individual. In this case, since there is only one good, a complete specification of the economy consists of the amount of beer consumed by each brother in Alpha Alpha and the corresponding amount consumed by each brother in Kappa Chino. Suppose that there are five alternative feasible economies, A through E. The beer allocations in each are:

	Economy				
	A	B	C	D	E
Alpha Alpha	2	2	1	3	3
Kappa Chino	2	3	5	3	1

(a) Which economies (if any) are efficient?

(b) What can you say (if anything) about the fairness of economy C for each of the categories of equity discussed in the text?

5. Joe Fix-It, a social entrepreneur, decides to establish an automobile repair shop that employs high school drop-outs and provides them with on-the-job training in automotive maintenance. What are the different ways that this venture can create new economic value? What prices observed in the marketplace can help to measure this value? Where do market prices fall short of measuring some of this economic value? State the reasoning behind your answers.

6. Yummy, a social business owned by Sally and Tony Spudnik, buys knishes, latkes and other potato delicacies at fair-traded prices from little old ladies struggling to make a living in Siberia, and sells them in upscale ethnic communities in Europe and the U.S. Yummy donates most of its profit to Oy!, a U.S. charity dedicated to preserving the Yiddish language. In what ways does Yummy create new economic value? And in what ways might Yummy be addressing concerns about horizontal and vertical equity? How would you decide if Yummy is efficient in addressing its social goals of helping struggling little old ladies and preserving the Yiddish language? What trade-offs might Yummy be making between these goals?

2

The place of nonprofits and social enterprise in the U.S. economy

I guess we shouldn't have given all of our money to Save the Typewriter, but at least we still have the warm glow!

2.1   Introduction

As these down and out business tycoons would easily recognize, there are, broadly speaking, three organized sectors in the U.S. economy: the private or for-profit business sector; the public or government sector; and the private, nonprofit sector. Each of these sectors is highly diverse internally, and highly interdependent and intertwined with the other sectors. Although the private nonprofit sector is the smallest of the three recognized sectors, it is still size-able with over 1.5 million nonprofit organizations ranging from hospitals to arts organizations to professional associations and religious organizations. However, the nonprofit form is no longer the only organizational vehicle for achieving social good in a market setting – over the last two decades social enterprise has grown both in prominence and impact. Social enterprises can take a variety of business, cooperative, nonprofit and hybrid forms. The purpose of this chapter is to give a general description of where the nonprofit sector and social enterprises fit into the overall U.S. economy. In the process of this excursion, we will become familiar with a number of important economic concepts that help us to understand the significance and functions of nonprofit and social enterprise organizations. We focus first on traditional nonprofit organizations and later consider other social enterprise forms.

2.2 Distinctive characteristics of nonprofit organizations

What distinguishes a private, nonprofit organization from a business or a government agency? In some ways, nonprofits share the characteristics of these other kinds of organizations:

- Like businesses, nonprofit organizations must break-even financially. That is, over a reasonable period of time (determined in part by their ability to borrow and the patience of their creditors) they must take in enough income to pay their bills. Like businesses, they are governed by private citizens rather than by public officials.
- Like government, they have purposes or missions that address aspects of the general public interest or the collective interests of particular groups.
- Like government, nonprofit organizations must observe the *nondistribution constraint* which stipulates that if the organization makes a profit (generates a financial surplus) it may not distribute that surplus to those who own or control it.

Because of this mixture of characteristics, nonprofit organizations have sometimes been called "businesses with public missions" (Bryce, 1987). This characterization identifies some ideas important to the economic analysis of nonprofits.

First, it is important to recognize the role of "profit" in the behavior of nonprofit organizations. Nonprofit organizations may indeed generate profits, but they must use those profits in ways consistent with the mission of the organization.

Second, the concept of *constraint* is important in economic analysis. Constraints are limits to the set of choices open to economic actors (e.g.

donors, purchasers of service, managers of nonprofit organizations and social enterprises). Budget limitations, government policy and technological feasibility constrain economic choices. For example, new forms of social enterprise such as U.S. *benefit corporations* allow profit distribution as well as distribution of assets to owners when they are dissolved; hence they are not subject to the same constraints as traditional nonprofits (Young, Searing, and Brewer, 2016). An important question, therefore, is how the economic behavior of these organizations will differ from nonprofits. Will they be more successful in mobilizing resources to devote to their social missions, or will they divert resources to private interests? Another example is the unrelated business income tax (UBIT) which taxes nonprofits on profits earned on business activities deemed not substantially related to their charitable missions. College sports are exempted from UBIT despite enormous profits earned from television rights and corporate sponsorships (McIntire, 2017). Eliminating this exemption would likely change the ways universities allocate their resources, compensate their employees, generate their income, and determine their academic and physical education programs. Economic analysis allows us to determine how the rational choices of economic actors change when technological progress, government policy, market conditions, and other factors alter constraints on their behavior.

Constraints also create *incentives*. As mentioned in Chapter 1, incentives, or inducements to behave in a certain way, are an important aspect of economic analysis. Taxes or subsidies provide incentives for consumers or taxpayers to do certain things or restrain from doing other things. In nonprofit organizations, the nondistribution constraint establishes conditions which encourage nonprofit organizations to become more "trustworthy" in their dealings with consumers. By prohibiting those in control from enriching themselves with the organization's profits, this constraint removes incentives for nonprofit managers or directors to increase those profits by exploiting consumer ineptness or ignorance. In addition to this "direct" incentive effect, the nondistribution constraint sends a signal to potential nonprofit managers and employees that there will not be stockholder pressure to maximize profits at any cost. Thus, nonprofits attract workers who are motivated more by altruistic or service goals than by money. This "sorting" effect amplifies the direct incentive provided by the nondistribution constraint and allows consumers and donors to place more trust in nonprofit than for-profit organizations (Hansmann, 1987). Similar effects may follow from "limited profit distribution" requirements of various forms of social enterprises such as community interest companies in the U.K. or social cooperatives in Italy (Young, Searing, and Brewer, 2016).

The generic concept of a nonprofit as a privately controlled organization that must observe the nondistribution constraint masks the full flavor and variety of this sector. Nonprofits carry out many different kinds of services, derive their funds from different sources, and benefit many different types of constituencies. As a result, public policy treats alternative categories of nonprofits differently. For example:

- *Public benefit nonprofits* (organizations classified as 501(c)(3) in the federal tax code) address the needs of broad segments of the public, while mutual benefit organizations (e.g., clubs, trade and professional associations) provide benefits primarily to their own members; contributions to public benefit organizations are deductible from personal income taxes while contributions to mutual benefit organizations are not.
- *Private foundations* have narrow bases of donor support, such as single individuals, families or corporations, while community foundations have many sources of donor support. Thus, community foundations are classified as public charities and treated more liberally in the tax code. So-called "social welfare organizations" (classified as 501(c)(4)) include civic leagues or organizations devoted to particular social causes (such as the National Abortion Rights Action League, the American Civil Liberties Union, or the Sierra Club) and engage substantially in political advocacy activities. Donations to these organizations are not deductible from income taxes. Because of constitutional considerations, religious organizations (e.g., churches, synagogues, mosques) are treated differently from other nonprofit organizations by public policy. In particular, contributions to these organizations are tax deductible even though the organizations need not file tax or registration forms with the government.

Note that government policy utilizes incentives and constraints to distinguish among the treatments of nonprofit organizations in various categories. Nonprofits that serve the public at large are eligible to receive tax deductible donations, while those serving only their own members, or engaging substantially in political advocacy are not. Thus, taxpayers have a special incentive to support public benefit organizations through their contributions. Other government policies, such as U.S. postal subsidies and exemptions from local property taxes and state and local sales taxes, provide similar incentives.

Private foundations are subject to payout requirements (constraints on how they can spend or accumulate their money) as well as excise taxes to support the regulatory system and penalty taxes to ensure compliance with the more restrictive set of rules applying to them. These policies encourage foundations to acquire broad sources of support in order to avoid being classified as private foundations, and they discourage close control of a foundation's resources by a few patrons. In part, such policies are designed to discourage the rich from using foundations as a tax shelter while continuing to control their wealth.

All nonprofits are exempt from paying corporate income tax on their profits if those profits derive from activity related to the mission of the organization. As noted above, profits from those commercial activities that do not directly contribute to the organization's mission are subject to an unrelated business income tax (UBIT) similar to the corporate income tax. Income from the sale of computers to the general public by a university bookstore is an example of unrelated business income. The differing tax treatment of related and unrelated income provides an incentive to shift revenue-raising efforts towards related ventures.

In these various ways, government policy utilizes incentives and constraints to encourage appropriate behavior by the various subcategories of nonprofit organizations as well as by the nonprofit sector as a whole. Similarly, policies and regulations applying to other forms of social enterprise affect the behavior and performance of those entities. For example, the degrees to which an enterprise is subject to an "asset lock" requirement wherein corporate assets cannot be appropriated by private owners, or a "limited profit constraint" that reduces returns on private equity, will undercut incentives for private individuals to invest in such enterprises. In contrast, however, the fact that social enterprises permit private returns on investment may discourage charitable foundations from investing in these entities for fear of violating the nondistribution constraint applying to nonprofits (Young, Searing, and Brewer, 2016). Still, allowing for-profit variants of social enterprise to provide services traditionally provided by nonprofits may increase that potential for attracting financial capital into the social sector.

2.3 The size and scope of the nonprofit sector[1]

The nonprofit sector is very diverse and continues to grow. Under the U.S. Internal Revenue Code, more than 30 types of legal entities are classified as 501(c) organizations; all are exempt from corporate income tax but not all are charitable. As we describe the part that nonprofits play in the overall economy, we will encounter several additional useful economic concepts. In particular, there is a variety of ways to measure the scope of nonprofit activity in economic terms.

One question we can ask is, how many nonprofit organizations are there in the U.S.? As of 2015, there were 1.5 million nonprofits registered with

Table 2.1 Size and financial scope of the nonprofit sector, 2003 and 2013

	2003	2013	% change
All Registered Nonprofits	1.38 million	1.41 million	2.8
Reporting Nonprofits	515,866	500,396	−3.0
Revenues	$1.36 trillion	$2.26 trillion	65.5
Expenses	$1.30 trillion	$2.10 trillion	61.2
Assets	$3.07 trillion	$5.17 trillion	68.1
501(c)(3) Public Charities	798,988	954,476	19.5
Reporting Public Charities	287,251	293,103	2.0
Revenues	$974 billion	$1.73 trillion	78.0
Expenses	$940 billion	$1.62 trillion	72.8
Assets	$1.75 trillion	$3.22 trillion	83.9

Source: McKeever (2015).

the IRS, ranging from charities, hospitals, educational institutions, day-care providers, social services agencies, arts and cultural institutions, research organizations, advocacy groups, international relief and development agencies, foundations, united funding organizations, to a host of other charitable and public-purpose nonprofit organizations. Not included in the 1.5 million registered nonprofits are religious congregations or their auxiliary groups, and smaller organizations that are not registered with the IRS. (Indeed, registered organizations are probably the tip of an iceberg constituting more than 5 million organizations, many of which operate informally as nonprofit organizations. If all religious congregations and smaller organizations were taken into account, the number of nonprofits would be closer to 2.2 million (McKeever, Dietz, and Fyffe, 2016).) Table 2.1 summarizes changes in the size and financial scope of the nonprofit sector between 2003 and 2013. Organizations in the 501(c)(3) category, which can receive tax-deductible contributions, include public charities and private foundations. This category accounts for the largest share of the nonprofit sector in number of organizations, expenses, and assets. The biggest industries in the nonprofit sector in terms of numbers of organizations are Human Services (34 percent), Education (18 percent), Health Care (12 percent), Public and Social Benefit (12 percent), and Arts, Culture, and Humanities (11 percent).

The second question is, what is the economic importance of these organizations? This question is complicated by a special factor – assessing the value of volunteer labor. As we will discuss in later chapters, volunteer time is an unpriced but nonetheless valuable resource that contributes directly to the production of services by nonprofit organizations (as well as other kinds of social enterprises).

Thus, it is conceptually correct and substantively important to include its value in the computation of national income accruing to nonprofit organizations. However, the value of volunteer labor is not obvious. As an approximation, researchers sometimes equate the value of an hour of volunteer time with the average hourly wage of nonagricultural workers in the U.S. economy, plus a 12 percent margin for fringe benefits (Hodgkinson et al., 1992). (See Chapter 6 for further discussion of this measurement issue.)

In addition to the challenges of measuring volunteer labor, estimates of the nonprofit share of the economy are also hampered by the fact that the value of output services delivered at zero or low cost is underestimated in national income accounts. With these caveats, we can use available information about the nonprofit sector to observe several trends in this sector and its relationship to the economy as a whole.

While smaller than the business or government sectors, the nonprofit sector contributes an important segment of GDP in the U.S. Including estimated volunteer contributions, nonprofit organizations of all types contributed an estimated $909.9 billion to the US economy in 2013, representing about 5.4 percent of GDP. The economic contribution of the nonprofit sector is concentrated in particular subsectors. In 2013, health organizations, which include hospitals, community health systems, and primary care facilities, accounted for 48 percent of nonprofit sector expenses and over a quarter of its assets. Education accounted for 13 percent of expenses and 20 percent of total assets. Approximately 90 percent of the national income earned by nonprofits was accounted for by public benefit type (501(c)(3) tax deductible) and social welfare advocacy (501(c)(4)) nonprofit organizations, including churches.

In 2014, nonprofits constituted an even larger share of wages and salaries than they did of GDP. Nonprofits paid $647.6 billion in wages and salaries, compared to $5.7 trillion paid by business and $1.1 trillion paid by government. This amounts to 9 percent of all wages and salaries paid to U.S. workers, at least partly reflecting the greater labor intensity of the nonprofit sector and its concentration in services versus goods, compared to the rest of the economy.

The major share of all nonprofit wages (57.1 percent) was paid by health care and social assistance organizations. Hospitals, residential care facilities, and ambulatory health care services accounted for just under half (49.4 percent) of all nonprofit wages. Wages for hospitals grew from $196.1 billion in 2003 to $313.2 billion in 2013, by far the largest absolute growth of any industry during the same period. If hospitals are removed from the employment trend, nonprofit wages would have grown more slowly from 2003 to 2013, 40.1 percent compared with 49.2 percent. The second largest subsector in terms of employment – which includes grant-making foundations, fund-raising or other supporting organizations, professional societies or associations, groups promoting or administering religious activities, cemeteries, human rights organizations, advocacy organizations, conservation and wildlife organizations – accounted for approximately 17 percent of nonprofit wages. The education sector, that includes organizations such as colleges, elementary schools, technical schools, exam preparation, hockey camps, and dance instruction, is the third largest wage sector at 16.2 percent. Higher education accounts for two-thirds of educational service wages and over 10 percent of total nonprofit sector wages.

The nonprofit sector's share of the economy changes only very slightly if supplements to salaries are included in the wage estimate. Supplements to salaries consist of employer contributions for employee pension and insurance funds and employer contributions for government social insurance. When these benefits are considered, nonprofits' share declines slightly, by about 0.1 percentage point. In comparison, government's share of wage and salary accruals increases by almost 3 percentage points (from 15.1 percent to 17.8 percent) and business's share declines by 2.5 percentage points.

Considering the value of volunteer labor is central to assessing the size of the nonprofit sector. In 2014, approximately 25.3 percent of US adults volunteered, contributing an estimated 8.7 billion hours, and generating a market value of $179.2 billion. The average wage value of volunteer time was $167.2 billion dollars. The combination of nonprofit wages and volunteer labor exceeded $801 billion in 2013, and volunteers accounted for more than 26 percent of this combined total (see Table 2.2).

Table 2.2 Nonprofit wages and the wage value of volunteer work, 2008–2013

	2008	2009	2010	2011	2012	2013
Wage Value of Volunteers ($B)	144.7	150.7	154.1	164.8	168.3	167.3
Nonprofit Wages ($B)	539.9	558.0	571.2	590.1	617.3	634.0
Total ($B)	684.6	708.7	725.3	754.9	785.6	801.2
Wage Value of Volunteers as % of Nonprofit Wage	27.0	27.0	27.0	27.9	27.3	26.4

Source: Calculations based on U.S. Census Data.

It is clear from the numbers that nonprofit organizations attract the bulk of volunteer labor in the economy. Why is this so? What is the special advantage that nonprofits have that attracts volunteers? This a question we want to deal with later when we discuss economic theories of nonprofit organizations. Interestingly, although public charities make up only 71 percent of the organizations in the sector (only 46 percent if we exclude churches) they account for more than 90 percent of the income, earnings, and employment of the sector. Thus, many other key functions of the nonprofit sector, such as advocacy and trade and professional representation, are underemphasized by these traditional measures, even if they are functionally very important.

Finally, it is worth observing that, overall, the nonprofit sector is small as a sector – only 5 percent to 10 percent of the economy by the various economic measures, compared to business and government. If we think of nonprofits as an "industry," however, commensurate with, say, public utilities, steelmaking, or food retailing, it is very large. Interestingly, while government and business wages and salaries fell between 2008 and 2009 during the recession, wages and salaries in nonprofit institutions serving households (NPISH) did not. Wages and salaries grew by 36.1 percent between 2006 and 2014 – faster than in any other sector of the economy (McKeever, Dietz, and Fyffe, 2016), suggesting that the nonprofit sector has a role to play in maintaining employment and job growth in the U.S., especially in difficult economic times.

2.4   The composition of the nonprofit sector

Like the business sector, the nonprofit sector is quite diverse, consisting of many "industries." However, because the nonprofit sector crosscuts industries, this is too simple a characterization. While it wholly contains certain "pure" nonprofit industries, it also contains a share of other "mixed" industries. Pure nonprofit industries include churches, trade and professional associations, foundations, and advocacy organizations. Virtually all organizations in these industries are nonprofit organizations. "Mixed" industries include health care, day care, education, nursing home, mental health services, and arts and culture. In some of these mixed industries, such as the arts, nonprofit organizations share the stage primarily with the for-profit sector, while in others, such as higher education, they primarily complement government provision. In still other mixed industries, such as hospitals and nursing homes, all three sectors are well-represented.

One puzzle for economists is the question of why certain industries are mixed. If the nonprofit form presents certain advantages in a given industry, why aren't all organizations in that industry nonprofit? And if in another industry, the form does not offer such advantages, why aren't all organizations in that industry of some other form? A related question is why the proportion of nonprofit organizations varies so widely from one mixed industry to the next. This is another issue for economic theory, and another way of posing the question, what competitive advantages do nonprofit organizations have in some situations that they do not have in others? Indeed, what advantages and/or market failures (see Chapters 3 and 13) are found in each of these sectors, and how might they interact to give us the current mixture of market structures found in the U.S. economy? (Steinberg, 2006).

Some insight can be gained from examining the proportions of various industries in which nonprofits participate. Salamon (2012) has compiled a variety of measures including shares of the number of organizations, industry employment, industry revenues or expenses, and enrollment or patient-days, where applicable and available (see Table 2.3). There are some interesting patterns found in these numbers. First, it is noteworthy that the nonprofit share varies so widely among industries. In particular, we see from Table 2.3 that nonprofits constitute over half the share, by various measures, of the hospital and various social services industries, and segments of the classical arts. Indeed, for emergency food and housing, vocational rehabilitation, and residential care, and for operas, orchestras, museums and dance companies, the nonprofit share exceeds two-thirds of their industries. Meanwhile, nursing homes and vocational education institutions constitute less than thirty percent of their respective industries. Economists ask what factors explain why such large variation exists among the mixed industries in which nonprofits participate. Perhaps more puzzling, even within broad categories of similar industries, there is considerable variation. Why, for example, is the nonprofit share so different between higher education and other education subfields (e.g., elementary education and secondary education), or between hospitals and nursing homes?

Another striking observation from the data is the different character of nonprofits versus other organizations in each industry. This is suggested by comparing alternative indicators of market share for particular industries. For example, nonprofit hospitals constitute half of the number of organizations but roughly two-thirds of industry expenses and patient days, indicating that nonprofit hospitals tend to be larger than other (for-profit) hospitals. Similarly, nonprofit nursing homes represent 18.7 percent of organizations but roughly 30 percent of employment and expenses. The same pattern emerges for social service organizations where shares of employment and expenses well exceed their shares of organizations in their industries. Such numbers raise questions for economists not only about why nonprofits co-

Table 2.3 Nonprofit sector shares in selected industries, 2007–2008

	% of organizations	% of employment	% of revenues [or % of expenses]	% enrollment [or % of patient-days]
Hospitals	50.5		69	[63]
Nursing Homes	18.7	29.3	31.1	
Higher Education	37.3		[39.2]	19.6
Elementary & Secondary Education	25		[8]	11
Vocational Education	18.9	24.5	27	
Emergency Food & Housing	95			
Vocational Rehabilitation	77			
Individual & Family Services	6			
Residential Care	67			
Day Care	29			
Operas	94	99		
Orchestras & Chamber Ensembles	95	98		
Museums & Historical Sites	88	91		
Dance Companies	78	90		
Theater Companies	61	61		
Sports & Recreation	16	21		

Source: Salamon (2012).

exist with for-profit and government organizations in the same industry, but why they are able to grow larger and attract relatively more resources than their (generally for-profit) counterparts. Similar questions arise in the higher education field where nonprofits constitute 37.3 percent of organizations and 39.2 percent of industry expenses, but account for only 19.6 percent of enrollments. What do these numbers suggest about the selectivity, quality, and efficiency of private (nonprofit) educational institutions compared to their (mostly public) university counterparts?

2.5 How do nonprofits interact with other sectors?

The presence of mixed industries suggests that nonprofit organizations either complement or compete with other kinds of organizations in the provision of particular goods and services. In fact, the question of whether they compete head-on by providing the same kinds of services to the same kinds of clients, or whether they occupy a different niche within the relevant market, is key to understanding the role of nonprofits in the economy. Although, the question of competition between for-profits and nonprofits has been a controversial public policy issue in recent years, economists believe that nonprofits and for-profits often occupy different market segments within industries. While nonprofits derive about half of their income, on average, from fees and service charges (excluding government reimbursements), relatively little of this sales revenue comes from commercially competitive ventures that are not directly related to their missions. Within their mainline or related service activities, many nonprofits address those market segments with a strong public-benefit component of little interest to for-profit business, such as legal services for the poor, social services for the disadvantaged, or high-cultural activities. In other industries, including hospitals, nursing homes, and child day-care centers, nonprofits appear to provide the same services and compete for the same paying customers as for-profit organizations. In these cases, however, there is evidence that nonprofits offer different qualities of service than for-profits (see Weisbrod, 1988).

In addition to competition, there are many different ways in which nonprofit organizations interact with other entities in the economy. For example:

- Nonprofits often serve as contractual agents for government, delivering public services that government pays for. In the fields of social services, employment/training, health, and arts/culture nonprofits delivered more than 40 percent of government-funded services in 2013.
- The supportive role of nonprofits in providing services desired by the government and business extends into other industries. For example, nonprofits contract with business to provide services such as mental health care for corporate employees. Nonprofits also operate fund-raising campaigns and payroll deduction plans within government agencies and corporations.
- While nonprofits serve the interests of business and government in many ways, the reverse is also true. Businesses establish corporate foundations and nonprofit trade associations, while governments regulate the behavior of nonprofit organizations in various ways. In addition, nonprofits form for-profit subsidiaries to separate commercial from mission-related activity.
- Corporate and government executives are involved as volunteers and board members of nonprofit organizations. Indeed, governments appoint board members to some nonprofit organizations in which they have a major interest. For example, the board of the Indiana University

Foundation, a private nonprofit that supports a public university, includes designated governmental representatives, elected alumni, and private citizens appointed by the board.

These examples illustrate that, while it is helpful to view the nonprofit sector as a separate and distinct part of the economy with its own unique characteristics, nonprofit organizations clearly do not operate in isolation from the rest of the economy. It is not an "independent sector" in an economic sense, but rather an "interdependent" sector that derives its support from a variety of sources and interacts with other sectors in many different ways.

Finally, economists are interested in why there is such wide variation in the sources of funds across nonprofit industries. Is the diversification of revenues practiced by many nonprofits a good thing? Does it provide protection against the risks of relying on a single source of support, or does it simply complicate the process of managing and accounting for multiple types of funds? Does heavy reliance on government funds imply a loss of autonomy and independence? That is, as government supplies more of the funding, do nonprofits lose their ability to decide for themselves what services to produce and how to produce them? Does a heavy reliance on fees make nonprofits too sensitive to market considerations and less able to focus on mission? As sales become a more important revenue source, do nonprofits gear their services more to paying customers at the expense of those who may need their services but are limited in their ability to pay? These are questions that economists try to address when they model the operations of nonprofit organizations as economic agents and ask what changes in policy (incentives and constraints) may be desirable.

2.6   Finances of nonprofits and allocation of funds

As documented by McKeever, Dietz, and Fyffe (2016), public charities reported $1.73 trillion in revenue, $1.62 trillion in expenses, and $3.22 trillion in total assets in 2013. Notably, the largest nonprofit organizations, primarily hospitals and universities, dominate the nonprofit financial landscape. Organizations with $10 million or more in annual expenses account for just 5 percent of all nonprofits but more than 86 percent of total expenses. Conversely, organizations reporting under $500,000 in total expenses account for approximately 66 percent of all charities but less than 2 percent of total expenditures. Larger organizations tend to be older. Approximately 53 percent of organizations with $10 million or more in total expenses report a founding date prior to 1980. Over two-thirds of organizations with less than $500,000 in total expenses report a founding date after 1989.

Nonprofit organizations derive income from various sources, including fees for service, from the government, and from donations. Fee-for-service revenue from private sources, which includes tuition payments, hospital patient revenues (excluding Medicare and Medicaid), and ticket sales, is the single largest source of funding for the nonprofit sector, accounting for 48 percent of total nonprofit revenues in 2013.

Fees from government sources, such as Medicare and Medicaid payments and government contracts, accounted for another 24 percent of revenue; private contributions, including individual contributions and grants from foundations and corporations, accounted for 13 percent; and government grants accounted for another 8 percent of total revenue. Funding from government, both fees for services and government grants, accounted for nearly one-third of all nonprofit revenue (32 percent). Other income, which includes dues and assessments, rental income, and income from special events accounted for less than 2 percent of revenue. Finally, investment income, which continued to recover from stock market losses caused by the 2008–2009 recession, accounted for 5 percent of nonprofit revenue in 2013. Researchers have tied the diverse income portfolios of nonprofit organizations to their missions, the kinds of public and private goods they provide, and the groups that they benefit (Young, 2017).

Consumption expenditures account for a large proportion of nonprofit expenditures (approximately 90 percent); the other component, transfer payments (discussed in Chapter 6), constitutes around 10 percent. Consumption expenditures by subsector are shown in Table 2.4. Health care organizations account

Table 2.4 Nonprofit expenditures, by subsector, 2014 ($ billions)

Subsector	Expenditures	Percent
Health	754.1	59.0
Education	174.4	13.6
Social Services	117.6	9.2
Religious Organizations	82.6	6.5
Recreation	43.6	3.4
Professional Advocacy	42.8	3.3
Foundations and Grant-making	32.8	2.5
Social Advocacy	21.1	1.7
Civil and Social Organizations	10.2	0.8

Notes: Excludes nonprofit institutions serving business and government. "Percent" is percent of total expenditures across subsections.

Source: McKeever, Dietz, and Fyffe (2016).

Table 2.5 Expenditures for nonprofit institutions, 2008–2014 ($ billions)

Year	2008	2009	2010	2011	2012	2013	2014
Revenue	1180.9	1191.3	1237.4	1237.4	1291.7	1294.6	1324.6
Expenditure	1251.1	1291.8	1311.9	1312.8	1346.5	1367.4	1394.5
Savings	−70.2	−100.5	−74.5	−78.4	−54.9	−72.9	−69.9

Note: Excludes nonprofit institutions serving business and government.

Source: McKeever, Dietz, and Fyffe (2016).

for more than half of expenditures (59 percent), followed by education (13.6 percent), and social services (9 percent). Expenditures of civic and social organizations were the smallest (0.8 percent, amounting to about $10.2 billion). In recent years, many nonprofits have had difficulty making ends meet. In 2014, U.S. nonprofits had a collective deficit of $69.9 billion. Savings have been declining since 2008 and nonprofit institutions have been running deficits between 4 and 8 percent of total revenue each year between 2008 and 2014 (see Table 2.5). Many nonprofits are spending more money than they are able to generate – highlighting a major concern for the sector. Nonprofits that run annual operating deficits either have to use reserves to fund their activities, borrow money to finance their operations, or cut expenses. In this connection, productivity is also a serious concern as wages and salaries rise over time. The ability to substitute capital (computers, networking, etc.) for labor in the nonprofit sector must be continually explored. Paid labor must itself be continually enhanced, through appropriate education and training. As discussed in Chapter 1, the cost disease associated with production of labor-intensive services can inhibit many nonprofits' abilities to significantly increase productivity.

Volunteer labor can sometimes substitute for paid employees. However, productive volunteers are scarce and must be trained. Nonprofit managers must decide how much to invest in volunteer recruitment and training and must determine the combination of paid and volunteer labor that is best for their organization. All these activities and initiatives must be managed efficiently to achieve their objectives.

2.7 Growth of the nonprofit sector

One reason that nonprofit organizations have received increasing attention in recent years is that their share of the economy is growing rapidly. Nonprofit sector employment has grown steadily over the last decade (McKeever, Dietz, and Fyffe, 2016). Between 2003 to 2013, the number of nonprofit organizations registered with the IRS increased by 28 percent, from 1.38 million to 1.41 million. Between 2000 and 2013, the number of employees in the nonprofit sector increased 22.6 percent while the government sector increased just over 5 percent and the business sector grew less than one percent. Indeed, excluding nonprofits, U.S. nonfarm employment grew by only 1.4 percent between 2000 and 2013. Wages in the nonprofit sector grew by 28.8 percent, faster than that of business, which grew 5.6 percent, and government, which increased 16.8 percent (McKeever, Dietz, and Fyffe, 2016).

Nonprofits' contribution to the U.S. economy has been steadily increasing over the past six decades. While government and business wages and salaries fell between 2008 and 2009 during the recession, wages and salaries in nonprofits did not. Nonprofit wages grew by 36.1 percent between 2006 and 2014, faster than in any other sector of the economy (McKeever, Dietz, and Fyffe, 2016). Nonprofit sector growth in wages and employees exceeded growth in both the government and business sectors during the recession and was only slightly behind business growth in the post-recession period. Similar growth and development, both of the nonprofit sector and social enterprise more broadly, has been experienced in countries around the world (Anheier and Salamon, 2006; Casey, 2016).

The relatively faster growth of the nonprofit sector in recent years again raises the question of what special advantages can be attributed to nonprofit organizations. Why are these organizations growing faster than government or business? Economists have proposed some ideas as to why this is happening.

First, nonprofit organizations operate in the services side of the economy rather than in the production of material goods. The services sector of the U.S. economy has been growing rapidly, and the growth of the nonprofit sector is comparable to the growth of the service sector as a whole.

Second, government has grown in recent years principally by increasing its expenditures, not by increasing public sector employment. Increasingly, government services have been delivered through private agencies. For example, in the post recessionary period 2010 to 2013 nonprofit growth in employment increased 3.6 percent compared to 2.9 percent for government. Rather than deliver services itself, government prefers more and more to deliver its services through contracts with private, largely nonprofit, organizations (see Smith and Lipsky, 1993; McKeever, 2015).

2.8   Commercial national charities and donor-advised funds

As the philanthropic landscape expands, diversifies, and shifts its priorities and preferences, billions of dollars are being set aside in commercial vehicles that are intended to facilitate charitable giving (Hurtubise, 2017). Commercial national charities, notably Donor-Advised Funds (DAFs) administered by commercial securities firms, now play prominent roles in philanthropy giving. There are also DAFs administered by nonprofit community foundations. DAFs are vehicles used by individuals to set aside funds for charitable use. A donor establishes a fund at a commercial national charity (such as Fidelity Charitable, Vanguard Charitable, or Schwab Charitable), donates cash or an appreciated asset such as stock or real estate to that fund, and takes an immediate tax deduction equal to the amount contributed. The commercial national charity then invests the liquid assets and awards grants to nonprofits at the recommendation of the donor. However, neither donors nor commercial national charities are obligated to distribute the funds to charities within any specific time frame.

According to Hurtubise (2017), during the next few decades approximately $30 trillion in Baby Boomer assets will transfer to their Gen X and Millennial children and grandchildren. An interesting question is whether DAFs will contribute a significant portion of these dollars to charity. In 2017, there were an estimated 285,000 DAFs with assets totaling around $85 billion. Total charitable assets in DAFs at commercial national charities grew by 134 percent (from $19.06 billion to $44.68 billion) between 2012 and 2016. During that same period, the annual payout rate from these funds decreased by 3.4 percentage points (from 24.1 to 20.7 percent). In 2016, more than $36 billion (approximately 82 percent of DAF assets) remained unallocated. The growth of commercial national charities affects many charitable institutions, in particular community foundations, which rely on their own DAFs, as well as those held by commercial charities, to support their work. Community foundations are dramatically falling behind commercial national charities in capturing donations for their communities (Hurtubise, 2017). In 2012, commercial national charities and community foundations nearly tied with respect to total charitable dollars in DAFs (around $18 billion each). By 2016, commercial national charities held $44.68 billion, while community foundations held $29.8 billion (National Philanthropic Trust's 2017 Donor-Advised Fund Report).

Donor-advised funds convey advantages to donors and enhance charitable giving. Wright-Violich (2008) provides the following reasons for the success of donor-advised funds:

- They democratize philanthropy. By aggregating donors and processing high numbers of charitable transactions, donor-advised funds have kept costs down, resulting in lower fees and lower account minimums.
- They leverage corporate-nonprofit partnerships. Donor-advised funds exemplify how a nonprofit mission can be linked with corporate knowledge to affect social change. They are, in effect, part of a revolution in the way nonprofits do business by engaging more closely with the business sector, in this case, large securities firms that attract substantial capital from individuals.
- They reduce barriers to giving. A study of high-net-worth philanthropy by Bank of America found that households with incomes in excess of $200,000 or assets in excess of $1 million cited red tape, the time it takes to give, lack of access to research on prospective nonprofits, and lack of knowledge about needy organizations as the greatest barriers to increasing their charitable giving (Wright-Violich, 2008). Institutions administering DAFs can potentially address these needs.
- They simplify and stabilize the flow of funds to charities. Donor-advised funds can be helpful to smaller nonprofits. Small and start-up charities are relieved of the hassle of accepting securities as contributions. Rather than having to deal with such assets, they get a check instead.
- The funds can serve as sources of stable funding for charities during an economic downturn. Even when contributions to the funds decrease, their assets continue to throw off earnings that can be granted to charities.

Despite the advantages presumed here, substantial concerns have been raised about DAFs. The major criticism is that too many of the funds hold their assets far longer than they should, thus squeezing the pipeline of charitable dollars that might otherwise have flowed to charitable causes more quickly.

2.9   Social enterprises: definition and distinction

The roles of government, conventional nonprofits, and for-profit businesses sectors are for the most part clearly understood. However, there is no definitional consensus in the relatively new field of social enterprise (see Steinberg, 2015). Different authors (Horton, 2006; Mook et al., 2015; Young, Searing, and Brewer, 2016) have used the term differently but there are common elements shared by the variety of categorizations and explanations. Some authors restrict attention to commercial activities with social benefits, emphasizing the word "enterprise" (e.g., Kerlin, 2006). Others focus on the word "social" to highlight provision of collective goods, redistributional issues and quality and affordability of essential services (e.g., Steinberg, 2015). The phrase "social business" as utilized by Yunas, Moingeon, and

Lehmann-Ortiga (2010) is defined as a private sector enterprise that primarily provides socially beneficial goods at no loss to investors. Mook et al. (2015) have done a comprehensive study of the social economy in the United States in which they analyze and categorize the role of social enterprises. According to this study, social enterprises include many types of organizations such as nonprofits, cooperatives, credit unions, limited liability companies (LLCs) and benefit corporations. There are approximately 30,000 cooperatives generating about $515 billion in revenues, over 856,000 million jobs, and more than $25 billion in wages and benefits. Americans hold an estimated 350 million memberships in cooperatives (Deller et al., 2009). In 2014, there were also 1037 low-profit limited liability companies (L3Cs), 1121 benefit corporations, and 746 certified B corporations in the U.S.

Despite their differences, these forms share common characteristics of prioritizing social objectives alongside economic objectives (profit generation). The social objective often assumes priority over economic purposes. According to Mook et al. (2015), social enterprises are intended to serve social needs that are unmet by the public and private sectors, and those objectives are often incorporated in their missions and organizational charters. The objectives are not a secondary consideration, as when a traditional business makes a decision to embrace corporate social responsibility to enhance profitability, but are intentional and central to the organization's purpose from its inception. The objectives take on different forms, depending on whether the social enterprise is meeting the needs of a membership group, pursuing charitable goals, or operating in the market in a socially responsive way. These goals underlie the following categorization of social enterprises (Mook et al., 2015):

- Social Enterprise for Public Benefit: Social enterprises have a long charitable tradition. Charitable social enterprises (primarily traditional nonprofits) constitute a heterogeneous mix of organizations that address public goals such as administering to the poor, advancing religion, education, or science; establishing and maintaining public monuments or works; reducing the burdens of government and neighborhood tensions; eliminating prejudice and discrimination; defending human and civil rights mandated by law; and combating community deterioration and juvenile delinquency.
- Social Enterprises Meeting Members' Needs: This form of social enterprise is based on the principle of mutual aid or self-help. The objective is to meet members' needs. Members of these social organizations usually share a common bond of association (e.g., common heritage, occupation, or location) and a common need that they address through service to

themselves and each other. The International Co-operative Alliance, the umbrella organization for all cooperatives and credit unions, embraces this objective. Self-help organizations are common among marginalized groups such as immigrants or racial minorities, and over the years people with common bonds such as workplace, profession, business, religion, ethnic and gender identity, have formed nonprofit mutual associations and cooperatives.

- Social Enterprises Operating in the Market: This form of social enterprise operates in the market with a social mission that is balanced with seeking profits for investors. For example, *work-integrated social enterprises* popular in Europe employ workers from marginalized groups with the intent of preparing them with skills to succeed in the labor market. Similarly, *fair trade* organizations seek to improve the welfare of low-income business entrepreneurs or farmers, often in less-developed countries, by purchasing their products and selling them at "fair prices" so as to lift the suppliers out of poverty. Another variation includes businesses such as Newman's Own and TOMS Shoes which sell commercial products and turn substantial portions of their profits over to charitable causes. Finally, some businesses make special efforts to accommodate low-income consumers with subsidized prices. These examples raise an interesting question as to the boundaries between social enterprise and ordinary businesses. For instance, are for-profit hospitals social enterprises? Indeed, they do provide a critical social service, sometimes at reduced market prices for the poor.

For our purposes here, there is no need to define the border between businesses and social enterprises, or between traditional nonprofits and social enterprises. Rather it suffices to recognize that economic analysis must take into account the different organizational objectives promoted, and the various constraints faced, by any of these forms as they seek to operate in economic markets.

2.10 Why social enterprises?

Social enterprises have emerged in the context of limitations of other forms of organizations to address the social needs of society. (In Chapter 13 we call this *market failure*). Here we will briefly consider four broad issues that help explain why social enterprises have developed in the contemporary economic landscape: efficiency issues, capital and financial issues, and demand issues.

Efficiency issues

Nonprofits can create their own kinds of productive and allocative ineffi-ciency. Recall from Chapter 1 that productive efficiency is about maximiz-ing charitable outputs from given levels of inputs, and allocative efficiency is about producing the right mixture of outputs. In the case of nonprofits, incompetence, inattentiveness, and indolence are possible because of the fol-lowing reasons:

- There may be hidden agendas to hire the friends of board members, expand board member résumés, or avoid hard work.
- There may be *agency* problems. The board (*principal*) hires managers (*agents*), and the managers hire employees (*chained agents*). The objectives of managers and employees may stray from the organization's mission, as it is costly to monitor employee performance and/or provide incentives to keep agents on task. Strategies such as profit sharing do not work as well in a nonprofit setting, but the agency problem may be smaller in social enterprises because the people who chose to work there are supportive of the mission and become more so through on-the-job socialization.
- In nonprofits, there is no threat of takeover bids or shareholders demand-ing higher dividends to check inefficiency. Still, there are many other sources of accountability for nonprofits, including donors, government overseers, and other stakeholders, to mitigate these issues (Steinberg, 1987; Peters, 2001). For example: nonprofit board members may be motivated by a passionate devotion to mission, and consumers of services are often on the board. Volunteers on site provide a strong check on per-formance and a helpful signal to other stakeholders. Monitoring is done by private certification and rating agencies such as the Wise Giving Alliance and Charity Navigator, combined fund-raising organizations (like United Way) and sometimes by trade associations. Debt holders and granting agencies also oversee the financial behavior of their nonprofit clients.

Capital and finance issues

Nonprofits are limited in certain ways in their access to, and costs of, rais-ing capital. For example, nonprofits cannot raise capital through initial public offerings (issuance of shares of stock) the same way for-profits can. Often, lenders require that nonprofits pay a higher interest rate than for-profits because there are no shareholders to bear the risk of default. The advantages of for-profits' ability to raise capital is a common reason for non-profits, particularly hospitals, to convert to for-profit status, and it is one factor behind the movement towards for-profit social enterprises. However, some of the problems limiting nonprofits' capacity to raise capital may be exaggerated. Nonprofits can secure donations and grants, while for-profits cannot. Nonprofits are exempt from the corporate income tax, which drains *retained earnings* as a source of capital, and they can obtain tax-exempt bonds in certain circumstances. They are also exempt from taxes on excess retained earnings applicable to for-profits.

Demand issues

Nonprofits may respond more slowly to changes in demand than for-profits, for a variety of reasons such as limitations in capacity to raise necessary capital; less incentive or desire to embrace market changes that are not clearly mission-related; and a proclivity to rally around historically-defined narrow and possibly shrinking missions rather than embrace a new set of emerging and growing societal needs. For example, many social service nonprofits were established to serve the needs of particular ethnic groups or immigrant populations whose welfare has improved over time, and have struggled to adjust their focus to serve the needs of newly emerging needy groups. Other nonprofits have had to adapt to new practices deemed more effective than old ways of doing things, such as the de-emphasis on institutional care in favor of community-based programming. In the for-profit sector, such adaptation often occurs by entry of new organizations to replace firms that have not maintained their currency, and through takeover of inefficient firms by successful ones. In the nonprofit sector, devotion to historical mission and substantial barriers to entry by new organizations inhibit the entry and exit process, while the special difficulties of combining independent nonprofit organizations in the absence of a market for corporate control slow the sector's response through mergers and takeovers (Fremont-Smith, 2004).

SUMMARY

The nonprofit sector is the smallest of the U.S. economy's three traditional sectors, but it is an extremely critical sector in terms of the kinds of services it produces and the functions that it serves. It is also the most rapidly growing sector as the U.S. becomes more and more of a service economy and government privatizes the delivery (if not the financing) of its services. The nonprofit sector is highly diverse in its composition and its reliance on different sources of funds, and it interacts closely with government and business in many important ways. Over the last two decades, social enterprise has grown in both prominence and impact and the nonprofit legal form is no longer the only organizational vehicle for achieving social good in the private parts of the economy. Economics helps us to understand the special advantages as well as the limitations of nonprofit organizations and the newer social enterprises in different service areas, and helps explains why these sectors have become so significant a part of the U.S. economy as whole.

NOTE

1 Most of the following statistics are taken from *The Nonprofit Almanac – Ninth Edition* (McKeever, Dietz, and Fyffe, 2016) and *The Nonprofit Sector in Brief* (2015) from the Urban Institute (McKeever, 2015).

SELECTED REFERENCES AND CITATIONS

Anheier, H.K. and Salamon, L.M. (2006). The Nonprofit Sector in Comparative Perspective. In Powell, W.W. and Steinberg, R. (Eds.), *The Nonprofit Sector: A Research Handbook* (2nd ed., pp. 89–114). New Haven: Yale University Press.

Bryce, H.J. (1987). *Financial and Strategic Management for Nonprofit Organizations.* Englewood Cliffs, NJ: Prentice Hall Publishing.

Casey, J. (2016). *The Nonprofit World: Civil Society and the Rise of the Nonprofit Sector.* Boulder and London: Kumarian Press.

Deller, S., Hoyt, A., Hueth, B., and Sundaram-Stukel, R. (2009). *Research on the Economic Impact of Cooperatives,* Madison: University of Wisconsin Center for Cooperatives. Retrieved from http://reic.uwcc.wisc.edu/sites/all/REIC_FINAL.pdf (accessed July 1, 2013).

Fremont-Smith, M.R. (2004). *Governing Nonprofit Organizations: Federal and State Law and Regulation.* Cambridge, MA: Belknap Press of Harvard University.

Grönbjerg, K. and Paarlberg, L. (2001). Community Variations in the Size and Scope of the Nonprofit Sector. *Nonprofit and Voluntary Sector Quarterly, 30(14),* 684–706.

Guidestar (no author listed). (2015). Nine Things You Might Not Know about U.S Nonprofits. Retrieved from https://learn.guidestar.org/news/publications/nine-things-about-us-nonprofits, p. 2 (accessed November 16, 2018).

Hansmann, H. (1980), The Role of Nonprofit Enterprise. *Yale Law Journal, 89(5),* 835–901.

Hansmann, H. (1987). Economic Theories of Nonprofit Organization. In Powell, W.W. (Ed.), *The Nonprofit Sector: A Research Handbook* (Chapter 2, pp. 27–42). New Haven: Yale University Press.

Hodgkinson, V., Weitzman, M.S., Toppe, C.M., and Noga, S.M. (1992). *Nonprofit Almanac 1992–1993: Dimensions of the Nonprofit Sector.* San Francisco, Jossey-Bass.

Horton, R. (2006). Thoughts on the Meaning and Field of Social Enterprise'. Columbia: Graduate School of Business. Retrieved from https://www8.gsb.columbia.edu/socialenterprise/about/meaningse (accessed November 23, 2018).

Hurtubise, M. (2017). The Problem with Donor-Advised Funds – and a Solution. *Stanford Social Innovation Review.* Retrieved from https://ssir.org/articles/entry/the_problem_with_donor_advised_fundsand_a_solution (accessed November 16, 2018).

Kerlin, J.A. (2006). Social enterprise in the United States and Europe: Understanding and learning from the differences. *Voluntas: International Journal of Voluntary and Nonprofit Organizations, 17(3),* 247–263.

Lilly Family School of Philanthropy – Indiana University (2017). The Philanthropy Outlook: 2017 and 2018. Retrieved from http://philanthropyoutlook.com/wpcontent/uploads/2017/01/Philanthropy_Outlook_2017_2018.pdf (accessed September 18, 2017).

McIntire, M. (2017). The College Sports Tax Dodge. *The New York Times: Sunday Review*, December 31, p. 10.

McKeever, B.S. (2015). *The Nonprofit Sector in Brief (2015)*. Washington DC: The Urban Institute.

McKeever, B.S., Dietz, N.E., and Fyffe, S.D. (2016) *The Nonprofit Almanac – Ninth Edition: The Essential Facts and Figures for Managers, Researchers and Volunteers*. Washington, DC: The Urban Institute Press.

Mook, L, Whitman, J.R., Quarter, J., and Armstrong, A. (2015). *Understanding the Social Economy of the United States*. Toronto: University of Toronto Press.

Paton, R., Nicholls, A., and Emerson, J. (Eds.) (2015). *Social Finance*. Oxford, UK: Oxford University Press.

Peters, G. (2001). By what Means? Accountability and the Law. *New Directions for Philanthropic Fundraising, 31 Winter*, 23–37.

Salamon, L.M. (1996). The United States. In Salamon, L.M. and Anheier, H.K. (Eds.), *Defining the Nonprofit Sector: A Cross-national Analysis* (pp. 280–320). Baltimore: Johns Hopkins University Press.

Salamon, L.M. (2012). *America's Nonprofit Sector: A Primer, Third Edition*. New York: Foundation Center.

Smith, M. (2017). Fundraising Expected to be Healthy in 2017. Retrieved from https://www.501c.com/fundraising-expected-to-be-healthy-in-2017 (accessed November 3, 2018).

Smith, S.R. and Lipsky, M. (1993). *Nonprofits for Hire*. Cambridge, MA: Harvard University Press.

Steinberg, R. (1987). Nonprofit Organizations and the Market. In Powell, W.W. (Ed.), *The Nonprofit Sector: A Research Handbook* (pp. 118–138). New Haven, CT: Yale University Press.

Steinberg, R. (2006). Economic Theories of Nonprofit Organizations. In Powell, W.W. and Steinberg, R. (Eds.), *The Nonprofit Sector: A Research Handbook* (2nd ed., Chapter 5, pp. 117–139). New Haven, CT: Yale University Press.

Steinberg, R. (2015). What Should Social Finance Invest In and with Whom? In Nicolls, A., Paton, R., and Emerson, J. (Eds.), *Social Finance* (Chapter 2, pp. 64–95). Oxford, UK: Oxford University Press.

Weisbrod, B.A. (1988). *The Nonprofit Economy*. Cambridge, MA: Harvard University Press.

Wright-Violich, K. (2008). We've Arrived. Now What? The Rise of National Donor-Advised Funds. *Stanford Social Innovation Review*, Summer.

Young, D.R. (2017). *Financing Nonprofits and Other Social Enterprises*. Cheltenham, UK and Northampton, MA: Edward Elgar Publishing.

Young, D.R., Searing, E.A.M., and Brewer, C.V. (Eds.) (2016). *The Social Enterprise Zoo*. Cheltenham, UK and Northampton, MA: Edward Elgar Publishing.

Yunas, M. (2007). *Creating a World Without Poverty: Social Business and the Future of Capitalism*. New York: Public Affairs.

Yunas, M., Moingeon, M.B., and Lehmann-Ortiga, L. (2010). Building Social Business Models: Lessons from the Grameen Experience. *Long Range Planning, 43(2–3)*, 308–325.

REVIEW CONCEPTS

Agency Problem: The difficulty supervisors or organizations have in aligning the behavior of their subordinates or contractors with their own objectives or missions.

Asset Lock: A legal prohibition against distributing the assets of an organization to unauthorized outside parties.

Benefit Corporation: A for-profit legal form in the U.S. that requires the firm to pursue a general public benefit, consider nonfinancial interests of its shareholders, and issue a report on how well it is achieving its social or environmental mission.

Charity: A nonprofit organization that meets a public benefit test, as determined by the IRS for such criteria as relief for the poor; advancement of religion, education, or science; erection or maintenance of public building, monuments, or works; lessening the burdens of government and neighborhood tensions; elimination of prejudice and discrimination; defense of human and civil rights secured by law; and combating community deterioration and juvenile delinquency (IRS-501(c)(3) (Mook et al., 2015).

Community Interest Company: A legal form of social enterprise in the United Kingdom that must pursue a community benefit, abide by a modified asset lock and profit distribution constraint, and include non-financial stakeholders in its governance.

Constraint: A specified limit on an economic quantity affecting behavior of an economic actor, e.g., a nondistribution of profits constraint, or an annual budget constraint.

Donor-Advised Fund (DAF): A fund administered by an institution such as a commercial charity or a community foundation that allows donors to donate cash or an appreciated asset such as stock or real estate and receive an immediate tax deduction.

GDP: The total economic value of traded goods and services produced by the economy of a country in a year.

Incentive: An economic reward or penalty that encourages an economic actor to behave in a particular way, for example, a tax incentive that encourages charitable giving or an unrelated business income tax that discourages unrelated business activity by a nonprofit organization.

Limited Profit Constraint: A legal requirement for a social enterprise to keep the amount of profit it can distribute to owners or financial investors within certain bounds.

Market Failure: Conditions under which a market fails to achieve an efficient allocation of societal resources (see Chapter 13).

Mixed Industry: An industry or field of service in which nonprofit organizations compete with for-profit firms and/or government agencies.

Mutual Benefit Organization: An organization whose mission is to serve its members as opposed to the public at large.

Nondistribution (of profits) Constraint: A legal prohibition against distributing financial surpluses to individuals who own or control the organization.

Nonprofit or Not-for-profit Organization: A self-governing organization that is formed to serve the public or a membership (Salamon, 1996). It is prevented from distributing profits to those individuals who control the organization (Hansmann, 1980), and many are classified by the IRS as tax exempt.

Operating Deficit: An annual shortfall of operating revenues to cover annual expenses of an organization.

Productivity: The output achieved from a given level of input resources.

Public Benefit Organizations: Organizations that address the needs of broad segments of the public; for U.S. nonprofits, classified under section 501(c)(3) of the federal tax code; also known as public charities.

Retained Earnings: Percentage of net earnings not paid out as dividends but retained by the company to be re-invested in its core business or to pay debt.

Social Business: A social business is designed and operated just like a "regular" business enterprise with products, services, customers, markets, expenses, and revenues. It is a no-loss, no-dividend, self-sustaining company that sells goods or services and repays investments to its owner, but its primary purpose is to serve society and improve the lot of the poor (Mook et al., 2015).

Social Economy: That part of the economy, outside government, consisting of many different types of self-governing organizations that balance social objectives with success in the marketplace.

Social Economy Organization: An organization that prioritizes its social objectives over its economic objectives.

Social Enterprise: A private organization or venture whose purpose is to include a social goal.

Social Welfare Organization: A U.S. organization (classified as 501(c)(4) in the federal tax code) devoted to a social cause and permitted to engage substantially in political advocacy activities.

Tax-exempt Bond: A bond issued by a government agency, possibly on behalf of a nonprofit organization, for which the bond purchaser is exempt from paying personal income tax on the interest.

Unrelated Business Income Tax: A tax on the profits of a nonprofit organization from business activity that is not substantially related to the organization's mission.

Work Integration Social Enterprise (WISE): A social enterprise that employs marginalized workers as a strategy to improve their economic welfare and employment readiness.

EXERCISES

1. Identify four industries in the U.S. economy as follows:

   (a) An industry in which all service-providing organizations are private, nonprofit;
   (b) An industry in which none or very few participating service providers are private, nonprofit;
   (c) An industry in which private, nonprofit providers co-exist with for-profit and governmental providers;
   (d) An industry in which private, nonprofit and for-profit providers co-exist but government does not participate as a provider of service.

In each case, offer an economic explanation of why we find the particular distribution of nonprofit versus other providers.

2. How would you classify the United Way of Cleveland according to the various taxonomies offered in the text? The American Cancer Society? The Sierra Club?

3. Discuss the size and scope of the nonprofit sector in the U.S. What is the economic importance of these organizations? Why are nonprofit organizations growing faster than government or profitmaking business?

4. Does it make sense to say that an organization that prioritizes its social objectives has economic goals as well? Explain and give an example.

5. Describe a range of organizational forms varying from ones that strongly prioritize their social objectives to those that weakly do so. If you are considering starting a new social venture or being employed by one, discuss the advantages and disadvantages of each organization in the range.

6. Joe Richguy is a *nouveau riche* philanthropist. Why should he consider putting his money in a donor-advised fund versus giving directly to his favorite charities or setting up his own charitable foundation?

7. Alice Dogood is board chair of the Community Foundation of Greater Gotham which administers its own donor-advised funds, has its own endowment and makes grants to local nonprofit organizations. What should she advise her board on whether the foundation should compete or collaborate with commercial charities?

3

Policy and management issues

Will they go away if we put in a deduction for policy advocacy?

3.1 Introduction

In this chapter, we sample some of the contemporary policy and management issues affecting nonprofit organizations and social enterprises and ask how economic analysis can contribute to the understanding and solution of some of these issues. As we have learned, the central concern of economic analysis is *efficiency – how resources can be put to their most highly valued uses.* While we will bump into other useful ideas and concepts from economics along the way, it is the essential focus on efficiency that will run through all of the discussion here.

3.2   Policy issues

In this section, we briefly discuss three areas of public policy affecting non-profit organizations and other social enterprises: the choice of institutional or legal forms for the provision of specific services, issues of competition, and tax policy issues. These broad policy areas are among the most important ones affecting the future of nonprofit organizations and social enterprises and they nicely illustrate how the ideas of economic analysis can help poli-cymakers and managers conceptualize the issues and think them through. Despite the predilections of the politicians in the above cartoon, these issues are unlikely to go away very soon.

Institutional choice

In Chapter 2, one question that arose consistently was: What is the com-petitive advantage of the nonprofit organizational form? That is, when are nonprofits more efficient than for-profit or governmental organizations and when are they not? Why are nonprofits found in some areas of the economy and not in others? Why are they found in greater numbers in some industries than in others? And why are they growing faster than other forms of organi-zation? Some of the answers to these questions are discussed in Chapter 2 where we learned about debates over the productive efficiency of nonprofit organizations versus other forms of social enterprise and about differences in access to financial capital. We also saw that nonprofit organizations are shaped by governmental policy which can encourage or discourage the flow of resources to particular nonprofit organizations. Here we go further in developing the theoretical foundations of sectoral advantages and disadvan-tages in order to discuss the desirability of government policies. Because government sets the rules of the game, the question of competitive advantage is highly intertwined with the public policy issue that we call "institutional choice" – that is, in what parts of the economy should government encourage the participation of nonprofits and other social enterprises and where should it not?

Emerging studies of the nonprofit sector around the world show that governments make different choices on this issue (Breen, Dunn, and Sidel, 2016). These choices are largely determined by historical develop-ments and by political and social traditions, but there are economic factors as well. We discuss two of these factors – informational asymmetry and heterogeneity – below.

1. *Information asymmetry and the inefficiencies of for-profit enterprises*

Economists have identified three types of goods and services for which consumers are less well-informed than sellers about the exact nature of their purchases. The resulting *informational asymmetry* is one economic factor underlying institutional choice.

First, a good or service may be so complex that the purchaser must rely on the provider's expertise to make decisions. A good example is medical care where the consumer must rely on the expertise and good-will of the care-providers to supply the appropriate quantity and quality of service. The pricing of medical services is also complex, and the consumer (or the consumer's insurance company) must rely, to some extent, on the provider's assertion that an appropriate amount is charged for the level of care supplied.

A second category of service with information asymmetry is where a donor contributes towards a *collective good*, such as aid for the impoverished, food for the hungry overseas, or cancer research. We define a good or service as collective when an added person can consume the good without the need to add to output. Cancer research that produces knowledge to help cancer victims is collective. No additional "knowledge" is needed to help an added cancer victim; the knowledge can be extended to help as many as need it. Aid for the impoverished is not a collective good for the impoverished (you need added aid to help an additional poor person) but is collective for those who care about the plight of the impoverished (if we help the poor, an added caring person can enjoy that fact without increasing aid). Nonprofit organizations, other social enterprises, and governments all provide collective goods as part of their missions. The collective nature of nonprofit outputs requires special funding (Chapters 11 and 13) and capital budget analysis (Chapter 14), but here we focus on the informational asymmetry aspect of such goods. Collective goods create an asymmetry between those who buy or donate and the organizations that they buy from or donate to. For example, you could pay a profit-maximizing firm or donate to a social enterprise or nonprofit organization that promises to feed the overseas hungry, but how could you tell if the recipient organization used your money for that purpose? You might be able, through remote observers who report to you by email, to confirm how much food the target group gets, but you won't be able to confirm how much food other customer/donors bought or supported. Maybe the food is there because of your contribution, or maybe it is there because of someone else's contribution. The key problem here is that the organization knows whether your purchase or donation *increased* the total amount they spent feeding the hungry or fattened the pockets of organizational owners, but you do not, and your ignorance can be exploited.

The third category of information asymmetry occurs when those who purchase services do so on behalf of others – for example, adults choosing among day-care centers for their children or nursing homes for their parents. The buyer can exact promises regarding the treatment of their loved ones but cannot experience that treatment. The person experiencing the treatment may not be able to credibly express that the promises haven't been kept. Information is asymmetric because the provider knows the quality of service experienced by the client, but the purchaser does not. Moreover, there is often a "lock-in effect" that makes it difficult or medically risky to move a client to another facility if it is later discovered that the promised quality of service has not been delivered.

In situations of asymmetric information, sellers may intentionally mislead buyers. Doctors that recommend unnecessary tests (or, more egregiously, unnecessary surgery) can pocket larger profits than their more scrupulous competitors. Nursing homes that overly sedate their residents do not need as large a staff to care for their customers, and this cost reduction adds to profits. This temptation for profit-maximizing organizations to mislead consumers is called *contract failure* (Hansmann, 1987, p. 29), which occurs when:

> Owing either to the circumstances under which a service is purchased or consumed or to the nature of the service itself, consumers feel unable to evaluate accurately the quality or quantity of the service a firm produces for them. In such circumstances, a for-profit firm has both the incentive and the opportunity to take advantage of customers by providing less service to them than was promised and paid for.

How does contract failure lead to inefficiency? If customers and donors cannot trust that the terms of the deals they make will be honored, they will not make such deals and mutually beneficial trades will be lost. Collective goods will be underprovided, particularly *nonexcludable* collective goods. A good or service is nonexcludable if there is no practical way to keep non-payers and nondonors from enjoying that good. There is no practical way to keep caring individuals from benefiting from the fact that the poor and hungry have been helped. In contrast, *excludable* collective goods, such as live artistic performances, can be restricted to paying customers and donors. When it comes to nonexcludable collective goods, consumers will not buy the good because they can enjoy it for free and consumers will not donate money and other resources because of contract failure. (See Chapter 13 for further discussion.)

Social efficiency is also lost because people are unable to get the quality level they would like within the constraints of available income and wealth. For example, nursing home residents would be treated with less loving kindness, and adult children would be denied the opportunity to purchase more-preferred levels of quality for their elderly parents. Providers may offer services that are easy to observe and convey the impression of high quality (such as nice lobbies and grounds at nursing homes) while cutting back on service qualities that are hard to discern (quality of nursing care). These providers will eventually drive out more scrupulous providers by offering a package of easy-to-observe and hard-to-observe quality characteristics that cost less and therefore can be sold at a lower price. Weisbrod (1988) calls these service characteristics "type 1" and "type 2," respectively. He concluded that contract failure causes allocative inefficiency: relative to the efficient quantities, type 2 attributes will be underproduced and type 1 attributes overproduced.

Can social enterprises and nonprofit organizations reduce the efficiency loss due to contract failure? If so, we have a clean theory of institutional choice. For-profit firms should be discouraged from operating in markets where contract failure is important and nonprofits and social enterprises encouraged. The superiority of nonprofits has been debated for a long time, ever since Hansmann first proposed the general theory of contract failure in 1980 (earlier arguments were made for the superiority of nonprofits in particular markets, but not for the nonprofit form as an institution). He argued that nonprofits are more likely to deliver the promised quality or quantity because those who control the nonprofit (governing board members) cannot benefit financially from delivering less and because the type of board member selected into the nonprofit sector is more interested in making the organization trustworthy. But the practical significance of contract failure is still contested (e.g., contrast Handy et al., 2010 with Ben-Ner, Hamann, and Ren, 2017).

2. *Heterogeneity, excess burden, and the inefficiencies of government*

The concept of information asymmetry helps illuminate the efficient choice between nonprofit, social enterprise, and for-profit institutional providers. But what about the choice between governmental and private provision? This too is a complex issue, clarified by focusing on economic efficiency, which we divide into productive and allocative efficiency.

Productive efficiency. Like nonprofits, governments must follow the nondistribution constraint, so our first thought is that government is as efficient (or inefficient) as private nonprofit organizations. But the budget constraint works differently in the two sectors, and this may result in efficiency differences. One reason nonprofit organizations strive for productive efficiency is that resources are limited, so that any waste limits the organization's ability to achieve its mission. Government resources are certainly limited, as any government grantmaker can testify, and so well-meaning bureaucrats will limit waste, but sometimes other forces dominate. First, governments have two options not available to private nonprofits that allow for increased spending: the ability to levy taxes and the ability to deficit spend. Nonprofits can raise prices but cannot compel anyone to buy at those higher prices whereas government can compel people to pay higher taxes. Nonprofits can borrow money or run down their endowments, which are sources like deficit spending, but most governments have a much larger line of credit. So, the financial pressures motivating productive efficiency are often lower for governments. All else equal, this factor makes government less productively efficient.

Second, the politics of productive efficiency are different between government and nonprofits for several reasons. Pressures to cut costs come from voters, and these pressures sometimes suffice to make government more efficient. However, neither voters nor the politicians that represent them are fully informed, and the bureaucrats that control the flow of information can slant information to make excessive expenditures look necessary. Regardless of information flows, politicians who wish to be re-elected sometimes pad government payrolls with supporters despite doubts about the social efficiency of doing so. So sometimes government expenditures are excessive and productive inefficiency can thrive. But sometimes the politics works differently. In the sound-bite logic that determines political fates, government cutbacks can also be excessive, and reduced spending on maintenance, training, technical infrastructure, and physical infrastructure also leads to productive inefficiency.

Allocative inefficiency. Governments have the power to fix all market failures and ensure that the economy is allocatively efficient. But governments are political beasts and often stray from that objective. Consider the provision of nonexcludable collective goods. We have already discussed the fact that for-profit firms will not try to provide these goods because they cannot receive revenues commensurate with costs. This means that if for-profits are the only option, these goods are under-provided and allocative inefficiency results. Governments could solve this problem at least two ways. First, they could directly produce collective goods, using tax revenue to pay for production. Second, government could pay others to produce collective goods, which is called contracting out. From this starting point, Weisbrod (1975) described what government *will* do, rather than what government *could* do, using median voter theory. The median-preference voter is the voting citizen in the middle if we line up people by how much they want government to spend on a particular collective good. Median voter theory says that "political equilibrium" (expected behavior after things settle down) is the most desired public expenditure level of the median preference voter. This is true because a majority of voters would oppose any other level of spending. Would the median-preference voter vote for the socially efficient expenditure level? Only by extreme coincidence because the answer depends on the exact distribution of voter preferences. If the distribution of citizen preferences (willingness to pay for a marginal increase in government spending) is symmetric around the median-preference voter and everyone votes, it can be shown that political equilibrium is socially efficient. But the average quantity of collective goods preferred by voters is generally higher than the median voter's preference, in which case it can be shown that governments undersupply collective goods.

Weisbrod (1975) was more interested in the positive question of predicting sectoral choice than the normative question of social efficiency. Regardless of whether median voter theory or some other model of political equilibrium is used, his model suggests that government action under-represents minority views of the public good. The minority of low demanders will be dissatisfied with government spending but have no recourse except to move to another jurisdiction. However, high demanders for collective goods will band together and support nonprofit organizations. Nonprofits supplement government, providing additional services and alternative types of services (e.g., religious education) on a voluntary basis. Dissatisfaction with government expenditure levels is larger when the electorate is heterogeneous and zero when everyone wants the same level of government expenditures. Thus, Weisbrod predicted that more heterogeneous societies will have lower government spending and higher private support for nonprofits.

A second source of governmental inefficiency stems from the side-effects of governmental finance. Governments that obey the nondistribution constraint may receive some voluntary donations, but many donors are reluctant to give to an entity that has taxing power. Therefore, governments must rely on taxes, which, unlike voluntary contributions, distort the economy. A tax on personal income serves as a work disincentive; a tax on corporate income serves as an investment disincentive, a tax on sales leads to a loss of mutually beneficial trades, and so on. Paying taxes is a burden for the taxpayer, but the distortionary effects of taxation produce an additional "excess burden" that reduces allocative efficiency.

3.   *Implications for policies on institutional choice*

In Chapters 11–13, we shall discuss voluntary support for collective goods in greater detail and conclude that donations will not be large enough to fully finance the allocatively efficient output level. Governments could solve this problem by either subsidizing those nonprofits that provide collective goods or by subsidizing collective good provision by organizations in any sector, but government action is less efficient if for no other reason than the excess burdens of tax-financed action. For social efficiency, governments should rely on donations to the maximum extent feasible, but also recognize that more spending is needed, and government should not scrimp in its added support. So, we might conclude from the viewpoint of social efficiency that in many European countries, the government share of public/private arts funding is too large. Government should rely somewhat more on voluntary donations in these countries. In contrast, the government's share of public/private arts funding is too small in the U.S., not large enough to counter the limits on voluntary support.

When government supplements voluntary provision of collective goods, is it better for government to produce these goods directly or contract out? Our discussion of productive efficiency suggests it is generally better to contract out, as private nonprofit organizations or for-profit social ventures will be more efficient than government. There are, of course, added complications, and here we emphasize the transactions costs of contracting out. Transactions costs are the costs of arranging a trade or other exchange of value. Contracting out includes the transactions costs of negotiating a contract or establishing and administering a competitive bidding system, monitoring contract implementation, and making payments. Competitive bidding for government contracts can make the productive efficiency advantage of contracting out even greater, but competition can worsen contract-failure problems (Steinberg, 1997). That is, competitive bidding will induce would-be contractors to streamline their operations to secure a competitive edge; however, increased competition for contracts may also incentivize such contractors to cut corners on quality.

Access to financial capital

In Chapter 2, we learned that there is a mixture of factors affecting nonprofit versus for-profit social-enterprise access to capital. Unlike nonprofits, for-profits can tap equity markets (selling shares of stock), and the risk-sharing that equitable ownership provides to lenders makes them willing to offer preferential rates on loans. Unlike for-profits, nonprofits can grow through retained earnings that are undiminished by corporate income tax, have access to donations and capital campaigns, and sometimes are eligible to issue tax-exempt bonds. But organizations in both sectors may need improved access to capital.

Although for-profit social enterprises have access to traditional equity markets, they cannot offer the same dividends as competitors that do not invest profits in support of the public good. This implies that share prices will be lower in the initial public offering, as investors that do not expect to receive market dividends need to see more capital gains through share price increases. The details differ between purely for-profit and hybrid social enterprises, but generally there is a trade-off between pursuing a nonprofit-maximizing mission and the amount of available equity capital (Steinberg, 2015). Therefore, some have argued that purely for-profit social enterprises should be tax exempt, allowing them to grow faster through retained earnings and finance the provision of nonexcludable collective goods (Posner and Malani, 2007). Others argue that personal donations to for-profit social enterprises should be tax deductible (Cohen, 2009). Others advocate that hybrid social enterprises should be tax exempt (e.g., Doeringer, 2010; Strom, 2011). Whether any of this is a good idea is beyond the scope of this book, but we note the disadvantages highlighted in Mayer and Ganahl (2014), who see no good way to restrict distribution of the exempted tax obligation to the social mission, rather than the pockets of shareholders.

Protecting the social mission

In the happy event that a non-collective (private) good produces social benefits for the buyer, profit-maximizing firms are socially efficient. Thus, we have no problems producing the efficient quantity of broccoli and doing so in a way that is productively efficient. We may have problems with the distribution of income that keep some unhappy children from eating the broccoli they love, but the mission of providing healthy vegetables is perfectly consistent with profit maximization. Problems appear when there is market failure – when the wrong quantities are produced by profit maximizers or mutually beneficial trades do not take place. In such cases, for-profit social enterprises sacrifice their social bottom line for their financial one. This can occur for three reasons.

First, the owners of the firm like having money and get to keep any profits generated by the firm they own. If there is a single owner (called a "proprietorship" in the U.S. and a "sole trader" in the U.K.), then the owner balances her desire to pursue the social mission against her desire to receive profits, and whatever choice is made is sustainable. But if there are multiple owners (as in a publicly traded "corporation" (U.S.) or "company" (U.K.)), it is harder to gain stable support for the social bottom line.

Second, there is a market for control. Takeover artists can buy a controlling share in the voting stock of a publicly traded for-profit corporation. They use that control to replace (or redirect) managers that want to pursue social objectives with those exclusively dedicated to profits. This is a very profitable activity because a firm that does not maximize profits will have a low share price. The takeover artist buys control at that low price, changes the firm's direction, share price rises, and the artist sells his control for a huge profit. Third, if the market is sufficiently competitive, for-profit firms that do not maximize their profits go bankrupt (see Chapter 7).

For-profit social enterprises find it difficult to pursue social missions for these reasons. Now it is true that the market for control is restrained by law in some countries and restrained by managerial self-protection strategies such as "poison pill" plans and "golden parachutes," so limited departures from profit maximization can occur. And sometimes proprietorships can stably protect their social mission. For example, actor Paul Newman created Newman's Own' to sell various food products with the promise that it will use "all profits for charity." Newman's Own was able to sustain that mission during Paul Newman's lifetime because he was a single owner and he valued the social mission more than the money he could have received if he sold his firm to someone else. Even so, he anticipated that after his death, new owners could end the social mission. To protect his vision, he bequeathed all shares in Newman's Own to The Newman's Own Foundation, a nonprofit corporation he founded. He selected the Foundation's initial self-perpetuating board, including only supporters of "all profits to charity." In effect, he sustained the social mission by converting a for-profit social enterprise into a hybrid social enterprise by making it a wholly-owned subsidary of a nonprofit (Steinberg, 2015).

Nonprofits are immune from financially-motivated takeover bids, and those in control of the organization cannot receive a distribution of profits. Thus, nonprofit organizations find it easier to sustain a social mission that is inconsistent with profit maximization. Even so, nonprofits sometimes face financial pressures that make it hard to pursue any mission that does not maximize profits. From a policy perspective, too much competition can destroy the social mission, but finding the right balance is difficult. Another problem occurs due to difficulty in enforcing the nondistribution constraint. If profits can be secretly distributed by an organization pretending to be nonprofit, we have a *for-profit in disguise* (FPID). Running an FPID is an ideal job for greedy people without too many ethical constraints. In addition to receiving profits from sales, the scam entrepreneur can receive donations, and all of this income is exempt from corporate income, sales, and property taxes. The scammer can increase those profits further when purchasers and donors trust him by practicing contract failure. From a public policy perspective, the biggest problem is not the scam itself, but the likelihood that people will lose trust in legitimate nonprofits, as they cannot tell a nonprofit from a FPID. Policies that improve enforcement of the nondistribution constraint are very important.

Hybrid organizations face many challenges sustaining their social bottom line. First, different legal forms of hybrids define the obligation to pursue two bottom lines differently, and there is considerable room to pursue one to the detriment of the other within the statutes. For example, a Benefit Corporation must pursue a "general public benefit" in addition to pursuing profits, but the statutes do not provide clear guidance on what qualifies as a general public benefit and do not require that the public benefit be balanced against the pursuit of profit in any particular way. Any independent and transparent third-party standard-setting organization can approve a firm's conversion or establishment as a Benefit Corporation, and the statutes do not require any minimum standards for third-party review. No part of the profit stream is specifically protected to serve the public interest, so there is nothing to stop contract failure. The only protection for long-run maintenance of the social mission is that a super-majority of shareholders must approve conversion to traditional for-profit status (Brakman Reiser, 2011). A similar problem affects Low-Profit Limited Liability Companies (L3Cs), which simply convert to a Limited Liability Company (LLC) if they fail to pursue their social mission. In contrast, the U.K. has a hybrid form called a Community Investment Corporation (CIC) that locks assets so that they must be used for community interests. Specifically, CICs cannot sell their assets at less than fair market value except in pursuit of their community mission or when transferring assets to another charity or CIC, including distribution of assets following dissolution or conversion to a different legal structure. However, CICs limit the payments of dividends to shareholders, reducing their ability to raise capital (Steinberg, 2015). Overall, the perfect form has yet to be found, but Brakman Reiser and Dean (2013, 2017) propose innovative designs and policies that they argue will solve the sustainability and capital issues. A key element of their proposal is to use a hybrid financial instrument, Flexible Low-Yield (FLY) Paper, that allows the investors and social entrepreneurs to make a credible commitment to pursue the charitable mission for a specified period of time.

Competition

Another key area of policy concern is competition within and across the sectors. There is a presumption, at least in the U.S., that competition is good because it fosters social efficiency. Major exceptions to this rule exist for some industries, such as utilities, where productive efficiency requires large-scale operations and the market may not have room for more than one efficient firm. Other exceptions exist for innovation, with patents and copyrights giving temporary protection from competitors to spur invention and composition. Finally, there are some goods and services whose characteristics prevent profitmaking businesses from operating profitably or in a manner that is efficient for society. (See Chapter 13 on market failure). First, we consider competition between nonprofits and for-profits, then competition between nonprofits and other nonprofits.

1.   *Competition with for-profits*

Nonprofit and for-profit organizations compete in two types of markets: in service areas directly related to the nonprofit's mission, and in commercial areas not directly related to the nonprofit's mission but directly competitive with some for-profit firms. Each type of competition raises complex efficiency issues.

For-profit firms regularly compete with nonprofit organizations in the nursing home, hospital, day care, arts and culture, hospice, and education subsectors, among others (see Chapter 2). Often, nonprofits and for-profits occupy different niches within a given industry rather than compete head-to-head. For example, for-profits concentrate on mass culture (rock concerts, blockbuster films) and nonprofits concentrate on high culture (opera, classical music, ballet) in the arts and culture subsector. There are no important efficiency issues resulting from this form of competition. Contract failure leads to a different form of niche specialization. If poorly-informed consumers prefer to use nonprofit organizations and are willing to pay a bit more, and better-informed consumers feel they can tell which for-profits are trustworthy, then the sectors complement each other as an efficient system of organizations. All consumers would find their most preferred service alternatives and could put their resources to their most highly valued uses. If instead there is a race to the bottom in delivering the promised quality or quantity of services, surviving for-profits and nonprofits would have to short-change consumers or go bankrupt. This would be inefficient, as those consumers wanting a trustworthy provider would be unable to buy what they want.

The second aspect of nonprofit/for-profit competition concerns the offering of commercial goods and services not related to the organization's mission. This competition may be healthy for three reasons: First, if nonprofits provide fair competition for businesses on their own turf then they help spur all providers to become more efficient. Second, nonprofits in some subsectors have economic advantages over their for-profit competitors that make them productively efficient. For example, university book stores or recreational facilities can more easily employ inexpensive student labor while offering students a convenient work location. Or, the photographic labs of medical schools can also process retail photos. In these cases, nonprofits enhance efficiency by offering selected commercial services at lower opportunity cost (see Chapter 6). Third, the most efficient way to subsidize mission-related services may be through profits from unrelated commercial activity. For example, in the hospital industry, nonprofits historically followed the practice of using profits from one area of service, say elective surgeries, to cross-subsidize public-benefit services such as care for the indigent, research, or medical education. This would be efficient if the best alternative way to cross-subsidize these services required tax-financed government money, as taxes create excess burdens. It is even possible that the efficient solution requires that we protect the nonprofit from for-profit competition. If the social losses from nonprofit monopolization are smaller than the excess burdens from taxation, nonprofit monopolies are superior to government finance for public-benefit services (Eckel and Steinberg, 1993). (See Chapters 8 and 9 for explanations of monopoly losses and impacts of taxation.)

Cross-sectoral competition is more difficult to analyze when nonprofits and for-profits are subject to different taxes and subsidies. When nonprofit and for-profit firms are treated the same way, those that are productively efficient can out-compete those that are not because they have lower costs. Long-run surviving organizations are all productively efficient, regardless of sector. However, if nonprofit hospitals are exempt from income, property, and sales taxes and their for-profit competitors are not, a moderately inefficient nonprofit can outcompete an efficient for-profit. The nonprofit will have lower costs if the added cost of productive inefficiency is smaller than the nonprofit tax advantage. This problem is important when nonprofits compete with for-profits in their mission-related goods, less important when they compete in unrelated business. This is due to the reduction in tax differences created by the unrelated business income tax.

2. *Competition among nonprofits*

Although there is a presumption favoring competition among for-profits, the opposite is sometimes true for nonprofits. Funders wonder why there are so many small nonprofits, urging them to merge or at least cooperate with each other in joint projects and partnerships. Government funders divide the service population into catchment zones where a single nonprofit has the responsibility to help. Nonprofit "combinations in restraint of trade" (to quote US antitrust law, which prohibits monopolies and restricts the growth of market power) can be harmful for the same reasons that for-profit combinations are harmful – they create allocative and productive ineffi-ciencies. But nonprofit combinations can also fix allocative inefficiencies, cross-subsidizing missions and leading to increased nonprofit provision of community benefits such as wellness education.

Another important area of competition policy is the domain of fund-raising. Nonprofits frequently recognize that they are fishing from the same donor pool as others, so that increases in solicitation by one organization raise the costs of fund-raising (amount that must be spent to raise a dollar) at other organizations. (See also, discussion of common pool goods in Chapter 13.) In the limit, Rose-Ackerman (1982) showed that organizations will spend nearly 100 percent of funds raised to successfully compete for donors. This is inefficient, because so much is spent just to counteract the fund-raising of others. Such inefficiency is hard to avoid without limits on entry of new nonprofits or combined fund-raising campaigns like United Way. Typically, combined campaigns require that member organizations accept a distribu-tion from the combined-campaign fund and refrain from conducting their own public campaigns. This reduces overfishing from the donor pool. In addition, combined campaigns enhance efficiency by making giving conveni-ent, auditing member organizations (which increases donor confidence) and saving donors the trouble of investigating alternative recipients. However, if competition with independent campaigns continues, combined campaigns cannot fully realize these efficiencies (Rose-Ackerman, 1980) and there is evidence of reduced returns from solicitation at current levels of competition (Paarlberg and Hwang, 2017).

Taxation and subsidy policies

It is unclear why the U.S. government exempted nonprofits from the corpo-rate income tax and introduced the charitable donations tax deduction from both the personal and corporate income taxes (Simon, Dale, and Chisolm, 2006), but after-the-fact rationalizations focus on the desire to subsidize the good works that nonprofits do or on the definitions of the tax base (what the tax is supposed to apply to). Under subsidy theories, the public policy question concerns the social efficiency of these policies and policies that directly subsidize nonprofits such as the reduced rate they pay for postage. We will mostly focus on the treatment of donations in the U.S. federal personal income tax.

1.   Income tax deductions

For those unfamiliar with the U.S. federal personal income tax, taxpayers start with a list of all income and calculate "adjusted personal income," in the jargon of the tax code. Before calculating their taxes, taxpayers can subtract specific expenditures (including charitable donations) from their adjusted personal income and the result is "taxable income." These subtractions from taxable income are called *deductions*. A preliminary tax is then calculated from tables and formulas provided by the tax authority. Once again, taxpayers can subtract specified expenditures directly from the preliminary tax to figure out the final amount of taxes owed to the government. These subtractions from tax, rather than from taxable income, are called *credits*.

Taxpayers have their choice of two types of deductions – the "standard deduction" or "itemized deductions." The standard deduction is a fixed dollar amount based on marital status set each year by the tax authorities, and rational taxpayers pick the standard deduction if it is larger than the alternative. Itemized deductions are calculated from the spending patterns of the household and include total donations to public benefit [501(c)(3)] organizations, interest paid on the primary home mortgage, certain state and local taxes, and several additional categories. To summarize, when U.S. taxpayers make sufficiently large donations or make donations on top of other deductions that are sufficiently large, they reduce the amount of taxes they owe by an amount proportional to the tax rate applied to their last dollars of income (the "marginal tax rate"). So, for example, an itemizer who makes a $1,000 donation and has a 30 percent marginal tax rate will thereby reduce her taxable income by $1,000 and her taxes by $300. In effect, it only cost her $700 (after tax) while the charity receives $1000. Following this logic, economists define the *price of giving* as the amount of after-tax income that must be sacrificed to provide the charity with a $1 added donation. In this example, the price of giving is $0.70. For nonitemizers, the amount they donate does not affect their taxes, so their price of giving is $1.00.

People consider many factors when deciding whether and how much to donate to charity. Undoubtedly the price of giving is one of these factors –

simply put, people like to buy more of anything when the price goes down, and the charitable donations tax deduction lowers the price of buying "warm glow." Debates continue, but only about the size of this price effect. Is the charitable donations tax credit an efficient solution for market failure in collective goods provision? That is a hard question that is not totally resolved (e.g., Roberts, 1987; Diamond, 2006). We shall consider some easier questions here, inefficiencies created because (a) different people face different prices of giving, and (b) the price of giving money is different from the price of giving time (volunteering).

On average, high-income taxpayers face a lower price of giving money for two reasons. First, high-income taxpayers are more likely to itemize, and only itemizers benefit from a reduced price of giving. Second, marginal tax rates are usually higher when income is higher (although the difference in how the tax code treats earned income and capital gains muddies this relationship). So, a rich itemizer in the 39 percent tax bracket enjoys a price of $0.61 while a middle-class itemizer in the 20 percent tax bracket has a price of giving equal to $0.80. This means that the charitable deduction is biased towards allocation of resources to charities favored by the wealthier members of society. Unless we are prepared as a society to make the judgment that such charities are more worthwhile, the charitable deduction is inefficient because it gives more to those charities and less to charities favored by the less wealthy than would be the case if the price of giving were the same for everyone. In addition to the issue of efficiency, there is a question of fairness when it costs more for a poor person to donate a dollar to charity than it costs a rich person. Some have called this an "upside-down subsidy." These are reasons why analysts such as Weisbrod (1988) argued in favor of replacing the tax deduction with a partial tax credit. If all taxpayers, itemizers and nonitemizers, are eligible for a 50 percent charitable donation tax credit, then everyone faces the same $0.50 price of giving and the pattern of charitable donations is undistorted by the tax system.

2. *Giving time versus money*

Let's now consider the case of volunteering. Suppose that a taxpayer is in the 25 percent tax bracket and earns $10 per hour when he or she works. Does the tax system distort the choice between volunteering and giving money? For itemizers:

- If the taxpayer volunteers one hour and is equally productive as a volunteer or as a paid worker, he or she gives a gift worth $10, but foregoes only $7.50 in after-tax income.

- If the taxpayer works for an hour and gives the $10 to charity, he or she deducts $10 and receives a $2.50 reduction in taxes. The net cost to the taxpayer is the same as if he or she volunteered, namely $7.50.

However, for nonitemizers:

- If the taxpayer works for an hour and gives $10 to charity, he or she receives no deduction. The net cost in this case is $10.
- If the taxpayer volunteers for an hour, he or she gives a gift worth $10 but foregoes only $7.50 in after tax income. Thus, the net cost is only $7.50.

Clearly, the tax code is biased in favor of gifts of time versus money for those who do not itemize deductions. But why is this inefficient? People volunteer for many reasons, but the costs of volunteering influence how much they volunteer. The tax code distorts the taxpayer's decisions to work and donate money versus volunteering. Even if the added donations resulting from an extra hour of working exceed the value of that person's volunteer time, the individual prefers to volunteer. And so, taxpayers will volunteer more and work less (and give less cash) than would be efficient.

3.   *Subsidy policies*

Direct subsidy policies also cause inefficiency. An example is the postal subsidy available to nonprofit organizations. This subsidy helps nonprofit organizations by lowering the cost of communicating with donors, clients, and other constituents. While this may be a laudable goal, the postal subsidy artificially reduces the price to nonprofits of one mode of communication. This distorts nonprofit communication mode choices from their free-market levels and inefficiency results. For example, suppose it costs 50 cents to raise a dollar by phone calls (telemarketing), and it cost 60 cents to raise a dollar by (direct) mail (for simplicity, assume that postage is the only expense incurred by direct-mail fund-raising). If the government subsidizes the use of the postal service by say 25 percent, then the price to the nonprofit for raising a dollar by mail will be only 45 cents (government pays the remaining 15 cents). Thus, the nonprofit will choose to use the mail rather than the phone, even though the full cost of the mail is higher. Scarce resources will not be devoted to their best uses.

Let's push this example further. How can the nonprofit be helped more efficiently? The value of the subsidy to the nonprofit is 15 cents per dollar raised by mail. Suppose the nonprofit were raising $100 by spending $45. This cost the government $15. Suppose the government were to just simply give the nonprofit $15. Then the nonprofit could spend $60 (the original $45 budget plus the unearmarked grant of $15) and could raise $120 by phone calls ($1 raised for each $.50 spent). Hence, the same resources are used to produce greater results and the inefficiency is eliminated.

The alert reader will note many complications we have ignored to make our point in the postal example above. One simplification we made was that the only costs of fund-raising are the costs borne by the charity. But tele-marketing imposes costs on those being solicited, such as the bother people experience by being called during the dinner hour. These external costs of fund-raising create their own market failures (Chapter 13), and if these costs are substantial, the postal subsidy might increase efficiency by shifting activ-ity from the telephone to the mail. On the other hand, there are also costs associated with producing, handling, and disposing of junk mail.

4.   *Tax exemption*

The exemption of nonprofit organizations from local property taxes creates inefficiencies as well. In suburbs and rural areas where property tax rates are low, tax exemption does not provide much advantage to nonprofit organi-zations. However, in central cities, where tax rates are higher, exemption provides a substantial subsidy, and this difference in subsidy rates makes nonprofit organizations more likely to locate in central cities than they oth-erwise would. This distortion in location can feed on itself, as the central city must raise tax rates to compensate for the loss of taxable property to exempt organizations. In turn, this may hasten the relocation of taxable businesses to the suburbs. Alternatively, nonprofit symphony orchestras and art museums may provide amenity values that enhance the desirability of locating taxable businesses downtown, slowing or even reversing the spiraling decay of the urban tax base. Thus, the level of inefficiency created by nonprofit exemp-tion from property tax depends on the difference between tax rates in nearby communities and the type of service provided by nonprofits. The exemption of nonprofits from sales taxes creates other distortions, as does exemption from state and local corporate income taxes (Clotfelter, 1988–1989). There remain substantial questions regarding whether tax exemption is the efficient way to subsidize nonprofit missions (Simon, Dale, and Chisolm, 2006).

3.3   Management issues

Nonprofit leaders and social entrepreneurs must remain aware of the policy issues affecting nonprofit organizations and other social enterprises, for these policies affect day-to-day operations as well as impel leaders to seek policy reforms. Nonetheless, of more immediate concern to nonprofit and social

enterprise leaders are the managerial decisions and strategies they must oversee within their own organizations.

Volunteer management

Managers are tempted to regard volunteer labor as "free" because volunteers
do not earn salaries. The implication of this view is that their organizations
should accept any and all volunteers that show up on their doorsteps. Is this
efficient? Careful economic analysis reveals that there are substantial costs
associated with taking on volunteers, and that it is important to account not
only for "explicit" or "out-of-pocket" costs but for all the foregone opportunities when volunteers are accepted and used for one purpose rather than
another. (We elaborate on these cost concepts in Chapter 6.)

Volunteers need supervision and guidance from paid staff. They may need
space and supplies, reimbursement for travel, and other kinds of support.
Volunteers may require training in the skills they need for tasks they are
asked to undertake. If they do not fit well within the organization, they may
be disruptive, causing losses in work effort and organizational effectiveness.
It may require special recruitment efforts to find the right kinds of volunteers (Brudney, 1990). Further, volunteer and paid labor responsibilities
must be carefully designed to minimize conflict between the two (Rimes et
al., 2017).

On the other hand, volunteers, properly selected and strategically deployed,
produce highly valuable benefits for nonprofit organizations and other
social enterprises. Using volunteers in telemarketing conveys the trustwor-
thiness and commitment of the campaign to the charitable mission. The
important questions include: "how much does it cost to recruit the right
kinds of volunteers;" "what is the value to the organization of particular
volunteer tasks;" and "what are the other costs and benefits of volunteer
employment." These are economic decisions, guided by the desire to put
limited resources to their best uses. Accepting all comers will be inefficient if
it produces more costs than benefits. Refusing all volunteers or committing
no resources to their development is also likely to be inefficient. Finding the
right level and mix of volunteers and deciding how much to invest in volunteers are decisions that nonprofit managers and social entrepreneurs must
face if they are to use their resources in the most efficient way (Brudney and
Duncombe, 1992).

Fund-raising

The development of charitable donations is a critical area for nonprofit managers, and it is a controversial one in many respects. Managers must decide how much to spend on fund-raising in an environment in which administrative overhead and fund-raising expenditures are misunderstood and misjudged. The pressure to cut administrative costs can reduce efficiency, because a poorly administered program will not direct resources to their highest uses. The pressure to cut fund-raising costs can reduce efficiency by distorting the use of scarce volunteers and reducing prospecting efforts. Prospecting is the search for new donors who will be long-term givers. Prospecting is expensive, shows up as a fund-raising cost not balanced by immediate donations, but is very helpful in terms of the lifetime value of newly found donors (Steinberg and Morris, 2010).

Donors correctly worry about whether charitable organizations are spending too much on fund-raising and administration. They prefer that their donations go to more efficient charities, and sometimes rely on watchdog agencies that try to judge fund-raising and administrative efficiency. While such inefficiency does occur, it is impossible for donors and watchdogs to detect using measures like the ratio of fund-raising costs to funds raised or the share of total expenditures spent on the charitable programs. These measures capture the average costs of fund-raising but say nothing about whether the right amount is spent (Steinberg, 1986). Economic analysis illuminates the proper efficiency test by distinguishing between the set-up costs of a fund-raising campaign and the incremental or *marginal* costs of solicitation, and by using marginal costs to determine the ideal fund-raising budget (see Chapter 5).

Other aspects of fund-raising can also benefit from economic analysis. In the discussion of postal subsidies above we referred to one aspect of the question of alternative means of asking for funds. Subsidies or not, this is an important issue – what combination of fund-raising methods will be the most efficient? Again, economic analysis can help by focusing on the incremental yields of different methods, and on how these yields vary with the size of the campaign. Other practical questions concern whether premiums (little gifts like coffee mugs or return-address stickers) bring in enough added donations to justify their costs, or whether, and how often, an attempt should be made to secure donations from a lapsed donor.

Finally, there is the interesting issue of joint or federated fund-raising versus fund-raising by individual organizations. We mentioned this issue above, in connection with competition policy. For the individual organization too, this may be an important economic decision. What are the benefits and costs to joining a federated campaign? How is this decision sensibly thought through? Again, economic analysis can help by asking about the best use of an organization's limited resources and its competitive advantage vis-à-vis other organizations.

Many other nonprofit managerial decisions can benefit from economic analysis to determine efficient choices. These include decisions about the level and pricing of services, pursuing alternative forms of revenues, and allocating resources among alternative programs. Addressing these issues more precisely, as well as the policy issues considered above, requires sharper tools than we have been able to apply thus far in the discussion. The next several chapters will develop these tools.

SELECTED REFERENCES AND CITATIONS

Ben-Ner, A., Hamann, D., and Ren, T. (2017). Does Ownership Matter in the Selection of Service Providers? Evidence from Nursing Home Consumer Surveys, Working Paper, Carlson School of Management, U. of Minnesota.

Brakman Reiser, D. (2011). Benefit Corporations – A Sustainable Form of Organization? *Wake Forest Law Review, 46*, 591–625.

Brakman Reiser, D. and Dean, S.A. (2013). Hunting Stag with Fly Paper: A Hybrid Financial Instrument for Social Enterprise. *Boston College Law Review, 54(4)*, 1495.

Brakman Reiser, D. and Dean, S.A. (2017). *Social Enterprise Law – Trust, Public Benefit and Capital Markets.* Oxford, UK: Oxford University Press.

Breen, O.B., Dunn, A., and Sidel, M. (2016). *Regulatory Waves: Comparative Perspectives on State Regulation and Self-Regulation Policies in the Nonprofit Sector.* Cambridge, UK: Cambridge University Press.

Brudney, J.L. (1990). *Fostering Volunteer Programs in the Public Sector.* San Francisco: Jossey-Bass.

Brudney, J.L. and Duncombe, W. (1992). An Economic Evaluation of Paid, Volunteer, and Mixed Staffing Options for Public Services. *Public Administration Review, 52(5)*, 474–481. doi:10.2307/976807.

Clotfelter, C.T. (1985). *Federal Tax Policy and Charitable Giving.* Chicago: University of Chicago Press.

Clotfelter, C.T. (1988–1989). Tax-Induced Distortions in the Voluntary Sector. *Case Western Reserve Law Review 39(3)*, 663–704.

Cohen, R. (2009). L3C: Pot of Gold or Space Invader? *Blue Avocado* (September 30, 2009). Retrieved from http://www.blueavocado.org/content/l3c-pot-gold-or-space-invader (accessed January 2, 2018).

Diamond, P. (2006). Optimal Tax Treatment of Private Contributions for Public Goods With and Without Warm-Glow Preferences. *Journal of Public Economics, 90*, 897–919.

Doeringer, M.F. (2010). Note, Fostering Social Enterprise: A Historical and International Analysis. *Duke Journal of Comparative and International Law, 20*, 291–322.

Eckel, C.C. and Steinberg, R. (1993). Competition, Performance, and Public Policy Towards Nonprofits. In Hammack, D.C. and Young, D.R. (Eds.), *Nonprofit Organizations in a Market Economy* (pp. 57–81). San Francisco: Jossey-Bass.

Gidron, B., Kramer, R.M., and Salamon, L.M. (Eds.) (1992). *Government and the Third Sector*. San Francisco: Jossey-Bass.

Handy, F., Seto, S., Wakaruk, A., Mersey, B., Mejia, A., and Copeland, L. (2010). The Discerning Consumer: Is Nonprofit Status a Factor? *Nonprofit and Voluntary Sector Quarterly 39(5)*, 866–883. https://doi.org/10.1177/0899764010362113.

Hansmann, H. (1980). The Role of Nonprofit Enterprise. *Yale Law Journal, 89*, 835–901.

Hansmann, H. (1987). Economic Theories of Nonprofit Organization. In Powell, W.W. (Ed.), *The Nonprofit Sector: A Research Handbook* (pp. 27–42). New Haven: Yale University Press.

Mauser, E. (1998). The Importance of Organizational Form: Parent Perceptions versus Reality in the Day Care Industry. In Powell, W.W. and Clemens, E.S. (Eds.), *Private Action and the Public Good* (pp. 124–136). New Haven: Yale University Press.

Mayer, L.H. and Ganahl, J.R. (2014). Taxing Social Enterprise. *Stanford Law Review, 66(2)*, 387–442.

Paarlberg, L.E. and Hwang, H. (2017). The Heterogeneity of Competitive Forces: The Impact of Competition for Resources on United Way Fundraising. *Nonprofit and Voluntary Sector Quarterly 46(5)*, 897–921.

Posner, E.A. and Malani, A. (2007). The Case for For-Profit Charities. *Virginia Law Review, 93*, 2017–2067.

Rimes, H., Nesbit, R., Christensen, R.K., and Brudney, J.L. (2017). Exploring the Dynamics of Volunteer and Staff Interactions: From Satisfaction to Conflict. *Nonprofit Management & Leadership, 28(2)*, 195–213.

Roberts, R. (1987). Financing Public Goods. *Journal of Political Economy, 95*, 420–437.

Rose-Ackerman, S. (1980). United Charities: An Economic Analysis. *Public Policy XXVIII*, 323–350.

Rose-Ackerman, S. (1982). Charitable Giving and "Excessive" Fundraising. *The Quarterly Journal of Economics, 97(2)*, 193–212.

Simon, J., Dale, H., and Chisolm, L. (2006). The Federal Tax Treatment of Charitable Organizations. In Powell, W.W. and Steinberg, R. (Eds.), *The Nonprofit Sector: A Research Handbook* (2nd ed., pp. 267–306). New Haven: Yale University Press.

Steinberg, R. (1986). Should Donors Care about Fundraising? In Rose-Ackerman, S. (Ed.), *The Economics of Nonprofit Institutions: Studies in Structure and Policy* (pp. 347–366). Oxford, UK: Oxford University Press.

Steinberg, R. (1997). Competition in Contracted Markets. In 6, P. and Kendall, J. (Eds.), *The Contract Culture in Public Services* (pp. 161–180). Aldershot, UK: Ashgate.

Steinberg, R. (2006). Economic Theories of Nonprofit Organizations. In Powell, W.W. and Steinberg, R. (Eds.), *The Nonprofit Sector: A Research Handbook* (2nd ed., pp. 117–139). New Haven: Yale University Press.

Steinberg, R. (2015). What Should Social Finance Invest In and With Whom? In Nicholls, A., Paton, R., and Emerson, J. (Eds.), *Social Finance* (pp. 64–95). Oxford, UK: Oxford University Press.

Steinberg, R. and Morris, D. (2010). Ratio Discrimination in Charity Fundraising: The Inappropriate Use of Cost Ratios has Harmful Side-Effects. *Voluntary Sector Review, 1(1)*, 77–95.

Strom, S. (2011). A Quest for Hybrid Companies That Profit, but Can Tap Charity. *The New York Times* (October 12, 2011). Retrieved from http://www.nytimes.com/2011/10/13/business/a-quest-for-hybrid-companies-part-money-maker-part-nonprofit.html.

Weisbrod, B.A. (1975). Toward a Theory of the Voluntary Non-Profit Sector in a Three Sector Economy, In Phelps, E.S. (Ed.), *Altruism, Morality and Economic Theory* (pp. 171–195). New York: Russell Sage Foundation.

Weisbrod, B.A. (1988). *The Nonprofit Economy*. Cambridge, MA: Harvard University Press.

REVIEW CONCEPTS

Asymmetric Information: When the two parties to a market transaction know different things about the quality or quantity of an exchange such that the more-informed party can take advantage of the less-informed party.

Benefit Corporation: A type of hybrid organization legal in some states in the U.S. that relies on third-party certification to balance the organization's social and financial bottom lines.

Collective Good: A good or service that a group of people can simultaneously consume.

Community Interest Company (CIC): A type of hybrid organization used in the U.K. that limits the distribution of dividends to below-market rates and insures that assets dedicated to the social mission cannot be distributed upon organizational conversion or termination.

Contract Failure: A kind of market failure resulting from asymmetric information in which the buyer (donor) is unable to verify whether the promised quality or quantity of a good is delivered.

Contracting Out: When government pays private organizations (for-profit, nonprofit, or hybrid) to deliver a good or service.

Excess Burden of a Tax: A dollar measure of the efficiency lost when taxes distort economic behaviors.

Excludable Collective Good: A collective good with the property that one can exclude those who don't pay from enjoying that good. For example, an opera performance. Antonym: Nonexcludable Collective Good.

Federated or Combined Fundraising: When several nonprofit organizations coordinate and share their fundraising through a central mechanism such as United Way and agree to forgo or limit their individual fundraising efforts.

For-profit-in-disguise: An organization that distributes profits to owners while pretending to be a nonprofit organization.

Low Profit Limited Liability Corporation (L3C): A type of hybrid organization legal in some states in the U.S. that prioritizes charitable over profitmaking purposes.

Market for Control: A market where ownership of (usually stock-issuing) organizations is bought and sold.

Price of Giving: The amount of after-tax income that a donor has to give up to transfer $1 to a charitable organization.

Tax Credit: A subtraction from the amount of taxes owed.

Tax Deduction: A subtraction from taxable income, that is, a subtraction before calculating taxes owed.

EXERCISES

1. If nonprofits arise to fix problems of asymmetric information, why are there no nonprofit automobile repair shops? Speculate on possible answers.
2. Elizabeth Mauser (1998) found that those parents who placed their children in nonprofit day-care centers actually spent more time researching their choice than those who put their children in for-profit day care. Is this what contract failure would predict? Does this evidence persuade you that contract failure theory is incorrect?
3. For each of the situations described below, would you expect the nonprofit sector to be relatively large or relatively small, compared to the government and/or for-profit sectors? Explain.

    (a) Preferences for public services differ substantially among local communities but are homogeneous within each local jurisdiction.
    (b) A new city has rapidly growing needs for social services, and the average person only lives in the community for a couple of years before moving out.
    (c) Property taxes are extremely high, but nonprofits are exempt.

4. A Taxing Problem: Suppose we were to eliminate the current tax deduction for personal donations and replace it with a matching grant system. At the end of each year, each nonprofit would mail an (audited) statement to the government indicating the total amount of personal donations they had received that year. The government would then mail a check to the nonprofit which matched donations by some fixed fraction. For example, if the matching rate were 30 percent, and a charity received $100,000 in donations, the government would mail a check for $30,000.

    (a) This system is similar to a tax credit system in terms of the resulting effective "prices" for giving. Explain.
    (b) There is at least one important difference between the effect of a tax credit and the effect of matching Identify and explain the difference.
    (Hint: Who would be able to use the tax credit?)
    (c) The matching grants would eliminate the pattern of "upside-down subsidy" in the current system of tax deductions. Explain why this is so and discuss whether this change is desirable.

5. Would you ever donate to a Benefit Corporation? To an L3C hybrid? To a CIC hybrid? How does the possibility of contract failure affect your answer?
6. In this chapter, we argued that the tax breaks given to nonprofit corporations lead to inefficiency. Does this mean we should get rid of these tax breaks? What are some pros and cons of doing so?

4

Analysis of economic functions: total, average, and marginal

I feel too much like a dependent variable!

4.1 Introduction

In economic analysis, we represent important relationships among economic quantities such as costs, revenues, prices, input resources, and output of goods and services by a mathematical construct called a "function." Accordingly, we need to delve into a little elementary mathematics, though perhaps not in time to relieve the distress of the trapeze artist flying above.

A *function* is simply a representation, in tabular, graphical or equation form, of how two or more quantities change in relation to one another. Before we

Figure 4.1 Student attention function

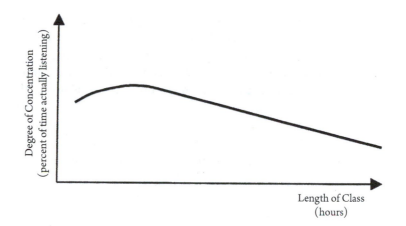

learn about functions in economic analysis, we must first become familiar with the building blocks of functions, namely "variables."

A *variable* is simply a quantity that takes on different values in different circumstances. Thus costs, revenues, prices or donations are all variables that can assume different positive or negative values measured in dollar terms. Alternatively, time is a variable that takes on different values as measured in hours, minutes or seconds.

In the construction of functions, we distinguish conceptually between two different types of variables – independent variables and dependent variables:

> A dependent variable *is a quantity whose value we want to explain or predict based on its relationship with other determining or influencing variables.*
> An independent variable *is one that determines or influences a dependent variable. We call these influencing variables independent variables.*

For example, suppose we were interested in what influences students' attention spans in class. The attention span of students (e.g., measured in the percentage of time actually listening to the instructor) would be our dependent variable. We might suppose that the length of the class (measured in hours) was an influencing or independent variable. If we graphed our dependent variable (usually on the vertical axis) against our independent variable (usually on the horizontal axis) it might look something like the picture in Figure 4.1. This graph shows that, past some point, as classes get longer and longer (yawn!), the attention of students will decrease. This example illustrates that a function can compactly describe, in this case graphically, the relationship between a dependent and an independent variable in a way that facilitates an informed choice on the duration of the class.

It is likely, however, that our dependent variable – student attention – is influenced by several variables, not just the length of the class. In general, it is important to distinguish among different types of independent variables – those under our control, which we call "choice" variables, and those which are not, which we call "environmental" variables. In the foregoing example, the length of the class is presumably a choice variable as we may select its value to influence student attention levels. However, other variables, such as the weather, may also influence student attention but are not subject to our control. These would be environmental variables.

An example from the economics of nonprofit organizations is the "donative revenue function" which relates how much an organization receives in donations in a given time period (the dependent variable) to such influencing variables as how much is spent on fund-raising (a choice variable) and the wealth of potential donors (an environmental variable). The relationship between dependent and independent variables is illustrated using graphs, tables or mathematical equations. We will use each of these approaches at different points in this text.

To focus on the variables under our control, we will usually depict the relationship between choice and dependent variables, while holding environmental variables constant at some pre-specified level. This idea of holding other variables constant while studying the relationship between a dependent and an independent variable, which economists call *ceteris paribus* (Latin for "holding all other things equal") plays an important role in economic analysis and will enable us to simplify our discussion considerably by breaking the analysis into a sequence of steps.

Figure 4.2 illustrates the idea of *ceteris paribus*. The lower curve in this figure represents a "donative revenue function" for a charity during a recession, when the level of the environmental variable Y, the level of income in the donor community, is held constant at a low level (Y_3). The upper curve illustrates the donative revenue function for that same charity in good times when donors enjoy high income Y_1. The middle curve illustrates the function when donor income takes the intermediate value Y_2.

Note, each curve in the figure shows that contributions increase (at a nonlinear rate) with increases in fund-raising expenditure. However, the level of income in the donor community also influences the level of contributions (height of the curves). At any given level of fund-raising expenditure, donations are higher when income is higher. Thus, if this organization spent $10,000 on fund-raising during ordinary economic conditions, it could

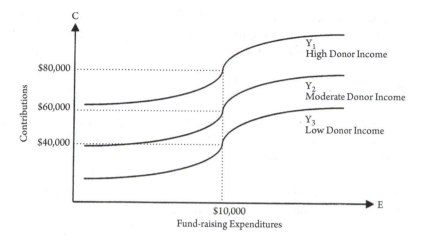

Figure 4.2 Donative revenue function at different income levels

expect donors to give $60,000. However, that same organization could obtain $80,000 in donations if it spent $10,000 on solicitation during an economic boom, but only $40,000 during a recession.

Now that we are familiar with dependent and independent variables, we can think of a function more precisely as a mathematical, tabular, or graphical representation that shows how a dependent variable changes in response to changes in the independent variables. We should be cautious about inferring causality, however. It is often unclear what causes what (does fund-raising expenditure increase donations or do increased donations cause excited fund-raisers to spend more?) or whether some third unidentified variable (a hunger crisis spurring both donations and spending on fund-raising) is influencing both the independent and dependent variables. Of course, correlation does not necessarily imply causation (one often sees ambulances at the scene of serious auto accidents, but that does not mean that ambulances cause auto accidents). Despite these caveats, the reader may find it useful to think in terms of cause and effect in understanding how a function summarizes the relationship between dependent and independent variables in an economic function.

In economics, there are many important functions, including cost and revenue functions, production functions that relate inputs to outputs, demand and supply functions, and others. In addition, the relationships between particular dependent and independent variables, such as cost and quantity produced, may be represented in several different important ways. In this chapter we will discuss three such ways – total, average, and marginal representations – for two significant types of economic functions – cost functions and revenue functions, both of which vary with the level of output produced by an organization.

4.2   Output

Economic functions depict the relationships among two or more economic variables such as costs, revenues, or amounts produced. One often-used variable is *output*. Output simply refers to the quantity of a good or service that is produced, per unit of time, as measured by some quantitative indicator. For example, we can measure production of beer in cans per week or six-packs per year. We will denote output by the letter Q.

In industries that produce physical manufactured goods, the concept of output is quite straightforward. We measure output by such indicators as the number of pairs of shoes, cans of fruit, tons of steel, or personal computers. Even when we are referring to goods, however, we must qualify output measurement by standardizing for *quality*. One personal computer is not the same as another, so we must indicate the quality or specifications that underlie our unit of output. In the provision of services, such as those offered by nonprofit organizations and social enterprises, we must also attend to the quality issue. In addition, the measure of output we select often requires more judgment than in the goods case and may depend on the purpose of our analysis. For example, in the performing arts we sometimes consider output as the number of performances given and other times the number of seats filled.

In general, we want to distinguish between *outputs* and *outcomes*: outputs are quantities that are directly controlled by the producer because they depend primarily on the input resources (labor, capital equipment, etc.) and the technology used by the producing organization. Thus, a *production function* depicts the dependent variable "quantity produced per unit of time" against independent choice variables for the quantities of each input employed per unit of time. Outcomes, by contrast, represent the societal impact of that output and depend not only on output but on other (environmental) independent variables as well. Thus, an *outcome function* frames outcome as the dependent variable and output and environment variables as the independent variables.

Outcomes often reflect the overall mission of a nonprofit organization or social enterprise. The following examples provide illustration:

The output of a meal program for children may be measured in terms of the number of meals served, or the number of children served. The desired outcome is better child health, which is dependent not only on proper eating but medical care, good housing and other factors not within the program's purview. Some of these variables are choice variables for the child (whether to eat broccoli), but as they are outside the organization's control, the organization regards these as environmental variables.

The output of a school may be measured by the number of courses offered or the number of students graduated. The desired outcome is a more highly skilled and educated population, which may depend not only on schooling but also on the upbringing of students and the economic opportunities to which they have access.

The output of a theater may be measured in terms of numbers of plays produced or number of theater goers served. The desired outcome may be greater arts appreciation in the community which also depends on the socio-economic character of the community as well as their access to theater.

The output of a social enterprise that employs challenged workers in the community may be the number of such workers who complete its training program and successfully work within the enterprise, but the outcome is the ultimate employment rate of its alumni who seek work in the broader economy, which also depends on economic conditions in the labor market.

The outputs of a community foundation or a United Way may be the number of dollars raised or the amount of money given as grants. The desired outcome is a more prosperous and well-functioning community, which also depends on many socio-economic factors.

Several comments about outputs and outcomes are relevant here. First, notice that in some of these examples, an organization or program has multiple outputs (courses offered, students graduated, etc.) and particular outputs are associated with multiple outcomes (employed workers, informed citizens). While multiple outputs and outcomes technically can be accommodated in our framework here, for explanatory purposes we focus primarily on single outputs and outcomes. In Chapter 9 we do consider multiple outputs explicitly. Second, the examples suggest the importance of clearly identifying a measurable unit of output that is thought to contribute to better outcomes. Analysis of costs, revenues and other important economic variables will all revolve around this measure. Output measures, which represent the direct products of organizations, are usually easier for an organization to define and measure than ultimate outcome measures. While we would often like to focus directly on outcomes, it is usually more practical to analyze managerial decisions as they affect output. Even where aggregate measures of outcome are available such as poverty, unemployment, or child mortality rates, it will be difficult for a manager to determine her organization's contribution to the aggregate outcome. Thus, practically speaking, the manager must make decisions in terms of output, even if the ultimate goal is one of outcomes.

Nonetheless, when making output decisions, it is important for managers to be sure that output affects outcome in the desired direction. If a clear case can be made that desired outcomes (unemployment rates) are negatively associated with increased output (number of clients served), then economic analysis can help us figure out the efficient level of output. Things are more difficult when the link between alternative outputs and outcomes is unclear. For example, schools have many alternative ways of producing the outcome of students' scientific literacy. Should schools produce more hours of classroom instruction, change the requirements for appointment as a science teacher, or offer more field trips? Economic analysis clarifies what we need to know and how we can use that knowledge, but resolving the problem itself will require advances in our understanding of educational programs.

The functions we study below are generic and apply to different measures of output. The important thing is to understand that output is simply a measure of how much of a good or service per unit of time an organization produces. Output is a dependent variable when explained by input use, but it is an important independent variable when we want to study such dependent variables as costs, revenues, demand, supply, and profits.

4.3   The concept of cost

The first type of function we will study is the *cost function* which relates the value of resources used in the production of a good or service (cost) to the amount of the good or service produced (output). In Chapter 6 we will delve more deeply into the nature of cost, because this is a very fundamental idea in economics. Here we provide just a brief explanation.

Fundamentally, we define economic cost as the value of the opportunities that are lost when resources are put to one use instead of another. For example, if we are buying toys for children in a day-care program, the cost is the value of that same resource in its *next best alternative use*. The money spent on toys is the cost to the organization because it is giving up the opportunity to buy other things with the same dollar value. The cost to society of using the toys in day-care programs reflects the value of the toys if used elsewhere. If those toys would otherwise have been bought by a family for its children, then the cost is also the money spent because that is what the family would have paid.

Note that this idea of *economic cost* is not the same as *accounting cost*. Accounting cost measures the amount of money that must be paid to get something, but sometimes you need to give up something that has value but is not money in order to get something. Then the amount paid for something (accounting cost) will not be the same as what the thing is worth in its next best use (economic cost). In the case of the toys, the two are identical because the only thing the day-care center gives up when getting toys is money and if the day-care center hadn't bought the toys, the family would have bought the same toys at the same price. On the other hand, suppose a worker in a hospital would be unemployed if he or she did not work at the hospital. In this case, the sum of the worker's wages and benefits (the accounting cost) is not an accurate estimate of the economic cost of using the worker's time because the worker cannot get an alternative job at that wage. Rather, an appropriate estimate would be the wage in the next best available job, or if there is no such job, the value that worker places on additional hours of "leisure." By contrast, the cost of a volunteer's time may be significant even though his or her wage is zero, since the volunteer is giving up scarce time that could be applied to other valued uses. In addition, despite their apparent cost of zero, it is likely that volunteers cost an organization something, as they will need to be trained and supervised as well as recruited and mentored.

This may seem an esoteric discussion for the hospital manager who still must pay the worker's wages and benefits, or the administrator of volunteer services who does not pay dollar wages to his or her charges. However, it is important to consider the volunteer's cost because, whether or not it shows up on the books, the volunteer knows intuitively that his or her work is not free. Rather, it uses valuable leisure time. Administrators who ignore this cost risk losing volunteer effort.

This brings us to still another critical point – that perspectives on costs vary, depending on the nature of the decision or decision maker involved. Economists make a distinction between *private costs* incurred by those who control market transactions (organizations, workers, or consumers), and *social costs* incurred by society as a whole. The social cost of employing a worker who would be otherwise unemployed is very low, but the private costs to his or her employer may be much higher. Alternatively, the private cost to the organization that employs a volunteer may be low, but the social cost of using that volunteer's time may be much higher. This difference can also apply to goods, as the social benefit of a good may be less (as in the case of a producer that pollutes in creating a good) or more (as when a good music student practices on a summer day when neighbors have their windows open and pay nothing for the privilege of listening). We will consider the distinction between such social and private costs further in Chapter 13 when we discuss *externalities*.

4.4   Cost functions

How do we represent the relationship between the output produced by an organization and the cost of producing that output?

Fixed and variable costs

To answer this question, we want to divide total costs into two components, Fixed Costs and Variable Costs:

Fixed Costs are those components of cost that do not vary or change with the level of output. *Variable Costs* are those components of cost that *do* vary with the level of output. Fixed costs are those costs that need to be expended before even the first unit of output can be produced. Variable costs are the additional costs incurred as more and more output is produced. Some examples:

- To produce a play, one needs a theater, costuming, stage sets, a rehearsed cast and crew, and a management team, before even one performance can be offered. These are the fixed costs. Then for each performance, additional costs are incurred for the daily wages of ticket takers, ushers, clean-up crews, actors, crew and other staff, printing of programs, utilities such as water and electricity, and various other supplies and services. These are the variable costs that increase with the number of performances.
- To run a fund-raising campaign, one needs an office, desk, telephone, computer, some basic information resources, and perhaps an allocation of a certain amount of administrative time. These are the fixed costs that need to be in place before a single dollar is raised. As more and more funds are solicited and secured, costs are incurred for the time spent by fund-raising volunteers and paid staff on phone calls and letters, rental of additional prospect lists, supplies, utilities, travel costs and time spent meeting with major-donor prospects, and so on. These are the variable costs that increase with the level of funds raised.
- To establish a resale shop to recycle and sell used items to low-income consumers, one needs a storefront and minimal staffing before anything

can be received, refurbished and sold. These are fixed costs. The additional staff time and processing costs required for sales are variable costs that increase with the level of sales.

It is important to note that the division of costs into the categories of fixed and variable depends on the period over which costs are being considered. Given enough time, the lease agreement can be canceled, actors left unrehearsed and disengaged, and phone lines abandoned. We refer to a time interval in which at least one element of production has a fixed quantity as *the short run*. The duration of the short run depends on the length of the lease, the repayment period of a loan, or any other physical restraints (like time to build a new factory) or contractual barriers to change. We refer to a time interval long enough that every input quantity can be varied as *the long run*. In the long run, there are no fixed costs because there are no fixed inputs. Fixed costs do not vanish, they get converted into variable costs. The size of the factory, amount of rehearsal time, and recruiting and training of staff can be adjusted to suit anticipated levels of output. Like short-run costs, long-run costs are a function of output. For a given level of output, long-run costs are lower than short-run costs because fixed costs can be adjusted to promote efficiency.

Consider the case of a primary school. In the short run, facility costs are fixed – there is no opportunity to expand or contract the building to accommodate more or fewer students within a year's time. However, over a ten-year period, the school's capacity can be changed, so that facility costs become variable. During that time, the school decides on a rebuilding plan to accommodate the anticipated number of students. Another factor that may be fixed or variable is staff costs. When annual contracts are used, the school may have to pay all staff for a year but can hire or lay off staff if given more than a year to adjust. Thus, classification of cost components as fixed and variable depends on the time for adjustment.

An additional measure of cost is introduced here, which reflects an important concept used by economists – that of the "margin," hence *marginal cost*. Just as a margin on a piece of paper is the strip along the edge, where the paper ends, so too is marginal cost a measure of the edge of cost, the extra cost that is incurred as output is expanded incrementally beyond its current level. We will see that marginal cost plays an important role in determining the optimal level of production for all kinds of organizations, including for-profit firms, nonprofit organizations, and social enterprises.

Total, average and marginal cost functions

Using the concepts of fixed and variable costs, we represent the relationship between costs and output in three different ways:

- *Total Cost* is the sum of fixed and variable costs at each level of output; the Total Cost function shows how total cost varies with the level of output.
- *Average Cost* (also known as *Average Total Cost*) is the *cost per unit* at each level of output. Average Cost is calculated by dividing Total Cost by the level of output at each output level; the Average Cost function shows how average cost varies with output. We divide the Average Cost function into two components: *Average Fixed Cost* (Fixed Cost divided by the level of output for each output level) and *Average Variable Cost* (Variable Cost divided by the level of output for each output level). At any level of quantity, Average Cost is the sum of Average Fixed Cost and Average Variable Cost. All three average cost functions measure costs in dollars per unit of output.
- *Marginal Cost* is the additional cost of increasing output by one unit starting at each level of output. The *Marginal Cost Function* shows how marginal cost varies with the level of output and is also measured in dollars per unit of output.

Consider a "dramatic" example of these various cost measures. Suppose the fixed cost of producing a high-school student play is $1000 and the cost of producing each additional performance is $100. Suppose further that five performances are initially being considered. At this level of output:

Fixed Cost = $1000,
Variable Cost = $500,
Total Cost = $1000 + $500 = $1500,
Average Cost = $1500/5 = $300 per performance,
Average Variable Cost = $500/5 = $100 per performance,
Marginal Cost = $100 per performance, the additional cost when Q is increased from 5 to 6.

How do we go from such calculations to representing total, average and marginal costs as functions, and how are these functions related to another? Let's consider a slightly more complicated example, represented in Table 4.1, adapted from a textbook by Apgar and Brown (1987/2011), depicting the costs and revenues of a Meals on Wheels program. The output measure for this program is the number of meals delivered per day to home bound people in need. The set-up or fixed cost is $15 for the availability of a van and driver

Table 4.1 Meals on Wheels: cost and revenue functions

Meals/ Day	Fix Cost $	Var Cost $	Tot Cost $	Average Cost $	AVC $	Marg Cost $	Tot Rev $	Average Rev $	Marg Rev $	Profit $
0	15.00	0.00	15.00							(15.00)
1	15.00	3.00	18.00	18.00	3.00	3.00	6.00	6.00	6.00	(12.00)
2	15.00	5.50	20.50	10.25	2.75	2.50	12.00	6.00	6.00	* (8.50)
3	15.00	7.50	22.50	7.50	2.50	2.00	18.00	6.00	6.00	(4.50)
4	15.00	10.00	25.00	6.25	2.50	2.50	24.00	6.00	6.00	(1.00)
5	15.00	13.00	28.00	5.60	2.60	3.00	30.00	6.00	6.00	2.00
6	15.00	16.50	31.50	5.25	2.75	3.50	36.00	6.00	6.00	4.50
7	15.00	20.50	35.50	5.07	2.93	4.00	42.00	6.00	6.00	6.50
8	15.00	25.00	40.00	5.00	3.13	4.50	48.00	6.00	6.00	8.00
9	15.00	30.00	45.00	5.00	3.33	5.00	54.00	6.00	6.00	9.00
10	15.00	35.50	50.50	5.05	3.55	5.50	60.00	6.00	6.00	9.50
11	15.00	41.50	56.50	5.14	3.77	6.00	66.00	6.00	6.00	9.50
12	15.00	48.00	63.00	5.25	4.00	6.50	72.00	6.00	6.00	9.00
13	15.00	55.00	70.00	5.38	4.23	7.00	78.00	6.00	6.00	8.00
14	15.00	62.50	77.50	5.54	4.46	7.50	84.00	6.00	6.00	6.50
15	15.00	70.50	85.50	5.70	4.70	8.00	90.00	6.00	6.00	4.50
16	15.00	79.00	94.00	5.88	4.94	8.50	96.00	6.00	6.00	2.00
17	15.00	88.00	103.00	6.06	5.18	9.00	102.00	6.00	6.00	(1.00)

(obviously a bargain!). The first column in the table shows the number of meals delivered. Note that, by definition, the fixed cost (second column) is the same in every row because fixed cost does not vary with output. The third column shows the variable cost of meals and fuel for the van which increases with the number of meals delivered. The remaining columns reflect the following calculations: column 4 shows the total cost (TC) which is calculated by adding the fixed cost in column 2 to the variable cost given in column 3; column 5 shows average cost (AC) which is found by dividing TC from column 4 by the output (number of meals) in column 1; column 6 shows the average variable cost (AVC) computed by dividing variable cost (column 3) by output. (Note that AC and AVC cannot be computed when output is at a level of zero, as a number divided by zero is undefined. Luckily, we don't ever need to know per unit costs when we are not producing any units.) Column 7 shows the marginal cost (MC) calculated by subtracting the Total Cost in column 4 in that row from the Total Cost in column 4 of the row below.

Let's take a closer look at the calculation of the marginal cost column, for greater clarity. We label the level of output (number of meals) by the variable Q. Now suppose that the number of meals delivered is 6, that is, Q = 6. What is the marginal cost of producing that last (sixth) meal? It is simply the total cost (TC) of producing six meals minus the TC for producing five meals, that is:

$$MC(6) = TC(6) - TC(5) = \$31.50 - \$28 = \$3.50 \qquad (4.1)$$

Thus, $3.50 appears in the table in column 6 at the level of output (Q) of 6 meals. Notice that in function notation, MC(6) means marginal cost when output is 6, it doesn't mean multiply marginal cost by 6. To generalize the above equation for any level of output, we write:

$$MC(Q) = TC(Q) - TC(Q\text{-}1) \qquad (4.2)$$

By making the above calculations for each level of output we compute the numbers in columns 4, 5, and 6 of Table 4.1 for all levels of output (rows of the table). Such a table is one way to represent cost functions. In particular, columns 4 and 1 together represent the Total Cost Function TC(Q), columns 5 and 1 represent the Average Cost Function AC(Q), and columns 6 and 1 represent the Marginal Cost Function MC(Q). In functional notation, here are the formulas for calculating each of the other cost variables from TC(Q):

$$FC(Q) = FC = TC(0)$$
$$VC(Q) = TC(Q) - FC$$
$$ATC(Q) = TC(Q)/Q$$
$$AVC(Q) = VC(Q)/Q$$

Another useful way to represent such functions is through graphs. For the Meals on Wheels program described in Table 4.1, the graphs in Figure 4.3A show the Total as well as the Fixed and Variable Costs as functions of output, while Figure 4.3B shows the Average, Average Variable, and Marginal cost functions. (The figures also contain revenue functions that we will come to later.) These graphs are obtained by simply plotting output (Q), that is, column 1 in the table, measured in meals per day, along the horizontal axis against the corresponding cost number, measured in dollars or dollars per meal per day, respectively, along the vertical axes and connecting the dots.

One may ask, "Why is it permissible in these graphs to connect the dots between the integral numbers representing different levels of output (whole

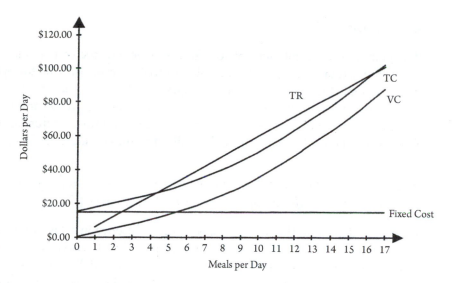

Figure 4.3A Meals on Wheels example

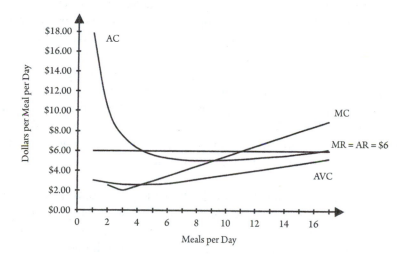

Figure 4.3B Meals on Wheels example

meals)?" That is, the graphs suggest that one can produce 2.5 meals as well as 2 meals or 3 meals. The answer is that we are measuring output on a per day basis so that, for example, 2.5 meals per day can be produced by producing 5 meals over a two-day period. Thus, every fractional output is producible because we are considering rates of production of output rather than absolute levels. (Even 3.1459 meals/day is permissible, though obviously Pi is just for dessert.)

Key relationships

The graphical representations of cost functions help us see certain relationships among total, average and marginal costs that are more difficult to appreciate by simply looking at tables or even equations. Here we want to take note of several of these relationships because they will help us understand these functions better and give us some new, intuitive insights into the nature of cost functions and how they can help us think about resource allocation decisions.

1. *The height of the marginal cost curve (MC) follows the slope of the total cost curve (TC) and the slope of the variable cost curve (VC)*

Recall our definition that marginal cost is the difference in total cost as one goes from one level of output to another. Where the TC curve is steep, TC moves up a lot when output increases by one unit and MC is high. This means the slope of a line connecting two points on the curve one unit apart from each other (rise over run) is the same as MC. Where the TC curve is flatter, the slope (and hence MC) is smaller. We can take this one step further by looking at how this slope changes as we increase output. Where the TC curve becomes steeper when we increase output, the MC curve will be upward-sloping (increasing marginal cost), and where TC becomes flatter, the MC curve will be downward-sloping (decreasing marginal cost). If it becomes less steep, then marginal costs are falling. In the graph (or table) we can see that from a level of output $Q = 0$ to $Q = 3$, total cost TC becomes less steep and MC declines. From $Q = 3$ on to higher levels of output, TC becomes steeper and steeper and MC rises over this range. Thus, marginal cost is reflected in the *slope* of the total cost curve.

Now observe that the slope of the Variable Cost curve (VC) is the same as that of the TC curve (see Figure 4.3A); these curves only differ in their height by the (constant) Fixed Cost. Thus, where the TC curve becomes steeper or less steep, the VC follows it exactly. So, if the slope of the TC curve reflects MC, the same is true of the slope of the VC curve. We can just as well compute marginal cost $MC(Q)$ by calculating $VC(Q) - VC(Q\text{-}1)$ as by calculating $TC(Q) - TC(Q\text{-}1)$ at each level of output Q.

One may wonder, however, why VC or TC do not increase uniformly with output, in this Meals on Wheels example, or in many other instances. This is the same as asking why marginal costs aren't constant over the whole range of output. A brief explanation is that it is uneconomical to prepare only one or two meals in a kitchen designed to produce more than that. It is almost the same effort for a cook and takes little more energy or cleaning costs to prepare two meals as one. This would explain why marginal cost declines from $Q = 0$ to $Q = 3$. However, as more meals are produced they may have to be delivered to more and more remote locations and this becomes increasingly costly. This shape is typical of short-run production, when, for example, we cannot simply build a remote kitchen for the remote locations. Past some quantity (here $Q = 3$), crowding more workers into a fixed facility becomes less productive on the margin, so MC becomes upward-sloping.

2. *Where the MC curve is above the AC curve, average costs are upward-sloping; where the MC curve is below the AC curve, average costs are downward-sloping*

Note in the graph (or table) that until an output of $Q = 8$ meals is reached, average cost (AC) is higher than marginal cost (MC), while at outputs above nine meals, MC is higher than AC. Note also that below eight meals, AC is downward-sloping while above nine meals AC is upward-sloping. This relationship between AC and MC *always holds*. Why? Because if the cost of an additional unit of output (meal) is greater than the average cost at the current output then the next unit of output will pull the average up. Conversely, if the cost of an additional unit is lower than the average cost, the next unit of output will pull the average cost down. To illustrate with our example, at an output level of five meals per day, average cost is $5.60 while marginal cost is $3.00. Thus, increasing output to six meals lowers the average cost to $5.25. In contrast, at an output level of 13, the average cost is $5.38 while the marginal cost is $7.00. Thus, increasing output to 14 increases the average cost to $5.54. This relationship between average functions and marginal functions always holds, whether we are talking about average variable costs or average total costs, whether we are talking about short-run costs or long-run costs, and whether we are talking about other kinds of functions like average revenue and marginal revenue. If you did better on the last test, your (average) grade in a class just increased, and if you did poorly, your grade fell.

In the short-run, average cost curves are usually U-shaped. This is because fixed costs per unit (average fixed costs) are always downward-sloping and never reach zero because overhead is "spread" over more units of output. Average variable costs are also downward-sloping because a large facility cannot be operated efficiently at low levels of output. Once output reaches the designed capacity of the facility, further increases in production become progressively costlier, so that average variable cost becomes upward-sloping. Eventually, the upward-sloping AVC curve dominates the downward-sloping AFC curve so that AC becomes upward-sloping.

Long-run average costs curves have diverse shapes. The most common case is constant costs, that is, the long-run AC curve is horizontal. The reason is that if one factory, operating at its designed capacity, can produce 100 units of output for $2 each, then two such factories would produce 200 units of output, still at an average cost of $2. Cloning facilities, only possible in the long run, allows the firm to produce any quantity at the same average cost. When long-run average costs are horizontal, the long-run marginal cost curve will overlap long-run average costs. Using our test-taking analogy, if you get a 70 on every exam, taking one more test will not change your average of 70.

Sometimes the process of production is such that long-run average costs are downward-sloping. For example, because we deliver electric power through a network of power lines, it is less costly, on average, to deliver power to every house than to every other house. Because every input can be adjusted in the long run, production changes are changes in the scale of operations. Downward-sloping long-run average cost curves exhibit *economies of scale*, where "economies" refers to a reduction in per-unit costs as the scale of operations gets larger. Sometimes long-run cost curves are upward-sloping, which we call *diseconomies of scale* (higher per-unit costs at larger scales). Cost curves can have economies of scale at some range of production levels and constant costs or diseconomies at other some other range of production. A common pattern is economies of scale up to some level of production, followed by constant costs. The level of production where the costs switch from economies to constant costs is called *the minimum efficient scale*. The logic of that label is clear – it is inefficient to produce small quantities because the costs are unnecessarily high.

3.   *The AC and MC curves cross each other where AC reaches its minimum*

Note in the graph of Figure 4.3B that the average and marginal costs curves cross each other where output $Q = 9$, and this is where AC reaches its lowest value. This follows from relationship No. 2 above: AC keeps getting smaller with additional output so long as MC is less than AC. When MC rises to the point where it is equal to AC, then producing the next unit of output will no longer lower the average cost. AC will have reached its minimum. At that point there is a cross-over: MC will become greater than AC, and AC will begin rising rather than falling with additional output.

The point of minimum average cost is an important one. It represents the level at which that output (meals in this case) can be produced at the least possible cost per unit, within the time frame considered. If the objective of a government agency were to produce a given level of output at lowest total cost, this has implications for the number of organizations the government should employ to deliver that number of meals. For the current example, where AC is minimized when $Q = 9$, the government should contract with 10 providers if it wants to provide 900 meals. Note, 900 meals could be supplied by eight providers or by twelve providers, but in these cases, it would be impossible for all suppliers to produce at the point where average costs are lowest.

Note the implication here for government policy: it is not always best for government to force consolidation of alternative service providers. Perhaps fixed costs could be reduced if each city had only one ambulance service or police station, but the added variable costs from longer travel distances would swamp this effect, not to mention the reductions in service quality that would occur. Similarly, one large soup kitchen might have lower average production costs for meals than a dispersed set of neighborhood centers, but if one counted the added variable costs of distribution incurred by recipients having to travel to the kitchen, the average cost of the kitchen might well be higher.

Finally, the question of what scale of production is most efficient is much more complicated than finding where average cost is minimized. For the individual organization, for example, the revenue as well as the cost side must be considered. To obtain some insight on how this works, we extend our Meals on Wheels example to include revenues as well as costs.

4.5   Revenue functions

In a manner very similar to the treatment of cost functions, we can represent how the revenues acquired by an organization change as the level of its output varies. The nature of revenue functions depends on the source of revenues and how the organization is paid. As with costs, we can make the distinction between "fixed revenues," that is, revenues that do not vary with the level of output, and "variable revenues," which do change with the level of output. Once again, we will encounter the word "marginal," this time to describe the extra revenue gained from providing another unit of a good.

Examples of fixed revenues include: grants or budget allocations given to an organization as a lump sum with no explicit tie to how much the organization produces; returns on investments or endowments that come in regardless of what a nonprofit organization or social enterprise produces; and a certain level of donations a charitable organization may attract on past reputation and current solicitation efforts, even if it produces no services. We are not saying that the organization is powerless to affect fixed revenues. The charity could seek more grants, change the return on investment, or increase donations through its other actions. The requirement is that fixed revenues do not change when we change output levels and nothing else.

Examples of variable revenues include those received per unit of sale of goods or services; reimbursements received from government or other third-party payers based on services provided; and incremental donations received as a consequence of providing additional levels of services.

Note that there are certain areas of ambiguity in classifying fixed versus variable revenues for nonprofit organizations and social enterprises. Some types of revenues, such as sales or reimbursements for services, are clearly variable. Others, such as income from (existing) endowment or invested funds are clearly fixed. But others, such as charitable contributions, while not explicitly connected to the level of output, are nonetheless likely to vary with output. Thus, part of charitable contribution revenue is probably fixed within some time period, while another component probably depends on how much service is produced, or how much donors perceive that the organization offers. Here again, the time period within which "fixed" and "variable" are defined becomes important. Within a short period of months or a year, charitable contributions probably do not vary much with the output level of services. Within a multi-year period they probably do.

In any case, as with costs, we can compute the three basic revenue functions:

Total Revenue (TR) is the sum of fixed and variable revenues at a given level of output.

Average Revenue (AR) is the revenue per unit of output, calculated at some given level of output. Average Revenue is computed by dividing Total Revenue by the level of output. This definition needs to be much more complicated when the organization produces multiple outputs, but we avoid this complication here.

If there is a component of fixed revenue, then it may also be worthwhile to compute average variable revenue (AVR):

Average Variable Revenue (AVR) is equal to variable revenue divided by output.

Finally,

Marginal Revenue (MR) is the added revenue obtained as a result of increasing output by one unit, for any given level of initial output.

Let's return to our Meals on Wheels example, shown in Table 4.1 and Figure 4.3. Suppose that the meals produced are sold at a uniform price of $6 each and that the organization can sell as many meals as it produces at this price. Under these conditions, columns 8, 9 and 10 display the TR, AR, and MR functions respectively. In this case, there is no fixed revenue, just variable revenue resulting from the sale of meals; thus, AR and AVR are the same. We can see also that since the meal price stays the same, that is, the price of each additional meal is the same regardless of how many meals are sold, MR remains constant at $6. And since there is no fixed revenue and MR is constant, AR (or AVR) is also constant at $6. That is, the average revenue brought in per meal is $6, no matter what the level of output. These relationships are shown graphically by the lines TR (an upward sloping line in Figure 4.3A) and MR and AR (a horizontal line in Figure 4.3 B, where MR = AR = price of $6.) Here, the TR function is just a straight line, and the MR and AC functions are just (the same) horizontal line at the $6 level.

This is the simplest imaginable revenue structure. We will analyze more general revenue functions later in the text. Yet it is a meaningful example because it represents the revenue opportunities of a small commercial organization in a large market, which must behave as a "price taker" (as in the case of perfect competition discussed in Chapter 7). That is, no matter how much it produces, within a wide range of output, the organization will have no influence on the market price. If it raises its price it will not be able to sell because other firms will sell at the lower ($6) market price. If it lowers its price, it will hardly be noticed by competing sellers and will spite itself by decreasing its revenues. This is also the revenue function for a nonprofit organization or social enterprise that is reimbursed at a fixed rate for all the output it can produce (such as a specific medical procedure reimbursed by a government or private health insurance program.)

4.6   The profit function

For any given level of output, we can calculate the profit by subtracting total cost from total revenue. Thus, in equation form, the *profit function* is:

$$\text{Profit } (Q) = TR(Q) - TC(Q) \tag{4.3}$$

We calculate profits and display them as the last column of Table 4.1 and graphically as Figure 4.4. Notice that the organization can make a profit by producing between approximately 4.5 and 16.5 units of output (meals). Producing outside this range produces net losses. At Q = 5 and Q = 16, the

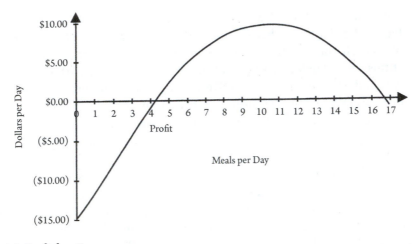

Figure 4.4 Profit function

organization barely breaks even. But the maximum profit is produced when the organization produces an output between 10 and 11 meals. There is an interesting and important relationship between the cost and revenue functions at the output where profit is maximized. Namely: *profit is maximized where marginal cost (MC) is equal to marginal revenue (MR).*

It is important to understand why this is so: if MR were greater than MC then expanding output would bring in more revenue than cost, and profit would be increased. (Here, when we increase output from 5 to 6 meals, profit is increased by $2.50. The added revenue ($6) covers the added cost ($3.50) with money left that adds to profits.) Therefore, profit cannot be maximal where MR > MC. Similarly, if MC were greater than MR then profit could be increased by reducing output. (Here, when we decrease output from 13 to 12, profit is increased by $1, the difference between the marginal revenue foregone ($6) and the saving of the marginal cost of the 13th meal ($7).) Hence, profits cannot be maximal where MC > MR. The only possibility then is that profit is maximal where MR = MC (around 11 meals in our example). If one wants to make as much money as possible, one keeps producing more output until one reaches the point where the added revenue taken in just offsets the cost of producing one more unit. To go further means producing additional units whose cost exceeds the revenue they bring in; not to go that far will forego additional profits from units that can be sold for more than they cost to produce. This rule for deciding how much to produce in order to maximize profits is just one example of what economists call "Analysis at the Margin." In the next chapter, we will explore how analysis at the margin can guide a variety of important resource allocation decisions.

Let's return to the Meals on Wheels example again and ask a different question. What if the organization decides that its mission is to produce and deliver as many meals as it possibly can? How much output will it be able to produce? Referring to Figure 4.4 we can see that it can produce up to Q =16 and still break-even. An agency with the objective of "maximizing output" subject to breaking even financially, will decide to produce 16 meals compared to 11 meals for the profit maximizing agency. This is one instance where the difference in motivations of a nonprofit or social enterprise versus a conventional for-profit may lead to different levels of service. However, we need to make two points clear.

First, the goal of pure output maximization is by no means universal among nonprofits or social enterprises. Nonprofit organizations may require some profits to build their endowments and reserve funds, to finance capital expansion, or to subsidize other outputs (e.g., using profits from sale of art reproductions to finance new acquisitions). Thus, a nonprofit may choose to make some profit rather than produce the absolute maximum level of service. Similarly, social enterprises may choose to make a minimum level of profit, albeit less than the maximum possible, to keep social investors on board.

Second, it is not clear that maximizing service is the best thing to do from the viewpoint of society. Note that every unit produced and sold after Q = 11 loses money because the marginal cost of producing it exceeds what is paid for it. If the price paid correctly indicates the value to society of additional production, then producing more than 11 units would be inefficient. However, if there are reasons to believe that such units have value beyond the price that purchasers pay, then from a social point of view, additional output beyond that which maximizes profit may be efficient. In Chapter 13, we will introduce the concept of "externalities" to deal with social benefits not incorporated in the price system.

The shutdown rule

The Meals on Wheels example shows that under some conditions, there is no level of output that allows the organization to make a profit or break-even. It may be seen from Table 4.1 that if the prevailing price is less than $5 per meal, there is no level of output for which average revenue (prevailing price) will exceed average cost (or where total revenue exceeds total cost). At the $5 price, the organization can sell nine units (the profit maximizing level where price equals marginal cost) and just break-even (both revenues and costs equal $45). However, even if the prevailing price were less than

$5 the organization may wish to continue operations in the short run if doing so would reduce losses. Operating at a loss is better than not operating, at a bigger loss. The key insight is that the firm loses its fixed costs if it shuts down but may be able to offset some of the fixed costs if operating profits (total revenue minus variable costs) are positive. That is, setting aside fixed costs, "operating profits" may be positive: thus, the organization should:

> *Stay open if average revenue exceeds average variable costs when you produce the quantity that makes MR = MC. Otherwise, shut down and accept losses equal to FC.*

In our example if the market price is more than $2.50, it will be possible to reduce losses by staying open. For example, suppose the prevailing price were $3 per meal. Then the organization would sell five units (where MC = $3), and revenues would exceed variable costs by $15 – $13 = $2 dollars. The two-dollar margin would pay part of the fixed cost, so the organization loses less ($13) staying open than shutting down ($15). In contrast, when the prevailing price is less than $2.50, there would be negative operating profits as well as fixed costs, so the organization is better off (financially) shutting down. In sum, when minimizing financial losses in any time period is an absolute requirement set by law or funders, we have this *shutdown rule*:

> *Cease production if, at the profit-maximizing production level where the prevailing price equals marginal cost (P = MC), that price (average revenue) is less than average variable cost (P < AVC).*

The shutdown rule represents an important idea for nonprofit managers and social entrepreneurs. In subsequent discussion, we will encounter other versions of the shutdown rule, including one that applies to fund-raising efforts. We have focused on profit maximization and loss minimization in this example, the natural thing to do in a traditional economics class, but when we consider the objectives and resource capabilities of social enterprises and nonprofit organizations, we may need to modify the rule. In particular, to avoid the likely result of shutting down – that clients would not be served by anyone else – the organization might stay open even when it could not cover its variable costs, provided it could find a new source of funding (an emergency appeal to donors or a bank loan).

4.7   The demand function

The Meals on Wheels example was particularly straightforward because it assumed a simplified revenue structure under which the organization could sell as much as it could produce at a given constant price. This is often not the case, especially when organizations produce large shares of the total output in the markets in which they sell. If the organization in the Meals on Wheels example were the only producer in its area it could choose its own price. If the organization wanted to sell more output, it would have to lower its price in order to sell that output.

Economists describe this phenomenon by saying that organizations face "downward-sloping demand curves." What they mean is that the price that people are willing to pay for a good or service declines as more of that good becomes available. Looked at in reverse, people will buy more if the price falls and less if the price rises. Thus, we could characterize the demand function as the quantity Q that people want to purchase at each possible price p. As shown in Figure 4.5, the demand function is usually represented by a curve or line sloping downward from left to right, with price p on the vertical axis and output Q on the horizontal axis. At any point (P, Q) on this curve, Q represents the amount that would be purchased if the price were set at P, so that in function notation, we write $Q^D = Q^D(P)$ (quantity demanded is a function of price).

Note that the inverse relationship – the maximum amount anyone is willing to pay (P) for each additional unit of output (Q) is the conventional way of specifying the *demand function*. You can obtain this by algebraically placing

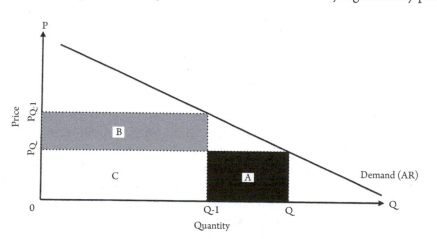

Figure 4.5 Demand function

P on one side of the equal sign and Q on the other side. Mathematically, this is represented as $P^D = P^D(Q)$ (demand price, or *marginal willingness to pay*, as a function of quantity). Marginal willingness to pay reflects how consumers attribute economic value to outputs that interest them, given their purchasing power or income. Hence, demand is not simply a function of what people need, but also what they can afford and what they prefer to have within the constraints of their resources. This is one reason market prices may not accurately reflect social valuations; social judgments sometimes incorporate distributional concerns and individual needs not reflected in what people are willing to pay in the marketplace. We will develop these ideas more fully in later chapters, especially Chapter 14 on cost–benefit analysis.

Consider now the relationship between demand and the revenue received by organizations selling the given output Q. When the price is set at P, all Q units are sold at this price so that P (the demand) is the average revenue AR(Q) brought in for these Q units. In general, we can see the following relationship between demand, total revenue TR(Q), and average revenue AR(Q):

$$TR(Q) = P(Q) \times Q, \text{ and} \tag{4.4}$$
$$AR(Q) = TR(Q)/Q = P(Q) \tag{4.5}$$

In short, the demand function represents the average revenue function, and total revenue is just average revenue (demand) multiplied by output. Note that this assumes that all output is sold at just one uniform price, P. In economists' terms, this means that there is no *price discrimination*, that is, sellers cannot charge different prices to different purchasers and cannot sell some units at one price and other units at another price to the same purchaser. When price discrimination is possible, revenue functions are more complicated but still useful. We will discuss various possibilities for price discrimination by nonprofits and social enterprises in Chapter 9.

In fact, for nonprofits and social enterprises, determination of pricing policies can be a complex issue. In traditional economics, profit-maximizing organizations always pick a price and quantity combination that is on the demand curve. However, selling at points (combinations of P and Q) below the demand curve is also feasible; it just means that the seller is receiving less for the output than consumers are willing to pay for the quantity sold. Profit maximizers would never do this, but a nonprofit that is concerned about distributional issues (for example, a university seeking a balanced

Table 4.2 Computing marginal revenue

Average Revenue (P)	Quantity (Q)	Total Revenue (TR)	Marginal Revenue (MR)
$10.00	1	$10.00	$10.00
9	2	18	8
8	3	24	6
7	4	28	4
6	5	30	2
5	6	30	0
4	7	28	(2)
3	8	24	(4)
2	9	18	(6)
1	10	10	(8)

student body) may indeed choose to do so. As we discuss later, this will require other ways of rationing services than just prices. Suffice it to say now that in such cases the revenue functions will take a different form.

Returning to the straightforward situation of selling output along a downward-sloping demand curve, how do we calculate marginal revenue (MR)? How much additional revenue does the organization receive if it sells another unit but in doing so, lowers the single price charged for all units sold? This is a somewhat tricky question which we will answer by referring to Table 4.2. This table shows the relationship between demand (AR or P), output Q, TR, and MR in a situation of downward-sloping demand. Column 1 represents the price required to sell different levels of output, column 2 is the output level Q, and column 3 is the total revenue TR (P × Q) obtained at different levels of output. Column 4 represents the marginal revenue MR(Q) calculated by subtracting TR(Q-1) from TR(Q) at each level of Q, in much the same way as we calculated MC(Q) from TC(Q) and TC(Q-1) in the previous discussion of marginal cost.

Notice that marginal revenue is different from demand or average revenue. Why is this so? Why isn't the incremental revenue from selling the next unit the same as the price that is paid for it? The answer is that every time another unit is sold, the price goes down and less revenue is obtained from all previous units that would have been sold at the higher price (again, assuming no price discrimination). So, if you sell three units you only receive $15 for each, and a total of $45, rather than $16 each and a total of $32, for selling two units. The (marginal) revenue added by the sale of the third unit is, thus, $13 (equal to $45 – $32).

In general, the marginal revenue is equal to the price obtained from the next unit sold (P), less the loss due to the price decrease for previous units (the change in price needed to sell an extra unit multiplied by the number of previous units).

This effect is illustrated graphically in Figure 4.5.

Total revenue (TR) at a given level of output (Q) is represented graphically by the area of the rectangle between the origin and the demand curve at that quantity. Two such TR rectangles are illustrated in Figure 4.5. The rectangle consisting of boxes B plus C represents total revenue when Q-1 is sold, because the area of this rectangle is length (here equal to P_{Q-1}) multiplied by width (here equal to Q-1). Similarly, the rectangle consisting of boxes A plus C represents the total revenue when amount Q is sold. The difference between these two TR rectangles, or (A + C) – (B + C) = A – B, measures the marginal revenue brought in by the sale of the Qth unit. Box A represents the extra revenue from the sale of the Qth unit. (Note that its length is, by construction, one unit so that the area equals 1 times P, or simply P.) Box B represents the loss in revenue obtainable from previous units of production. (Its width is the change in price necessary to sell the next unit $(P_{Q-1} - P_Q)$ and its length is the number of units previously sold (Q-1).)

Every time this organization increases output, this produces gains (like the area of box A) and losses (like the area in box B). Figure 4.6 shows that except for the first bit of output, the marginal revenue function MR(Q) is always below the average revenue or demand function AR(Q) because of the losses represented by box B. In fact, it is very possible that for some range of output, MR will be negative (when box B exceeds box A). Under these conditions, the revenue gained by selling an additional unit will be more than offset by

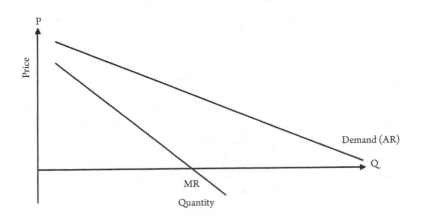

Figure 4.6 Average and marginal revenue functions

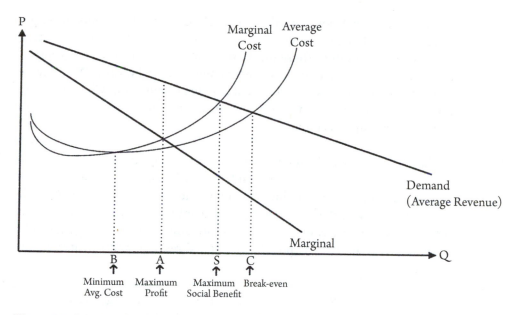

Figure 4.7 Output under different organizational objectives

reductions in the price of previous units. In Chapter 8 we will investigate the conditions under which this will occur.

The fact that MR is, in general, different from demand has important implications for pricing and output decisions. This is illustrated in Figure 4.7 which depicts the cost and revenue functions for an organization that faces a downward-sloping demand function. Here again, the choice of output level depends on the objective of the organization. But the rules of analysis are the same:

> *To maximize profit, increase output Q until MR is no longer greater than (just equal to) MC; this occurs at output level Q = A in the diagram.*
> *To maximize output, increase output until TC = TR, or AC = AR (break-even point). This occurs at level Q = C in the diagram. Recall, this is where the organization just breaks even.*

Again, the profit-maximizing level of output is considerably less than the maximum output that can be produced while breaking even. However, the more interesting result here is that the level of output at which profit is maximized is different from the level at which demand P(Q) is equal to MC (in contrast to the previous example). This is point S in the diagram. This is an interesting point because up until this level of output additional units can be sold at prices higher than they cost to produce. Thus, it can be argued that society places a net positive value on producing the added units of output from A to S, and thus such expansion would be efficient. A profit-maximizing firm would not produce those units. A nonprofit firm (or social enterprise) attempting to maximize societal benefits might do so, however. And if there were further reasons (such as external benefits discussed in Chapter 13) to produce even more, the nonprofit or social enterprise might continue to expand output up to C units.

In the Meals on Wheels example earlier, there were no fixed revenues and the price was independent of the quantity sold. Thus, price, average revenue, average variable revenue, and marginal revenue were all the same. We have just seen that when the price depends on quantity sold, marginal revenue is distinct from the price, but price is still the same thing as average revenue. Now, we also consider the possibility of fixed revenue and revisit the *shut-down* rule.

Average revenue (AR) consists of two components – average fixed revenue (AFR) and average variable revenue (AVR). When fixed revenues are present, the price is the same as average variable revenue, but both are less than average revenue. Therefore, we must be much more specific for our *shutdown* rule:

> *An organization should shut down if, at the profit-maximizing level of positive output, AVR < AVC.*

The earlier *shutdown* rule is a special case of this general rule. With no fixed revenues, price is identical with average variable revenues. Even though marginal revenues are generally lower than the price, this rule involves average variable revenues that are identical to the price even with downward-sloping demand. As before, an organization might want to remain open even though it is losing money. This would occur when the net revenues from operating offset a share of fixed costs. The interesting and new implication here is that, assuming its sales are intended solely as a means of raising funds, an organization might want to shut down its sales operation even if it were possible to stay open and operate at an overall profit! Specifically, if at the profit-maximizing level of (positive) output (where MR = MC), variable revenues are less than variable costs, an organization could nonetheless enjoy positive overall profits if the excess of fixed revenues over fixed costs outweighed the difference between variable costs and revenues. Despite its ability to stay open and avoid bankruptcy, this organization would do better to shut down and devote its entire (non-operating) profit, unencumbered, to direct pursuit of its organizational mission.

Regardless of whether the organization is making or losing money, operating losses will hurt and can be avoided by shutting down. An example illustrates this possibility. Suppose that an organization can sell its services at a fixed price of $10, and the best level of production at this price (when it stays open) is five units of output. Suppose further that fixed costs are $5, the total costs of producing 10 units are $60, and fixed revenues are $100. Under these conditions, the organization would have profits of $95 if it shut down (calculated by subtracting fixed costs from fixed revenues). Staying open, its total revenues would be $150 (from 5 × $10 + $100), its total costs would be $60, so its maximal profits would be $90 (from $150 – $60). By eliminating its money-losing sales activity the organization has more to spend on its organizational mission. Our shutdown rule provides correct guidance in this case, because average variable revenue (price) is $10, which is less than the average variable cost of $11 (which is calculated by subtracting fixed costs ($5) from total costs ($60) and dividing the result by the quantity (10)).

The alert reader will have noticed two related problems with this analysis. First, the organizational mission may be to sell the service in question, rather than use it to finance some other charitable activity. Second, when the output is mission-related, short-run fixed revenues may evaporate if the organization stopped producing that mission-related service. What would be the point of donating or making grants to support an activity the organization discontinued? We deal with both these possibilities in the section on advanced pricing issues in Chapter 9.

SUMMARY

We have covered a lot of territory in this chapter. We have defined output and cost, and we have shown how economic variables such as cost, revenue, and demand can be related to the level of output through the construction of cost, revenue and demand functions. We have described the different forms of these functions – total, average, and marginal. And we have demonstrated some ways in which these functions can be analyzed to arrive at decisions about the quantity of output to produce. One analytic principle we applied to output decisions was *analysis at the margin*. This is a powerful principle that we will continue to apply to various economic decisions in subsequent chapters.

SELECTED REFERENCES AND CITATIONS

Apgar, W.C. and Brown, H.J. (1987/2011). *Microeconomics for Public Decisions*. Menlo Park, CA: Askmar Publishing.

Gill, R.T. (1993). *Economics*. Mountain View, CA: Mayfield Publishing Company.

Mankiw, N.G. (2018). *Principles of Microeconomics* (8th ed.). Boston: Cengage Learning.

Mansfield, E.W, Allen, B., Doherty, N.A., and Weigelt, W. (2016). *Managerial Economics* (8th ed.). New York: W.W. Norton & Company.

REVIEW CONCEPTS

Accounting Cost: The costs reported in the firm's official financial statement.

Ceteris Paribus: Latin for "all other things held constant." Commonly assumed in economics when analyzing the impact of a change in one particular variable on another.

Demand Function: The relationship that exists between the number of units of a good or service that consumers are willing to buy, and a given set of conditions that influence the willingness to purchase, such as price, income level, and advertising.

Dependent Variable: A quantity whose value we want to explain or predict based on its relationship with other determining or influencing variables that we call independent variables.

Economic Cost: The value of an input in its best alternative employment; that is, the opportunity cost of using the input.

Fixed Cost: Costs that do not vary with the quantity of output produced.

Function: A representation, in mathematical, tabular, graphical, or other form, of how two or more quantities change in relation to one another.

Independent Variable: A variable used to describe, predict, and control the dependent variable.

Marginal Analysis: A basis for making various economic decisions by computing the additional (marginal) benefits derived from a particular decision and comparing them with the additional (marginal) costs incurred.

Marginal Cost: The incremental increase in total cost that results from a one-unit increase in output.

Marginal Revenue: The change in total revenue that results from a one-unit change in quantity demanded.

Outcomes: The social impact or result of a decision, representing the combined impact of outputs and other (environmental) independent variables.

Output: The level of a good or service that is produced, as measured by some quantitative indicator.

Production Function: The relationship between quantity of inputs used to make a good or service and the quantity of output of that good or service.

Sunk Cost: A cost that has already been committed and cannot be recovered.

Total Costs: The market value of inputs a firm uses in production.

Total Revenue: The amount of money received by sellers of a good or service, computed as the price of the good or service times the quantity sold.

Variable: A quantity that takes on different numerical values in different circumstances.

Variable Cost: The cost of all the inputs whose level varies with output.

EXERCISES

1. The following cost data apply to concerts by Little Falls Symphony Orchestra:

Q	FC	VC	TC	AVC	ATC	MC
0	100	0	____	X	X	X
1	____	60	____	____	____	____
2	____	85	____	____	____	____
3	____	105	____	____	____	____
4	____	120	____	____	____	____
5	____	138	____	____	____	____
6	____	163	____	____	____	____
7	____	200	____	____	____	____
8	____	239	____	____	____	____
9	____	300	____	____	____	____
10	____	400	____	____	____	____

(a) Fill the blanks in the table. Note: Place the marginal cost *between* any consecutive quantities next to the higher quantity. For example, if you decide that the marginal cost between the quantities of 12 and 13 was $45, and if the table were a bit longer, you would put $45 next to a quantity of 13. You may find that doing this part in a spreadsheet such as Excel is more efficient and insightful.

(b) On a graph, plot and label the Average Variable Cost, Average Cost, and Marginal Cost curves. Fractional outputs are allowed, so you can connect the dots when drawing these curves.

(c) If your diagram is correct, AVC declines at first and then rises. Why is this pattern so typical?

(d) What is the level of output that leads to the minimum Average Variable Cost? Why is this level important to managers?

(e) Does the marginal cost curve intersect the average cost curve where AC is rising, falling, or at its minimum point? Explain.

(f) If fixed costs were $300 instead of $150, how would your MC curve be affected?

(g) Given the cost data above, how many concerts per season should this orchestra produce if the goal is profit maximization and the market price for a concert is $40.00? How much profit will the orchestra make if they do that?

(h) Given the cost data above, how many concerts per season should this orchestra produce if the goal is output maximization subject to a break-even constraint and the market price for a concert is $40.00?

(i) Given the following data on demand, fill in the blanks below (placing Marginal Revenue between any two quantities next to the higher quantity and assuming that there is no fixed revenue).

The Orchestra faces the following demand (downward-sloping) curve:

Q	P	TR	MR
0	50	____	x
1	49	____	____
2	48	____	____
3	47	____	____
4	46	____	____
5	45	____	____
6	44	____	____
7	43	____	____
8	42	____	____
9	41	____	____
10	40	____	____

(j)   How many concerts should this orchestra produce if it faces the cost and revenue functions given above, wants to maximize profits from concerts, and can choose its price? How much will profits be at this maximum?

(k)   In the long run, the $100 in fixed costs becomes a variable cost rather than a fixed cost. Suppose that there are no other long-run changes in the cost or demand functions. With this added information, what would the orchestra do when it reached the long run if:

- It faced a market price of $40.00 and wanted to maximize profits?
- It faced a market price of $40.00 and wanted to maximize output subject to breaking even?
- It was free to choose its price and wanted to maximize profits?

2. Suppose you were to organize a fund-raising campaign for Save the Park, an environmental advocacy group in your community. Consider the costs of organizing and running a campaign and answer the following questions:

(a)   Choose a single method you will use to raise funds (e.g., a direct mail campaign, special event dinner, telemarketing, crowd sourcing on the Internet or social media, etc.) and specify the time period over which this activity will take place.

(b)   List all of the different types of costs you will incur in carrying out the fund-raising campaign.

Assume that "number of dollars raised" is your output measure. Now identify:

(c)   The components of cost which are fixed; i.e., do not vary with output.

(d)   The components of cost which are variable, i.e., which do vary with the level of output.

(e)   Explain which of the fixed costs would become variable if you considered operations over a longer time period.

(f) Using your best judgment, or data to which you may have access, make quantitative estimates of the fixed and variable costs at different levels of output and display these costs in a table.

(g) From the numbers in your table, calculate Total, Average, and Marginal costs at each level of output, and display these as three additional columns in your table or in a separate table.

(h) Draw on a single graph, the total, average, and marginal cost curves which show how these quantities vary as output changes.

(i) Using your graphs or table, determine the optimal level of the campaign if your goal is to maximize the financial returns (donations minus cost of solicitation). How much should you spend and how much money will you make?

3. Suppose you are organizing a conference for the Professional Society of Association Professionals. The society finances the conference with participant registration fees (the same for every attendee) plus a foundation grant explicitly designated for the conference. The grant is a fixed dollar amount, rather than a subsidy for each attendee, and must be returned to the foundation if the conference is canceled for any reason. Registration covers all conference materials and meals. The costs of the conference involve renting a facility, organizing the program and arranging for speakers, and providing materials and meals for each participant.

(a) Using graphs, describe the total, average and marginal revenue functions.

(b) Classify costs into fixed and variable components and graph the total, average, and marginal cost functions.

(c) Using (a) and (b) as a guide, graph a circumstance where the conference loses money but the society is better off financially if the conference is held than if it is canceled.

(d) Graph an alternate situation in which the society should cancel the conference if it insists on minimizing losses.

(e) Show a circumstance where the conference makes a positive profit. What can you say about the relationship of the conference fee to marginal cost, and the relationship between average variable cost and the conference fee in this case?

4. The social enterprise Laptops for Littlekids (LFL) provides a basic laptop computer for a child in a low-income community for every laptop it sells to the public. The company sells into a competitive market where it can sell as many computers as it wants at a price that is 10 percent more than the market price because it appeals to socially-minded consumers. LFL's marginal cost for producing a basic laptop is constant at $50 and its marginal cost for the (fancier) laptop that it sells is constant at $100. There are no fixed costs or fixed revenues to worry about (at least for now).

(a) What must the market price for a laptop in the market be in order for LFL to break-even?

(b) How would this change if LFL were to receive a lump-sum grant of $1000 from the MacroHard Foundation to support its operations? How many units could it sell at the price you calculated in (a)?

(c) Using a graph or equation describe the Total Cost, Average Cost and Marginal Cost functions of LFL.

(d) Assuming it receives the grant and the market price for computers is $150, describe the Marginal Revenue, Total Revenue and Average Revenue functions.

(e) What should be LFL's shutdown rule for its computer sales, assuming that it continues to follow its gifting policy? Should LFL follow the rule?

5

Thinking at the margin

Big marginal benefit, low marginal cost!

5.1 Introduction

Marginal analysis is considered one of the most useful concepts of economic decision making. In Chapter 4, we introduced the economic concept of the "margin." We learned how to calculate *marginal costs* and *marginal revenues* and demonstrated how the analysis of these marginal functions could help a manager decide how much of a good or service to produce. This mode of analysis, which we call "analysis (or thinking) at the margin," is one of the most powerful ideas underlying microeconomics. In the marginal analysis framework, resource allocation decisions are made by comparing the marginal (or *incremental*) benefits of a change in the level of an activity with the marginal (or incremental) costs of the change. This marginal (or incremental) decision criterion is useful when all alternatives to a decision are considered and the outcomes associated with these alternatives are understood. In this chapter, we look further into the application of this concept to resource allocation decisions that face nonprofit and social enterprise managers.

5.2 Output and pricing decisions

First, let us review and extend what we learned earlier about analyzing marginal costs and marginal revenues in order to determine how much to produce and what price to charge. Recall that such decisions hinge on the organization's objective in providing a particular good or service. In Chapter 4 we considered several possibilities, including maximum profit, maximum output, minimum cost, and maximum societal benefit.

Let's dispense with two of these objectives – maximum output and minimum cost because, as we explain below, these generally are not very satisfying criteria. We need to ask, "Why produce at maximum output? What is the underlying reason for producing as much as possible?" There may well be a virtually unlimited need for some service such as day care or artistic performances, but in allocating scarce resources to such services we want to be sure that the services are valued enough to justify whatever level of production is chosen. The objective of maximizing output, which only seeks the highest level of production that is financially possible and says nothing about the value of that production, or the efficiency of such a decision (i.e., whether resources would be put to their most highly valued use if we maximized output), doesn't make that clear.

To understand the problem better, we can apply our idea of thinking at the margin. If a nonprofit organization or social enterprise produces as much output as possible and then allocates that output according to established priorities based on some indicator of client needs, it presumably will allocate the last unit it produces to the least needy of its clients. If, instead, the organization cut back the production of that last unit, resources are freed for other uses that may be more important. For example, suppose a nonprofit employment agency offers training courses to unemployed individuals, giving priority to the financially neediest. If the agency simply maximizes the number of courses it offers, it will be accommodating clients whose financial needs are less and less pressing as it nears its maximum capacity. Thus, it should begin to ask itself whether it should invest its funds elsewhere, such as in a job placement service that would more heavily benefit its needier clients, instead of in yet another course offering.

A similar argument applies to the minimum average cost rule. As we observed earlier, the average cost may reach a minimum point at a fairly modest level of service. Should we resist expanding beyond that point even if people highly value the provision of additional units? Should we even produce that much if people do not value the service very much? Again, the minimum cost rule says nothing about the most efficient level of provision (i.e., the level that would put resources to their most highly valued uses).

The two remaining rules are more meaningful because they do juxtapose the value of services produced with the cost of producing those services. The maximum profit rule asks that services be expanded until the producing organization achieves its maximum financial surplus, while the maximum societal benefit rule asks that overall net value of services be maximized. Application of each of these rules involves thinking at the margin. Either or both rules may be applicable to nonprofit and social enterprise organization services, depending on circumstances.

Maximizing profit

Social enterprises and nonprofit organizations engage in multiple activities, some that further the mission and some that simply raise funds that are applied to that mission. It is also possible that some social enterprises engage in certain profit-seeking activities for the benefit of shareholders. For these latter types of activities, profit maximization is usually desirable. Thus, museum gift shops, university bookstores, social enterprise restaurants or laundries, and church cake sales should consider profit maximization to guide their output and pricing decisions. Any explicit *fund-raising* activity, including donor solicitation and capital campaigns, is also an exercise in maximizing profit. As we mentioned earlier, the rule for maximizing profit is as follows:

> *To maximize profit, expand output to the point where marginal revenue just equals marginal cost.*

This point is illustrated by output level Q_1 in Figure 5.1A. This output level would be sustained by charging a price P_1 corresponding to Q_1 on the demand or average revenue function. (Recall that a profit maximizer will always choose a price on the demand curve, not below it, because that is the highest price that consumers will pay for the selected quantity.) Note that at Q_1, MR equals MC and production beyond this point would result in units of output (at the margin) that cost more than they command in revenue. Failure to reach this level of production would forego marginal units of output that would bring in more revenue than they cost. Thus, either deviation from the point where marginal revenue just offsets marginal cost will reduce profit.

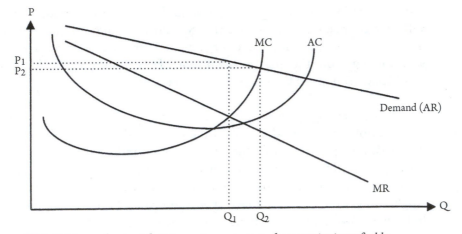

Figure 5.1A Pricing and output decisions: circumstances where service is profitable

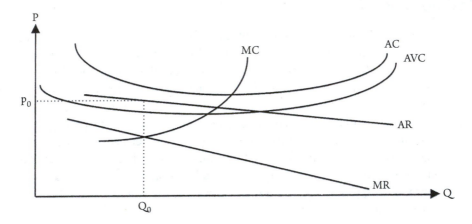

Figure 5.1B Pricing and output decisions: circumstances where service is unprofitable

As suggested by the shutdown rules discussed in Chapter 4, there is one important caveat to this rule: in some circumstances it may not be possible to make a profit at all. That is, setting MR equal to MC results in a negative profit because the demand function (AR) lies below the average (total) cost curve (AC) for all levels of output. While setting MR equal to MC results in the smallest possible loss, given that production takes place, it may be better in this instance for the organization to shut down production entirely. Figure 5.1B illustrates the case where the organization runs a loss but the profit maximizing (loss minimizing) price P_0 is greater than the average variable cost (AVC) at corresponding output Q_0. Here, continuing to produce can help pay for part of the fixed costs, and the organization will do better to continue production. If this were not the case, the organization should shut down.

Maximizing societal benefit

The computation of social costs and benefits is a major subject that we will discuss in detail in our treatment of cost–benefit analysis in Chapter 14. For now, we already have some analytical tools that allow us to examine how a nonprofit and social enterprise organization wishing to maximize benefits for society might approach decisions about output and pricing. Depending on the circumstances, we can assume one of two things about the demand function (AR) in Figure 5.1A. One possibility is that the function accurately represents how society values the good or service at issue. A second possibility is that the function does not represent the full value of the good or service.

Consider the first possibility. As we discussed in Chapter 4, the demand function can be interpreted as the maximum amount consumers are willing to pay for additional units of the good or service. For example, the value placed on art reproductions sold in a museum gift shop may be closely approximated by the demand (willingness to pay) on the part of museum visitors. Under this assumption, the museum shop could use the following output and pricing rule:

> *To maximize social benefit when the demand function adequately represents the value that society places on the good or service, choose a level of output at which demand is equal to marginal cost.*

The rationale here is that producing any less would mean that some consumers – those who are willing to pay more for additional (marginal) units of the good or service than it costs to produce them – would not be accommodated. So, too, producing any more than the level at which demand equals marginal costs would mean production of marginal units that cost more than anyone is willing to pay for them. Either deviation from the level at which demand equals marginal cost would therefore be inefficient.

In Figure 5.1A, this solution is represented by output Q_2 and price P_2. It is interesting to observe that applying this rule results in higher output and a lower price than if one were to apply the maximum profit objective (where MR equals MC). One can thus argue that when an organization faces a downward-sloping demand curve (and therefore can influence the price it charges by varying its output), the profitmaking objective will result in a less efficient allocation of resources than the "demand equals marginal cost" rule. In particular, the profit maker will not produce the additional output from Q_1 to Q_2 even though those units provide more benefit than they cost to produce.

This raises a perplexing question for nonprofit managers. Should they sacrifice additional profits in a service such as a museum gift shop in order to increase societal benefit, or should they try to make as much profit as possible? The answer of course must depend on how the additional profits would be used to produce other benefits, whether alternative funding can be procured to produce those benefits, and how those other benefits compare to those foregone by restricting the output level of the gift shop (Eckel and Steinberg, 1993). Social enterprise managers who are clear and explicit on objectives can deal with these perplexities because of the dual nature of their *objective function* – maximize a mix of social benefits and economic profits. Their objective spells out the trade-off they are willing to make between the loss of benefits to buyers when profit is pursued and the gain in social benefits to others financed by profits.

One additional nuance of the output and pricing rule is important for nonprofit organizations. In some cases, the organization may choose to charge prices below the demand curve even though the demand curve properly indicates the social benefits of production. This occurs when affordability or distributional justice is part of the organization's mission (Steinberg and Weisbrod, 1998, 2005). For example, for reasons of equity it might decide to charge a lower price or to give the good away free, rationing it some other way than by charging fees. The rule still applies in principle, however: the same level of output should be selected as that which would be chosen if demand were set equal to marginal cost. What counts for selecting the quantity of output is what people are willing to pay, not what they actually pay.

What about cases where demand is not an adequate measure of social benefit? This is probably more the rule than the exception for nonprofits, since many nonprofits serve needy clientele or produce collective goods whose value is greater than the amount their consumers demonstrate they are willing to pay. For example, while there is a clear market demand for preschool education, part of the benefit from that service flows to society in the form of healthier, better educated, less disruptive children who ultimately become more productive citizens. But market demand reflects only what parents themselves are willing to pay, not what other citizens may also be willing to contribute. Thus, making price and output decisions based solely on market demand is likely to under-allocate resources to this important service.

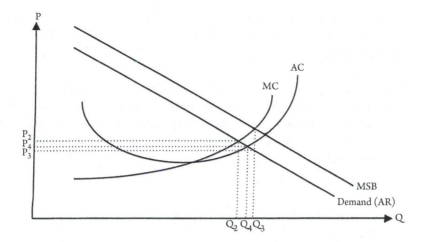

Figure 5.2 Maximizing social benefits when demand does not include all benefits

We can extend our thinking at the margin to address this case. One way is to supplement the market demand curve with estimates of additional public benefits associated with each unit of service. For example, for each additional child served in day care, how much does society benefit? This might be estimated by the level of subsidies government provides, or it might be an internal estimate of what the nonprofit organization calculates to be this value, and what it may be willing to provide in subsidy from its own sources. (See the discussions of these approaches in Chapters 6 and 13.) Figure 5.2 graphs such a situation by drawing a line above the demand curve which is labelled MSB (*marginal social benefit*). Marginal social benefit is determined by adding the estimated marginal external benefit to the private demand (average revenue) curve. If we can estimate such a function, we can subscribe to the following rule:

> *To maximize social benefit where external as well as private benefits are involved, choose the level of output where marginal social benefit is just equal to marginal cost.*

Indeed, we can adopt this as the universal rule (superseding the one above) with the caveat that sometimes the MSB is the same as the demand curve and sometimes it is not. Figure 5.2 shows that using this rule leads to producing even more output (Q_3) than if we simply set price (private benefit) equal to marginal cost (Q_2). Consumers won't buy Q_3 unless the price is lowered further to P_3. However, as the graph suggests, we must be careful in using this rule so that the organization is not jeopardized financially. In the figure, for example, AC exceeds AR at the output level Q_3 where social benefit is maximized. Unless the organization can subsidize the difference from other sources, it will set output at level Q_4, the most it can produce while still breaking even.

The possibility that, when external benefits are considered, a nonprofit agency or social enterprise may want to produce beyond its financial means we must briefly revisit the rule about maximizing output. If the external benefit is sufficiently large (as illustrated above), the rule for maximizing social benefits becomes the same as the rule for maximizing output. Again, we can apply thinking at the margin:

> *If, at the maximum affordable output level (absent subsidies, the financial break-even point where AR = AC), producing another unit of service yields a marginal social benefit greater than or equal to marginal cost, then the agency should choose the maximum affordable output level and a price that yields zero profits.*

This condition holds in Figure 5.2. Producing another unit of output beyond Q_4 does yield a marginal social benefit greater than marginal cost. This situation may well apply to services for which there is a strong need and of which there is limited supply, such as emergency relief for hurricane victims, supplies of rare blood, or health care or preschool services in poor, rural areas. The key, however, is to ask the question about the last unit of production to ensure that maximum output is justified. Essentially, we are still using analysis at the margin to make the decision, even though the maximum output rule may be a handy shortcut in some instances. However, caution should be used in maintaining a maximum output objective over a long period of time, even if that objective is initially justified by the above rule. Maximizing output may become part of the organization's culture and may persist even after circumstances have changed and the rule no longer warrants pursuit of that objective.

Let us revisit the Meals on Wheels problem from Chapter 4. Suppose that society puts an extra value on each dinner delivered equal to $6 over the going price; it matters to the community that old and sick citizens who cannot drive to the store still have access to healthy food. While maximizing social benefit when the demand curve accurately reflects social benefit will lead to the organization producing where MC = MSB = 6 at Q = 11, maximizing social benefit when this extra value of each meal is included would require Q > 17; however, output would have to be limited to a maximum of Q = 16 to ensure breaking even.

In Chapters 13 and 14, we will study the concepts of collective goods and external benefits and costs, and we will develop the methodology of cost–benefit analysis. This will introduce more sophistication into decision making about output levels where market demand is an insufficient (often absent) indicator of value. In this wider framework, we will again employ thinking at the margin to equate *marginal social costs* with marginal social benefits. For the present, however, we summarize this discussion by reiterating that one of several rules may be appropriate for the nonprofit or social enterprise manager wishing to set price and service levels efficiently. For activities explicitly intended for fund-raising or commercial purposes, the maximum profit rule would apply. For an activity intended as a public service, the rule of setting demand equal to marginal cost will apply where demand accurately reflects social benefit. Where it does not, a more general rule of setting marginal social benefit equal to marginal cost, using additional estimates of public benefits to supplement private demand, is appropriate. All of these cases employ thinking at the margin to ensure that the last unit of output produced has a value that exceeds its incremental cost.

5.3 Fund-raising

Fund-raising activity is the classic example of a situation in which the profit-maximizing rule can be applied to the operations of a nonprofit organization. If we characterize the output of fund-raising as *the number of dollars raised*, then profit from this activity is simply donations minus solicitation costs. How much should an organization spend on fund-raising? Once again, the answer requires thinking at the margin, using the profit-maximizing rule developed above. Consider the diagram shown in Figure 5.3, which shows the average and marginal cost functions and the average and marginal revenue functions for a fund-raising program.

Since the output is dollars raised, the revenue functions are very simple. The average revenue received per unit of output (i.e., per dollar) is, by definition, $1. Thus, the AR function is just a constant horizontal line at the level of $1. Similarly, the marginal revenue associated with each additional unit of output (i.e., $1 raised), is the same constant horizontal line at the level of $1. The cost curves are more conventional. As drawn, they illustrate that the initial dollars to be raised may cost more than $1, but that eventually the marginal cost of raising a dollar, and subsequently the average cost of raising a dollar, dips below $1. It is in this region, where average cost is below the average revenue of $1, that fund-raising activity is worthwhile (unless one enjoys fund-raising just for the sport!). Eventually, at higher levels of (output) Q, dollars become more difficult to raise and the marginal and then average

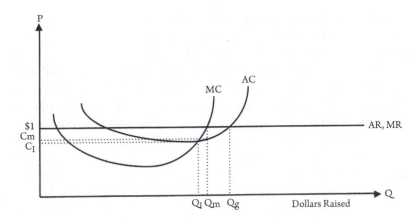

Figure 5.3 Optimal fund-raising

costs of fund-raising again rise above the average and marginal revenue line. At this level of activity, additional fund-raising is no longer worthwhile.

Following our principle of thinking at the margin, we can see that net funds raised (profits) will be maximized at the point where marginal cost equals marginal revenue (i.e., where the marginal cost rises to \$1 and donations equal Q_m). Up to this point, the nonprofit accumulates financial surplus because it costs less than a dollar (MC) to raise an additional dollar. Beyond that point, it costs more than a dollar to raise an additional dollar, subtracting from the accumulated surplus from earlier dollars raised. Clearly, the logic of thinking at the margin determines the fund-raising level Q_m that will bring in the largest amount of funds for the charitable mission. At this level, raising a dollar costs C_m dollars (AC), so the net proceeds are $Q_m \times (1 - C_m)$ dollars.

Again, we have the caveat of the shutdown rule to ensure that the solution produced by comparisons at the margin is better than not producing at all. Like any production activity, campaigns have fixed costs in the short-run, and unless donations stemming from the campaign exceed average variable cost, the campaign should be shut down. The revenue function adds an additional complication, however, because there are both fixed and variable donations. Fixed donations are those that occur even when the campaign is shut down, and occur due to ongoing payroll deductions, board member giving, and other campaigns conducted by the organization, ongoing or completed. Fixed donations are irrelevant when deciding whether to shut down any particular campaign. Instead, we focus on variable donations, donations that change when expenditures on the campaign change. We can amend our previous statement of average revenues to state that the average variable revenue from a unit of fundraising is $1. In general, the shutdown rule is:

> *If, at the level of fund-raising where marginal contributions received equals marginal fund-raising costs, average variable contributed revenue is less than average variable fund-raising cost, the fund-raising campaign should be suspended.*

Viewed in the light of optimal fund-raising, the ongoing debates about fund-raising costs are very interesting. Charities are criticized when fund-raising costs are too high a percentage of funds raised and applauded when average fund-raising costs are low. This focus on average costs represents a failure to think at the margin. The goal of a campaign is to maximize the net surplus because the charitable mission requires more money, not a lower ratio. As Figure 5.3 shows, maximizing net surplus is inconsistent with minimizing the average costs of fund-raising. Average costs are minimized when Q_I is raised, so the organization is failing to obtain the financial surplus resulting from increasing donations to Q_m.

One can argue, of course, that if the average cost of fund-raising is too high, donors may become wary and give less money. If so, the cost curves would look different, becoming steeper due to a feedback loop – higher average costs make it more difficult to raise an additional dollar. But the analysis is the same; we simply calculate marginal costs from a differently shaped total cost curve.

Of course, there is also a danger that an organization will err in the other direction. Charities often set fund-raising goals or targets and then focus simply on funds raised, not on how much it cost to raise those funds. Thus, an organization that sets its goals so high that it essentially seeks to maximize the gross level of funds it could possibly raise may actually bring in as much as Q_g in Figure 5.3, where AC = AR. This could occur if an unscrupulous Director of Development wanted to look good, so he could get a new job elsewhere at a higher salary. Unfortunately, too many search committees look at the candidate's record of raising gross donations, and the question, "How much did it cost your organization to raise that much?" never gets asked. Whether gross donations are maximized by mistake or maximized to advance the Director of Development's personal agenda, this process of raising funds spends all the funds raised! Unfortunately, this has been known to happen.

Finally, it is important to realize that one cannot simply compare one charity with another in terms of the costs and levels of fund-raising, since each charity faces different fund-raising conditions and hence different cost functions. To suggest that a given charity should minimize its fund-raising costs or is inefficient simply because its average ratio of costs to revenues raised is high is not correct. The appropriate approach is to determine if the last dollar allocated to fund-raising brings in $1, no more and no less. Note that this again is an example of making decisions on the margin. This rule can be adjusted to account for many real-world complications: the time lag between solicitation and receipt of funds (especially in connection with bequests and other forms of planned giving), the effects of fund-raising on volunteers, and the opportunity to advocate and educate while raising funds (see Steinberg, 1991). Although it is not possible to discuss all the nuances in this volume, the principal lesson is clear: thinking at the margin can help avoid the traps of "average thinking" in fund-raising management, assessment, and regulation.

It is also possible for charities to be inefficient in their fund-raising by using the wrong combination of fund-raising techniques or by not making the most efficient use of their input resources. Next, we will see how analysis at the margin helps us to avoid such situations.

5.4 Allocating resources to alternative inputs and programs

Another important application of thinking at the margin relates to the decisions nonprofit managers and social entrepreneurs must make about allocating resources to alternative uses within their organizations. These types of decisions fall into two categories. The first is *input* choice for a given service. For example, telephones, supplies, people, and physical space are needed to run an advocacy campaign. What combination of such programs is most efficient in producing as much output (measured, say, by the number of citizens contacted) as possible for a given budget expenditure?

The second type of decision is the choice between different programs designed to achieve the same goal. For example, a Meals on Wheels program and a cafeteria program in which disabled people are brought to a common location for meals, are two different ways of delivering food to those who cannot shop and prepare meals for themselves. What combination of such programs is most efficient in delivering as many meals as possible for a given expenditure of funds?

Both decision problems have the same structure: allocate a given budget between two alternative uses (inputs or programs), which we will label t and v, in order to maximize output Q. The decision maker knows the productivity of combinations of inputs or programs (the *production function*), and also knows the price of a unit of each input or program (we shall return to the exact meaning of "price of a program" shortly). The prices of each are labeled P_t and P_v. This is one way to describe the problem, focused on maximizing the productivity of spending on production or programs. But we can think of the problem another way for additional insight. What combination of inputs will have the lowest cost for producing a given level of output? Both questions have the same answer in the form of a rule for resource allocation, and marginal thinking gets us the answer. But first, we need some new terminology. We define the *marginal product* associated with each input as follows:

> *MPT = the marginal product of t, is the additional output (Q) produced by employing an additional unit of input t (with all other inputs held constant).*

Similarly,

> *MPV = the marginal product of v, is the additional output (Q) produced by employing an additional unit of input v (with all other inputs held constant).*

For example, if t were telephones and v were volunteers in an advocacy campaign, and Q were the number of contacts made per day, then MPT would be the number of additional contacts that could be made if we added one telephone but did not change the number of volunteers. Similarly, MPV would be the number of additional contacts that could be made if we added one volunteer but did not change the number of telephones.

Note that the marginal product of a given input is a function not only of the level of that input but of all other inputs as well. For example, suppose a public radio station has ten phones for its fund-raising drive. Holding the number of phones constant at this amount yields one level of marginal product (additional output) for the eleventh volunteer (say $100) and a different level for the twelfth volunteer (say $90). However, if the number of phones is increased to 12, the marginal products of the eleventh and twelfth volunteers will be different again (perhaps $120 and $105, respectively, because they no longer have to share a phone).

Now that we understand the concept of marginal product, let us see how it can help in the decision to allocate alternative inputs efficiently. We can allocate inputs efficiently if we are guided by the following rule:

> *For a given level of budget expenditure, select levels of t and v such that:*
> $MPV/P_v = MPT/P_t$

Note that the ratios of marginal product to price (MP/P) on either side of the equal sign is the amount of additional output per additional dollar spent on that input. For example, if it costs 50 cents (P_v) to attract an additional full time equivalent (FTE) volunteer, and that volunteer increases output by five units (MPV), then $1 spent on volunteers will bring in two FTE volunteers, yielding an increase in output of approximately 10 units (twice the marginal product for volunteers). Alternatively, if it costs $5 to attract a FTE volunteer, then an additional $1 spent on volunteers will bring in only 0.2 FTE volunteers and will increase output by only one unit (a fifth of the marginal product for volunteers). So, another way of stating the above rule is:

> *Choose levels of inputs t and v such that the additional output (Q) obtained by spending another dollar on t is the same as the additional output that results from spending another dollar on v.*

The logic here is just another application of thinking at the margin. When the marginal product of a dollar spent on one input is greater than the marginal product of a dollar spent on a second input, we can increase output at no additional cost by spending more on the first input and less on the second. Suppose that the additional output (contacts made) produced by an additional dollar spent on recruiting volunteers is six, while an additional dollar spent on telephones brings two additional units of output. If we spend one less dollar on telephones and one more dollar on volunteers, output goes up by four units (6 – 2) while spending is unchanged. That initial split in spending is clearly not efficient. As long as we can make more additional contacts spending a dollar on volunteers than on telephones, we should continue to shift dollars, and we cannot increase output by shifting when the two are equal. Therefore, we obtain maximum output by following the rule and the rule selects the efficient way (input combination) of producing the output.

How do we get from our starting point (an additional dollar spent on volunteers is more productive than an additional dollar spent on telephones) to our ending point where the two are equal? The answer is the *law of diminishing marginal product*. This law states that as we increase spending on an input past some point, the marginal product of that input gets smaller, so the name of the law is practically the law itself. To see this, suppose we start with two telephones and no volunteers. Obviously, we will contact no one. Add one FTE volunteer, and perhaps we contact 80 prospects per day. Add a second FTE volunteer and we would presumably contact an additional 80 prospects, for a total of 160 per day. Add a third FTE volunteer (but no new telephones) and maybe that volunteer can fill in during breaks taken by the first two, producing few additional contacts. Marginal product assumes the quantity of the other input is fixed, and past some point, the fixed factor becomes a bottleneck.

So, from our starting point we transfer a dollar of spending from telephones to volunteers, and the number of contacts goes up by four. This changes the marginal products – the marginal product of volunteers goes down (because we have more volunteers) and the marginal product of telephones goes up (because we have fewer volunteers, but we are moving from a lower productivity to a higher productivity). This makes the gap between the marginal product of a dollar spent on volunteers (say five) and the marginal product of a dollar spent on telephones (say three) narrower. Each additional dollar beyond that narrows the gap further until it disappears, when we stop shifting funds.[1]

In this example, both inputs are "essential" in that you cannot produce any contacts if you do not have at least one phone and one volunteer. But sometimes, when inputs are not essential, you can transfer the last dollar from the low marginal-product-per-dollar input to the high marginal-product-per-dollar input and the gap remains. In this case, the efficient thing to do is to not use the low productivity input at all.

The logic is the same when we choose between two programs that contribute to the same goal, but we are faced with an immediate difficulty when we try to apply the rule above. What is the marginal product of a program? When we expand a program, we are increasing multiple inputs at the same time, so that even though we may be holding the amount spent on the other program constant, we are not "holding all other inputs constant." To get around this problem, we use the trick of treating this as a two-stage problem. In the first stage, we find the efficient mix of inputs for each total amount we might spend on the first program, then do the same for the second program. In the second stage, we use the first stage to calculate the extra amount of output we get when we spend an extra dollar. The answer to this question depends on how we spend that dollar, on which inputs and in what proportions; however, the first stage already tells us how to spend the dollar optimally. Once we have calculated the extra output from spending an additional dollar on each program, we compare the results and transfer spending from the lower productivity to the higher productivity program. We continue to transfer spending until the two programs' marginal products are equal or until there is no money being spent on the low marginal product program; the result is then economically efficient.

For example, suppose we could obtain two meals per dollar by spending one more dollar on a cafeteria program, whereas we would obtain only one meal by spending that dollar on Meals on Wheels. How do we know this? We have calculated how to divide that dollar between inputs in the cafeteria program, then calculated the resulting extra output from the production function. We have done the same for the Meals on Wheels program. Then, to obtain the greatest possible output for our budget, we should shift a dollar from Meals on Wheels to the cafeteria program. After doing this, we should ask the same question again: should we shift another dollar from cafeteria to Meals on Wheels? As long as it is possible to obtain more meals by shifting dollars from Meals on Wheels to the cafeteria program, we should continue to do so.

Eventually, we expect to reach a point where another dollar for the cafeteria program will produce the same number of additional meals as the Meals on Wheels program. This is the point of *efficient allocation*. If we went further, we would find that we could obtain more meals from an additional dollar allocated to Meals on Wheels than to the cafeteria program. This would be inefficient, and we would have to cut back allocation for the cafeteria program until our two allocations were once again equally productive.

Unlike the case of allocating two inputs to one output, we have no law of diminishing marginal product that applies to program expansion. If, for example, there are economies of scale in the cafeteria program, then when we transfer money from Meals on Wheels to the more productive cafeteria program, the marginal products would grow less equal and although we are enhancing efficiency, we do not end up with equal marginal products for the programs. There are many complications that require more advanced mathematical techniques for formal analysis (see, e.g., Panzar and Willig, 1981), but careful use of marginal thinking, shifting resources from less productive to more productive programs, can guide decision makers to the correct decisions in most cases. The next section provides an example of this approach.

5.5   Applications to fund-raising

Consider a fund-raising program that uses two means of soliciting funds: direct mail and telemarketing (solicitation over the phone). The output of this program, Q, is measured in dollars raised. Table 5.1 displays the marginal products MPM and MPT for each mode of fund-raising at different levels of expenditure. The trajectory illustrated in this table assumes that each additional dollar is spent on the input with the highest marginal product at that level of total expenditure. For example, at a level of expenditure of $6, $4

Table 5.1 Allocating fund-raising expenditures among alternative methods

Direct Mail		Telemarketing	
Expenditure	MPM	Expenditure	MPT
		$1 ↓	$20
		$2 ↓	$18
		$3 ↓	$15
		$4* ↓	$10
← ← ← ← ← ← ← ← ← ←			
$1 ↓	$10		
$2 ↓	$9		
$3 ↓	$8		
$4 ↓	$7		
$5 ↓	$6		
$6* ↓	$5		
→ → → → → → → → → →			
		$5 ↓	$5
		$6 ↓	$4
		← ← ← ← ← ← ← ← ← ←	
$7 ↓	$4		
$8 ↓	$3		
$9 ↓	$2		
→ → → → → → → → → →			
		$7 ↓	$2
		$8 ↓	$2
		$9 ↓	$2
← ← ← ← ← ← ← ← ← ←			
$10 ↓	$1		
$11 ↓	$0.5		

Note: * Optimal expenditure on fund-raising programs for a $10 total budget.

on telemarketing and $2 on direct mail, an additional dollar on direct mail would bring in $9 in funds. Similarly, at an expenditure level of $11, $6 on direct mail and $5 on telemarketing, an additional dollar on telemarketing would bring in $5 in funds. Note also that the numbers in the table illustrate the effect of *diminishing returns*: the marginal product of each solicitation method declines as more is spent on it.

How can we apply the marginal product rule to determine how much we should invest in direct mail as compared to telemarketing? The answer depends, of course, on how much money we have to spend. Suppose we had a budget of $10. We can determine how to allocate this $10 by considering one dollar at a time. Where should the first dollar go? Since a first dollar devoted to telemarketing brings in $20 (as compared to only $10 for direct mail), we should put that first budget dollar into telemarketing. Similarly, we should allocate the second and third dollars to telemarketing. Once we reach the level of the fourth dollar, the situation becomes a toss-up. The next dollar spent on either telemarketing or direct mail brings in $10. Since we are already using telemarketing, we may as well allocate the fourth dollar to this method, but the fifth dollar should be allocated to direct mail, which will bring in $10 (compared to only $5 for the next dollar for telemarketing). Similarly, the sixth through ninth dollars should be allocated to direct mail. The tenth dollar is a toss-up again, since at this level another dollar to either method will bring in $5. We may as well allocate this last dollar to direct mail rather than switching back to telemarketing. This uses up our $10 budget. In all, we have allocated $6 to direct mail and $4 to telemarketing, and we have brought in a total of $108, found by adding up all the marginal products MPM from 1 to 6 and MPT from 1 to 4 in the table. The most money we can raise with a $10 budget using the best combination of the two alternative programs is $108.

We can follow this logic for any given level of fund-raising budget. Table 5.2 shows the results of doing this. Note that total revenue is $108 for a budget of $10, as we have just calculated. Note also that the optimal combination of direct mail and fund-raising changes as the budget changes. Finally, note that Table 5.2 lists the marginal revenue (MR) and total revenue (TR) associated with each level of budget up to $21. At any given level of budget, MR is the same as the MP for the alternative method selected for additional allocation at that level. Thus, at budget level $5, the last dollar is spent on direct mail, bringing in $10, and so on.[2]

The marginal revenue column is revealing because it brings us back to our previous analysis of how much we should spend and how much output (funds raised) we should seek to attain. In particular, note that up through a budget of $18, an additional dollar spent on one method or another brings in more than a dollar of funds raised. If we were to increase the budget to $19 by allocating an additional dollar to fund-raising, we would bring in only one more dollar in return. Thus, the optimum fund-raising budget in this case is $18, yielding the highest net return of $132 – $18 = $114. Actually, if we spend $18, $19, or $20, we have the same net revenue because we are spending and receiving one more dollar for no net change. The optimal budget is a toss-up in this range, but if we spent $21, our net return ($113.50) is lower.

Table 5.2 Donations production using two fund-raising programs

Budget	Dollars Spent On		Dollars Raised	
	Direct Mail	Telemarketing	Marginal Revenue	Total Revenue
1	0	1	20	20
2	0	2	18	38
3	0	3	15	53
4	0	4	10	63
5	1	4	10	73
6	2	4	9	82
7	3	4	8	90
8	4	4	7	97
9	5	4	6	103
10	6	4	5	108
11	6	5	5	113
12	6	6	4	117
13	7	6	4	121
14	8	6	3	124
15	9	6	2	126
16	9	7	2	128
17	9	8	2	130
18	9	9	2	132
19	9	10	1	133
20	10	10	1	134
21	11	10	0.5	134.5

5.6 Applications to social enterprise and social investment

A distinguishing feature of social enterprises is that they pursue various combinations of social benefit and economic profits. In popular terms, they pursue a *double bottom line*. Social investors also pursue dual objectives. Social investors include individuals with a social conscience and institutions such as foundations that seek to invest their endowments in organizations that can return a financial as well as social return. In these various instances, the "objective function" to be maximized is a stipulated mix of social benefits and economic profits. Alternatively, we can think of this situation as having two "margins" along which the decision maker seeks to make the best choices.

Various combinations are possible. For a traditional nonprofit organization, the underlying purpose of financial profit is support for maximizing social impact. Charitable foundations that offer *program-related investments* (PRIs) provide zero or below-market-interest loans to traditional nonprofits. PRIs support the foundation's social mission directly while leveraging additional financial resources for future social investments. At the other end of the double bottom line spectrum are traditional businesses and corporations that seek to maximize profits but view social impacts as a means to that end. Here, programs of corporate social responsibility are ultimately judged by their contributions to profits.

Between these extremes we have social enterprises that are intended to generate financial returns to their investors while contributing directly to the organization's social mission. Here, social entrepreneurs must ask how best to allocate investment funds to achieve the desired combination of these goals. What can we say about social enterprise with the tools at hand?

First, let us clear up a common misunderstanding. It is impossible to simultaneously maximize profits and social benefits when they are not identical. There is an inevitable trade-off, else we would not need social enterprises. If social benefits could be maximized at no cost to profits, for-profit firms would already be doing that. The concept of efficiency puts the proper interpretation on double bottom lines: the output of a social enterprise is economically efficient if, given the level of profits, there is no way to produce more social benefits. Equivalently, the output is efficient if given the level of social benefits, there is no way to increase profits. When a social enterprise is inefficient, it can make changes that either improve social benefits while holding profits constant, improve profits while holding social benefits constant, or improve both without maximizing each one.

Before we continue, we need to be a bit clearer on net social benefits. Social benefits are the total benefits to everyone in a society, including producers, consumers, and third parties. Owners of for-profit enterprises receive a distribution of profits, and we count this distribution as part of net social benefits. Consumers and clients receive value if they obtain goods and services at a price that is less than the maximum they are willing to pay, and this is part of net social benefit. Third parties are those affected by the production, consumption, or trading of goods and services by others. Visitors to a park and breathers of polluted air are third parties, obtaining benefits in the first case and costs in the second from the activities of others. These too are part of net social benefits.

With the clear definition of net social benefits provided by economics, we can clarify the missions of double-bottom-line organizations and the trade-offs they face.[3] Profits are part of net social benefit, so we need to look at profits and *other* social benefits (for consumers and third parties) as bottom lines. The right mixture of the two requires that we consider both trade-off and non-trade-off situations. Providing some amount of other social benefits may add to profits, and that is one reason for corporate donations and corporate social responsibility. This is because consumers may be willing to pay a little extra for the products of good corporate citizens, and because top management and line workers may be willing to work for less, with less turnover, if the corporation is providing other social benefits.

To increase other social benefits beyond this point, the decision maker must trade benefits of increasing one bottom line against the necessary cost to the other bottom line. It is no longer enough to say, "we care about both;" explicit overarching preferences are necessary. Does the organization value a dollar of marginal profit the same, more than, or less than a dollar of other social benefits? Does the value of marginal profit depend on how much profit and other social benefits we start with? If the organization can make this explicit, marginal thinking can guide social entrepreneurs to the best decision. This occurs when the marginal value of an additional dollar spent on profit-seeking equals the marginal value of an additional dollar spent on other social benefits.

To illustrate this point, consider four different types of enterprises with both social and economic goals – a *conventional nonprofit organization*, a *new-era social enterprise* that is willing to sacrifice some profits to increase its other social benefits, a *sustainable business* which seeks to maximize profits while avoiding social harm, and a *traditional business* which seeks to maximize profits by practicing strategic corporate social responsibility. These organizations should engage in the following logics to determine the combinations of social and economic goals to invest in.

The conventional nonprofit organization's mission is to maximize its social impact. To this end it will invest in commercial activity (such as gift shop sales) so long as its return at the margin produces a financial return that is larger than other ways of raising capital that it can use to finance its social programs. At this point the marginal profit from commercial sales would equal the marginal profit from charitable fund-raising, and so on. However, this calculation can be more complex if the commercial activity also has a direct mission impact – for example, if the gift shop is staffed by volunteers who help articulate the mission and sell products reflecting that mission. In this case, the organization may decide that marginal commercial output should be greater than that which maximizes financial profit, in essence recognizing the external benefits of this activity (see Chapter 13).

In contrast, the traditional business's mission is profit maximization. It engages in programs of corporate social responsibility and other charitable activities only insofar as these activities add to profits. The public relations benefits from these programs allow the firm to charge higher prices and increase profits. These programs can also lower costs, as executives and line workers may accept lower salaries, with less turnover, when working for a responsible firm. Therefore, corporate social responsibility spending, charitable donations, and the like are programs that enter the firm's profit function. Thinking at the margin, the firm will increase its investment in corporate social responsibility to the point where the marginal profit contribution is equal to that of other commercial and charitable programs it engages in.

The sustainable corporation is a bit more complex. This is an organization that has pledged to do no harm in the community, to the environment or to its labor force. It is therefore committed to fair labor practices and prevailing environmental standards governing air and water pollution and land use. An example might be an eco-tourism company interested in helping poverty-stricken native populations in an exotic region of Central America while developing a profitable resort hotel. To a certain extent such a project can be environmentally friendly, provide needed income and economic skills to local people and build local community. But at a large scale, it can become environmentally damaging and culturally disruptive. The challenge for this sustainable corporation is to think at the margin, to find the point where the marginal social or environmental benefits begin to decline, even as marginal profits continue to rise.

A new-era social enterprise values the other social benefits created by its programs as well as profits according to some internal blended-value calculus, and therefore will sacrifice some profits in order to produce more social benefits than a profit-maximizing business would. For example, a social business in an inner city might choose to invest in a set of local educational programs, each of which produces social benefits as well as financial profit or loss. Thinking at the margin, the enterprise should invest in these programs incrementally and sequentially, in priority order of highest combined marginal value of social benefits and profits, until this blended marginal value is equal across programs. In some cases, it will be impossible to reach a point of equality because highest blended value programs at the margin may provide large social benefits but also large financial losses, potentially bankrupting the firm. Here, the investment of dollars should stop where total profits are zero or reach some minimum pre-determined amount.

Some cases are simple. Newman's Own seeks to maximize profit in order to give all that profit to charity. It needs only to follow the rules of profit maximization. But other social enterprises face a more nuanced calculation. Consider an organization like TOMS, which uses a one-for-one model: "Every time a TOMS product is purchased, a person in need is helped." (http://www. toms.com/, accessed March 31, 2018). Some of this help comes in the form of donations of TOMS products, as in its Gift of Shoes and Gift of Eyesight programs, and some comes in the form of services, as in its Gift of Water and Gift of Safe Childbirth programs. TOMS must think at the margin across the double bottom line by ensuring that each component program contributes the same combined value of profits and social benefits at the margin.

SUMMARY

In this chapter we have employed the logic of "thinking at the margin" to analyze two important kinds of decisions facing managers of nonprofit and social enterprise organizations. The first type of decision involves choosing the most efficient levels of services and the prices that correspond to those levels. The second type of decision involves allocating a limited budget among alternative inputs or programs to achieve the highest level of output. We observed, as in the case of fund-raising, that the two kinds of decisions are interrelated: for any particular level of budget, resources should be allocated among inputs (or alternative programs) in the most efficient way possible to achieve maximum output. We concluded by discussing social enterprises as organizations that pursue two objectives simultaneously. Sometimes, the activities of social enterprises serve double duty, because activities that produce other social benefits also add to profits. But social enterprises that wish to provide higher-than-profit-maximizing social benefits face a margin of trade-offs, where further gains to the social objective require a loss of profits and further gains to profits require a loss of other social benefits. Marginal profits must be weighed against marginal social benefits to make these decisions.

NOTES

1 Mathematically advanced readers may note that at the same time we are changing the marginal product of volunteers because we have one more volunteer, we are changing the marginal product of volunteers because the volunteers are working with fewer phones. This cross-effect could be positive or negative, and it is even possible that the gap between a dollar spent on the high marginal product input and the low marginal product input would grow when spending is shifted from low to high. The topic is a bit advanced for this text, but when growing gaps occur, the second-order conditions are violated, and the rule finds the least efficient way of spending a fixed amount rather than the most efficient way.

2 In this example, we assumed that there are no spillover effects, i.e., that conducting a direct mail campaign does not affect the returns from a telemarketing campaign. If, for example, the same client list is used for both, this assumption is incorrect. Thinking on the margin then requires a correction – where the marginal product of each method needs to be adjusted to reflect the amount of spending on the other method.

3 Sometimes those who use the language of double bottom lines have other things in mind than the social

efficiency approach taken here. The other definition adds fairness and the just distribution of income as social benefits, and these are not captured by the economic definition of social efficiency. Some divide social benefits further, into profits, environmental, and other social benefits to produce a "triple bottom line."

SELECTED REFERENCES AND CITATIONS

Eckel, C.C. and Steinberg, R. (1993). Competition, Performance and Public Policy Towards Nonprofits. In Hammack, D.C. and Young, D.R. (Eds.), *Nonprofit Organizations in a Market Economy* (pp. 57–81). San Francisco: Jossey-Bass.

Friedman, L.S. (2002). *The Microeconomics of Public Policy Analysis*. Princeton: Princeton University Press.

Krugman, P. and Wells, R. (2018). *Economics* (5th ed.). New York: Worth Publishers.

McGuigan, J.R., Moyer, C., and Harris, H.F. (2016). *Managerial Economics: Applications, Strategy, and Tactics* (14th ed.). New York: South-Western College Publishing.

Panzar, J.C. and Willig, R.D. (1981). Economies of Scope. *The American Economic Review, 71(2)*, 268–272.

Steinberg, R. (1991). The Economics of Fundraising. In Burlingame, D. and Hulse, M. (Eds.), *Taking Fund Raising Seriously* (pp. 239–256). San Francisco: Jossey-Bass.

Steinberg, R. and Weisbrod, B.A. (1998). Pricing and Rationing by Nonprofit Organizations with Distributional Objectives. In Weisbrod, B.A. (Ed.), *To Profit or Not to Profit: The Commercial Transformation of the Nonprofit Sector* (pp. 64–82). Cambridge, UK: Cambridge University Press.

Steinberg, R. and Weisbrod, B.A. (2005). Nonprofits with Distributional Objectives: Price Discrimination and Corner Solutions. *Journal of Public Economics, 89(11–12)*, 2205–2230.

REVIEW CONCEPTS

Diminishing Returns to an Input: When the quantity of one input is increased while other inputs are held constant, the resulting change in output is called the marginal product of that input. Diminishing returns means the marginal product gets smaller as the quantity of that input gets larger.

Double Bottom Line: The twin goals of social enterprises to maximize profits and to maximize other net social benefits.

Fund-raising: The process of requesting and gathering voluntary contributions of money and property from individuals, businesses, charitable foundations, or governmental agencies.

Incremental Profit: The profit gain or loss associated with a given managerial decision.

Inefficient: A situation where there is a way of reallocating resources to make at least one person better off without making anyone else worse off (see Chapter 1).

Input: A resource or factor of production, such as a raw material, labor skill, or equipment employed in the production process.

Law of Diminishing Marginal Product: Says that once the quantity of the input is greater than a particular amount, diminishing returns occur. For example, assume that when the number of workers increases from 10 to 11, 6 additional units of output are produced. Then, according to the law, if the number of workers increases from 20 to 21, output will increase by less than 6 units.

Marginal Analysis: A basis for making various economic decisions that computes the additional (marginal) benefits derived from a particular decision and compares them with the additional (marginal) costs incurred.

Marginal Cost: The incremental increase in total cost that results from a one-unit increase in output.

Marginal Product of an Input: The change in total output associated with a one-unit change in the input, holding other inputs fixed.

Marginal Revenue: The change in total revenue that results from a one-unit change in quantity demanded.

Marginal Social Benefit: The change in total social benefit caused by a one-unit increase in an economic activity. Includes benefits to the buyer and to others affected by the activity.

Marginal Social Cost: The change in total social cost resulting from a one-unit increase in an economic activity. Includes costs to the buyer and to others affected by the activity.

Objective Function: A mathematical function used to measure success in meeting organizational goals.

Production Function: A formula specifying the maximum amount of output that can be produced for each level of inputs.

Program-Related Investments (PRIs): Social lending or investment by foundations as a way to further their charitable mission as well as generate income.

Rule for Profit Maximization: Choose the quantity that makes marginal revenue equal to marginal cost.

EXERCISES

1. Explain how you would apply the principle of "thinking at the margin" to the following nonprofit management situations:

   (a) Determining how many volunteers to recruit for a fund-raising event.
   (b) Deciding on the size of a committee to develop a strategic plan.
   (c) Deciding on the size of an ad in the newspaper to recruit for an open position in your organization.
   (d) Deciding how to allocate an increase in the annual grant from United Way to a variety of organizational uses.
   (e) Deciding how to distribute an annual budget cut across different departments of your organization.
   (f) Determining whether to undertake a fund-raising campaign or a commercial venture in order to increase organizational resources.

2. Why do organizations (nonprofits) frequently diverge from "optimal" performance and pursue some objective other than (or in addition to) the efficiency objective? Would you expect a greater divergence from the efficiency objective in:

   (a) A small nonprofit – like a day-care center?
   (b) A nonprofit hospital?
   (c) A government agency?
   (d) A social enterprise organization – like the Grameen Bank founded by Muhammad Yunus?

3. For the fund-raising example discussed in the text and illustrated by Tables 5.1 and 5.2, explain why the alternatives of direct mail and telemarketing may be subject to diminishing returns.

4. Explain why charities with the lowest average fund-raising costs are not necessarily the most efficient or making the best use of their fund-raising resources.
5. Some charitable service programs have diminishing returns and others do not. Give an example of each, explaining why there are or are not diminishing returns in each case.
6. Save the Wales is a nonprofit organization dedicated to the welfare of the Welsh people. Their costs of fund-raising are as follows:

Donations	Total Cost	Average Total Cost	Average Variable Cost	Marginal Cost	Net Revenue	Cost Ratio (TC/D)
$0	$1.00	–	–	–		–
1	1.20					
2	1.30					
3	1.50					
4	1.80					
5	2.30					
6	3.10					
7	4.20					
8	6.00					
9	8.00					
10	10.00					
11	12.00					

(a) What is their fixed cost of fund-raising?
(b) Fill in the missing cells in the table above (except those cells with a dash).
(c) What is the marginal revenue when we move from one row to the next row?
(d) What amount of donations yields the largest net revenue? (Hint: if there is no row where the marginal revenue exactly equals marginal cost, pick the highest level of donations for which marginal revenue is greater than marginal cost.)
(e) What amount of donations leads to the lowest cost ratio?
(f) How much net revenue would Save the Wales give up if it minimized the cost ratio rather than maximizing net revenue?
(g) Suppose Save the Wales chooses to maximize gross donations, subject to at least breaking even on the fund-raising program. How much would be donated?

6

The concept of cost

My donors just don't understand my opportunity cost!

6.1   Introduction

In Chapter 4 we introduced the definition of economic cost as the value of opportunities lost from the use of resources because they cannot also be applied to their *next best use*. This idea of *opportunity cost* is fundamental to economics – both implicit and explicit costs are opportunity costs. Although this is a chapter about measuring costs, it is also a chapter about measuring benefits. This is because the opportunity costs for using resources in one application are equal to the benefits these resources would produce in their next best use. Thus, the manager in the above cartoon frets over the recreational benefits he is losing by being chained to his desk!

In this chapter, we first discuss fixed costs in greater detail and make some additional distinctions between various kinds of costs. Next, we catalog the major differences between accounting and economic costs that lead to much confusion. Accounting costs omit most implicit costs, but there are also differences in the treatment of functional cost allocations, joint costs, sunk costs, and historic costs. Next, we consider assigning costs to the organization, stakeholders, and society in general. In standard introductory economics courses, this topic is unimportant because these costs are the same in classical market situations where many marginal equalities occur, for example, the cost to the buyer of the last unit bought equals the cost to the seller of the last unit sold, or the cost to the employer for the last hour of worker time equals the cost to the worker of the last hour worked. This is not necessarily the case in nonprofit and social enterprise contexts.

Continuing the second example, the value of what a firm gives up for another hour of worker time is the hourly wage rate. The value of what the worker gives up for that last hour of paid employment is the value of the last hour of leisure (or sleep, or whatever the next best use of the worker's time is). What is that time worth? Thinking on the margin, let us simplify by assuming the worker can choose the exact amount of working time per day and there is no tax on income. Then, the last hour of leisure is worth the wage rate, because otherwise the worker would want to work more (if wages had a higher value than the last hour of leisure) or less (if wages had a lower value). The picture is very different in nonprofit economics, because so many things are chosen without that kind of market interaction. The cost to the employing nonprofit of the last hour of a volunteer's time does not equal the value of the volunteer's last hour of leisure except by coincidence. Therefore, the phrase "volunteer cost" has no meaning unless we specify whose cost we are referring to.

Next, we discuss how to combine future costs (or benefits) resulting from today's decisions with current costs to measure the value of foregone opportunities. This complication arises frequently, for example, when deciding how much to spend prospecting for new donors that will remain loyal for several years or deciding whether to build a new durable facility. The "present discounted value" of a stream of costs over time produces a single number for cost.

6.2 Some distinctions

Recall from Chapter 4 that costs are associated with inputs. More specifically, we want to distinguish inputs that last more than one period from inputs that, once used, are used up. A headquarters building is an input to charitable output that lasts, and so it is called a *factor of production*. Workers, land, and human capital (trained and experienced workers) are also factors of production, but inputs that are used up (like paper, electricity, ink cartridges, and staples) are not factors of production. This leads to a more precise definition of fixed costs. Fixed costs are those costs resulting from a fixed factor of production. Whether a cost is fixed or not depends on the time we are considering – the short run is a period of time when we cannot change the amount of at least one factor of production, and the long run is long enough that all factors of production are variable. By definition, all costs are variable in the long run.

If the organization has bought a treatment center for $1 million, it is giving up the right to claim interest or investment earnings on that sum of money until it sells the center. This opportunity cost is due to ownership and is fixed while that ownership continues, regardless of how much the organization produces. There is also another kind of cost that is not associated with the number of clients served or any other measure of output called *quasi-fixed costs*. Fixed costs are associated with owning a fixed factor of production, while quasi-fixed costs are associated with *using* what you own. Before the treatment center can be used, you must turn on the lights and heat, two inputs that are not factors of production. So, the discrete cost of using the facility is not a true fixed cost, but a quasi-fixed cost. Although there are no fixed costs in the long run, quasi-fixed costs are always present.

Quasi-fixed costs are part of variable costs because variable costs are all costs that are not fixed. This means we do not have to alter the shutdown rule when quasi-fixed costs are present. Indeed, quasi-fixed costs are the reason that the shutdown rule is needed, why the organization wouldn't always want to operate when the best it can do is lose money. Quasi-fixed costs explain why the average variable cost curve can be negatively sloped for small quantities of production – as the costs of heating and lighting the facility get spread among more units of production, the cost per unit falls. By shutting down, the organization avoids paying quasi-fixed costs, so it only makes sense to stay open if revenues are sufficient to cover at least the quasi-fixed costs of production.

The owners of factors of production are "overpaid" when they supply those factors to the market at a price exceeding the minimum they would accept. Consider a farmer who owns his land and grows vegetables which he sells for $1000 per acre. When a company wants to rent his land for some other use and offers $5000 per acre, this is $4000 in excess of the minimum acceptable bid (the farmer needs at least $1000 or the opportunity cost of renting would be too much). This excess payment is called an *economic rent*. In the case of land, the terminology is confusing because the rental contract would obligate the company to pay $5000, so we call that $5000 a "contract rent," rather than an economic rent. Any factor of production can receive an economic rent. The owner of a mine can sell it for a price exceeding opportunity costs, the owner of a patent can receive royalties in excess of opportunity costs, and a star basketball player can earn far more using her scarce talent in the game than working anywhere else. All are examples of economic rents.

Sunk costs are costs that have already been paid and cannot be recovered. Thinking at the margin means that sunk costs should be ignored – decisions should consider the costs and benefits of change from your starting point. Here are some examples of costs that have been paid and should not be further considered:

- Payments to a consultant who conducts a feasibility study on building a new facility are sunk once the build/don't-build decision is made and implemented.
- Previous expenditures on worker training are sunk and should not be considered in a decision to reassign workers.
- Past donations to a charity are irrelevant when a donor decides on whether to make a new donation.

However, coworkers and other stakeholders are not members of the *homo economicus* species, which creates complications. Rational managers should ignore sunk costs themselves but should consider irrational responses by others when making decisions. Perhaps morale will suffer when a project goes ahead that looks unprofitable when sunk costs are included but are worth doing when sunk costs are omitted. Perhaps donors will react negatively to such decisions as well. The point is that economic decisions should be forward-looking, considering sunk costs only as far as they affect the decisions of relevant others.

In making real estate, or any other durable asset decisions, historical costs are irrelevant. The asset may have depreciated or been revalued by inflation or demand, and all these factors make the relevant resale price different from historical costs. When an equivalent asset is trading today, the opportunity cost should be "marked to market." However, some assets are unique or rarely bought and sold, like paintings in an art museum or fossils in a university collection. Various methods exist to estimate the likely resale price, and this practice is called the "mark to market model," which depends on varying assumptions necessary for estimation. For this reason, universities value collections using historical cost, replacement cost, resale value on liquidation, or productivity in current use (Hansmann, 1990). There is controversy over the best approach in both economics and accounting (Greenberg et al., 2013).

The last distinction is between costs and *transfer payments*. Costs are incurred when resources are consumed or transformed. In contrast, a transfer payment is a shift of resources from one person or group to another, without consuming or transforming resources. Examples of transfer payments are taxes, gifts and donations, and welfare payments.

6.3   Economic versus accounting costs

Economists and accountants both measure costs, but their goals are different. Economists measure costs in order to allocate resources efficiently, while accountants measure costs in order to provide useful information for a variety of stakeholders. Some stakeholders find one way of displaying financial information most useful, others find another way useful, but there is only one set of accounting standards in any application. This means compromises are necessary between the competing needs of economic decision makers, lenders, donors, and regulators, so that accounting definitions of cost are not identical with economic cost definitions. The fundamental logic of foregone opportunities defines economic costs, so there is only one way to define economic costs. In contrast, accounting conventions vary across countries, evolve over time, and apply differently to for-profit and nonprofit entities. Despite this variation, some differences between generic accounting and economic costs stand out.

First, perhaps in a bid to address the needs of financial investors, accountants do not include implicit costs in their cost measures. In contrast, economic costs include both implicit and explicit costs, and are therefore generally higher than accounting costs. In most cases, it is clear whether a given cost is implicit or explicit, but the distinction is less clear for tangible assets. For example, the organization's headquarters building can be preserved (through maintenance expenditures, an explicit cost) or allowed to depreciate (in that the resale value of the building goes down over time, an implicit cost). If the building is sold, depreciation becomes an explicit cost, a capital loss, but if it is not sold, depreciation is included in accounting cost only by convention. So, accountants list this one implicit cost, but not others.

Sometimes the definitions of costs are set by the taxing authority, and these definitions do not fit neatly into either economic or accounting conventions. For example, many U.S. nonprofits file informational tax returns (form 990) that require the division of costs into three categories: program service expenses, management and general expenses, and fund-raising expenses. Other government agencies provide different rules for functional classifications, and the various rules differ from those of the Financial Accounting Standards Board (National Council of Nonprofits, n.d.). Accounting standards are designed "To help donors, creditors, and others in assessing an organization's service efforts" (FASB, 1993, p. 10), rather than to guide economic decision making. Foundations have their own standards for calculating overhead costs, and there is considerable confusion among grant and contract recipients about this (Berlin, Masaoka, and Schumann, 2017).

Some resources used by nonprofits and social enterprises contribute to the provision of more than one service, activity, or output of the organization. For example, the office of financial administration in a university serves multiple departments, centers, and programs. *Joint costs* are those attributable to a shared resource like financial administration, libraries, computer infrastructure, and physical plant. Once again, the accounting approach to joint cost allocations is different from the economic approach.

When a cost is truly joint, attributing parts of the cost to each service, activity, or output is an arbitrary act. Accounting standards generally allow an organization to use any reasonable, fair, or proportional allocation of costs provided the rules for dividing costs are consistent and transparent. For example, library costs may be divided among departments in proportion to the number of majors, number of faculty, share of university floor space, or overall departmental budget. The rules for making joint cost allocations become institutionalized through formal internal budgeting systems. For example, some nonprofit universities use "responsibility center budgeting," which means that each "responsibility center" (typically a school or department) keeps the bulk of resources it generates but pays a tax to support the university's joint costs. The rule dividing joint costs across responsibility centers has real consequences that may distort decisions, leading to social inefficiency. Accounting rules serve the accountability goal of insuring that someone handles each part of joint costs but serve as a poor guide for economic decision making.

The opportunity-cost approach does not require any division of joint costs, focusing instead on the changes in joint costs resulting from economic decisions. For example, suppose a university is considering expanding the Economics Department by hiring new faculty. This may appear to be very costly in the accounting framework because the new program is required to pay a substantial proportion of central administrative costs. Instead of using an arbitrary but reasonable share of joint costs, the opportunity cost approach focuses on how joint costs would change if the Economics Department expands. Most likely, this expansion would not require a proportional increase in the amount of joint resources, so the accounting allocation is misleading.

Finally, accounting and economic treatments of transfer payments differ. Transfer payments are entered as costs in a book-keeping sense but are not costs in an economic sense because they do not signal the use of valuable resources. They merely move resources from one organization or individual to another. However, whoever pays the transfer payment bears a cost, and the fact that this cost cancels out in the broader economy leads us directly to the next section.

6.4   Whose cost?

Recall from the first section of this chapter that when market participants trade, there is a single number for marginal cost because the buyer's marginal cost is equal to the seller's marginal cost. Buyers pay the cost of the seller's production and employers pay the costs of workers' foregone leisure. Marginal costs of trading partners are equal when both parties are free to choose the amount they buy or sell or the number of workhours per week. When choice is restricted, the two marginal costs are not equal, and we cannot answer questions about cost without knowing whose cost we are referring to. In this section, we first discuss restricted trade, then the curious case of nonprofit organizations whose mission includes minimizing costs imposed on others.

The following examples illustrate some of the complexities:

What is the opportunity cost to a worker who takes a job?

- If he is otherwise employed, the opportunity cost is the wage he would have earned in his next best job. If he is free to choose the number of hours, we know that this wage rate is the same as the value placed on the last hour of leisure. Whether the opportunity cost to the employer will be the same as the opportunity cost to the worker depends on the compensation level chosen by the employer.
- If the employer pays the lowest wage (and other compensation) the worker will accept, the usual starting point in the analysis of for-profit firms, then the opportunity cost to the worker will be the same as the opportunity cost to the employer.

- If the employer pays a wage higher than necessary, the opportunity cost to the employer will exceed the opportunity cost to the worker. This sort of "overpay" may be part of a nonprofit organization's mission (if the organization believes in paying a living wage to those who would otherwise be paid the minimum, or if the organization hires former felons or people with disabilities). "Overpay" can also result from union wage-setting and other factors.

- If the worker is currently unemployed or out of the labor market, the opportunity cost is the value placed on "leisure," defined to include all use of time other than paid employment. If he is free to choose the number of hours worked, and he chooses non-employment, we know that the wage rate in the next-best job is lower than the value he places on his last hour of leisure. It will cost the employer more than the wage rate in the next-best job to attract this worker.

- If the worker is otherwise employed and offered a forty-hours-per-week job on a take it or leave it basis, his opportunity cost will differ from the value of the last hour of leisure. However, if the best foregone alternative is working elsewhere for forty hours per week, the opportunity cost to the worker will equal the opportunity cost to the organization.

- Income and wage taxes also cause the marginal cost of using a worker (pre-tax wage) and the opportunity cost of an otherwise employed worker taking this job (after-tax wage) to differ.

- "Compensating differentials" further complicate labor costs. Wages for desirable jobs are lower than wages for jobs that are unappealing. Safe jobs pay less than dangerous ones, interesting jobs pay less than boring ones, all else equal. Suppose the next best opportunity for a nonprofit worker is to work in the for-profit sector at an average quality job. If this worker finds nonprofit employment especially attractive, she will accept a lower nonprofit wage than her wage in the next best opportunity. In effect, she is spending some of her alternative wages to buy better job characteristics. This is the argument behind the partial volunteering model of nonprofit labor supply. Her nonprofit wage (and the organization's cost of employing her) is less than the opportunity cost of her time.

What is the cost of volunteering?

- Recall from Chapter 2 that gross estimates of the value of volunteer resources in the U.S. economy were obtained by multiplying estimates of hours worked by the average (after tax) wage rate for nonagricultural workers (Hodgkinson et al., 1992). This is probably the best we can do at the aggregate level, but all the issues regarding the cost of an employee apply here as well.

- In addition, perhaps the next-best alternative for the volunteer is volunteering for another organization. In this case, all the complications for calculating the cost of volunteering apply as well to the foregone benefit.
- The cost of employing a volunteer is not zero for the employer, as we discussed in Chapter 3. There are both one-time (recruiting, training) and continuing costs (supervision, non-wage benefits) to the organization. However, because the employer costs are not paid to the volunteer, there is no effective market that equilibrates marginal values. A successful lawyer who volunteers to help stuff envelopes is not worth the compensation he would receive in his next-best use of time practicing law.
- Volunteers may substitute for paid labor, complement paid labor, or create conflict with paid labor, affecting the cost of employing paid labor (Brudney and Duncombe, 1992; Rimes et al., 2017). The marginal cost of a volunteer to the employer should account for these side effects.

What is the cost of taxation or payments-in-lieu-of taxes?

- The direct cost of taxation is a transfer from the taxpaying organization to government, creating a cost from the standpoint of the organization but not from the standpoint of society.
- The organization faces additional costs of administration (special accounts need to be kept to meet tax authority definitions of financial variables) and also pays the cost of finding and applying strategies designed to reduce the tax burden.
- The government faces additional costs enforcing the tax laws and processing the data. The marginal cost to the government would equal the marginal cost to taxpayers only by coincidence.
- Society faces additional costs known as *excess burdens* because they are added to the direct burden of paying the tax. These costs count negatively when taxes distort behavior away from social efficiency (such as the combination of property tax on for-profits and exemption for non-profits) or positively, as benefits, when taxes correct market failures (as in deductibility of donations from personal income tax). Chapter 3 develops these arguments. Hence, the costs to society differ from the costs to tax authorities and the cost to taxpayers.

What is the cost of donating goods and services?

- The direct cost to the donor is the same as the direct value received by the recipient, so when complications are ignored, this is a transfer payment.

- However, as noted in Chapter 3, tax credits or deductions reduce the donor's price of giving money to charity and so reduce the marginal cost of donating. However, volunteer services are not deductible in the U.S. This complicates things, but if the opportunity cost of volunteering is the after-tax wage rate, volunteering is subsidized by the opportunity to avoid taxation of paid labor income. Gifts of goods and other services also have their costs reduced by deductions and credits, but there are a variety of special rules designed to reduce gaming of the system by, say, valuing obsolete computers at their original list price.

- Accepting a gift is costly for the recipient organization. Sometimes the costs are limited to processing and saying thank you, but sometimes (as in gifts of historical artifacts) restoration, preservation, and storage costs can be substantial. For example, the New-York Historical Society was almost bankrupted by the costs of collections that grew faster than the organization could properly accommodate (Guthrie, 1996).

- Donated goods are internally scarce, and there is an opportunity cost of using them. To estimate that cost, you can look at prices in the marketplace. When market goods are very similar to those donated, market prices are an accurate estimate of opportunity cost. If the organization uses a donated computer instead of selling it, it is forgoing the market price it would get by selling. If the donated goods were substandard, used, obsolete, or different in some other way from those sold in actual markets, then some downward adjustment is needed. The proper "price" would be what the organization would have been willing to pay to get one more unit of the donated good. Whenever we calculate a price for goods that are not actually traded, we call this calculated value the *shadow price*.

- Donated goods are particularly hard to value when they are restricted from resale. For example, there is a small market for lithographs (high quality copies produced by the artist in limited numbers), but if the donor requires that the lithographs not be resold, then the market price is irrelevant for two reasons. First, the organization has no opportunity to sell the lithograph, so the sales price is not foregone revenue. Second, the organization would not buy the lithograph at the market price because the market price is higher than it would be willing to pay. In this case, the proper opportunity cost would be used only for internal allocation (who gets it for their office) and would be based on the highest willingness to pay for an alternative use.

What is the cost of publicly-provided services such as police, social and educational services, roads, or the legal system?

- The cost of producing these services is a cost to the government. But even though organizations pay a portion of these costs through their taxes, there is no direct link between the two because taxes are the same whether the organization uses the service a lot, rarely, or not at all. Thus, there is no opportunity cost to the organization.
- User fees for government services can link the costs to the government with the costs to the organization. But fees are set by government bureaucrats and politicians, rather than the market, so there may be a mismatch between the costs to government and the costs to the organization using those services.
- The cost of service production differs from the cost of service use when government services are collectively consumed. A highway is expensive to build, but the only cost of allowing an additional driver on an uncrowded highway is minor wear and tear. Highways are collectively consumed, but also *congestible* which means that although the same highway is available to users, when we let another car on the road at some point the highway becomes less usable due to traffic jams. Police services are partly rival, partly collectively consumed. When one organization calls on the police, some officers and squad cars are not available to help other residents. However, when the police visibly come to the organization's door, this deters crime throughout the neighborhood so that there is collective consumption of public safety. (See also, the discussion of varieties of public goods in Chapter 13.)

What is the cost of using facility space?

- When an organization owns a facility, the decision to allocate space within that facility is made administratively instead of through a market. However, there are opportunity costs when part of the facility is used to provide day care for the children of employees, or a phone bank for volunteer fund-raisers, or a fancy lobby to impress potential donors.
- Opportunity costs are not based on simple measures like how many square feet are devoted to a use. Rather they consider the value in the next best use, which may be that the space is used for some other activity within the organization or perhaps rented to outside users. These opportunity costs are independent of whether the facility is paid off or mortgaged.

In standard economics courses, for-profits are the only kind of organization and it is very clear what they consider a cost. For example, a power plant would consider the costs of fuel, facilities and equipment, and any other cost that affects the bottom line, but would not include the costs they impose on others through the pollution they generate. There is a difference between *private costs* – borne by the buyer and seller – and *external costs* – borne by those with no control over the market transaction. The sum of private and external costs is called *social costs*. All three kinds of costs are functions of the level of production and private consumption (denoted Q for quantity) and the summation occurs for total, average, and marginal costs. Therefore, the following are true for every Q by definition:

Total Social Costs(Q) = *Private Costs*(Q) + *External Costs*(Q)

Average Social Costs(Q) = *Average Private Costs*(Q) + *Average External Costs*(Q)

Marginal Social Costs(Q) = *Marginal Private Costs*(Q) + *Marginal External Costs*(Q)

Things are more complicated in nonprofit and social enterprise economics, because organizational missions may include some or all costs imposed on others. Some organizations consider the environmental costs of their actions to be part of their own costs. Some human service organizations would off-load costs on clients if they were for-profit firms but instead consider client costs as part of their mission to help. For example, converting from a Meals on Wheels program to a central cafeteria service off-loads transportation costs from the organization's budget to the budgets of consumers. Moving from an institutional program for handicapped children to a program that provides in-home family-based care imposes additional costs on family members such as lost work time and costs of additional supplies or equipment. For-profits would ignore these off-loaded costs, but social enterprises with related social objectives would consider them as part of their costs. Put another way, the proper distinction between private and external costs is determined by who the organization cares about, rather than who bears the costs.

6.5 Some examples

For illustration, let us consider the various kinds of opportunity costs associated with programs and initiatives that may be undertaken by nonprofit organizations and social enterprises. Later, in our study of cost–benefit analysis (Chapter 14), we will be more detailed in our approach to such matters. For the present, we simply want to get the flavor of these considerations.

A residential treatment program

Suppose a nonprofit family service agency administers a program for teenage delinquents that provides residential and treatment services. The costs associated with providing this program are likely to include:

- Direct budgeted costs such as salaries and benefits of paid workers, supplies, food, maintenance and other expenses;
- Cost of administration by the host organization;
- The time costs of individuals who volunteer in the program;
- Indirect costs falling on other agencies, such as security provided by police in the neighborhood, court costs associated with the referral process, costs of services provided by the school system, etc.;
- The costs to offenders including lost employment while in the program and the value they put on lost liberty; and
- Costs to families associated with visiting and other obligations that may be imposed on them.

Note that the organization may choose not to take account of all of these costs if it makes decisions from a narrow organizational perspective. In particular, indirect costs falling on other agencies, costs to offenders and cost to families might be ignored in this instance. However, if the organization takes a wider view of its social responsibility it should include these costs in its decision making.

A deaccessioning program in a library or museum

Suppose a library or museum is considering selling off part of its collection. What are the costs associated with such a decision?

- The benefits that may be lost to researchers, connoisseurs or others for lack of access to the sold inventory. Those benefits would be the smaller of (a) the value researchers place on access and (b) the added transportation and other costs associated with visiting the collection in its new private locations (if such visiting is possible).
- The labor and other costs associated with administering the deaccession process.
- The value of the time of volunteers who provide assistance.

On the other hand, what are the costs of not undertaking the deaccession program?

- Lost benefits associated with alternative use of the space for housing the current inventory. For example, if the current inventory is not sold, there may be no space for new acquisitions.
- Loss of benefits that can be obtained from the funds received by selling part of the current inventory. For example, the proceeds from deaccessioning may be used to purchase new items for the collection, or to fix a leaky roof.

6.6 The opportunity value of time

A very important application of the concept of opportunity cost applies to situations in which costs are incurred at different points in time. In these circumstances, we must ask the question – does a dollar spent now have the same value as a dollar spent a year from now? This is a very important issue for nonprofit managers and social entrepreneurs because different projects or programs may have very different profiles of cost over time, and the profile of costs may be significantly different from the profile of services or benefits. Thus, we need a method to weigh costs incurred at different times against one another.

A host of different nonprofit or social enterprise managerial decisions involve choosing whether to expend resources at one time versus another:

- How much should be spent now to reap returns later from planned giving?
- In a crisis, should part of an endowment be spent now, or should it be preserved to generate future investment returns?
- What share of fund-raising expenditures should be focused on prospecting for new donors as opposed to retaining and upgrading current donors?
- Should the headquarters building be bought or leased?
- What educational benefits should workers get in order to increase their future productivity?
- In a budget crunch, is it wise to defer routine maintenance of plant and equipment?
- Should time be taken out for a staff retreat when staff are needed to service clients?

Managers of nonprofits and social enterprises must decide on an almost daily basis when scarce resources should be invested for future returns. This requires a time value for money, which incorporates two factors – lost opportunities and inflation.

Lost opportunities

Consumption of money or other scarce resources today has the opportunity cost of foregone investment in future capabilities. If money is saved instead of spent, the organization can earn interest and investment returns that offer more money tomorrow. Consider the following example.

Suppose the annual interest rate is 10 percent. An organization has $100 that it can spend now or earn interest for a year. The "future value" of that $100 would be $100 × 1.1 = $110. If the organization waits for a year to spend that $100, it can do so and have $10 left over. The number 1.1 comes from the fact that it gets back its original investment plus 10 percent interest on that number. In general, to determine the value of money in a year you multiply that amount of money by $(1 + r)$, where r is the annual interest rate expressed as a decimal value. Simple algebra based on that calculation enables us to go from future value to *present value*. How much would we need to invest today in order to spend $100 next year? The present value of spending $100 in one year is $100/1.1 or $90.91. As a rule, to calculate the present value of money in one year, you divide that money by $(1 + r)$. The greater value of an expense incurred this year versus next year results from the loss of the opportunity to invest it rather than spend it now.

The calculation we made above is called "discounting" because money spent in the future has a lower cost than money spent today, so sometimes people call the current value the *present discounted value* instead of present value. What is the present value of $100 invested for two years? Assuming that the interest rate remains constant, that $100 would become $110 in one year and $121 in two years ($110 × 1.1). Interest compounds, as interest is paid in the second year on both the original amount saved and the first-year interest received. Because $100 invested now has a future value of $121 ($100 × 1.1 × 1.1 or $100 × $(1.1)^2$), the present value of $100 in two years is $100/(1.1)^2$ or $82.64. The same logic applies to money invested for three or more years, so that the general formula for calculating present value when the interest rate remains constant over time is:

$$PV = A_0 + \frac{A_1}{1 + r} + \frac{A_2}{(1+r)^2} + \frac{A_3}{(1+r)^3} + \cdots \qquad (6.1)$$

where: A_0 is the cost or benefit in the current year.
A_t is the cost or benefit t years from now.
r is the interest rate.

The same calculation can be written more compactly as:

$$PV = \sum_{t=0}^{T} \frac{A_t}{(1+r)^t} \tag{6.2}$$

where: T is the last year of costs or benefits.

Present value calculations become tedious when many years are involved, but many calculators and online freeware speed up the calculations by including present discounted value buttons and tables. Nonetheless, it is often useful to approximate the present value of $A received for many consecutive years with a constant interest rate by the following formula:

$$PV = \frac{A}{r} \tag{6.3}$$

This formula is exactly right if the number of years is infinite, but close to accurate whenever A is paid for 20 or more years. It is simple and convenient for figuring out the present value of a 30-year mortgage, and reasonably useful for calculations involving endowments that disallow spending from the charitable corpus. The reason this equation works in terms of future value is clear in the following example. Once again, suppose we can spend or invest $100 today or save it forever and the interest rate is 10 percent. At the end of one year, we could spend $10 and leave $100 in the bank. That $100 left in the bank would generate the same $10 interest at the end of two years, so we could spend $10 in the second year and leave $100 in the bank. At the end of the third year, well, hopefully you get the picture. So, the present value of $10 per year forever is $100 because that amount generates an infinite stream of annual $10 payments (and is computed as $10/0.1). Similarly, suppose a donor promises to give $100 per year in perpetuity, and that the interest rate is 10 percent. The present value of this stream must be $1000, for if the donor had $1000 today it could be placed into an endowment which draws off $100 each year in interest, and never exhausts the principal. (The donor strategy of providing grants in perpetuity in place of an endowment has been called "an evergreen grant.") Conversely, if the recipient organization borrowed $1000 today, its credit rating would remain sound if it paid $100 in interest each year forever.

Inflation

If we use "dollars" to measure cost, then we need to be sure that this measuring rod remains constant. Unfortunately, the purchasing power of the dollar (or any currency) changes over time because of inflation (or deflation).

Economists measure the purchasing power of a dollar by calculating different price indices. The best-known price index, the *consumer price index* (CPI), measures the average cost of a market basket based on typical consumer purchases. The CPI is set to 100 in some base year (e.g., 2015), and in all other years the CPI reports the ratio of the cost of the market basket in that year divided by its cost in the base year. Continuing our example, if the CPI is 104 in 2017, it means that prices are 4 percent higher in 2017 than they were in 2015.

Banks and other lenders face the opportunity cost of foregone interest and investment earnings if they make loans and need to be compensated for this cost. They would not lend money at a loss, and so charge an interest rate that at least covers their opportunity costs. Part of the opportunity cost of lending is inflation and part is foregone interest in excess of inflation, and both are built into the interest rate. We call the interest rate that is charged the *nominal interest rate*, and the part that is in excess of inflation the *real interest rate*, with the following relationship:

Nominal interest rate = Real interest rate + Expected inflation

Note that this is only approximately true, because the arithmetic of calculating rates of change from price levels creates complications, but the approximation is very good unless the rates involved are very large. For example, a bank that wants to earn 2 percent on its loans beyond the inflation rate would charge the borrower 7 percent if it expected the inflation rate to be 5 percent. To see this, suppose someone borrows $100 in a CPI base year for one year. The next year, the CPI is 105 (5 percent inflation), and the borrower pays the bank $107 to repay the loan. In base year dollars, that converts to $107/105 = 101.90, a payback in constant dollars of just under 2 percent. (The approximation error is ten cents here.)

With this in mind, how do we calculate present value when inflation is expected? One way is to report future costs and benefits without building in any inflation. But if we do this, we should use the real interest rate for discounting. The other way is to report future costs and benefits using expected future prices, building inflation into our annual costs. Since inflation is now included in costs, we should use the nominal interest rate for discounting. What we don't want to do is mix the two approaches up, using a nominal interest rate without building inflation into costs.

An example

Suppose a development officer of a foundation is given the following choice by a donor: An endowment of $100,000 given in a lump sum now, or as an annual gift of $30,000 per year (in current dollars, that is, the $30,000 won't go up or down with inflation) for the next four years. Which alternative should the development officer choose? The answer depends on the interest rate at which the foundation can invest the funds. But before we calculate present values, there are timing complications to deal with. Is the first annual gift given at the beginning of this year, the end of this year, or somewhere in between? If $30,000 is given immediately, we don't have to discount this, and we would discount only the next three years. If the $30,000 is given at the end of this year, we would discount all four payments. For our calculation, we assume that the first installment comes at the beginning of the current year:

- If the nominal rate r = 5 percent, the present value of the annual gift is: PV = $30,000 + $30,000/(1.05) + $30,000/(1.05)^2 + $30,000/(1.05)^3 = $111,697. Since this is greater than $100,000, the present value of the endowment, the foundation officer should choose the annual gift plan.
- If the nominal rate r = 15 percent, the PV of the annual gift is $98,497. In this case, the foundation officer should choose the endowment of $100,000.
- Conversely, if this example is considered from the viewpoint of the donor wishing to preserve as much value for herself, she would choose to give the money up front if the rate is 5 percent and in installments if the rate were 15 percent.

This example illustrates an important principle: as the discount (interest) rate rises, future costs (or benefits) become less important than near term costs. As we will see in more detail later, the choice of an appropriate discount rate can have profound effects on decisions. If we use a low rate, we will count future costs and benefits more prominently. If we assume a high rate, we discount the future heavily and count near-term costs more prominently. Because alternative program initiatives differ in their time profiles of benefits and costs, the choice of discount rate will influence our assessment of a program's efficiency.

SUMMARY

All costs are opportunity costs. However, some costs are not well gauged by prices observed in the marketplace. In particular, there is a variety of circumstances in which prices are either absent or misleading. In these circumstances, one must explicitly determine the opportunity value of the use of such resources by specifically calculating their value in the next best alternative use.

Aggregating costs incurred over different periods of time also involves consideration of lost opportunities. Such costs can be measured on the common scale of present-year dollars by calculating the "present value" of the stream of costs incurred at different times in the future. The present value calculation takes into account the lost opportunities associated with dollars spent or received in the future versus the present.

SELECTED REFERENCES AND CITATIONS

Berlin, N., Masaoka, J., and Schumann, M.J. (2017). Two-Legged Stool: New Findings from California on Nonprofits and Overhead. *Nonprofit Policy Forum, 8(2)*, 165–181.

Brudney, J.L. and Duncombe, W.D. (1992). An Economic Evaluation of Paid, Volunteer, and Mixed Staffing Options for Public Services. *Public Administration Review, 52(5)*, 474–481.

Financial Accounting Standards Board (FASB). (1993). *Statement of Financial Accounting Standards No. 117: Financial Statements of Not-for-Profit Organizations*. Retrieved from http://www.fasb.org/pdf/fas117.pdf (accessed February 8, 2018).

Greenberg, M.D., Helland, E., Clancy, N., and Dertouzos, J.N. (2013). *Fair Value Accounting, Historical Cost Accounting, and Systemic Risk*. Santa Monica, CA: Rand Corporation.

Guthrie, K.M. (1996). *The New-York Historical Society: Lessons from One Nonprofit's Long Struggle for Survival*. San Francisco: Jossey-Bass.

Hansmann, H.B. (1990). Why do Universities have Endowments? *Journal of Legal Studies, XIX*, 3–42.

Hodgkinson, V.A., Weitzman, M.S., Toppe, C.M., and Noga, S.M. (1992). *Nonprofit Almanac 1992–1993*. San Francisco: Jossey-Bass.

National Council of Nonprofits. (n.d.) *(Mis)Understanding Overhead*. Retrieved from https://www.councilofnonprofits.org/tools-resources/misunderstanding-overhead (accessed February 8, 2018).

Rimes, H., Nesbit, R., Christensen, R.K., and Brudney, J.L. (2017). Exploring the Dynamics of Volunteer and Staff Interactions: From Satisfaction to Conflict. *Nonprofit Management and Leadership, 28(2)*, 195–213.

REVIEW CONCEPTS

CPI: The most widely used measure of inflation, the consumer price index.

Economic Rent: Payment to a factor of production in excess of the minimum required to induce the owner of that factor to offer it to the market.

Excess Burden of Taxation: The loss in value when taxes move behavior away from social efficiency.

External Costs: Costs borne by those who do not control an economic transaction.

Factor of Production: An input that is not used up when it is used, such as labor, capital, or land.

Joint Cost: Cost that supports two activities, such as the cost of a direct mail solicitation that both asks for funds and educates the public.

Nominal Interest Rate: The posted interest rate, which includes expected inflation.

Present Value or Present Discounted Value: The amount of money today that is equivalent to a stream of money in the future.

Private Costs: Costs borne by those controlling an economic transaction.

Quasi-Fixed Cost: The discrete cost of operating a fixed factor of production, such as the cost of turning on the lights in the headquarters building.

Real Interest Rate: The interest rate adjusted for inflation. Approximately equal to the nominal interest rate minus expected inflation.

Shadow Price: The price that would be charged for a nontraded resource if it were for sale. Equal to marginal willingness to pay.

Social Costs: The sum of private and external costs.

Sunk Costs: Costs that have been paid and cannot be recovered.

Transfer Payment: A shift of resources from one person or group to another that neither consumes nor transforms the resources.

EXERCISES

1. Select a service program or initiative provided by a nonprofit organization or social enterprise with which you are familiar.

   (a) By talking to someone in charge of the program or reading reports, make a list of all the different kinds of costs associated with providing the program.
   (b) Which of these costs are well-measured by market prices?
   (c) Which of these costs require indirect estimates because they are not adequately represented by market prices? How would you make those estimates using the concept of opportunity cost?
   (d) What expenses, if any, are incurred that are really transfer payments rather than actual costs?

2. A nonprofit cemetery offers families of the deceased two options for maintenance of graves: (1) an annual fee of $25 per year; or (2) a one-time immediate charge of $500 for perpetual care.

   (a) If families are able to earn an interest rate of 10% on their savings, which plan is most economical for them?
   (b) What plan would be the most economical if the interest rate were 4%?

3. Ralph's Pretty Good Charity decides to sell raffle tickets to raise funds. The winner of the raffle will receive a total of $1 million, payable in twenty annual installments of $50,000 each. Unfortunately, Ralph is only able to sell 900,000 raffle tickets at $1 each. Upon consulting his banker and learning that the nominal interest will remain at 10% over the next two decades, Ralph's face breaks out in an enormous smile. Has he gone crazy or has Ralph's raffle produced a financial bonus? Explain.

4. A nonprofit social service agency is trying to decide if it should put its resources into a residential treatment program rather than a day program for the elderly. It has a limited budget and can undertake only one of these options. In calculating the cost of the residential program should it count the benefits lost by not opening the day program? Explain.

5. Easy Ed is a talented volunteer. He is paid $1000/day at the Acme corporation, where he does quality control for roadrunner traps, but still volunteers one day a week to help Charity for Dummies, a registered 501(c)(3) organization dedicated to training crash-test dummies. Dummies could use him to help with fund-raising or to supervise the day-care center for Dummies employees. Both tasks are essential. Ed has passed the state-required training program for child day-care work and aced all his courses at The Fund Raising School®. Here is some other information you may (or may not) need to answer the questions below:

   • All the other volunteers cannot be assigned to either task, and Ed cannot do both tasks.
   • It would cost $300 to recruit and train a new talented volunteer.
   • The cost of supervising and insuring volunteers is $10/day.
   • It would cost $800/day to employ a professional fund-raiser who is exactly as competent as Ed but gets paid.
   • It would cost $80/day to employ a paid day-care worker who has the same qualifications as Ed.

   (a) Is it rational for Ed to volunteer at Dummies? Why or why not?
   (b) If Dummies does not choose to recruit a new talented volunteer, should it ask Ed to work in fund-raising or day care? Why?
   (c) Should Dummies recruit and train a new talented volunteer? Why or why not?

6. Tony Teacher has a steady job as an instructor in a local public high school, but he is unhappy with the progress of his students and thinks he has a better way to educate them with the educational software he has developed and a new philosophy of fun-based learning. However, the school district won't allow him the flexibility to implement his methods, so he contemplates establishing his own school as a for-profit social enterprise. To do this he must leave his position, raise venture capital, rent some space, hire teachers and secure state approval. All of this is costly but so is the option of staying put.

   (a) What are the various explicit and implicit costs that Tony should consider in evaluating the option of undertaking the new venture?
   (b) What are the costs associated with continuing as a public-school teacher?
   (c) If Tony chooses to undertake the venture, how are his costs likely to change over time? What costs are short term, and which are long term?
   (d) If Tony is able to secure a below market, low cost loan in the form of a program-related investment from a local foundation, how will this affect the valuation of his costs and his decision?

7

Analysis of competitive markets

I tried as hard as I could, but she just wouldn't give us any more sugar pops!

7.1   Introduction

One cannot fully appreciate the behavior of individual nonprofit organizations, for-profit firms, workers, volunteers, consumers, entrepreneurs, or donors without understanding the economic environments and markets in which they interact. First, we define and explain what we mean by a "market" and identify several different markets important to the functioning of nonprofit organizations and social enterprises. Some of these, such as the market for volunteers, might not be immediately identifiable as markets to the reader not familiar with this concept. We will model these markets with some broadly familiar concepts such as supply and demand, and some less familiar but highly useful notions such as point measures of demand and supply "elasticity," for example, the price elasticity of supply which reflects how much more supply of a product or service might be forthcoming as its price rises. (It seems, for example, in the above cartoon that Mom's supply of sugar pops is price inelastic, unlikely to expand no matter what the kids offer her.)

While there are various market structures, we focus in this chapter on perfectly competitive markets. *Perfect competition* is a market structure where there are many sellers and many buyers, indeed, there are so many of both that no one buyer or seller, or any small group of such, has an influence on the prevailing price charged in that market. In this context, we examine the forces that determine prices and quantities exchanged, we introduce the idea of a supply function, and we elaborate further on the demand function. It is the interaction of supply and demand that determines market outcomes under perfect competition. This discussion allows us to understand how nonprofit organizations and social enterprises should make price and quantity decisions under a market condition of perfect competition and it sets the stage for analyzing market conditions that differ from perfect competition, as discussed in Chapter 8.

7.2   Types of markets

A market is not necessarily a physical entity; fundamentally a market is a "conceptual space" where items of value are exchanged. Usually, we think of markets, such as supermarkets where groceries are purchased, as places where goods or services are traded for money. In the nonprofit and social enterprise world, this sort of market is commonplace, but other forms of exchange also occur in markets:

- Donors exchange their money for premiums, prestige, tax breaks, and the warm glow of having done a good thing. Nonprofit organizations compete in the market for donations.
- Volunteers trade their time for experience, training, camaraderie, knowledge about the internal workings of the organization, and the warm glow of working for the common good. Nonprofit and social enterprise organizations compete in the market for volunteers.
- Skilled managers, service providers, entrepreneurs and fund-raisers are scarce. Nonprofit organizations and social enterprises compete in various labor markets for the available talent.
- Nonprofit hospitals, day-care providers, nursing homes, universities, and counseling centers compete with for-profit and/or government

providers as well as with each other in the markets for their respective mission-related services.

- Universities compete in the markets for housing services, food services, and bookstores. Many other nonprofits sell commercial goods and services peripherally related to carrying out their organizations' missions.
- Nonprofit lobbyists and advocacy organizations compete in the public policy arena which may be thought of as a market for ideas and influence over legislation.
- Government contracts are awarded to nonprofit and for-profit providers in a bidding market. Government and foundation grants are also scarce and competed for in markets.

Effective nonprofit and social enterprise management requires an understanding of the competitive structures in the various markets in which their organizations participate. There is a well-established terminology to describe the various possible structures for monetized markets (where goods, services, or inputs are traded for money), which we discuss below. Analyses of market structures for donations, volunteers, and ideas are less well developed and represent frontier areas for research. Nonetheless, the basic concepts presented here apply and will be illustrated in our discussion of these topics below.

We focus on the market structure known as perfect competition, where no sellers or buyers believe that they can safely depart from the price established in the broader market by the interaction of supply and demand. Why would an organization believe that it had no control over price? The usual assertion in elementary economics textbooks is that price-taking results when the number of firms is large, and the product being sold is homogeneous (that is, there are no differences in real or perceived quality or in the convenience of purchasing that would lead consumers to think twice before turning to a lower-priced competitor). Similarly, no consumer would believe they could bargain for a lower price because the organization would simply sell to someone else at the market price. In addition, no organization would gain financially by lowering its price below the market level, because (as we shall see) each organization can sell all that it wants to at the prevailing price. Moreover, offering a lower price in this situation will lead to financial ruin in the long run since prevailing competitive prices will provide the minimum revenue needed to break-even. Finally, no consumer would seek to pay a higher than market price to any organization if she regards the seller market as homogenous.

Although perfect competition emerges when there are many sellers, it is possible for a market to behave like a perfectly competitive market even when there is only one seller in the market. If there is only one seller at the current time, but that seller has no particular advantages – such as brand name loyalty, proprietary production techniques, control of some essential input, legal protection against competition, and so on, then that seller would have to take the price as given. Should this seller attempt to raise prices, other providers will enter the market and force the price back down. Thus, the number of *potential* competitors may say more about market structure than the number of actual, competitors. Markets in which there are many potential, but few actual competitors are said to be *contestable*, and managers in contestable markets must behave as if they were in a perfectly competitive market. Alternatively, a market that is not contestable in which there is only one seller of a product is known as a *monopoly*, as discussed in the next chapter.

Day care for children is probably not perfectly competitive in most local markets. Day-care centers differ in convenience of location, hours, services provided, religious orientation, child-care philosophy, quality, and the like. There is no single market price for day-care centers. In contrast, it was not too long ago that retail textbook sales in large cities with many book stores was close to perfectly competitive, so that there would have been little difference between *Economics for Nonprofit Managers* (the first version of this book) sold by one bookstore or another, and stores would have competed on price alone. These days, however, the book selling market has been substantially consolidated, with many fewer off-line and on-line sellers, so that sellers of this new edition, such as Barnes and Noble, university bookstores and Amazon, may determine their own prices and compete on other variables as well, such as convenience and amenities. Consumers in competitive markets are price takers provided the goods are homogeneous, and there is no combined market for the same good sold by a very socially responsible company or by an irresponsible company. (In the latter case, the consumer can choose a higher price to buy from the responsible company or a lower price to buy from the irresponsible company, but within each of these two submarkets the consumer is a price taker.)

Clearly, the perfectly competitive and monopoly market structures are extreme; it is hard to think of many real-world goods that are traded in perfectly competitive markets, or even by pure monopolies. However, many markets are close in structure to one or the other of these extremes, so that by describing these two endpoints, we can say something meaningful about the real-world in-between cases. We will defer further discussion of monopoly and other less competitive market structures to Chapter 8.

7.3 Concepts of equilibrium

In this section we examine how nonprofit and social enterprise organizations choose price and output levels when a market is perfectly competitive. We begin by discussing the concept of equilibrium.

Equilibrium values are the prices and quantities we expect to see in a particular market once it reaches a stable level of operation. We use the term equilibrium to describe what we expect during a time period when both demand and the technology of production are relatively firmly established and any changes in demand or supply are predictable. There are equilibria in competitive markets, monopoly markets, and even in economic games. This construct is usefully applied in most for-profit market situations and works for most nonprofit markets as well. For example, the methods for providing emergency shelter care are well established and even the need for such shelter varies predictably with the weather, government policies, and the state of the local economy. Equilibrium may be the resting point of a series of market adjustments or it may be a set of prices and quantities that, if reached, is stable.

In perfectly competitive markets, each seller and buyer takes the price of the product or service as given. The seller only has to decide the quantity to offer for sale and the buyer has to decide the quantity to seek to buy. The equilibrium price is the one that harmonizes these respective offers, that makes the quantity offered for sale and the quantity desired for purchase the same. At this price, we say that the "market clears," and the traded amount is the equilibrium quantity.

When markets are not perfectly competitive, equilibrium can be more complicated than a single price that clears the market and the resulting quantity. For example, nonprofits may offer different prices and free care, based on the income (or insurance coverage) of the purchaser, such as the sliding-scale fees charged by some nonprofit day-care centers or the net-of-financial-aid price charged to individual students at a university. The prices charged may be too low to clear the market, and some other way of restricting access has to be found. A nonprofit health clinic would not provide free medical care to the wealthy and well-insured despite the possible eagerness of these patients to "purchase" at a price of zero. Harvard University sells its educational services only to those who best advance its elite mission, using a competitive admissions process to do so. Some social-service agencies ration access to care by putting people on a wait list instead of expanding facilities to clear the market. We discuss some of these nuances further in later chapters, after perfect competition is understood.

An important distinction is made between short-run and long-run equilibrium. As suggested in Chapter 4, the *long run* is defined not by any specific length of time but by the speed with which fixed costs can be converted into variable costs in the particular industry being studied. During the period of a lease, rental costs are fixed. When the lease comes up for renewal, an organization can avoid these costs by not renewing, or it can choose to renew and pay rent. If this were the only fixed cost, the long run would be reached the day after the lease expired. There are as many short runs as there are sources of fixed costs, but we can simplify by assuming only one (aggregate) source of fixed costs (and hence one short run). Usually, we will assume that the size of physical facilities is fixed, but the number of employee hours is variable. Then, short-run equilibrium results from market forces operating on workers but not facilities, and long-run equilibrium results from market forces operating on both.

For-profit firms derive most of their revenues strictly from sales, so that the amount of revenue varies with the quantity of output produced and sold. For that reason, revenues from sales are called *variable revenues*. Revenue from capital gains and dividends on the firm's investments do not change with the quantity produced and sold, and so constitute *fixed revenues*. Fixed revenues are more important in the nonprofit and social enterprise setting, as grants and donations are not usually tied to the quantity of output. Thus, it makes sense to extend the definition of "long run" and "short run" to fixed versus variable revenues as well as costs. Precisely how we will divide revenues into fixed and variable depends on the decision problem and the context. For example, a donative nonprofit (one that receives most of its revenues from donations) produces charitable solicitation (letters, phone calls, visits with major prospects), and we will define variable revenues in this case as the portion of donations that varies with the current production of solicitation. Donations that flow in without current production of solicitation are fixed revenues, and may come from board members and loyal donors attracted by past campaigns. For the revenue side, the short run ends when donations would cease without new solicitation efforts such as the next capital campaign.

Long-run equilibrium is determined by using long-run cost and demand functions, and short-run equilibrium is determined by short-run functions. However, the difference in equilibria does not depend solely on differences in the cost functions of individual firms or on long-term shifts in demand, but also on differences in the number of organizations in the market. The number of organizations can be thought of as a fixed quantity in the short run, but we need to make additional assumptions to determine how this factor is limited in the long run. For-profit sector economists define a market as having *free entry and exit* when the number of organizations is perfectly variable, new organizations have the same cost functions as incumbents and hence can produce as cheaply as old firms, and no special penalty is paid by exiting firms. When entry and exit are not free, we identify the reasons why as barriers to entry and exit. Barriers to entry are discussed further in Chapter 8. Barriers to exit might include bond forfeiture, laws requiring maintenance of employment, and tax penalties. However, we know relatively little at this time about the nature and determinants of nonprofit and social enterprise entry and exit, although speculations and hints abound in the ongoing work of researchers. For this book, we will analyze the two extremes (open versus restricted entry) without a clear notion of where these fence posts lie in most nonprofit and social-enterprise industries.

7.4 Short-run perfectly competitive equilibrium

Earlier (Chapters 4 and 5) we studied the market demand curve which describes how consumers adjust their desired purchase quantities when faced with alternative prices. Here, we develop the corresponding "supply curve," which describes how producers and sellers adjust their desired production and sales levels when faced with alternative prices. Then we show how supply and demand interact to determine market equilibrium in both the short and long runs.

Under perfect competition, both buyers and sellers are price-takers. Marginal revenue for a price-taking firm is particularly simple. The extra money that the firm derives from the sale of an additional unit is simply the price at which that unit is sold. For example, recall the Meals on Wheels example from Chapter 4. In this situation, the organization will choose to produce at the point where the revenue received from selling another unit of their product is just equal to the marginal cost of producing that last unit of output. As illustrated in Table 4.1, the selling price of $6 leads the organization to choose to produce 11 units of their service, where price (which is identical with marginal revenue for price takers) is equal to marginal cost. Alternatively, if the selling price was equal to $3.50 (substituting $3.50 for $6 in column 10 of the table), this would lead the organization to produce only six units of service. Similarly, at a selling price of $7.45, it would choose to produce 14 units. Price takers do not have to worry that by selling an extra unit, they will have to drop the sales price for all the earlier (infra-marginal) units they sell. In the Meals on Wheels example, the government may be setting this price.

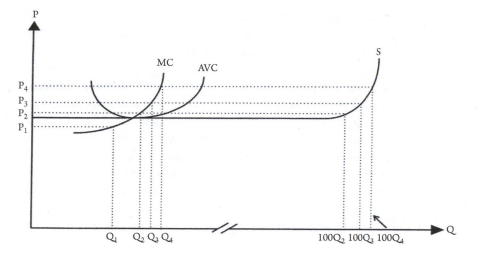

Figure 7.1 Determination of organization and market supply

For the general situation of perfect competition, there are so many firms in the marketplace that individual firms have negligible impact on the overall market. In effect, individual firms see such a small slice of the market demand curve that it looks horizontal (at the given price) over the range of potential firm production levels, so that price, average revenue, and marginal revenue are all identical and do not depend upon the firm's decisions. Recalling the profit-maximizing rule from Chapter 5 (set Q to make $MR = MC$), this simpler marginal revenue function leads to a simpler rule for profit-maximizing firms under perfect competition:

> *Choose a quantity of production that equates price with marginal cost*
> *($P = MC$). Produce this quantity if at this level, price exceeds average variable*
> *costs ($P > AVC$); otherwise, shut down and produce nothing.*

We derive an organization's supply curve by repeated application of this rule at different prices that the organization might be faced with. Figure 7.1 illustrates the cost functions for a single competitive firm on the left half of the chart. Facing a price of P_1, the quantity that makes $P = MC$ is Q_1. However, P_1 is lower than the average variable cost at Q_1, so the best this organization can do when faced with such a low price is to shut down. At prices P_2, P_3, and P_4, the candidate quantities are Q_2, Q_3, and Q_4, respectively, and all these quantities are worth producing because the price exceeds average variable cost. Continuing the process with additional prices, it rapidly becomes clear that:

> *The competitive organization's short-run supply curve is the same as the MC curve for all prices greater than or equal to AVC. Competitive suppliers will offer a quantity of zero for all prices lower than the minimum of AVC.*

Now, suppose that this organization is one of 100 identical suppliers in its industry, each possessing the same cost curve. This allows us to construct the short-run supply curve for the industry. If all organizations faced a price of P_1, they would each produce Q_1, so the total supplied would be $100 Q_1$. Repeating this process for other prices yields the market supply curve illustrated in the right half of Figure 7.1. To derive this curve, we added the quantities produced by each organization at a given price, a process known as *horizontal addition*. If all the organizations are identical, this addition is the same as multiplying the quantities produced at each price by any one supplier; but even if costs are not identical across organizations, we have the following result:

> *The short-run market supply curve is the horizontal sum of the short-run firm-level supply curves.*

Figure 7.2
Equilibrium of supply
and demand

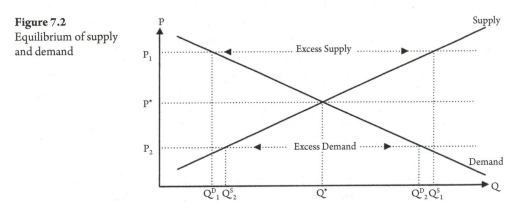

Now that we have described supply – how sellers respond to alternative prices – we are ready to show how prices harmonize the interests of buyers and sellers to determine an equilibrium. Figure 7.2 illustrates the typical short-run supply and demand curves in a competitive market. P^* is the equilibrium price, because at that price, the quantity that sellers would like to offer for sale (Q^*) is exactly equal to the quantity that buyers would like to buy. P_1 is not an equilibrium price, because at that price the quantity supplied (Q_1^S) greatly exceeds the quantity demanded (Q_1^D), and goods will pile up on the shelves or potential services will be unused. If all organizations are faced with a rapidly accumulating inventory or excess capacity at some price, we do not expect that price to persist even in the short run. Some seller will drop its price, competitors will be forced to follow suit, and the price will drop to P*. As the price falls, sellers reduce the quantity they offer, and buyers are willing to buy a larger quantity. This process continues until the two offers match. Likewise, P_2 is not an equilibrium price, because at that price the quantity demanded (Q_2^D) greatly exceeds the quantity supplied (Q_2^S). If consumers are lining up to buy a product or service, competitive for-profit sellers will raise prices a bit and still sell out because consumers cannot find the product available from a lower-priced competitor. As prices rise, sellers increase the quantity they offer for sale and buyers reduce their desired purchase quantities, until once again we reach the short-run equilibrium price and quantity. Thus, we conclude that:

> *Equilibrium prices and quantities in perfectly competitive markets are determined by the intersection of supply and demand curves.*

While supply and demand are defined in terms of desired quantities to sell or buy at given prices, either can be interpreted in inverse fashion. We have already noted that the height of the demand curve can be interpreted as the maximum marginal willingness to pay, that is, as the most a consumer would willingly pay for a one additional unit of output. Similarly, the height of the supply curve can be interpreted as the minimum marginal willingness-to-sell, that is, the minimum payment that would lead the supplier to offer an additional unit for sale.

7.5   Comparative statics

Equilibrium is (by definition) stable, but not eternal. We have assumed that many factors remain constant while price adjusts to equilibrate the market. If the positions of the supply and demand functions change, then the market moves to a different equilibrium based on the new conditions.

A comparison of the equilibrium level of P and Q for different supply and demand curves is called *comparative statics analysis*. The comparative static approach simply compares these two equilibria, without trying to understand the dynamic adjustment process that moves a market from one equilibrium to another. While this approach has the disadvantage of ignoring possible speculative price spirals, selling panics, and other chaotic and sometimes catastrophic adjustment paths, it has the virtue of simplicity and is descriptively accurate for most markets where speculation is not the driving force. In addition, while little is known about price dynamics in for-profit markets, even less is known about dynamics in nonprofit markets. We don't yet know whether, as some allege, nonprofit organizations are too slow to recognize and react to changing market conditions or, alternatively, whether they just take a longer-term perspective than for-profit managers when choosing their patterns of adjustment. (There is some evidence that nonprofits do react more slowly, for example, when for-profit nursing homes expanded much faster than nonprofit homes at the advent of Medicare and Medicaid. See Vladeck, 1980 and Eaton, 2000.)

At least five different kinds of factors or conditions affect the positioning of the demand and supply functions.

Factors affecting supply curves

1.   *Changes in the price of inputs*

The price of inputs enter into the calculation of each supplier's marginal and average variable cost functions and hence move both the firm's and market supply. For example, if labor contracts mandate an increase in the wage rate, this would raise each organization's marginal and average cost functions. Hence, the schedule of minimum marginal willingness-to-sell (supply curve) would shift to the left and we would say supply (meaning the whole curve) has decreased. This decrease in supply (from S_1 to S_2 in Figure 7.3A) would lead to a new equilibrium with a higher price and a lower quantity exchanged. In contrast, if formerly paid workers agreed to perform their regular duties as volunteers, supply would shift to the right (increased supply), equilibrium price would fall, and a larger quantity would be sold. Remember that an increase in supply is a shift to the right. When supply is upward-sloping, a rightward shift looks like a downward shift, but focus on left/right movement.

2.   *Changes in technology that improve the productivity of variable factors of production*

The increase in worker productivity resulting from improved technology would move the organization's marginal and average cost functions downward. With lower costs, the quantity that makes P = MC would move to the right and supply would increase from S_2 to S_1 in Figure 7.3A.

3.   *Changes in the number of firms*

An increase in the number of firms increases market supply, as this is the horizontal sum of firm supply curves, so when one more is added the total moves to the right (from S_2 to S_1 in Figure 7.3A), leading to a larger quantity

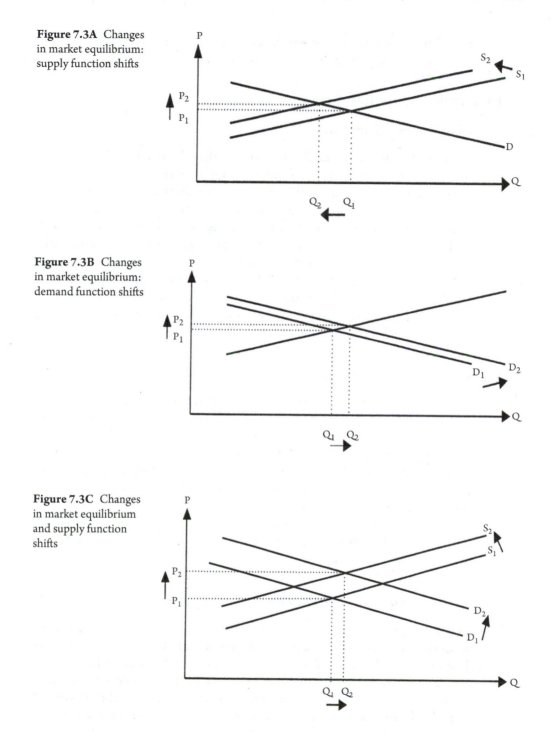

Figure 7.3A Changes in market equilibrium: supply function shifts

Figure 7.3B Changes in market equilibrium: demand function shifts

Figure 7.3C Changes in market equilibrium and supply function shifts

and a lower price in equilibrium. A decrease in the number of firms reduces S, lowering the equilibrium quantity and raising the equilibrium price.

Factors affecting demand curves

1. *Changes in consumer tastes*

   Tastes can shift the demand function in either direction. If, for example, the music of Chopin enjoyed a sudden surge in popularity, the number of classical-music concert tickets that would be bought at any given price would increase, and the demand curve would move to the right. This case is illustrated in Figure 7.3B, showing that an increase in demand (from D_1 to D_2) leads to an increase in both equilibrium price and quantity. Alternatively, if newly environmentally conscious consumers switched to products without extensive packaging, the demand curve for waste management services would shift to the left. Again, this is illustrated in Figure 7.3B if we think of D_2 as the initial demand curve, showing that a decrease in demand reduces both the equilibrium price and quantity.

2. *Changes in wealth or income*

   When people become wealthier, they wish to purchase more of most goods and services at any given price, increasing the market demand in these markets. Theater tickets, vichyssoise, luxury cars, and cosmetic surgery fall in this category, where an increase in wealth would shift demand to the right and thereby increase the equilibrium price and quantity of these goods. These are *normal goods*. However, the demand for some goods falls when income or wealth increase: bleacher-seat tickets, cold watery gruel, bus tickets, and medical treatment for malnutrition. An increase in income would decrease demand, equilibrium price, and equilibrium quantities for these goods and services; thus, they are known as *inferior goods*.

3. *Changes in the price of related goods*

   When the price of Coke (Coca-Cola™ that is) falls, some people that used to drink Pepsi™ at each Pepsi price will now want to buy Coke. Because less Pepsi is demanded at any Pepsi price, this shifts the demand for Pepsi to the left, a decrease in demand, with consequent lower equilibrium price and quantity of Pepsi. When one good is used instead of another (like Coke and Pepsi), we call that pair of goods *substitutes*. An increase in the price on one good causes an increase in demand for substitute goods, and a decrease in the price of one good causes a decrease in demand for substitute goods.

When the price of rum goes up, less rum will be bought, and this too has a side effect on demand for Coke (at least among consumers that like the mixed drink rum and Coke). In this case, demand for Coke would decrease. When one good is used together with another (like rum and Coke) we call the pair of goods *complements*. (We don't call them compliments – that is a different word. Two goods are complimentary if they are free, or if they say to each other "you are a really nice good."). An increase in the price of one good causes a decrease in demand for complementary goods, and a decrease in the price of one good causes an increase in demand for complementary goods.

The way in which we describe movements is important, because we must distinguish between a movement along the supply or demand curve from a movement of the whole curve itself. When the whole curve moves, we use language like "demand changes" or "supply increases" or "demand shifts to the right." When the curve stays where it is, and the price of the good changes, we are moving from one point on the curve to another and use the words "quantity demanded" or "quantity supplied." In the example above, when the price of rum goes up, demand for rum is unaffected. The curve doesn't move, we move from one point on the curve to another, and we use words like "the quantity demanded has changed" to make this distinction. Price determines the location of demand for other goods, but not demand for the good whose price changes.

4.   *Changes in expected future prices or income or quality*

A demand curve shows the rate at which consumers wish to buy a good at a point in time. Expected changes in the future price of a good affect the timing of consumer purchases and so move the current demand curve. For example, current demand for iPhone X depends on how soon iPhone XI will be released for sale in the market for two reasons. First, everyone knows that the price of X will fall when XI is released. If XI won't be offered for 10 years, well, you need an iPhone X now to get you through, but if XI will be offered in a week, you might hold off on buying a new X, anticipating that its price will drop, hence lowering current demand for X. Indeed, if XI will be offered in a week, you might instead buy a new XI, again lowering the current demand for X.

Expected future income also affects current demand for goods. The day you learn that you have won the lottery is the day you start splurging, increasing the current demand for luxury goods even though your current income and wealth have not changed. Finally, expected future quality affects current demand. If Pomegranate announces that iPhone XI will be released with new killer apps that won't work on any other phone, that would decrease current demand for iPhone X.

5. *Changes in the number of consumers*

This one is obvious or will be shortly. With more consumers in the market, demand increases.

6. *Changes in the decision-making climate*

Whenever a major snowstorm is predicted, milk, bread, salt, shovels, and hot chocolate tend to disappear from grocery market shelves because of the increase in demand for these items. A forecast of rain increases demand for umbrellas. Lead in the water supply increases demand for bottled water.

Factors affecting both supply and demand

1. *Changes in tax, subsidy, or regulatory policy*

These changes can shift either or both curves and do so in any combination of directions. For example, a housing-code regulation requiring group homes for the developmentally challenged in a particular locality to meet minimum space and fire-prevention standards would increase cost and hence decrease supply. This same regulation would increase the quality of the product, which would increase demand (Figure 7.3C).

A decrease in supply increases the equilibrium price and an increase in demand also increases the equilibrium price. However, when supply decreases, equilibrium quantity decreases while the demand increase works in the opposite direction. The overall effect on quantity depends on which of the curve changes has greater effect, which in turn depends on how much each curve moves as well as on the relative slopes of the two curves. In Figure 7.3C, the effect of the demand change is greater than that of the supply change, so the equilibrium quantity went up from Q_1 to Q_2, but if we moved supply a little more, equilibrium quantity would have decreased.

2. *Changes in determinants of demand occurring at the same time as changes in the determinants of supply*

In the previous example, a single factor caused both curves to move, but two different factors work just as well. We could have an increase in income (which increases demand for normal goods and decreases demand for inferior goods) occur at the same time as an improvement in worker productivity that increases supply. Working through the variety of combinations, the reader can verify that for some combinations of moves, the price moves in a definite direction but the direction of change in quantity is uncertain; for other combinations of moves, the direction of change in price is uncertain but quantity moves in a definite direction.

7.6 Elasticity

Defining and measuring elasticity

Elasticity is a way to measure how sensitive one dependent variable (an effect) is to a change in an independent variable (a cause). There are many kinds of elasticity that interest us here including:

- *Price elasticity of demand* which measures the response of desired purchases of a product to a change in the price of that product while holding all other determinants of demand constant.
- *Income elasticity of demand* which measures the response of desired purchases of a product to changes in consumer income while holding all other determinants of demand constant.
- *Cross-price elasticity of demand* which measures the change in the quantity of one product demanded due to a change in the price of a different product while holding all other determinants of demand for both products constant.
- *Price elasticity of supply* which measures the response of desired sales quantity for a product to changes in the price of that product while holding all other determinants of supply constant.
- *Income elasticity of supply* which measures the response of desired sales quantity to a change in supplier income holding all other determinants of supply constant. We shall see that this measure is irrelevant for profit-maximizing organizations but matters for mission-driven organizations.

Elasticity measures are functions that depend on all the underlying determinants of the relevant curves. For example, the price elasticity of demand depends on what the price is before it changes: consumers may respond one way to a price increase when the price starts out high, and quite another way when the price starts out low. Each elasticity measure is also a function of the other determinants of demand or supply, which we hold constant. For example, in computing the price elasticity of demand, we measure consumer responsiveness to price changes while holding income, prices of other products, tastes, expectations, the number of consumers, and the decision-making environment constant at particular levels. If we change one of those factors, say income, then the price elasticity of demand could take a different numerical value at each possible price.

All the elasticity measures use the same formula to calculate numerical values, although they differ in which variables are inserted into those formulas:

$$\varepsilon = \frac{\text{percentage change in some effect}}{\text{percentage change in some cause of that effect}} = \frac{\%\Delta\text{effect}}{\%\Delta\text{cause}}$$

where: ε (the Greek small letter epsilon) is the symbol for elasticity and $\%\Delta$ is shorthand for the percentage change in.

The formulas measure responsiveness in proportional, rather than absolute terms, for several reasons. First, our intuition about responsiveness suggests that proportions should be used. A one-penny increase in the price of chewing gum is different than a one-penny increase in the price of a 2018 Rolls Royce Phantom (with prices starting at $420,325). Measuring in percentages captures the essence of this difference. Second, proportional changes have a meaning that is not linked to the units of measurement employed, allowing one to compare the elasticity of six-packs of beer with liters of Pepsi and with 1000s of dollars of insurance coverage. Whether we measure the price in pennies, dollars, rubles, or yen, and whether we measure quantities in gallons, pounds, liters, or six-packs, a 10 percent change means the same thing.

Specifically, the *price elasticity of demand* has this formula:

$$\varepsilon_p^D = \frac{\%\Delta Q^D}{\%\Delta P} \text{ between two points on the same demand curve.}$$

The subscripts and superscripts on epsilon indicate that this is a price elasticity (P) of demand (D). This is a function of the two points chosen, and the fact that the two points are on the same demand curve indicates that no other determinant of demand is allowed to vary. A little thought reveals that since the demand curve is always downward sloping, the price elasticity of demand must always be a negative number. If $\%\Delta P$ is positive (a price increase) then $\%\Delta Q$ must be negative (quantity demanded decreases as price increases, whether measured in absolute or percentage terms); if $\%\Delta P$ is negative (price fall), then $\%\Delta Q$ must be positive (increase in quantity demanded), and whether you divide a positive number by a negative number or a negative number by a positive number, the result is always negative. The real question is how negative this elasticity is. Negative numbers are awkward to describe in words, because a number is larger whenever it is to the right on a number line, so -1 is larger than -100. To ease this awkwardness, we work with the absolute value (-1 is smaller in absolute value than -100), but the negative sign of elasticity should not be forgotten in practical applications. The larger the absolute value of elasticity, the more sensitive the quantity demanded is to changes in price. If the absolute value of price elasticity is 1, it means that a 1 percent increase in price causes a 1 percent decrease in quantity demanded, which is moderate responsiveness. But if the absolute value of price elasticity is 100, it means that a 1 percent increase in price leads to a 100 percent decrease in quantity demanded, very sensitive indeed.

We will find it useful to distinguish among five ranges for the value of elasticity of demand, three of which are found on a typical downward sloping demand curve, and two of which are found only in extreme limiting situations:

- If the absolute value of ε_p^D = infinity, we say that demand is *perfectly price elastic*. In words, when demand is perfectly price elastic, it means any change in price causes an infinite percentage change in quantity demands. The tiniest price rise drops quantity demanded to zero, and the tiniest price fall increases quantity demanded to infinity, which, if you think about it, means that the demand curve is horizontal (Figure 7.4A). This is a logical extreme if we are talking market demand curves, approximated perhaps but never seen in reality. But an individual seller in a perfectly competitive market regards the relevant portion of demand as horizontal (otherwise, their quantity decision would affect the price), and that is a realistic application.
- If the absolute value of ε_p^D is between 1 and infinity at some pair of points, we say that demand is *price elastic*.
- If the absolute value of ε_p^D = 1 at some pair of points, we say that demand is *unit elastic* with respect to price; in this case, a 1 percent change in price brings about a 1 percent change in quantity demanded.
- If the absolute value of ε_p^D is less than 1 at some pair of points, we say that demand is *price inelastic*.
- If ε_p^D = 0, we say that demand is *perfectly price inelastic*. This is a limiting situation, which might occur if patients need a specific medicine and are willing to pay any price necessary to obtain it. Even so, as price keeps rising, there comes a point where even Bill Gates cannot afford to buy the medicine. So, we can have perfectly price inelastic demand only for a limited range of prices. Sections of the demand curve that are perfectly

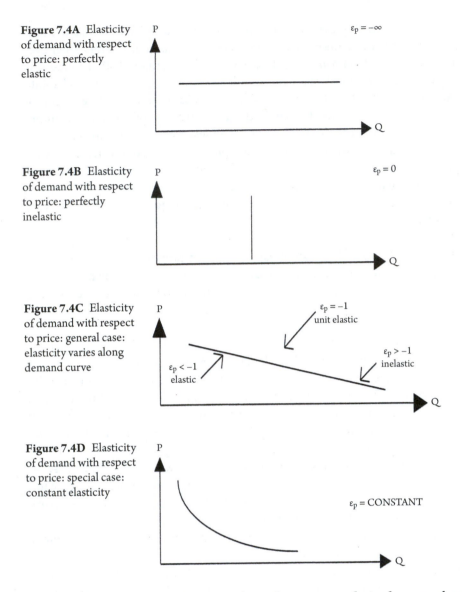

Figure 7.4A Elasticity of demand with respect to price: perfectly elastic

Figure 7.4B Elasticity of demand with respect to price: perfectly inelastic

Figure 7.4C Elasticity of demand with respect to price: general case: elasticity varies along demand curve

Figure 7.4D Elasticity of demand with respect to price: special case: constant elasticity

inelastic will be vertical, as the quantity desired never changes for a vertical demand curve (Figure 7.4B).

The alert reader will note that we have not yet specified how to calculate a percentage change. Economists use a different way to calculate percentage changes than is usually taught in school. The traditional formula for a percentage change is:

$$\frac{\text{ending value} - \text{starting value}}{\text{starting value}} \times 100$$

For example, if the price of a share of stock goes from $100 to $150, that is a 50 percent increase in price ({[$150 – $100]/$100} × 100 = 50%). The problem with using this way of calculating is that it is sensitive to which value you label as the starting value and which you label as the ending value. If the price of a share of stock falls 50 percent starting at $150, the ending price will be $75 ({[$75 – $150]/$150} × 100 = -50%). In other words, if the price of a share of stock rises by 50 percent one day and falls by 50 percent the next day, you have less money than you started with ($75 vs. $100)!

When we calculate elasticities, we do so between two points. It is a way of describing the curve, and neither point can be labeled as "ending" or "starting." Therefore, in economics, we usually calculate percentage changes this way:

$$\frac{\text{one value} - \text{the other value}}{\text{the average of the two values}} \times 100.$$

In turn, you calculate the average of the two values by adding them up and dividing by 2. This leads to the scariest way of portraying the formula for calculating the price elasticity of demand between the points (P_1, Q_1) and (P_2, Q_2) on the same demand curve:

$$\varepsilon_p^D = \frac{\left[\dfrac{(Q_2 - Q_1)}{\left(\dfrac{Q_1 + Q_2}{2}\right)}\right]}{\left[\dfrac{(P_2 - P_1)}{\left(\dfrac{P_1 + P_2}{2}\right)}\right]}$$

but it looks less scary if you break it down into steps as we have. Simplifying this complex fraction and rearranging terms gives the following:

$$\varepsilon_p^D = \frac{\Delta Q^D}{\Delta P} \times \frac{\overline{P}}{\overline{Q^D}}$$

where: $\overline{Q^D}$ is the average quantity demanded.

$\overline{P}$ is the average price.

This version of elasticity is convenient for demonstrating that unless demand is horizontal or vertical (Figures 7.4A and 7.4B), the price elasticity of demand is different at every average point on a straight-line demand curve. The first factor in the formula is just the reciprocal of the slope of the demand curve between the two points (e.g., if the slope is 2/3 then the reciprocal slope is 3/2). Like the slope, the reciprocal of the slope is also constant between any two points on a straight line. However, the second factor, the ratio of average price to average quantity, varies from a limit of infinity (when one point is on the y-intercept of demand and the other point gets closer and closer to it) down to a limit of zero (when one point is on the (horizontal) x-intercept of demand and the other point gets closer and closer to it). We can speak of these limits as elasticity at a point, rather than elasticity between two points, so when we calculate the elasticity at the y-intercept, we have the reciprocal of slope times some P divided by zero. A straight-line demand curve with any slope (other than zero or infinite) is perfectly price elastic at the (vertical) y-intercept of demand. When we calculate elasticity for other points moving downward along the demand curve, the (absolute value of) elasticity falls continuously, reaching 1 (unitary elasticity) halfway down the line and 0 (perfect inelasticity) at the x-intercept (Figure 7.4C).

It is also possible to draw demand curves that have constant elasticity but are neither vertical nor horizontal. As we move along the curved demand illustrated in Figure 7.4D, each time the price to quantity ratio gets smaller, the inverse slope gets larger (in absolute value) and the two changes cancel out. The formula for a constant elasticity demand curve is:

$$\ln(Q) = a + b \times \ln(P)$$

where: ln means the natural log.
b is the constant elasticity that describes every point on demand.

When two straight-line demand curves with differing slopes intersect, we can quickly compare their relative elasticities – but only at the point of intersection. Because P/Q is the same at this point, the comparison hinges only on the relative (inverse) slopes, so that the steeper the demand curve, the smaller the elasticity (in absolute value). But we can't say that the steeper curve is less elastic than the flatter curve because there are points on both curves where elasticity ranges from infinity to zero.

Factors that determine the price elasticity of demand

We have already considered several factors that affect the price elasticity of demand.

1.   *Availability of substitutes*

When close substitutes become available, demand becomes more price elastic at each given price, for then even a moderate price increase would induce many to switch their purchases to the substitute good or service. For example, the demand for orchestra performances may be elastic because people can attend other kinds of concerts, purchase compact-disc recordings or buy their music from an Internet service. On the other hand, certain services such as organ transplants and disaster-relief services have few good substitutes and are highly necessary. The demand for such services would be highly price-inelastic, as consumers would not substantially reduce their purchases in response to a price increase.

2.   *Time frame*

When consumers are given a longer time to adjust to a price change, their demand becomes more price-elastic at each given price. This is directly related to the availability of substitutes. What may be a unique service in the short run may allow the cultivation of alternatives in the long run. For example, in the short run one may be highly dependent on the services of a public police force or a private security agency to provide protection from crime. In the longer run, one can install an electronic security system or move to a safer neighborhood. Or, the demand for acute medical care may be more elastic in the long run than the short run, because preventative alternatives can be developed to lessen the need for acute care. Or demand for gasoline can become more elastic when consumers are given the time to switch to more fuel-efficient cars, begin carpooling, and shorten their commutes.

3.   *Importance of the good in the consumer budget*

If the price of bubble gum were to increase 50 percent, consumers would not cut their purchases of this product by very much. They can afford to ignore the price of bubble gum in their decision making because their expenditure on this product is a trivial part of their total expenditures. On the other hand, a modest increase in the price of subsidized rental-housing for the indigent would likely provoke a large decrease in applications for this subsidy. Even a slight increase in the rent would have major budgetary implications for the indigent, requiring them to spend less on other necessities or find alternative places to live. Thus, demand would be more elastic. In general, demand for a good or service is more elastic when expenditure on the product (price times quantity) is a large fraction of available resources.

Why is price elasticity of demand important?

The price elasticity of demand is a very useful tool for setting prices. In general, an increase in price will decrease the volume of sales, but the revenue collected on each unit sold will go up. A decrease in price will increase the volume of sales but reduce revenue on each unit sold. With these opposing forces at work, can we raise more revenue by increasing or decreasing price? The answer depends upon the numerical value of the price elasticity of demand at the current price:

> *When demand is price elastic, an increase in price will decrease total revenue and a decrease in price will increase total revenues.*
>
> *When demand is inelastic, an increase in price will increase total revenue and a decrease in price will reduce total revenues.*
>
> *When demand is unit elastic, neither an increase nor a decrease in price will change total revenues.*

This result can be proven mathematically, but it is not simply a mathematical artifact. Rather, it really is quite an intuitive result. For if demand is price-elastic then a price decrease will result in a proportionally greater increase in quantity sold, more than offsetting the loss of revenues from the price decline. Conversely, if demand is price inelastic, the increase in quantity sold will be proportionally less than the price decrease and will not make up for the revenue loss of that price reduction. These results are illustrated in Figure 7.5A. The top diagram shows the effect of a price reduction when demand is elastic. The slender rectangle labeled "Revenue Loss" has an area equal to the decrease in revenues from those who would have bought the good at the high price but now pay a lower price, while the rectangle labeled "Revenue Gain" has an area equal to the revenues $(P \times Q)$ from new customers who only buy at the lower price. When demand is elastic around the two prices as shown, the area of the loss rectangle is smaller than the area of the gain rectangle, so

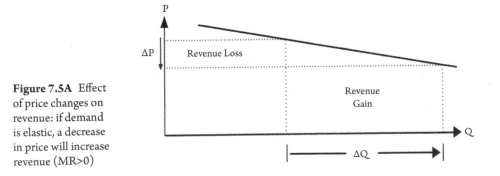

Figure 7.5A Effect of price changes on revenue: if demand is elastic, a decrease in price will increase revenue (MR>0)

Figure 7.5B Effect of price changes on revenue: if demand is inelastic, a decrease in price will decrease revenue (MR<0)

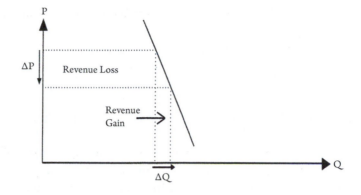

total revenues are higher at the lower price. Figure 7.5B shows the case of inelastic demand. Here, the rectangle representing the loss from the price decrease is larger than the rectangle representing the revenue increase from additional sales.

In short, when demand is price-elastic around the current price, more revenues can be generated by lowering the price and selling more. Where demand is price inelastic, total revenues can be enhanced by increasing the price and selling less.

7.7   Various kinds of elasticity

Each of the other kinds of elasticity is also a ratio of two percentage changes:

Income elasticity of demand:

$$\varepsilon_Y^D = \frac{\%\Delta Q^D}{\%\Delta Y},$$

where: Y is the average income of consumers.

Cross-price elasticity of demand:

$$\varepsilon_{P_a}^{Q^D_b} \text{ (or, more compactly) } \varepsilon_a^b = \frac{\%\Delta Q^D_b}{\%\Delta P_a},$$

where: a and b are two different goods.

Price elasticity of supply:

$$\varepsilon_P^S = \frac{\%\Delta Q^S}{\%\Delta P},$$

where: superscript S means pick two points on the supply curve.

Income elasticity of supply:

$$\varepsilon_Y^S = \frac{\%\Delta Q^S}{\%\Delta Y}$$

where: Y is average organizational income, including grants and donations.

The income elasticity of demand measures the impact of changes in income on desired purchases at a given price. For example, if the income elasticity were 0.7, then a 10 percent increase in income would result in a 7 percent increase in the quantity desired for purchase (all other determinants of demand, and, in particular, the price held constant). Unlike the price elasticity of demand, the income elasticity is usually (but not always) positive. A positive income elasticity indicates that the good is normal as defined in economics – people want more of it when their income rises. A negative income elasticity indicates that the good is inferior – people want less of it when their income rises. Public transit may be an inferior good within a certain range of income; when people's income rises they often buy cars and abandon the transit system. If income elasticity exceeds unity, a percentage increase in income causes a more than proportionate percentage increase in demand, providing a numerical test to label goods as *luxuries*. In contrast, a normal good whose income elasticity is less than unity could be classed as a *necessity*. Jewelry and food prepared in the home are classic examples of luxury and necessity goods, respectively. So, too, may be arts performances and health care respectively.

The cross-price elasticity of demand measures the interrelationships between two products. When the two goods are regarded by consumers as substitutes (e.g., outpatient care in a nursing facility and home nursing care), then the cross-price elasticity of demand will be a positive number. This is because if the price of facility care goes up and the price of home care stays constant, some consumers will switch to home care. Thus, the demand for home care will increase and in particular, the quantity of home care demanded will increase (at the constant price of home care) so we have a positive number divided by another positive number, resulting in a positive number. If the price of facility care instead went down, the quantity of home care demanded would also go down, but whether you have a positive number divided by a positive number or a negative number divided by a negative number, the result is a positive number. In the nonprofit arena, dance and opera, direct mail and media advertising in fund-raising, or donations to alternative environmental charities are substitutes. The size of this cross-price elasticity is important to managers, whether both products are sold by the same organization (in which case it predicts how pushing one product will reduce revenues from another product) or by different organizations (in which case it predicts how actions of competitors will affect an organization's revenues).

Other pairs of goods, like symphony tickets and beverages sold during intermissions, are complements, consumed together. If the price of symphony tickets were to rise enough to reduce the number of tickets sold, then the demand for intermission beverages would fall, as would the quantity demanded at the constant price of beverages. Thus, the cross-price elasticity is negative for complements. In the nonprofit sector, preventive health care and social-work counseling services, or music education and music performances, are probably complements. Nonprofit and social enterprise managers would also like to know about the extent of complementarity revealed by the cross-price elasticity of demand, because when an organization raises the price of one of its products, it will reduce sales not only for that product but also for any complementary products it markets. Even if demand is price-inelastic, so that the increase in price adds to the total revenues from sales of the first product, the total of revenues from both products would go down if the cross-price elasticity were sufficiently negative. On the other hand, when another organization lowers the price of a complementary good, the cross-price elasticity helps to predict the size of the increase in revenues to your organization.

Finally, a relationship of independence characterizes most pairs of goods and services – charitable donations and pencils, cheese and trips to Tahiti, Beatles posters and health-care services. The cross-price elasticity of demand is zero for these pairs of goods. It is harder to guess what the relationship between some other products of interest to nonprofit managers and social entrepreneurs is, and so empirical study is needed. For example, it is still an open question as to whether volunteering and giving to charity are complements, substitutes, or independent activities. There is some evidence that the two are complements, so that the easier one makes it for people to volunteer (the lower the price of volunteering) the more they will give to charity (e.g., Hodgkinson and Weitzman, 1992; Hartmann and Werding, 2012). Other studies (e.g., Andreoni et al. 1996; Feldman, 2010) find evidence that the two are substitutes. If the government were to raise the after-tax price of gifts of money (as it did in the 1986 Tax Reform Act by cutting marginal tax rates, reducing the number of taxpayers who itemize, and eliminating the charitable deduction for non-itemizers; or the 2017 federal tax legislation that also cut marginal tax rates and reduced the number of itemizers), this would not only reduce gifts of money but also gifts of time, if the two are complements. Obviously, this is a matter of importance to nonprofits and one where improved information may be quite helpful.

Figure 7.6 Elasticity of supply

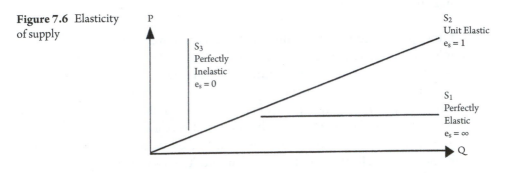

The price elasticity of supply is generally positive. Again, we can distinguish between elastic and inelastic cases:

- If $\varepsilon_p^S < 1$ then supply is price inelastic;
- If $\varepsilon_p^S > 1$ then supply is price elastic.

Figure 7.6 illustrates three supply functions with different elasticity characteristics. Again, these are all special cases where the price elasticity of supply is the same at all points on the curve. In general, however, as with price elasticity of demand, elasticity will vary along the supply function. The horizontal function S_1 in Figure 7.6 illustrates the case of a perfectly price-elastic supply curve. We can imagine this function to be rising to the right, but ever so slowly. Thus, any increase in price (P) will lead to a very large increase in the quantity supplied (Q^S). The opposite case is S_3, where supply is perfectly price-inelastic. Here we can imagine the curve leaning ever so slightly to the right as it rises. Thus, an increase in price will lead to only a miniscule increase in the quantity supplied. Or we can use the limit arguments we made for the price elasticity of demand. Finally, supply curve S_2 is unit-elastic between any pair of points on the curve. Since S_2 is a straight line through the origin (0,0), any change in price will be met with a proportional change in quantity supplied. (In fact, any supply function that is a straight line through the origin will have an elasticity value of 1, no matter how steep or shallow it is.) And, regardless of the shape of the supply curve, if two supply curves intersect at any point other than the origin, we can conclude that the flatter curve will be more elastic at the point of intersection.

As with demand elasticity, the time frame is an important factor that influences the price elasticity of supply. If an industry depends on certain resources that are difficult to adjust quickly, such as large physical plants, highly sophisticated equipment, or a highly-trained labor force, then it will have difficulty responding vigorously to price changes in the short run and supply is less elastic. However, if the price change is expected to endure for a long time, the industry will be able to adjust by investing (or disinvesting) in plant and equipment, training (or phasing out) sophisticated workers, and entry (or exit) of organizations, and supply is more elastic. If the industry faces an absolute constraint on expansion (due to a strictly limited supply of some resource needed in production or restrictions imposed by government), even the long-run supply curve will be inelastic.

In the nonprofit sector, the supply of services such as heart surgery, graduate-level higher education, or top-quality orchestral performances, are constrained by the available supply of appropriately trained professional people and the capacity of appropriate physical plants. In the short run, say one year, therefore, the supply of such services is inelastic. In the long run, say ten years, medical schools, academic departments, and experienced musicians can be expanded and supply is more elastic.

In economics for the business sector, we rarely use the concept of the income elasticity of supply, for the stockholders who own a for-profit firm would seek a profit-maximizing level of production. This depends on marginal revenue and marginal cost, not on the level of retained earnings, the amount of profits received, or capital gains in the firm's investment accounts. In contrast, maximizing an objective based on a charitable or social mission is often mathematically identical to a consumer choosing what to buy, and for both, income affects the optimal choice. Income matters because it determines what can be spent on advancing the mission. Publicly-held corporations are more tightly constrained to maximize their profits (because of the threat that straying managers face from profit-motivated takeover bids) but there is a little more room for other objectives to play a role in privately-held corporations, partnerships, and proprietorships. This is true because the number of owners in these forms of for-profit organizations is small, making it more likely that they can stand firm against takeover bids. The same clearly holds for new forms of "social business" such as low-profit, limited-liability companies (LC3s), benefit corporations, and other new hybrid forms used by social entrepreneurs (see Young, Searing, and Brewer, 2016). Nonprofit organizations are immune from takeover bids because nondistribution of profits make them wholly unattractive to buyers. So, they can pursue their missions provided they break-even in the long run. In any case, the nondistribution of profits constraint opens the door for the pursuit of missions that do not involve the maximization of distributable profits. For example, when a symphony orchestra has low income, it might need to perform mostly familiar works by Beethoven and Mozart. If that same symphony were to receive a grant, it may choose to supply more contemporary and experimental musical programs at any given ticket price (Rose-Ackerman, 1987). Thus, familiar works would be inferior goods, having a negative income elasticity of supply, and contemporary works would be normal, having a positive income elasticity of supply.

One minor detail is worth commenting upon. The income elasticity of supply is defined in terms of "owner" income. Although the directors or trustees of a nonprofit organization are essentially the legal "owners," they do not have full ownership rights to the income of the organization. Full ownership allows owners to direct the use of the resources owned, receive any profits generated by those resources, and transfer ownership to others who are willing and able to pay for it. Nonprofits cannot distribute profits or transfer ownership rights for financial gain, so ownership of nonprofit firms by their boards is a muted one. In this situation, it is best to think of owner income as the income the controllers of the organization have the right to allocate, presumably in support of mission. Hence, any income received by the organization counts in this category.

7.8   Perfect competition in the long run

The analysis presented above examines perfect competition in the short run, when at least one factor of production is fixed. We now look at this market structure in the long run, when all inputs, as well as the number of firms in a market, are variable. As a market enters the long run, four changes occur: fixed costs become variable costs; fixed revenues become variable revenues; the size of physical facilities (and the amount of other fixed factors of production) change; and the number of supplier organizations changes.

The first two changes have already been addressed in Chapter 4. An organization should shut down in the long run if its long-run average variable cost exceeds its long-run average variable revenue. With no fixed costs, long-run average variable costs are synonymous with long-run average total costs. With no fixed revenues, long-run average revenues include both revenues from sales and donations. The shut down rule in the long run makes eminent sense – shut down if you cannot at least break-even, but it is better to call shutting down for the long run "exit" because no fixed assets will remain.

We postpone for a moment, discussion of the third source of change – facility size. We first need to say more about the impact of entry and exit on long-run equilibrium. If there are sufficient barriers to entry and exit, the number of firms is fixed in the long run. But, if there is free entry and exit, we have the following paradoxical result:

> *Economic profits are zero in long-run competitive equilibrium with free entry and exit.*

Why would anyone, especially a for-profit firm, remain in business if it expected to receive zero profits? The key is that we are talking about *economic profits*, which count the value of all foregone activities and investments as costs. To say that profits are zero is to say that there is no other economic opportunity offering a greater return. Any time profits in an industry are positive, it means a new entrant could do better in this industry than it could do anywhere else. Any time profits are negative, entrepreneurs could profit by switching to another line of business. Thus, the conclusion that long-run profits are zero with entry and exit follows directly from our definition of profits. For example, if the interest rate paid on savings is higher than the expected return from investing those savings in a business enterprise, then the economic profit earned on that business enterprise is negative. If the two values are equal, then profit is zero. It is only if expected return from investing in an enterprise is greater than that of any other option, such as putting that money in a bank, that economic profit is positive.

We are now ready to illustrate how a market adjusts from one long-run equilibrium to another. Suppose, as in Figure 7.7, the day-care market is perfectly competitive and in long-run equilibrium, where the typical organization produces q_0 at price P_0 (left-hand side of the diagram). In turn, the price P_0 is determined by the intersection of market supply and demand curves (right-hand side of the diagram) and the market equilibrium quantity Q_0 results. Because we have supposed that this is a long-run equilibrium, we know that profits are zero, so P_0 must equal the AC at firm equilibrium quantity q_0. Prices and quantities will remain at these equilibrium values until one of the curves moves.

Now suppose that a sudden in-migration of families with young children increases the demand for day-care services to D_1. In the short run, this will increase the equilibrium price to P_1. Why? Because at the initial price with the new demand curve, we have a shortage that bids the price up. This price increase will increase the firm and market quantities to q_1 and Q_1, respectively. The typical supplier earns positive economic profits, because the new price is greater than average total cost at the new quantity.

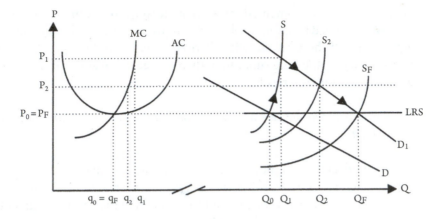

Figure 7.7 Market adjustments to new long-run equilibrium

As we move towards the long run, these positive profits will attract new entrants to the day-care industry. At the same time, some incumbent suppliers may wish to adjust their facility sizes. In order to keep things simple, assume that there is only one facility size available, so that long-run and short-run costs curves are identical. Then, the increase in the number of firms moves the market supply curve to the right to position S_2. Why? Because at any given price, 101 identical suppliers will produce a greater total quantity than would 100 firms. The horizontal summation moves to the right as we increase the number of organizations over which we sum. With the new supply curve, the equilibrium price falls to P_2, each supplier reduces its production to q_2, but the increase in number of organizations dominates the reduction in production at each organization so that the market equilibrium quantity increases to Q_2. As illustrated, profits, although smaller, are still positive so that entry of new suppliers would continue, and the supply curve would continue to creep to the right.

When will this process end? It will end when profits are once again zero, but what price and quantity does this lead to? The answer depends upon whether the entry of new suppliers causes a change in the cost functions of existing suppliers. The simplest, and most common assumption is that the cost functions are unaffected by entry. We have been implicitly assuming this by not changing the location of the curves on the left half of Figure 7.7 as the market supply curve moved to the right. Under this assumption, the long-run equilibrium price with the new demand curve is the same as that with the old demand curve (P_0), and each supplier produces the same quantity (q_0) as well. However, market quantity goes up to Q_F. Connecting the intersections, we derive the long-run supply curve, which illustrates the quantities willingly supplied in the long-run when the number of suppliers can adjust. Here, the long-run supply curve is horizontal.

An alternative possibility is that the increase in the number of suppliers raises the price of production for all suppliers. This could occur if one essential input were scarce (for instance, well-adjusted adults who are good at nurturing other people's children), so that expansion of the industry would drive up the wages of day-care workers. This would result in an upward-sloping long-run supply curve, although it would still be flatter than the short-run supply. An increase in demand would cause a small increase in the long-run price.

Another possibility is that an increase in the number of suppliers would lower the costs of production. This could occur if there were sufficient economies of scale in supplying a crucial input. For example, it is quite expensive to produce solar power cells on a small scale, so that if the solar electric-generating industry contained only a few firms, each would have to pay a high price for raw materials. If the number of firms increased, it would be possible to use more efficient assembly-line techniques for production of power cells, lowering their price and making solar generation of power possible at lower cost. In the nonprofit world, a similar situation may occur with ticket sales services for arts organizations. Automated ticket purchasing systems are expensive but become more efficient as volume increases. If more arts organizations enter the market, demand for this service will increase and costs will decline. In these cases, the long-run supply curve is downward-sloping even though the short-run supply curves are upward sloping. This is the only case where an increase in demand would cause a decrease in the long-run price.

This discussion of long-run competition points to the importance of profits in the performance of competitive industries, even those involving nonprofit organizations and social enterprises. We can conclude that:

> *When there is free entry, profits are a temporary phenomenon. Profits signal that demand has increased in a particular market and will attract the added resources necessary to meet the increase in demand.*

Thus, even for nonprofits and social enterprises, profit can serve the function of helping markets adjust to new levels of demand. Conversely, we can also see the importance of economic losses in helping markets adjust to reduced demand in the long run. For an industry that starts in long-run equilibrium but then experiences a permanent decrease in demand, losses signal that resources should move away from that industry towards more highly-valued uses. In the example illustrated in Figure 7.7, the exit of suppliers will then raise the price back to its initial level. (As an exercise, the reader should trace the path of adjustment in Figure 7.7, from Q_F to Q_0, assuming demand drops from D_1 to D.)

SUMMARY

In isolation, it is not hard to figure out how a given for-profit firm, social enterprise or nonprofit organization should decide on a price and quantity to produce for any set of goals it might want to pursue. However, organizations operate in markets in which competition restricts their market options to a smaller set of "survivable behaviors" that may or may not support their objectives. In the present chapter, we analyzed the limiting case of perfect competition wherein all organizations are price takers. This analysis highlighted several concepts crucial to the understanding of competitive markets, including market equilibrium, comparative statics, long run and short run, and the construct of elasticity. In the next chapter we consider situations of monopoly and oligopoly, in which producers have market power and can influence the prices at which their services are sold, as well as the quantities they produce to achieve their goals.

The analysis offered in this chapter demonstrates that competition can have important benefits for society. Competition can force even malevolent organizations to contribute to society or go out of business. Notably, competition keeps suppliers from charging exorbitant prices for shabby services. However, competition can also destroy the ability of nonprofit organizations or other social enterprises to provide unique social benefits. For example, a day-care center wishing to extend its services to all unserved preschoolers in its vicinity will find itself losing money unless it has alternative sources of funds. Indeed, nonprofit organizations and other social enterprises must remain aware of their competitive environments – including actual and potential competitors – in all the markets they participate in, not just the market for sales of goods and services but the markets for inputs, donations, volunteers, and grants.

SELECTED REFERENCES AND CITATIONS

Andreoni, J., Gale, W.G., Scholz, J.K., and Straub, J. (1996). Charitable Contributions of Time and Money. *University of Wisconsin–Madison Working Paper.*

Eaton, S.C. (2000). Beyond "Unloving Care": Linking Human Resource Management and Patient Care Quality in Nursing Homes. *International Journal of Human Resource Management, 11(3),* 591–616.

Feldman, N.E. (2010). Time is Money: Choosing between Charitable Activities. *American Economic Journal: Economic Policy, 2(1),* 103–130.

Hartmann, B. and Werding, M. (2012). Donating Time or Money: Are they Substitutes or Complements? *CESifo Working Paper*: Behavioural Economics, No. 3835. Munich: Center for Economic Studies and Ifo Institute.

Hodgkinson, V.A. and Weitzman, M.S. (1992). *Giving and Volunteering in the United States*. Washington, DC: Independent Sector.

Rose-Ackerman, S. (1987). Ideals Versus Dollars: Donors, Charity Managers, and Government Grants. *Journal of Political Economy*, 95(4), 810–823.

Steinberg, R. (1993). Public Policy and the Performance of Nonprofit Organizations: A General Framework. *Nonprofit and Voluntary Sector Quarterly*, 22(1), 13–32.

Steinberg, R. (2015). What Should Social Finance Invest In and With Whom?, in Nicholls, A., Paton, R., and Emerson, J. (Eds.) *Social Finance* (pp. 64–95). Oxford: Oxford University Press.

Vladeck, B.C. (1980). *Unloving Care*. New York: Basic Books.

Young, D.R., Searing, E.A.M., and Brewer, C.V. (Eds.) (2016). *The Social Enterprise Zoo*. Cheltenham, UK and Northampton, MA: Edward Elgar Publishing.

REVIEW CONCEPTS

Comparative Statics: Analysis of changes in equilibrium outcomes when the underlying determinants of supply and demand change, without consideration of the adjustment paths over time.

Complements: Products used together, so that when use of one product falls due to a price increase, use of the other product also falls. Complements have a negative cross-price elasticity of demand.

Contestable Market: A market with zero costs of entry and exit, so that even if there is only one organization supplying the market, that organization must behave as if it had many competitors.

Cross Price Elasticity of Demand: The percentage change in the quantity demanded of one good divided by the percentage change in the price of a different good.

Economic Profit: The difference between the total revenue received by the firm from its sales and the total opportunity costs of all the resources used by the firm.

Elastic Demand: When the absolute value of the price elasticity of demand is greater than 1. This implies that a given percentage price change will cause a larger percentage change in quantity demanded. The concept also applies to other demand elasticities, e.g., demand is income elastic when a given percentage change in income causes a larger percentage change in quantity demanded.

Elasticity: A way of calculating how responsive one variable (the effect) is to a change in another variable (the cause) based on a ratio of percentage changes.

Equilibrium: The outcome of a market situation that is predicted to occur by economic theory. A balancing of forces, such that no individual or organization wants to change its behavior given the behavior of others in the economy.

Fixed Revenue: Revenue available to an organization that is independent of the level of production, like investment returns, royalties, rents received, and at least a portion of donations and grants.

Free Entry and Exit: Free entry is a circumstance where, if a new organization enters a market, it will have the same cost curves as other organizations in the market. Free exit is a circumstance where organizations do not pay a cost to leave the market.

Horizontal Sum of Curves: A way of adding curves (graphed functions), rather than numbers, that involves adding the x-coordinates of each curve for each y-coordinate. Market demand is the horizontal sum of individual demand curves, meaning at each price, we add the quantities that each individual wants to buy and plot that sum against the price.

Income Elasticity of Demand (Supply): Measures responsiveness of quantity demanded (quantity supplied) to changes in income, holding constant the effect of all other determinants of quantity demanded (supplied).

Inelastic Demand: When the various elasticities of demand are between 0 and 1 in absolute value. Demand is price inelastic when the absolute value of elasticity is in this range, and income inelastic when the income elasticity is in this range. When demand is price inelastic, a given percentage change in price causes a smaller percentage change in quantity demanded.

Inferior Good: A good or service with a negative income elasticity of demand, which means when income goes up and all other determinants of demand are held constant, the quantity demanded goes down.

Long Run: The long run occurs when enough time passes that all factors of production can be varied. Organizations can adjust plant capacities, train and engage more labor, replace old machines, purchase new equipment, and so on. New organizations can enter the market in the long run.

Luxury: A normal good that is income elastic, so that a given percentage increase in consumer income causes a larger percentage change in quantity demanded.

Necessity: A normal good that is income inelastic so that a given percentage increase in consumer income causes a smaller percentage change in quantity demanded.

Normal Good: A good or service with a positive income elasticity of demand, so that when consumer income goes up and all other determinants of demand are held constant, the quantity demanded increases.

Perfect Competition: An idealized market in which there are many buyers and sellers of a homogeneous good or service, no single buyer or seller controls a noticeable share of the market, and all buyers and firms are fully informed about the prices of each and every firm. Some markets come close to this ideal and are analyzed as if all buyers and sellers are price-takers.

Price Elasticity of Demand: Responsiveness of the quantity demanded to a change in the price of the product, holding constant the values of all other determinants of demand. Computed as the percentage change in the quantity demanded divided by the percentage change in its price.

Price Elasticity of Supply: Responsiveness of the quantity supplied to a change in the price of the good, holding constant the values of all determinants of supply. Computed as the percentage change in the quantity supplied divided by the percentage change in price.

Price Taker: An individual or organization who believes their own actions cannot influence the price of its product. Price takers view the market price and decide how much to buy or sell at that price.

Short Run: A time period in which there is at least one fixed factor of production. Usually, in simplified economic models, we assume that labor is variable, but capital is fixed in the short run.

Substitutes: Products that can be substituted for other products, so that when the quantity demanded of one good falls due to a price increase, buyers will switch away from the other good and demand for the substitute product will fall. Substitutes have a positive cross-price elasticity of demand.

Supply Curve: A graphic illustration of the quantity offered for sale at each possible price, holding other determinants of this quantity constant.

Unitary Elasticity: When elasticity (of any kind) is equal to 1. When the price elasticity of demand is unitary, a given percentage increase or decrease in price causes an equal and opposite percentage change in quantity demanded, so that total revenue remains constant.

Variable Revenue: Revenue available to an organization that depends on the level of production. Sales revenue is variable, and sometimes a portion of donations and grants is also variable.

EXERCISES

1. Think of the process of charitable giving as a market in which nonprofit organizations compete for the funds offered by donors. In particular, nonprofits supply satisfactions to donors in exchange for financial contributions. If Q is the supply of donor satisfactions (tangible expressions of recognition, services provided for which the donor can claim credit, etc.):

   (a) Draw a typical organization's supply curve for these satisfactions, using Figure 7.1 as a model.
   (b) What assumption(s) did you make about the objective function for nonprofit organizations in this situation? Are they reasonable for real-world nonprofit organizations?
   (c) Add the short-run market supply curve for these satisfactions to your graph from part (a), using Figure 7.1 as a model. Make the assumption that there is no "commons externality" (Chapter 13) in the short run. That is, an increase in fund-raising by one nonprofit can make it more expensive for competing organizations to succeed in their fund-raising. Charities fishing in the same donor pool and getting in each other's way is the essence of the commons externality. Please ignore that effect here.
   (d) If, instead, there is free entry and exit for nonprofit organizations and the commons externality is important in this donor market, what would the long-run market supply curve look like? Upward-sloping, horizontal, or downward-sloping, and why?

2. If the market for donations is perfectly competitive, with free entry and exit,

   (a) How will this affect the ability of individual nonprofits to raise funds in the long run?
   (b) How does your reasoning in this case help us to understand the justification for united fund-raising organizations like United Way?
   (c) Can you use the set of categories for market structures (perfect competition, monopoly, and oligopoly) to accurately describe this market? If so, how would you classify this market. If not, why?
   (d) Compare the likely long-run net proceeds from fund-raising with and without a united fund-raising organization. In your answer, consider the difference between what would happen if all nonprofits (including those that might enter the market later) must conduct their fund-raising through the combined campaign and what would happen if some nonprofits choose not to join the combined campaign.

3. There are several dozen nonprofit and for-profit theaters in the entertainment district of the city of Thespian that offer serious dramatic performances. However, ever since Computers, Inc. closed its nearby facility and many citizens moved away, these theaters have all run annual deficits. In this market, how are the strategies and objectives of nonprofits likely to differ from those of the for-profit theaters? In the long run, what are the likely ways for this market to adjust, in terms of the number of theaters, how much they produce, what they will charge, and how well they do in terms of profit or loss? Use a graph such as that in Figure 7.7 to illustrate your reasoning.

4. *Beans for Economic Justice* (BEJ) is a social enterprise that sells fair-traded coffee in its café, in a market where demand is $Q^D = 3 - P$. Calculate the price elasticity of demand at each of the following price points (think of these prices as the average price for two bracketing adjacent values on the demand curve). At each point, explain whether total revenue increases, decreases or remains the same as BEJ increases or decreases the price of a cup of coffee near the starting price:

   (a) $P = \$2$
   (b) $P = \$1.50$
   (c) $P = \$1$

5. In each instance below calculate the relevant elasticity. Explain what the calculated value means, and why the sign makes sense in this context.

   (a) Income elasticity of demand, if $Q^D = Y + 10$, between two points with average income of $2.
   (b) Cross-price elasticity of demand, if $Q_a^D = 100 - P_a + 2P_b$, between two points where the average quantity of good a that is demanded is 115, the average price of good b is $10, and the price of good a is held constant at $5.
   (c) Cross-price elasticity of demand, if $Q_a^D = 100 - P_a - P_b$, between two points where the average quantity of good a that is demanded is 85, the average price of good b is $10, and the price of good a is held constant at $5.
   (d) Elasticity of supply, if $Q^S = P + 4$, between two points with an average price of $2.
   (e) Income elasticity of supply, if $Q^S = Y + 10$, between two points with an average income of $2 million. Explain what Y means in the context of nonprofit and social enterprise organizations.

6. For each of the following nonprofit services, discuss whether demand is likely to be price-elastic or price-inelastic at various levels of output:

   (a) Shelter care for the homeless.
   (b) Emergency medical clinics.
   (c) Girl Scout cookies.
   (d) Opera performances.
   (e) Meals on Wheels programs.

   How would your assessment in each case influence how the producing nonprofit should price these services?

8

Market power

I think we need to find a new market niche. Maybe the Shorties League where we'll have more market power!

8.1   Introduction

The structure of markets can vary from the most highly decentralized perfect competition (many buyers and many sellers, as considered in Chapter 7) to the most concentrated forms of *monopoly* (only one seller), *monopsony* (only one buyer) or *bilateral monopoly* (one buyer and one seller). Monopoly and monopsony are the extreme cases of *market power* that we consider in this chapter. In addition, on the supply side of the market, between monopoly and perfect competition, we consider a variety of *imperfectly competitive* types of markets. When there are two suppliers, we have a *duopoly*. Three suppliers make a *triopoly*, and any small number of suppliers greater than one constitutes an *oligopoly*. We understand far less about how oligopolies behave than we do about perfectly competitive markets or monopolies because oligopolists can adopt a wide variety of different strategies and counterstrategies. For example, a duopolist can raise prices above those of its competitor, but if the competitor does not match the price increase, it could lose all its customers. However, if both competitors raise prices together, they might each prosper. Thus, oligopolists may behave like perfect competitors, or like monopolists, or in a more complicated and fluid fashion than either of these, as discussed below.

Another intermediate case is *monopolistic competition*, in which each producer has a monopoly on its particular version of a common product (such as a brand of toothpaste), but producers with new versions of the product can enter freely. New versions of the product or service differ from the older versions in real or perceived quality, style, convenience of selling location and hours, or indeed association with charitable causes. For example, in the financial industry, one credit card seems just like another, but corporations differentiate their cards in terms of service quality (e.g., how widely the card is accepted, rewards programs, how easily complaints are serviced) as well as how usage benefits charitable causes through cause-related marketing arrangements such as money paid to a designated charity for each purchase transaction. In higher education, many colleges and universities also offer similar services, but each provides a different combination, style and quality of coursework, and colleges differ in the extent to which they help low income students or emphasize community service. The same may be said of hospitals.

Monopolistic competitors can raise their prices a bit without losing all their customers because they each produce a unique version of the product. Nonetheless, they cannot raise their prices too much to secure very high profits, because at some point people will switch to substitute versions of the product. Regardless, the free entry of new firms for each version of the product means that long-run profits are zero. Any market like this, where there is free entry and exit of firms, is called a *contestable* market.[1]

Market structures are also defined for cases where the number of buyers is limited. A single buyer, as noted above, constitutes a monopsony, and a situation with only a few buyers is known as an *oligopsony*. When a single buyer confronts a single seller, we have *bilateral monopoly*. For example, when the government purchases social services by inviting competitive bids, there is one buyer (the government) and many sellers (bidding nonprofit or for-profit firms) so the market is *monopsonistic*. But when there is only one potential bidder for a government contract, we have a bilateral monopoly. Monopsony can also arise in input markets such as labor services – one cannot be employed as a Catholic priest unless one has been ordained and therefore indirectly works for a branch of the Vatican. Here, the Catholic Church is effectively a monopsonist in the market for Catholic clergy. Likewise, if there is only one hospital in a town, then it will act like a monopsonist in the hiring of certain specialized medical personnel, such as radiological technicians, who cannot relocate for family or other reasons.

As we discuss below, just as monopoly gives the seller control over price, monopsony gives control over prices (which are, in this case, wages and other contract conditions) to the buyer. This usually leads to fewer workers being employed at lower wages than would be found under perfect competition (with a notable exception seen when there is a minimum wage in a labor market in which a monopsony operates; see Chapter 9). There are no clear-cut predictions for the outcome of negotiations under bilateral monopoly, for, as in the case of a duopoly, a variety of patterns of strategic interaction is possible. Similarly, game theory is needed for bilateral monopsony, where a single employer negotiates with a labor union that "sells" all the labor employed there. The methods of game theory discussed in Chapter 11 apply here (see also, e.g., Brams, 2003 for more on bargaining games).

While these examples outline different types of markets, defined by the number of firms in each market, it is also possible for markets to differ in the mix of types of supplier organizations. A *mixed-sector duopoly* consists of one for-profit and one nonprofit firm selling the same product, as when a for-profit and a nonprofit private school compete for students in the same community. We could also have nonprofit duopolies (two nonprofit firms, such as two nonprofit day-care centers in a given town), for-profit duopolies (two for-profit firms, such as two for-profit auto dealers within an hour's drive), mixed-sector monopolistic competition (a variety of for-profit and nonprofit firms each occupying a different niche, as is often the case with higher education or health care), and any other sectoral combinations one could imagine. Finally, we can have various structures of collaboration that alter the competitive nature of a market. For example, under united fund-raising arrangements, such as United Way, members agencies refrain from competitive solicitation efforts but otherwise compete in service markets; with public–private partnerships, separately incorporated for-profits, nonprofits, and government agencies share decision making and risks for specified projects or programs; in mixed-sector joint ventures, such as university collaborations with for-profit medical-technology and pharmaceutical companies, suppliers who might otherwise compete work together to develop new products and services; and so on. While economic theory is not as well-developed for some of these possibilities, the basic principles of analyzing markets where participants have significant market power will nonetheless help nonprofit managers and social entrepreneurs gain important insights.

8.2   Monopoly

When there is only one firm producing a good, that firm will no longer be a price taker. A monopoly may consider operating at any point along the entire demand curve, that is, it can choose a combination of price and quantity from among all combinations that consumers are willing to consider. Accordingly, it will select the optimal point which, for a conventional for-profit firm at least, would be where profits are maximized. Analysis at the margin tells us where that point will be.

Monopoly pricing depends on the nature of the good or service being sold and the circumstances under which it is sold. We will consider two polar opposite cases: A "single-price monopoly" sells all units of its output to all buyers at the same price. At the other extreme, a "perfectly price-discriminating monopoly" chooses a different price for each unit sold to each person. In this chapter, we consider single-price monopolies; in Chapter 9 we cover the perfectly price-discriminating monopoly. In between these two poles are many kinds of *price discrimination* such as charging a different single price to different groups of buyers, sliding-scale fees, free distribution with eligibility requirements, admission and usage fees, and quantity discounts. These are beyond the scope of this book but see Steinberg and Weisbrod (1998) and Seaman (2018) for more on price-discrimination by nonprofit organizations.

We saw that in the case of perfect competition, firms produce the level of output at which marginal cost (MC) equals the selling price (P) given by the market, provided that this price is higher than the minimum of the average variable cost curve (AVC). For price-taking firms, price, average revenue (total revenue divided by Q), and marginal revenue (extra revenue if an additional unit is sold) are all the same horizontal line, so we can equivalently state that the competitive firm's equilibrium Q is where $MC(Q) = MR(Q)$. Profit-maximizing monopolies also follow this rule, setting marginal revenue equal to marginal cost. However, the calculation of marginal revenue is different for a monopoly.

Single-price monopolies must lower the price to sell an additional unit because the demand curve is downward-sloping. Thus, marginal revenue is no longer a constant price determined by the interaction of supply and demand.

Figure 8.1 Monopoly

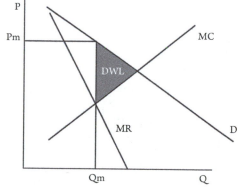

Instead, marginal revenue is a function of Q involving two parts. The first part is the extra revenue from selling the last unit, which is the price on the demand curve. The second part is a reduction in revenue from selling all the previous units, because each of these receives a lower price (see Chapter 4). This second term means that marginal revenue at each Q is lower than the price on the demand curve by an amount that increases with the number of previous units sold (Figure 8.1). For example, if a firm lowers its price from $11 to $10 and, as a result increases its sales from 1000 units to 1500 units, it receives added revenue of $5000 from the additional 500 units sold and reduced revenue of $1000 from the first 1000 units sold, for a net gain of $4000.

In summary, as for the perfectly competitive firm, the profit-maximizing monopoly will choose to operate at the quantity that makes $MR(Q) = MC(Q)$, where the parentheses indicate that both are functions of Q rather than multiplication by Q. Figure 8.1 illustrates the relevant curves and the profit-maximizing price and quantity. Importantly, the price it chooses, P_m, is on the demand curve above that intersection, the highest price at which the chosen quantity can be sold.

At this point, we have discussed how a monopoly can maximize its profits, but sometimes social enterprises and nonprofits have a different goal in mind. The logic of thinking at the margin can be extended to other objectives (Chapter 4 touched upon this), but sometimes social organizations maximize the profits from some activities in order to spend those profits advancing other, mission-related, activities. In this case, the profit-maximizing monopoly model applies directly.

How does this compare with the perfectly competitive output and price? In Chapter 7 we showed that the supply curve is the horizontal sum of firm marginal cost functions above AVC. If the curve labeled MC in Figure 8.1 were

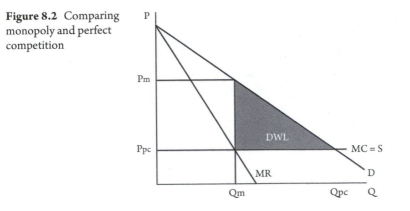

Figure 8.2 Comparing monopoly and perfect competition

such a horizontal sum as well as being the only MC curve for a monopoly, we could make the comparison directly, but justifying these assumptions is unnecessarily complicated. Instead, we shall consider long-run marginal cost curves that are identical and horizontal for each firm in perfect competition. Then the horizontal sum of infinitely long horizontal lines at the same height is that same infinitely long horizontal line. This line can do double duty as the supply curve (were the market perfectly competitive) and the MC curve for a monopoly (Figure 8.2). Assuming constant costs is the natural thing to do for this comparison, because if there were economies of scale, competitive firms would be outcompeted by larger competitive firms until a single firm was left. This is called a *natural monopoly*, and it is illogical to compare a natural monopoly with un-natural competition. If, instead, there were diseconomies of scale, the monopoly would be outcompeted by competitive firms that have lower costs. So, the only sensible comparison in the long run is between perfect competition and monopoly under the condition of constant costs.

Figure 8.2 makes it clear that the total quantity produced is larger under perfect competition and the price is lower, compared with monopoly. But there is also a reduction in *allocative efficiency* – a *deadweight loss* (DWL) – caused by organizing this market as a monopoly. To see this, consider the value of producing an additional unit, starting at the quantity Q_m. This produces a benefit to the buyer and a benefit to the seller whenever that unit is sold for any price between P_m and P_{pc} because the buyer gets the good for less than she is willing to pay, and the seller sells the good for more than it cost to make. That unit would be produced and sold under perfect competition, but not under monopoly because the seller would have to drop the price for the last unit and also lower the price for all the earlier units. Adding up these "foregone mutual gains to trade" for all the units between Q_m and Q_{pc}

produces the shaded area, which is a dollar measure of the lost allocative efficiency due to monopoly.

Single-price monopolies create a form of "market failure," a general term for any situation in which market equilibrium is not socially efficient (other sources of market failure are discussed in Chapter 13). This is why public policies like antitrust laws generally try to eliminate monopolies where feasible. U.S. antitrust law ignores the nonprofit/for-profit distinction, but combinations in restraint of trade do not always produce deadweight losses for social organizations that do not seek to maximize their profits. The case of monopolistic nonprofits is more complex because nonprofits may use their financial surpluses for social purposes such as subsidizing loss-making, but socially beneficial, activities. Monopoly finance of these activities creates a deadweight loss, but the gain in efficiency due to these socially beneficial activities can outweigh the deadweight loss created by monopoly finance.

8.3 Monopsony

A *monopsony* arises when there is only one buyer of a good or service for which there may be many sellers. Monopsony may occur in various markets, such as that for professional-grade athletic equipment where there are many producers but only one professional sports league, or in the market of new apps for iPhones that require Apple approval. Most commonly, however, monopsony occurs in labor markets where there is only one employer for certain skill types. This holds often in the nonprofit sector, such as when there is only one hospital in an area that employs people with very specialized medical skills, or when there is only one institute of higher education that hires instructors with certain advanced degrees. In these various cases, the market no longer clears at an equilibrium price that equates marginal benefit to marginal cost. Rather, as in the case of the monopoly, a monopsony exhibits market power.

Before discussing any examples of monopsonistic labor markets, we need to discuss the nature of labor markets, where, in a sense, the roles of organizations and individual people as buyers and sellers are reversed. Individual people, who buy many products, will sell their labor (or more accurately, collect rent for use of their time by the employer). In a competitive labor market, there is a supply of labor curve that represents the willingness of workers to rent out their time to an employer at each possible wage rate. This is an oversimplification, because real workers have complicated compensation packages – salaries that are independent of hours worked, taxes, bonuses, benefits, and advancement opportunities. The full compensation package cannot be easily summarized by a single "wage" number, but the full compensation package determines labor supply. For our purposes, we can safely ignore such complications but interested readers should consider a course in labor economics and/or human resource management (with a textbook like Ehrenberg and Smith, 2018) to learn how to incorporate these factors into formal analysis.

Firms, nonprofit organizations, and social enterprises are sellers of many products but are buyers (renters) of labor. Hence, the labor demand curve comes from the desired hiring by organizations and shows the number of worker hours that employers would like to hire at each possible wage rate. Again, there are many simplifications built into this economic model. For example, firms care both about the number of workers and the number of hours that each worker spends on the job, but in our simplified model it is just total hours that matter. That is, the firm is indifferent between having one worker working eight hours a day or two workers working four hours or eight workers working one hour. Also, firms care about the entire compensation package, not a single summary measure like the wage rate. For our purposes here, those are unnecessary complications. But we note that unlike the market for coffee (where all the suppliers offer the same product for sale), the market for various kinds of labor includes sellers of many products. For-profit car dealerships and nonprofit theater companies both demand accountants, so both are part of the labor market for accountants. What is the same across sellers and buyers is the type of labor. Skilled workers and unskilled workers are in two different labor markets, a factor behind growing inequality of income in recent years.

Competitive equilibrium in this "factor market" occurs at the wage rate that "clears" the market – the wage that makes the number of hours offered by workers equal to the number of hours desired by employers. Excess demand for workers causes market wages to rise and excess supply causes market wages to fall until that excess is eliminated. Every buyer and seller of labor takes the wage rate as given, determined by market forces rather than anything they control. There is no "wage discrimination," i.e., a single wage rate for identical workers in comparable settings prevails. Workers do not have to work more than they want to and there is no special pay for overtime. There is no unemployment in our simplified model of labor markets, in contrast to the real world. The contrast between this simple model and the real world is the subject of macroeconomics, but we can learn a lot by comparing a competitive labor market equilibrium with a monopsony labor market equilibrium, and that is what we do here.

Figure 8.3
Monopsony in the
labor market

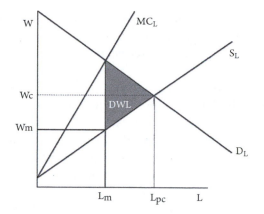

In single-price monopoly, the monopolist chooses a price/quantity combination from the market demand curve. This causes the marginal revenue function to fall more and more below the price as the quantity of output increases. In monopsonistic labor markets, the single employer chooses a wage/hours combination from the market labor supply curve, which, as we shall see, causes the firm's marginal cost of adding a labor hour to exceed the wage rate, with a consequent deadweight loss.

For example, suppose that an art museum is the only organization in a city that hires skilled workers who can restore paintings, and that these workers are unwilling to move to another city with an art museum when market power is utilized to their disadvantage. Were this market perfectly competitive, the museum could hire as many labor hours as it wanted at the same prevailing market wage rate, but as a monopsony facing an upward-sloping labor supply curve, it recognizes that to acquire more labor, it must increase the wage rate. This situation is illustrated in Figure 8.3.

In more detail, when the monopsonist contemplates hiring an extra hour of labor, this employer must pay all workers a higher wage than previously. This means that the marginal cost to a monopsony of hiring another worker[2] (MC_L) is greater than the wage represented on the market supply curve (S_L), much as the marginal revenue from selling another unit of a good is lower than the price seen on the demand curve for a product sold by a monopoly. Like marginal revenue, the marginal cost of labor has two parts. The added worker must be paid the new wage rate, but all the earlier workers get a raise, and the two costs added together are greater than the new wage rate. The profit-maximizing monopsonist chooses the number of hours to hire by equating the marginal cost and marginal benefit of the last hour hired. In turn, the marginal benefit of a unit of labor is given by the height of the labor demand curve. Having picked L_M, what wage rate would the monopsonist pay? Clearly, the answer is the lowest it could get away with, W_m on the labor supply function beneath this intersection.

Comparing the monopsonistic and perfectly competitive labor-market equilibria, we find that the monopsonist pays a lower wage and hires fewer units of labor than the competitive market would. This results in the illustrated deadweight loss, because each worker to the right of the monopsony equilibrium adds more in social value (the height of the labor demand curve) than she adds in social costs (the height of the labor supply curve). However, in economics, sometimes two wrongs make a right. We will show in the next chapter that an increase in the minimum wage (bad in perfectly competitive labor markets) may cause the deadweight loss of monopsonistic labor markets to fall.

Finally, some markets may feature only one buyer and one seller, both monopsony and monopoly. This is called a *bilateral monopoly*. In the labor market, this happens when a monopoly labor union negotiates with a monopsony employer – for example, a teachers' union versus a local public-school system, or a musicians' union in a city with one philharmonic orchestra. The equilibrium wage in markets like these will fall somewhere between the monopoly wage demanded by the union and the monopsony wage offered by the employer. Within that range, the wage is determined by the relative market power wielded by each side and the stubbornness of each side. As we note above, such markets are best analyzed using game theory (see Chapter 11).

8.4 Oligopoly

Recall that an *oligopoly* is a market structure in which there are only a few firms, all selling goods that may be seen as perfect or close substitutes. In such markets, the actions of one firm affect the decisions of other firms, and although game theory is required, there is no clear model predicting behavior in all circumstances. Here we describe four alternative game-theoretic models of how firms behave in oligopoly: the Cournot–Nash model, the Bertrand–Nash model, the Stackelberg model, and the Cartel model. In each case, we focus on the interaction between just two firms or organizations (duopoly), but comment that the results usually generalize to oligopolies with more than two competitors. (The reader may get more out of this discussion if she first reads Chapter 11, but we omit enough technical details to allow her a basic understanding here.)

Models of duopoly

Prices and quantities chosen by both firms are interdependent strategies. Consider two firms in the legal defense industry – Alibis Unlimited (Firm A) and Bail Bonds for All (Firm B). If Alibis can figure out what Bail Bonds will do, it can calculate a best response – a price and/or quantity for Alibi that will maximize profits against Bail Bond's choice. But to figure out what Bail Bonds will do, Alibi needs to recognize that Bail's decision depends on what Bail thinks Alibi will do. Attempts to think this through involve a train of logic that never ends: "If A knew B would choose 1, A would choose 2. But if B knew A would choose 2, B would never have chosen 1. The best choice by A depends on what A thinks B thinks A will do, and the best choice by B depends on what B thinks A would choose when A thinks B thinks A will choose . . .."

The first economist to tackle this problem carefully was Antoine Augustin Cournot, who was way ahead of the discipline when he published his work in 1838. He assumed that firms pick a quantity to produce, and that the quantities chosen by each firm would form a sequence over time. In the first time period, firm A chooses an initial quantity that will maximize A's profits if B were to continue producing some initial quantity. Then, in the second period, Firm B picks a new quantity that will maximize B's profits if A were to continue producing its first period quantity. In the third period, A picks a new quantity that would maximize A's profits if B were to continue producing its second period quantity, and the firms continue to take turns maximizing against the past. Cournot showed that this process converges to a set of quantities Q_A^*, Q_B^* such that Q_A^* maximizes A's profits when B chooses Q_B^* and at the same time, Q_B^* maximizes B's profits when A chooses Q_A^*. Thus, the final outcome is stable – neither firm wants to change its quantity given the quantity produced by the other firm. The price is calculated by adding these two equilibrium quantities and substituting that number into the formula for the demand curve. This was known, prior to the invention of game theory, as the "Cournot equilibrium."

Many years later, in 1883, Joseph Louis François Bertrand criticized the Cournot model, arguing that the back and forth process was logical, but it was arbitrary to have firms picking production quantities rather than sales prices. In the alternative known as the "Bertrand model," A picks a price that maximizes A's profits if B were to continue selling at its previous-period price, then B picks a price that maximizes B's profits if A were to continue selling at its previous period price. Again, the two firms alternate price adjustments, and the process converges on a pair of prices and a market quantity that is stable, the "Bertrand equilibrium."

In 1934, Heinrich Freiherr von Stackelberg found a way to circumvent the infinite chain of logic for some duopolies. In his model, one of the two firms is a leader and the other is a follower. In the first stage, the leader picks a quantity, and the follower knows what quantity was picked. In the second stage, the follower uses that information to pick a quantity, and then trade occurs. The follower just maximizes profits, no game theory required. The leader has a forward-looking problem to solve: he knows how the follower will respond to each possible quantity choice made in the first stage, so he picks the first-stage quantity that maximizes leader profits based on that predictable reaction by the follower. The pair of quantities chosen and the resulting price from the demand curve constitute the *Stackelberg equilibrium.*

For a long time, economists remained disturbed by the logics of both Cournot and Bertrand equilibrium. In both models, firms never learn from their mistakes, which is logically unsatisfying. Firm A is wrong about B holding its quantity equal to the last period quantity and B is wrong about A holding its quantity constant in every period. The same is true with respect to prices in the Bertrand model. Although limited progress was made in the interim, it wasn't until 1950 that John Forbes Nash Jr. provided a general answer to the problem. He noted that firms can act logically by jumping immediately to the stable points of Cournot or Bertrand processes, because these equilibria can be computed from the beginning. His concept of stability as equilibrium applies to many other games (discussed in Chapter 11) and stable points have been called "Nash equilibria" ever since.

Duopolies are games without natural rules. In the Cournot model, the implicit rule is "pick a quantity and let the market determine a price." The modern, game-theoretic approach to such a rule produces the *Cournot–Nash equilibrium.* In the Bertrand model, the implicit rule is "pick a price, then produce what consumers demand at that price," and this rule produces the *Bertrand–Nash equilibrium.* In the modern game-theoretic version of Stackelberg equilibrium, the rule is that the two firms proceed sequentially, and firms are appointed to the positions of leader and follower. Nash's name never got attached to the game-theoretic version because his original formulation of Nash equilibrium was not appropriate for multi-stage games like this one. Reinhard Selten made the necessary adjustment in 1965 when he defined "subgame-perfect Nash equilibrium," but calling the result a Stackelberg–Nash–Selten equilibrium never caught on.

Finally, the two firms may enter into a legally-binding agreement to restrict total production to the monopoly level, dividing up the profits in some mutually-agreeable way. Such an agreement is called a cartel. Cartels are illegal in many countries due to antitrust laws, but firms may be able to act as if they were members of a cartel without a cartel agreement (see the discussion of indefinitely repeated games in Chapter 11) and without legal consequences. Thus, this kind of duopoly deserves discussion.

Unfortunately, we do not have much theory predicting the rules of the game that will be played by each particular duopoly. All we can say with confidence is that each of these models have been observed in practice. It is even possible that one competitor thinks he is in a Bertrand game and the other thinks she is in a Cournot game, with weird outcomes. Nonprofit and social entrepreneurs need to be tolerant of this ambiguity, but the four models may help them assess the upside- and downside-risk of particular strategies they might choose. For example, in a local community dominated by two large nonprofit theaters that are simultaneously deciding how many shows to put on in the upcoming fall season, it is natural to think of the Cournot model. But there is some risk – if the first theater is picking a quantity thinking that the second theater is doing so simultaneously, it will err in its choice if the second theater waits to decide. Mistakes will also be made if one theater calculates its Cournot equilibrium quantity while the other calculates its Bertrand equilibrium price. The four models give the manager a picture of what might happen due to such mismatches.

Some details

1.   *Reaction functions and Nash equilibrium*

Unlike the games summarized in Chapter 11, duopoly games allow the players to pick any number from a continuous number line. Technically these are games with "continuous action spaces," and although the logic and definition of Nash equilibrium is the same in both kinds of games, we need a new tool, *reaction functions*, to solve duopoly problems numerically. Reaction functions specify the best response to a choice by the other player. In a Cournot model, the reaction function for firm A specifies the profit-maximizing quantity for A to produce as a function of each possible quantity that B might choose. There is also a reaction function for firm B, specifying the profit-maximizing quantity for B as a function of each possible quantity that A might choose. Cournot–Nash equilibrium occurs wherever these two quantity-based reaction functions intersect. In a Bertrand model, A's reaction function specifies the profit-maximizing price for A as a function of each possible price B could choose, and Bertrand–Nash equilibrium occurs wherever these two price-based reaction functions intersect.

2. *The Cournot model*

The Cournot model of duopoly assumes that there are two firms that split a market for a homogeneous good between them. In this model, each firm chooses its level of output, constrained by its competitor's choice and the demand curve for the total output of that good or service. We simplify and represent total demand by the linear function $P = a - bQ$, a conventional downward-sloping demand curve. If the outputs chosen by firm 1 and firm 2 are Q_1 and Q_2, respectively, then the market price is found by $P = a - b(Q_1 + Q_2)$. We shall further simplify by assuming $TC_1 = cQ_1$, which has constant $ATC = c$.

To find firm 1's reaction function, we write out its profit function:

$$\text{Profits}_1 = TR - TC$$

$$= Q_1 \times (P - ATC)$$

$$= Q_1 \times [a - b \times (Q_1 + Q_2) - c] \tag{8.1}$$

Hence, firm 1's profits depend on its own choice variable, Q_1 and the choice of its rival, Q_2. To get 1's reaction function, we treat Q_2 as some unknown constant, leaving its value open. For each value of that constant, we calculate the profit-maximizing Q_1 by setting $MR_1 = c$. The result is a reaction function: an optimal Q_1 as a function of the value taken by the unknown constant Q_2.

It is a bit difficult to compute MR_1 here, and easier to use calculus to solve this (see the Methodological Appendix in the Online Companion https://www.e-elgar.com/textbooks/young and, e.g., Stewart, 2011). Either way, we get firm 1's reaction function:

$$Q_1^* = \frac{a - c - bQ_2}{2b} \tag{8.2}$$

Proceeding similarly, we get firm 2's reaction function:

$$Q_2^* = \frac{a - c - bQ_1}{2b} \tag{8.3}$$

We find the Cournot–Nash equilibrium by solving these two reaction functions simultaneously, or by graphing the two functions and seeing where they intersect, as shown more generally in Figure 8.4. Doing so yields the Cournot–Nash quantities: $Q_1^* = Q_2^* = (a-c)/3b$. Substituting the sum of the two quantities into demand gives the equilibrium price: $P^* = (1/3)a + (2/3)c$.

Figure 8.4 Nash equilibrium as the intersection of reaction functions

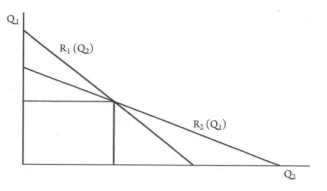

It is not surprising that both firms produce the same quantity and have the same profits because both firms have the same costs and share the same market demand curve. But if instead the cost functions were different for the two firms, equilibrium quantities and profits would also be different.

To illustrate, let's choose values for a, b, and c. Consider a market in which there are two very similar nonprofit day-care centers that both have constant marginal cost (per week) per child of $100, and face a demand curve for day care of:

$$P = \$400 - (Q_1 + Q_2) \tag{8.4}$$

This is the model above where we have chosen values for the parameters of the model: a = $400, b = $1 and c = $100. Substituting these numbers into the formulas above we find that in Cournot–Nash equilibrium, each day-care center cares for 100 children, charges a price of $200, and earns profits of $10,000.

Note that we have, perhaps callously, found the equilibrium quantities that would maximize each center's profits, although this might not be the objective for these nonprofit organizations. However, profit maximization might indeed be a means to an end that is appropriate for nonprofit organizations in some circumstances. For example, if the day-care centers' real goal was early childhood education, and they wanted to maximize the profits from simple care in order to have more resources available for educating their resident children, a profit-based duopoly model is the appropriate one. In other cases, when profit-maximization does not help or even hurts the organization's pursuit of mission, it is possible to use thinking at the margin to calculate more appropriate reaction functions. The same approach can be used for nonprofit or mixed-sector duopolies that follow any of these models, calculating reaction functions based on mission rather than profits.

3. *The Bertrand model*

When both firms choose prices rather than quantities, and both firms have the same cost function, we have the surprising Bertrand–Nash equilibrium in which the price is equal to both marginal and average total cost and profits are zero. So how many firms does it take for a market to behave perfectly competitively? In the Bertrand case, only two. The reason is that the best response to any price with positive profits is to choose a lower price, and this kind of price war ends when neither competitor is willing to drop the price further because it is better off exiting the market than accepting negative profits in the long run.

In the day-care centers example discussed above, the Bertrand–Nash equilibrium has both centers charging $100 per child per week. At that price, 300 children will be served, although with price and quality the same, the split in quantities across the two centers is indeterminate. Like perfect competition, there is no deadweight loss because no family willing to pay more than the costs of service will be frozen out of the market.

Bertrand–Nash equilibrium is more interesting when the two cost curves are different, or the goods produced by each are imperfect substitutes for each other. In the former case, the price leads to zero profits for the high-cost firm and positive profits for the low-cost firm unless the low-cost firm would rather operate as a monopoly and the law allows it to do so. The low-cost firm could drive its competitor out of business by charging a price lower than its competitor's costs. The latter case is sometimes used to model markets with oligopolistic competition.

4. *The Stackelberg model*

The *Stackelberg* model is a variation of the Cournot model, in which output choices are made sequentially. To calculate Stackelberg equilibrium, we work backward from the second stage. This method is called "backward induction." Using backward induction, we first calculate how the choice in the last stage depends on the choice made in the next-to-last stage, and so on until we reach the first stage decision. Although this looks very much like the Cournot model, it gives a different result.

The Stackelberg leader knows that the follower will do whatever the follower's reaction function tells it to do in the second period. If both firms know the demand curve, and their own and the rival's cost function, the leader can use that knowledge to calculate the exact form of the follower's reaction function.

Letting subscripts L and F denote the leader and the follower respectively the follower's reaction function has the form:

$$Q_F^* = f(Q_L) \text{ which we will simplify as the linear function } Q_F^* = d - eQ_L$$

Substituting that into the leader's profit function yields

$$\text{Profits}_L = Q_L[a - b\,(Q_L + Q_F) - c]$$
$$= Q_L[a - b\,(Q_L + d - eQ_L) - c] \qquad (8.5)$$

This removes the follower's quantity from the profit function, so the leader has an ordinary maximization problem of choosing the Q that maximizes his profits. First we can solve this maximization problem to obtain Q_L^*, the profit-maximizing leader quantity, then substitute this value into the follower's reaction function to get Q_F^*. Adding these and plugging the result into demand gives the equilibrium price and then each firm's profits can be calculated. In our day care example, we found that the parameters of the follower's reaction function are $d = (a - c)/2b = \$150$ and $e = -1/2$. One can show, most easily using calculus, that in Stackelberg equilibrium, the leader cares for 250 children, the follower for 25 children. The price is $125, the leader's profits are $6250, and the follower's profits are $625.

5.   *Cartel behavior*

It is possible that two firms such as the day-care centers in our example, would do better by acting as a *cartel* and deciding between themselves what the best level of output would be, and then splitting the resulting profits. Such "collusion" is illegal under antitrust laws in the United States and many other countries, so we will first discuss what happens when cartels are legal, then discuss how to act like a cartel without violating antitrust laws.

If the two day-care centers in our example acted as a cartel, they would select quantities, Q_1 and Q_2, that would maximize total profits. Because the price depends on the sum of quantities and both centers have the same horizontal ATC functions, the solution is the same as that for a monopoly. They would pick a single combined Q to maximize the function $Q[(a - bQ) - c]$, and would find the solution by setting $MR(Q) = MC(Q)$, where in this case $MC(Q)$ is identical to c. It doesn't matter how Q is divided between the two firms because the costs are the same at each. Using all the numbers from this example, the optimal combined production quantity $Q = 150$, the price is $250, and combined profits would be $9000. The cartel agreement would typically specify how these combined profits are split, and the obvious solution is $4500 to each.

More generally, if the cost functions are different, different quantities will be produced at each firm. This complicates the decision on how profits should be split, although the natural outcome is "in proportion to production." However, the decision on profit-splitting comes from a two-party bargaining situation where anything can happen, depending on the power and stubbornness of the two parties. Another problem occurs if it is costly to observe whether parties are sticking to the cartel agreement that restricts production at each firm. Cheating on that agreement is profitable to the cheater (though harmful to the other cartel member), and the cartel may fail to achieve its goal (see the discussion of prisoner's dilemma games played once or repeatedly in Chapter 11).

Antitrust law is extremely complicated, and volumes have been written on the subject. It is clear that an explicit cartel agreement is illegal, but the law allows each firm to independently respond to the competition as they see fit. This gives the firms some wiggle room to act as if there was a cartel agreement even if nothing is in writing and representatives of the two firms never talk to each other. This is called "conscious parallelism." All the same problems that apply to cartels apply to firms practicing conscious parallelism, but to a greater extent. Deciding how to split production and profits is more difficult, and unlike a cartel, one cannot separate the production split from the profit split. Profit distribution is strictly in proportion to production. Detecting cheating is harder, so it is less likely that the two firms will be able to maintain their collusion over time.

6.   *Summary of oligopoly models*

The various oligopoly models yield different results with respect to the prices and levels of outputs in the markets in which they participate. We can rank the levels of output as follows:

$$Q_M = Q_{CA} < Q_{CT} < Q_S < Q_B = Q_{PC}$$

where: Q_M is the monopoly quantity,
Q_{CA} is the total quantity produced by cartels,
Q_{CT} is the total quantity produced in Cournot–Nash equilibrium,
Q_S is the total quantity produced in Stackelberg equilibrium,
Q_B is the total quantity produced in Bertrand–Nash equilibrium, and
Q_{PC} is the total quantity produced in perfectly competitive equilibrium.

Prices vary inversely to quantities, so:

$$P_M = P_{CA} > P_{CT} > P_S > P_B = P_{PC} = MC \qquad (8.6)$$

where MC is marginal cost.

It is an empirical question as to which of the oligopoly models applies best to specific situations in markets involving nonprofit organizations and social enterprises. Essentially, the issue is how well the assumptions of each model apply in particular contexts. First, to what extent is the assumption of profit maximization a reasonable approximation for the participating nonprofit firms or social enterprises? Second, what are the rules of the game: prices or quantities? Simultaneous or sequential? Third, do the organizations act independently or cooperate to achieve their common objectives despite the presence of antitrust laws? The analysis of oligopolistic nonprofit and social enterprise markets is as much an art as a science when it comes to discerning the best assumptions to make. However, the variety of models together offer a range of possible outcomes that bracket what we can expect to see in real markets. Moreover, the different models offer a guide to how other organizations might respond to a strategy taken by a particular nonprofit or social enterprise manager, allowing that manager to calculate the upside- and downside-risks of each available choice.

SUMMARY

Monopolies, oligopolies and monopsonies are market structures that depart from perfect competition. In these markets, individual sellers or buyers do not have to take the market price as given; instead, they make choices that affect prices. Frequently, inefficiency results. In the for-profit world, inefficiency results in all cases other than Bertrand–Nash equilibrium. Among nonprofits that attempt to fix market failures, collusive behavior can actually reduce inefficiency in some circumstances. The field is underexplored, but Eckel and Steinberg (1993) show that when two nonprofits produce a commercial good solely to finance an underprovided collective good, the Cournot–Nash equilibrium is more efficient than perfectly competitive equilibrium; they also show that a nonprofit monopoly like this is more efficient than perfect competition.

Except for a cursory mention of antitrust laws, we have neglected the influence of public policies, such as taxes, subsidies and regulations. The next chapter addresses those policies, but generally does so for competitive markets. In addition, the next chapter considers price discrimination. The alert reader may wish to combine the insights of these two chapters in some management situations.

NOTES

1 A contestable market is one consisting of only a few firms where the possibility of other firms entering the market leads to outcomes similar to those found under perfect competition.

2 More generally, there is an additional cost of employing an additional unit of any factor of production (such as capital), and this is called (in most other economics textbooks) the marginal factor cost (MFC). For labor, we have MFC_L, the marginal factor cost of labor. We don't discuss other kinds of marginal factor costs here, so we just call it MC_L.

SELECTED REFERENCES AND CITATIONS

Allen, B., Weigelt, K., Doherty, N., and Mansfield, E. (2013). *Managerial Economics, Theory, Application and Cases* (8th ed.). New York: Norton Publishing.

Andreoni, J. (1998). Toward a Theory of Charitable Fund-Raising. *Journal of Political Economy, 106(6)*, 1186–1213.

Andreoni, J. (2006). Leadership giving in Charitable Fund-Raising. *Journal of Public Economic Theory, 8(1)*, 1–22.

Brams, S.J. (2003). *Negotiation Games: Applying Game Theory to Bargaining and Arbitration* (2nd ed.). London: Routledge.

Dixit, A.K. and Nalebuff, B.J. (1991). *Thinking Strategically, The Competitive Edge in Business, Politics and Everyday Life*. New York: W.W. Norton & Company.

Dutta, P.K. (1999). *Strategies and Games, Theory and Practice*. Cambridge, MA: MIT Press.

Eckel, C.C. and Steinberg, R. (1993). Competition, Performance and Public Policy Toward Nonprofits. In Hammack, D.C. and Young, D.R. (Eds.) *Nonprofit Organizations in a Market Economy* (pp. 57–81). San Francisco: Jossey-Bass.

Ehrenberg, R.J. and Smith, R.S. (2018). *Modern Labor Economics* (13th ed.). London: Routledge.

Gwartney, J.D., Stroup, R., Sobel, R., and MacPherson, D. (2015). *Economics: Private and Public Choice*. Stamford, CT: Cengage Learning.

Hodgson, A. (n.d.). *Bertrand Oligopoly Model*. Retrieved from https://www.bing.com/videos/search?q=video+on+Bertrand+duopoly+model&view=detail&mid=470BFF2F4B0637C9545E470BFF2F4B0637C9545E&FORM=VIRE (accessed April 2016).

Polak, B. (n.d.). *EC 159, Yale University Course on Game Theory, fall, 2007*. Retrieved from http://oyc.yale.edu/economics/econ-159 (accessed May 2016).

Policonomics (n.d.). Bertrand duopoly. Retrieved from http://www.policonomics.com/bertrand-duopoly-model/ (accessed April 2016).

Policonomics (n.d.). Cournot duopoly. Retrieved from http://www.policonomics.com/cournot-duopoly-model/ (accessed April 2016).

Policonomics (n.d.). Stackelberg duopoly. Retrieved from http://www.policonomics.com/stackelberg-duopoly-model/ (accessed April 2016).

Seaman, B.A. (2018). Static and Dynamic Pricing Strategies: How Unique for Nonprofits? In Seaman, B.A. and Young, D.R. (Eds.), *Handbook of Research on Nonprofit Economics and Management* (2nd ed., pp. 199–224). Cheltenham, UK and Northampton, MA: Edward Elgar Publishing.

Steinberg, R. and Weisbrod, B.A. (1998). Pricing and Rationing by Nonprofit Organizations with

Distributional Objectives. In Weisbrod, B.A. (Ed.), *To Profit or Not to Profit: The Commercial Transformation of the Nonprofit Sector* (pp. 65–82). Cambridge: Cambridge University Press.

Stewart, J. (2011). *Calculus* (7th ed.). Belmont, CA: Brooks/Cole Publishing.

REVIEW CONCEPTS

Allocative Efficiency: The part of social efficiency concerned with producing the right quantity of each good. Absent externalities and collective goods (which are discussed in Chapters 13 and 14), the allocatively efficient quantity results where the marginal benefit (height of the demand curve) equals the marginal cost.

Bertrand–Nash Model: A duopoly model where organizations compete by simultaneously choosing prices.

Bilateral Monopoly: A market structure consisting of a monopsonist buying from a monopolist, such as a firm in a company town renting workers represented by a labor union.

Cartel: An organization of sellers designed to coordinate supply decisions so that the joint profits of the members will be maximized.

Contestable Market: A market is contestable when entry and exit of new competitors is costless. Potential competition, rather than the number of competitors at a point in time, determines the behavior of incumbent firms when a market is contestable.

Cournot–Nash Model: A duopoly model where organizations compete by simultaneously choosing quantities.

Deadweight Loss: A measure of allocative inefficiency. It represents the reduction in social value that occurs when mutually beneficial trades do not take place. In Chapter 14, this concept is more precisely defined in terms of consumer and producer surplus.

Duopoly: A market structure in which two producers of a good or service compete.

Imperfect Competition: Any market structure other than perfect competition.

Marginal Cost of Labor: The additional cost to an employer when it rents an additional unit of labor. Approximated by the wage rate when factor markets are perfectly competitive, but higher than the wage rate in monopsony markets.

Market Power: The ability of a firm to profitably raise the market price of a good or service above marginal costs.

Mixed-Sector Duopoly: A market where a single for-profit firm competes with a single nonprofit organization. Other "mixes" are also covered by this term, such as when a single government agency competes with a single nonprofit organization.

Monopolistic Competition: A market structure with many sellers, each producing a different version of the good or service in question, with low barriers to entry and exit.

Monopoly: A market where there is only one seller of a good or service with no close substitutes. For monopoly to be sustainable, there must be barriers to entry or exit of other firms, including economies of scale or scope (see Natural Monopoly below).

Monopsony: A market structure with a single buyer and many sellers. The buyer has market power.

Natural Monopoly: A firm with decreasing costs (downward-sloping ATC) up to the quantity that serves the entire market. Such firms can outcompete any smaller firms so that they eventually become the sole provider. The shape of the cost curve provides a barrier to entry.

Oligopoly: A market structure characterized by few sellers and interdependent price/output decisions.

Price Discrimination: The practice of charging different consumers different prices for the same product.

EXERCISES

1. The gift shops in both the art museum and the natural history museum in Museum Park in Centralville, USA sell identical sweatshirts featuring Museum Park logos. The managers of the gift shops see themselves as competitors and both institutions rely on gift shop revenues to support their programs. These managers make their decisions independently according to the same fiscal year calendars.

   (a) What model of duopoly is most likely to apply to this situation? What can you say about the resulting prices and sales levels of the sweatshirts?

   (b) Suppose the museums decided to put their own individual logos on their sweatshirts? What impact would this have on prices and quantities sold? Explain.

   (c) Suppose the managers of the two gift shops were instructed by their chief executives to collaborate on their sweatshirt sales? What model of imperfect competition would apply in this case, and what impact would the collaboration have on resulting prices and quantities sold?

2. Several optometrists in Buena Vista fashion themselves as social entrepreneurs who provide eyeglasses at a low cost to needy patients. Each of their enterprises faces a constant marginal cost of $10 per pair of eyeglasses. An economist on the faculty of Buena Vista University estimates that the demand for low cost eyeglasses in this market can be modeled as:

   $P = \$140 - \$2Q.$

   (a) If there are many competing optometrists in this market, what price would be charged if the marginal cost of production is equal to $10? What if the marginal cost was equal to $20? What quantity would be produced in each case?

   (b) If, instead, there were only one such optometrist social entrepreneur, what can we say about the quantity that will be produced and the price that will be charged, relative to your answers to (a)?

   (c) If there are two such optometrists sharing the market, what price and output decisions would they make, under the various assumptions of the Cournot, Cartel, Bertrand and Stackelberg models? Which model seems most appropriate in this situation? What can we say about deadweight loss in this situation?

3. Suppose Healthy General Hospital (HGH) is the only place of employment in town for people trained to interpret MRIs.

   (a) What can we say about the number of MRI health specialists that HGH will hire, relative to the amount they would hire if there were many local hospitals where such people could find work.

   (b) What can we say about the wage HGH will pay such employees?

   (c) Suppose the minimum wage is increased. How might the result in this market be different from what we would expect from an increase in the minimum wage in a perfectly competitive labor market? (Hint: see discussion in Chapter 9).

9

Applications of market analysis

We've just never been able to charge extra for the good weather!

9.1 Introduction

Competitive markets are socially efficient provided there are no other market failures, which we will discuss in Chapter 13. Sometimes, otherwise efficient markets will fail because of government policies such as taxes, subsidies, and price controls. In this chapter, we first expand on how sales taxes affect market equilibrium and briefly consider subsidies as negative taxes. We look next at labor markets – how they work in general and how traditional labor-economic models should be modified to account for special features of non-profit and social enterprise. For example, we consider interactions between paid and volunteer labor markets. We also illustrate the fact that government policies that would otherwise cause market failure (with the example of the minimum wage) can fix markets that are already failing (because of monopsony). Our third set of applications concerns pricing and price discrimination, developing some of the differences in for-profit and social/nonprofit pricing. These include price discrimination to achieve social missions rather than profit maximization, adjusting for the effect of commercial activity on donations, considering the effects of subsidized prices on recipient behavior, and the use of profits from one activity to cross-subsidize an unprofitable activity that advances the organizational mission. While managers can't control the weather, it might indeed affect the demand for their products and services. So, the lemonade vendors in our cartoon, and managers and entrepreneurs of all stripes, would do well to pay attention here to some nuances of market pricing under different conditions.

9.2 Taxes and subsidies

Taxes are a complex but necessary evil. We touched on some of the equity notions involved in tax design in Chapter 1. Here we examine competitive markets with taxes, focusing on how the burden of a tax is passed on to people who are not responsible for paying the tax. The way the burden of a tax is split after markets adjust to taxation is called *tax incidence*. Nonprofit managers that care about the well-being of their customers or have vested interests in various tax policies (such as taxes on tickets for performances in the arts) need to understand tax incidence. Next, we analyze government subsidies that are proportional to sales using the same framework, for these subsidies are, in effect, negative excise taxes.

Tax incidence is a broad topic that can easily occupy half of a course in Public Economics, but we limit our discussion to sales taxes in order to illustrate the kinds of things that happen. First, some definitions. The term "sales tax" is usually used to refer to a general tax, applied to many products. When a tax is attached to a narrow group of products, it is usually called an "excise tax." Sales and excise taxes are of two types: *ad valorem*, and *per-unit*. An ad valorem tax is a percentage markup on the price, such as a 6 percent sales tax. A per-unit tax is a fixed dollar-amount markup on the price, such as a tax of $.06/gallon on gasoline. Under either approach, the tax on an item priced at $1/unit would be the same (in this case, 6 cents), but if the price rose to $2/unit, the sales tax liability would increase to 12 cents while the per-unit tax liability would remain at 6 cents.

In the U.S., the federal government does not impose any sales taxes, but does impose excise taxes on gasoline and other fuels, alcohol, firearms, indoor tanning services, and a variety of business purchases. Nonprofit organizations are not exempt from these taxes. However, general sales taxes and many excise taxes are levied by state and local governments, and each state has its own rules. Nonprofits are exempt from paying a sales tax on purchases in some states, exempt from paying a sales tax on sales in other states, exempt from both in some states, and exempt from neither in some states. Sales and excise taxes may apply to some products sold by nonprofit organizations, but not other products that are generally taxable; for example, computers sold by a nonprofit university's bookstore may be taxable, but textbooks may be exempt. This greatly complicates our discussion, so we simplify by assuming that all sellers – nonprofit, social, or for-profit – are equally taxable. We will now show that the shapes of market demand and supply curves completely determine tax incidence.

Without taxes, there would be no difference between the price paid by the consumer and the price received and kept by the seller. Taxes drive a wedge between these two prices. For each unit purchased, the consumer pays a price that includes the tax, whereas the seller receives a price that does not. To understand tax incidence, it is essential to understand that the consumer price (P_C) is distinct from the producer price (P_p). Letting t represent the tax rate for a per-unit tax, we have an identity (which means it is true by definition for all values of the variables, rather than an equality where we are finding the one value that makes it true when we solve an equation):

$$P_C = P_p + t \qquad\qquad (9.1)$$

When consumers decide upon a quantity to purchase, they care about their out-of-pocket costs, including the tax. They generally do not care what percentage of that price is kept by the seller and what percentage is turned over to the government. Once we know the consumer price with the tax imposed, we know where we are on the demand curve. When producers decide on a quantity to offer for sale, they care only about the per-unit revenues they can keep. They do not care what the consumer is paying or what the government is getting except insofar as these factors affect the equilibrium producer price they will receive. Once we know the producer price, we know where we are on the supply curve.

An equilibrium with a per-unit tax is a quantity, a consumer price, and a producer price. In order to clear the market, we need a pair of prices that makes the quantity demanded the same as the quantity supplied while obeying the identity above. In other words, all we have to do is to look for a quantity where the price on the demand curve is greater than the price on the supply

Figure 9.1 Panel A: When supply and demand have equal but opposite slopes

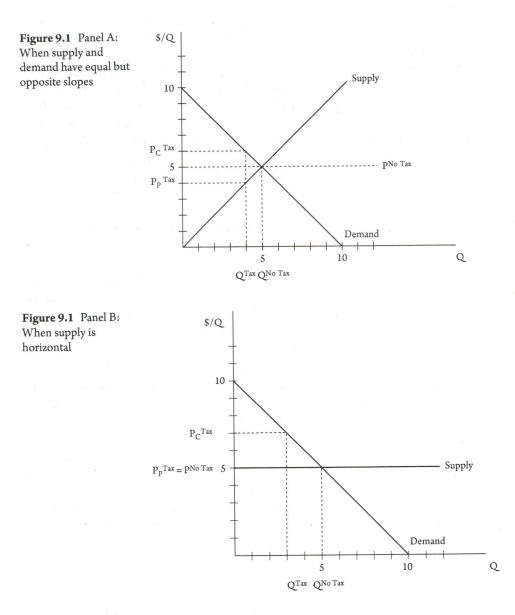

Figure 9.1 Panel B: When supply is horizontal

curve by the amount of the tax. Figure 9.1 illustrates this for a $2 per unit tax. In panel A, we illustrate what will happen when supply and demand have equal but opposite slopes.

Panel A shows that in the absence of a tax, this good would sell for a price of $5 and 5 units would be sold. To impose the tax, we look for a $2 wedge between the supply and demand curves, which happens for a quantity of 4. In the new equilibrium, the price consumers pay increased by $1, the price

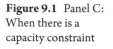

Figure 9.1 Panel C:
When there is a
capacity constraint

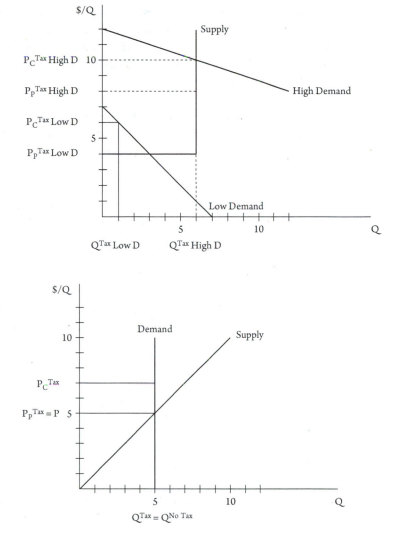

Figure 9.1 Panel D:
Vertical demand curve

Figure 9.1A–D Incidence of tax on sales

producers keep went down by $1, so the incidence of the tax places a 50 percent burden on each. We got this result without knowing anything about the "statutory incidence" of the tax, that is, about who pays the tax according to the law. For most sales and excise taxes, the statutory incidence is 100 percent on the producer – firms and organizations are responsible for collecting the tax and sending it to the government. Why did the economic incidence of the tax differ? Because if producers did not raise the before-tax price and paid the tax out of the $5 that consumers pay, they would get to keep only $3 per unit. At such a low producer price, they are only willing to supply three units of the good to the market, which is less than the five units consumers want to buy. As we have seen, when the quantity supplied is less than the quantity demanded, the price rises until the market clears. The relative slopes of supply and demand, rather than statutory incidence, determines the economic incidence of the tax.

Panel B shows what happens when the same $2 per-unit tax is imposed on a market with a horizontal supply curve. Such industries are rare in the short run, but as we saw in Chapter 7, quite common in the long run with free entry. Now, the consumer price goes up by the full amount of the tax, so 100 percent of the burden is on consumers. Market forces are the reason – with a horizontal supply curve, the sellers would not accept any producer price lower than $5 and so would produce zero if forced to accept any part of the tax burden.

In panel C, we consider the interesting case of a market in which the supply curve is first horizontal, then vertical as there is a capacity constraint preventing production of a larger quantity. Although it is not a perfectly competitive industry, you might think of the Metropolitan Opera, which sometimes sells out and other times has seats available. When demand is low, supply and demand cross on the horizontal section of supply, so, like the previous example, the burden of the sales tax falls 100 percent on consumers. However, with high demand and an intersection on the vertical part of the supply curve, the only way to draw the wedge is along the supply curve and the graph shows us that 100 percent of the burden falls on producers. The reason is that a vertical supply curve says, in a sense, that suppliers are easy. If they bear 100 percent of the burden, they supply the same quantity they would if there were no tax. The consumers are not so easy – so if the consumers bore any part of the burden, they would buy less of the good. The resulting excess quantity supplied puts downward pressure on the price, all borne by the producers.

The last case we consider is that of a vertical demand curve. It is impossible that the demand curve for any product would be vertical over its entire length, because at some (very very very high) price, even Bill Gates cannot afford to buy the good, but it is reasonable for a demand curve to be vertical over some range of prices. For example, the demand for medicines by consumers that have health insurance plans that cover drugs without co-pay would be vertical over a range of prices. The demand by addicts for addictive substances is very steep, and we may approximate it with a vertical demand curve. Nonprofit hospitals likely face vertical demand curves over a range of prices in their markets for highly essential services with no available substitutes, such as kidney dialysis or organ transplants. An excise tax on these services would not hurt the hospitals, nor would it reduce the equilibrium quantity of care provided. However, it would raise the price paid by the patient (or the patient's insurer). Panel D illustrates this. Here, the only way to insert a $2 wedge is along the demand curve, and the result is that 100 percent of the burden is on consumers (or at least on their insurance companies). The reason is that the vertical demand curve signals that consumers are easy. They will buy the same quantity even if the consumer price rises by the full amount of the tax, whereas producers would sell a lesser quantity if they bore a portion of the burden. The excess demand whenever producers bear a burden would force prices up until the entire burden is on consumers.

We need to stress one important point, not so much for the student reader but for their instructors. Most textbooks describe tax incidence in terms of the price elasticities of demand and supply because many of the instructors that select textbooks have been mis-educated and would not buy a textbook that presented the material correctly. Perhaps a bit altruistically, we seek to push back. As we explained in Chapter 7, a straight-line demand curve has the same slope everywhere while containing every value of elasticity from zero to infinity somewhere on the line. A little experimentation with diagrams will prove that if you move the intersection of supply and demand without changing either slope, tax incidence remains the same. Therefore, it is slope rather than elasticity that matters. You can only speak in terms of elasticity when slope and elasticity correspond throughout the curve, which happens only in two cases. When demand or supply is a vertical line, the curve exhibits perfectly inelastic demand or supply everywhere on the curve. If it is the demand curve that is vertical, 100 percent of the burden will be on consumers, and 100 percent will be on producers when the supply curve is vertical. The other case is when demand or supply is perfectly price elastic, a horizontal line. If supply is horizontal, the burden falls on consumers and if demand is horizontal, it is easy to show that the burden falls on producers. One prominent textbook tried to compromise by using constant elasticity supply and demand curves, but these curves do not have constant slope so that tax incidence depends on exactly where the curves intersect. Thus, this compromise fails.

A per-unit subsidy is just a negative excise tax, as, for example, when the government gives a per-unit subsidy for school lunches. Like taxes, the incidence of a per-unit subsidy will vary with the slopes of the supply and demand curves in the subsidized industry. Schools could use the entire subsidy to supplement their per-student fees for lunches, or they could pass on all or part of the subsidy by reducing the fees charged. To see which occurs, we simply look for a wedge equal to the per-unit subsidy, but this time with the producer price on top and the consumer price on the bottom. For markets like panel A of Figure 9.1, the benefit of the subsidy is split 50–50 and the quantity traded increases. For markets like panel B, consumers gain the full benefit of the subsidy; for markets like panel C producers gain the full subsidy if the show sells out, and consumers gain the full subsidy if it does not. Consumers also gain the full subsidy in markets like panel D. Some other examples of per-unit subsidies (or their logical equivalent) include vouchers for day-care service, scholarships for higher education, Medicaid reimbursements for health-care services, or food stamps for purchase of essential food.

While the amount of a service to provide and the price to charge for it are certainly important decisions that must be made by managers of nonprofit organizations and social enterprises, other decisions include the type and amount of inputs that will be used in producing a good or service. We focus here on the decision to use labor, with the understanding that many of the concepts presented here can be applied to studying markets for other factors of production, such as land and capital.

9.3　Analyzing factor markets: labor

We began this discussion in the previous chapter. A factor of production is a durable input, one that can be rented and used for a period of time. Some factors of production can be bought or rented (land), but when slavery was prohibited, labor became a factor of production that can only be rented. The people who offer their own labor for rent are the workers, and their willingness to supply this labor constitutes the labor supply curve. The people who wish to employ workers are the firms, social enterprises, nonprofit organizations, and government agencies, and their willingness to rent workers constitutes the labor demand curve. In this section, we first provide more details on labor supply and demand and competitive equilibrium in the labor market. Then we discuss the minimum wage and show how it operates in competitive and monopsony labor markets. We conclude by looking at the volunteer labor market.

The supply of labor

The supply function for labor relates the quantity of hours that people offer for work to the (after-tax) wage rate paid for that work. Different supply functions would, of course, apply to different types of labor – nurses, social workers, legal-aid lawyers, or managers of arts organizations offer differing hours of work at any given wage. Labor supply functions are often upward-sloping, indicating that people offer to work more hours when the wage rate

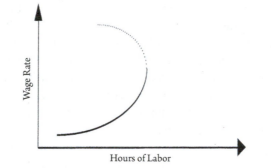

Wage Rate

Hours of Labor

goes up. However, theoretical and empirical studies suggest that, in many occupations, the labor-supply curve for prime-age men (between 25 to 54 years of age) tilts backward. This may be because a higher wage-rate allows one to work fewer hours to reach a target income level, for example, enough to pay the monthly bills, or because the increase in income resulting from a wage increase is spent on consuming larger quantities of all normal goods, including the good "leisure." Figure 9.2 illustrates a typical upward-sloping labor supply curve, and the dotted-line extension of this curve illustrates the backward bending possibility.

The demand for labor

The demand for paid labor is what economists call a "derived demand," which means that the demand for labor is a function of the demand for the products made by labor. Thinking at the margin allows us to describe the determinants of labor demand more precisely. Additional worker hours are added whenever the marginal value of a worker hour exceeds the marginal cost. What are these values and costs?

First, we need a little background on production functions. A *production function* has a dependent variable measuring the amount of a product produced per unit time, the rate of production, and independent variables measuring the quantities of each factor of production. We define the *marginal product of labor* (MPL) as the extra output produced when an extra unit of labor is added, holding constant all other factors of production. Further, we define the *value marginal product of labor* (VMPL) as the additional revenues from sales when an additional unit of labor is added (see below). For simplicity, we assume that there are two factors of production, labor (L) and capital (K, because C is used for other things in economics) and we are in a short run situation with labor as the variable factor and K = 2 as the fixed factor. Table 9.1 provides an example of a production function and the marginal product of labor.

The marginal product of labor is a function that is first upward-sloping then downward-sloping. This is because the amount of capital is fixed, and one person cannot run an assembly line by herself. This means adding labor increases average productivity up to some point. Past that point, there are too many workers to use the fixed stock of capital effectively, so average productivity declines. Average productivity does not decline because the added worker is incompetent; it declines because with one more competent worker, there just aren't enough machines to go around. The marginal product of labor is a short-run concept, as we fix the quantities of all other factors of production. In the long run, we could build a larger factory, and for the new factory size (with more K), we would have a new MPL curve.

For profit-maximizing firms or organizations, the value of an added worker hour is the product of the extra output produced because of that hour (MPL) and the extra revenue that the added output will fetch when sold. If the organization's output market is competitive, each extra unit of output sells for the same market price and the added revenue per unit is constant and equal to P; more generally, however, the added revenue is simply MR:

$$VMPL(L) = P \times MPL(L) \text{ if the output market is competitive}$$

$$= MR(Q) \times MPL(L) \text{ otherwise.}$$

These two are identities, equations that define the columns in Table 9.1. The (L)'s above indicate functional dependence, rather than multiplication, and writing the identity this way is equivalent to multiplying two columns in a

Table 9.1 Production function, marginal product of labor, and value of the marginal product of labor

Q	L	K	MPL	P	VMPL
0	0	2	–	$5	–
10	1	2	10	$5	$50
25	2	2	15	$5	$75
38	3	2	13	$5	$65
49	4	2	11	$5	$55
58	5	2	9	$5	$45
65	6	2	7	$5	$35
70	7	2	5	$5	$25
73	8	2	3	$5	$15
74	9	2	1	$5	$5

spreadsheet. In the table, we have assumed that the output market is perfectly competitive with a market price of $5.

Given the prevailing market wage w in a perfectly competitive labor market and the VMPL curve, we obtain the profit-maximizing quantity of labor by solving:

$$VMPL(L) = w \qquad (9.2)$$

This rule follows directly from the logic of analysis at the margin. Any worker whose VMPL exceeds the wage rate should be hired because doing so will add more to organizational revenues than to costs, supplementing the profits earned from earlier hires. As more and more workers are hired, VMPL eventually declines and the firm or organization stops hiring when VMPL declines enough to equal w. In Table 9.1, if the wage rate = $20/hour and Q is also measured per hour, the organization would hire between seven and eight units of labor per hour. The seventh unit of labor adds $25 in revenues and costs $20, adding $5 of profit to the accumulated total; the eighth unit is not worth hiring because this would add $15 of revenues and $20 of costs, subtracting $5 from accumulated profits. VMPL = w for the 7.5th unit of labor, through interpolation because the table does not have rows for fractional employment.

Repeated use of this rule for alternative values of w produces all the points on the organization's demand for labor curve. Thus, organizational labor demand is the downward-sloping part of the VMPL curve. In turn, the market demand for labor is the horizontal sum of organizational demand curves (the sum of workers desired by each organization at each given wage). If the wage is high, employment of few workers will bring equality between VMPL and w; and if the wage is low, more workers are needed to attain this equality. Thus, the demand for labor is downward-sloping, as illustrated in Figure 9.3.

Figure 9.3 Labor demand

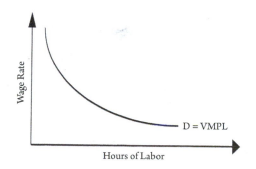

Of course, nonprofit managers and social entrepreneurs have a mission, and sometimes the mission requires using a number of workers that does not maximize profits. For example, a sheltered workshop for the visually challenged might hire fewer challenged people if concerned solely with profits. In such cases, the labor demand curve must be modified to take account of the mission, and the value of an extra worker will not be MPL x P but some other estimate of marginal social benefit resulting from an additional unit of labor. Nonetheless, in many other cases, mission-driven organizations view workers as a means to an end and will find profit-maximizing appropriate. For example, if the workers are producing a commercial product unrelated to the organizational mission, then the organization wants to maximize profits from that activity in order to subsidize its mission-related activities. In all cases, thinking at the margin is the appropriate mode of analysis.

Labor market equilibrium

Figure 9.4 pictures the demand and supply for (paid) labor on the same graph. Following our usual market analysis, we can determine that, left to its own devices, this labor market will equilibrate at a market-clearing wage of w_0 with H_0 hours worked. This assumes that the input market is competitive, with many employers and workers, so that no individual organization employs so many workers that they have significant market power (i.e., monopsony) and that there are no labor unions with sufficient strength to enhance the market power of workers (i.e., no monopoly).

Now suppose the government sets a minimum wage. This appears as a horizontal line at the minimum required wage rate, for the same minimum is required regardless of the number of units of labor. Legal wages are above this line and illegal ones are below it. If the minimum is set below the free

Figure 9.4 Labor market equilibrium

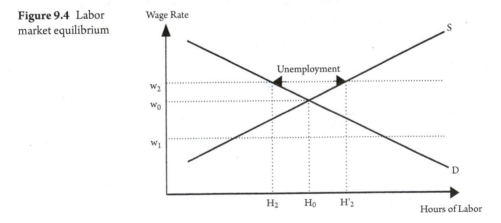

market equilibrium (say, at w_1) the law will have no effect because the free market wage is on the legal side of the line. But if the minimum wage is set above the free market equilibrium (say, at w_2) the law binds and affects economic behavior. More hours are offered by workers (H_2') than are desired by employers (H_2), and unemployment equal to $H_2' - H_2$ results. This is the basic story, and we are neglecting a lot of complications in order to focus on those most relevant to nonprofit and social managers.

Labor unions can also affect equilibrium. If the union negotiates a wage rate (w_2) higher than the free-market equilibrium, it would have the same effect as a minimum wage – those lucky enough to keep their jobs would receive a higher wage, while others would be laid off. To protect long-standing union members, unions often negotiate seniority rules that mandate the last hired are the first fired. But there are other ways that unions can increase wages. If they can move the VMPL curve upward by promoting union products with "Buy the union label" or "Buy American" campaigns, and thereby allowing unionized firms the opportunity to sell their products at a premium price, then both wages and employment will increase.

Monopsony and the minimum wage

The minimum wage, when binding, distorts markets and causes unemployment and inefficiency in competitive labor markets. Things are different in monopsonistic labor markets. As discussed in Chapter 8, when a monopsony employer of labor wishes to hire more labor, it moves up along the labor supply curve, increasing wages not just for the new workers but for all incumbent workers as well. This means that the marginal cost of labor curve (MC_L) lies above the labor supply curve (Figure 9.5). The logic of thinking at the margin tells us that instead of picking the quantity of labor that makes $VMPL(L) = w$, monopsony employers should choose the quantity of labor

Figure 9.5 The minimum wage can increase employment in monopsonistic labor markets

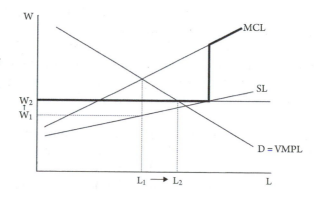

that makes $VMPL(L) = MC_L(L)$, then pay the wage rate below that intersection on the labor supply curve.

In Figure 9.5, absent a minimum wage, the monopsony would employ L_1 units of labor and pay them a wage rate of w_1. Imposing a minimum wage of w_2 would increase the wage rate, but also increase employment to L_2 units of labor. This is because the minimum wage changes the marginal cost of labor to the monopsony. Instead of having to raise wages on all earlier units of labor to get one more unit, all the earlier units are already at the minimum wage and need no further increase. In effect, the horizontal minimum wage line becomes the MC_L curve for all levels of labor employment less than or equal to the quantity of labor that makes the minimum wage line intersect the labor supply curve. Past that point, the MC_L curve jumps up to its usual level, because now everybody gets a raise when the firm hires an additional unit of labor.

Volunteer labor

By definition, volunteer labor lacks a conventional supply and demand curve because there is no explicit money wage or price paid for this labor. However, we can analyze volunteer labor in much the same way as paid labor because organizations do pay a price for volunteer labor consisting of the costs incurred for supervision and the costs of benefits provided to volunteers such as awards, training opportunities, and the like. Moreover, volunteers contribute to the organization's production of services in much the same way that paid workers do. Therefore, the demand for volunteer labor will be determined by the value of the marginal product of that labor and will decline with total hours worked in much the same way as that of paid labor. The function illustrated in Figure 9.3 may also be a reasonable representation of the demand for volunteer labor, with an appropriate modification of the scale on the vertical axis to reflect the effective unit-costs of volunteer administration and reward rather than the wage rate (Emanuele, 1996). Volunteers do receive benefits that are non-monetary in nature. But some are also tangible, in the form of training and benefits, rewards, and opportunities to socialize with other volunteers or enjoy the services of the organization. As these benefits are increased by the organization, people will generally increase the hours they offer to volunteer.

The analogy is not exact, and we speak somewhat metaphorically, but market analysis does provide insight into volunteering and volunteer utilization. The costs and benefits to the organization of using volunteers implicitly determine a demand curve for volunteers. The costs and benefits to individuals of volunteering implicitly determine a supply curve for volunteers. Their interaction helps determine the number of volunteers used, equilibrium expenditures on maintaining a volunteer force, and equilibrium benefits received by volunteers. The usual tools of comparative statics can be applied to this equilibrium. Thus, for example, if the after-tax wage rate received by workers in their paid employment rises, the opportunity cost of volunteering is increased, which would move the volunteer labor supply curve to the left, all else held constant. Assuming that the volunteer supply curve is upward-sloping, the equilibrium number of volunteers used would fall, organizations would devote more resources per volunteer towards recruiting, training, and volunteer perquisites, and, on average, volunteers would receive greater benefits from their volunteering experience.

Without a better empirical understanding of these phenomena, we cannot be very confident of our conclusions. In particular, when the after-tax wage rate goes up, the income of potential volunteers would also go up (unless the paid-labor supply curve were very backward bending), and this too would affect their willingness to volunteer. Available evidence suggests that at least for some forms of volunteering, higher-income people are more likely to volunteer and to volunteer more hours. This "income effect" of an increase in wages pushes the supply curve for volunteers to the right, decreasing or even reversing the leftward shift in volunteer supply due to the increased opportunity cost of volunteering. Unfortunately, we do not yet have sufficient evidence on the relative sizes of these opposing effects to produce firm qualitative conclusions about the impact of increased wages on volunteering.

Interactions between the paid and volunteer labor markets

We have already indicated that the minimum wage creates some interactions between a nonprofit organization's use of paid and volunteer labor by prohibiting a range of intermediate wage rates. There are much simpler interactions as well. If we neglect the possibility that the same person could work as either a paid or volunteer worker or both, then we can regard paid and volunteer labor as two distinct factors of production used in the nonprofit production process. The general analysis of multiple factors is quite developed in for-profit economics, which distinguishes complementary factors (factors that are more effective when used together, like carpenters and sanding machines) from substitutable factors (factors that can be used instead of other factors to accomplish a task, like teachers and substitute teachers). When the equilibrium price for one factor of production increases, the demand for the other factor will shift to the left for complements and to the right for substitutes. This analysis probably applies equally well to nonprofit organizations and social enterprises, but we have little evidence on whether particular types of nonprofits regard volunteers as a substitute or a complement for particular types of paid labor. One interesting study by Duncombe and Brudney (1995) estimated some of the necessary parameters to characterize the optimal mixture of paid and volunteer workers in firefighting companies. That study found that the costs of training, recruiting, and retaining volunteers must be balanced against the wage rate to determine the best proportions of these inputs. Further evidence of the relationship between paid and volunteer labor was highlighted by Simmons and Emanuele (2010).

9.4 Advanced issues in nonprofit pricing

In this section, we consider five advanced issues in nonprofit pricing. First, since nonprofit organizations derive income from different sources, we consider interactions between sales and other sources of revenues – chiefly donations. Second, since organizations often market several products, we explore the scope for cross-subsidizing one output using profits from another. Third, since organizations may charge different prices to different customers (price discrimination), we investigate how nonprofit organizations with different objectives should design their pricing policies. Fourth, we consider "niche behavior," where an organization chooses its quality, ideological bent, and product line with a strategic eye towards pricing implications. Finally, we observe that price plays multiple roles. While the price determines who will buy and how much revenue the organization will collect, it may also have direct effects on organizational mission attainment.

Interactions between sales and other revenues

In earlier chapters, we noted that the principal source of revenues in the nonprofit sector is sales of goods or services, including sales of items directly related to the organizational mission, sales of items to generate revenue in support of the organizational mission, and contracts to provide goods and services for governments. However, donations, including time, money, and in-kind gifts, dues, bequests, and foundation, corporate, and government grants, are important supplements to sales for most nonprofits, and the principal source of support for some of these organizations. Until this point, we have examined nonprofit pricing in isolation. Now we will consider the possibility that the volume and mixture of sales activities can affect the volume and mixture of donations, and we will see how pricing rules must be altered when these interactions are important.

Sales of any sort may *crowd-out* donations (an increase in sales causes donations to fall) or *crowd-in* donations (an increase in sales causes donations to rise). Why is this? One argument for crowd-out is perceived need: donors may feel that there is less need for their donations when an organization is able to fund its activities through sales of goods and services. Another is perceived deservedness: donors may feel that commercial activity is crass and undermines the organizational mission or that the organization may lose sight of the fact that it is in fact nonprofit. One argument for crowd-in, particularly in social enterprises that can accept donations, is that foundations and major donors want to have lasting impact. They get this if the recipient organization uses their gifts to branch out into the commercial realm and become self-sustaining. Because these arguments depend on the information provided to donors and how donors interpret this information, a lot of details may matter: whether the commercial activity is related or unrelated to the organizational mission, whether markets are segmented (so that donors are at a separate location from purchasers and unlikely to perceive the connection, or the commercial venture is spun-off in a manner that makes donors unlikely to perceive a connection), whether the product is unique and reminds donors of the organizational mission (as in sales of art posters by museums), whether donors are motivated mostly by altruism or by a desire for personal gain (e.g., the chance to receive a sweepstakes/raffle ticket), whether similar charities are engaged in similar commercial activities, whether the governance structure of a social enterprise insures that the social mission will be maintained, and whether the product is of high quality and sold at a fair price. Different donors may respond to nonprofit commercial activities in different ways, and the pattern of responses may be sensitive to historical and cultural factors. Careful empirical studies to determine the signs and magnitudes of these interactions are rare (exceptions include Schiff and Weisbrod, 1991; Kingma, 1995; Segal and Weisbrod, 1998; Okten and Weisbrod, 2000; Yetman and Yetman, 2003; and Herzer and Nunnenkamp, 2013), so nonprofit managers will have to rely on their experience and intuitions in applying the following analysis.

Commercial activity may have both fixed and marginal effects on donations. The mere fact that the organization is engaging in unrelated business activity at any scale may cause donations to change by a substantial amount. Suppose that there are positive net donations (donations minus fund-raising costs) before and after the commercial activity begins, and that net donations change by $K if the organization engages in commercial activity (K can be positive or negative). If the organization wishes to maximize the sum of profits from sales and from fund-raising in order to generate maximal resources for pursuing its mission, this changes the shutdown rule for the unrelated business activity:

Cease unrelated commercial activity if MR < AVC – K/Q

The shutdown rule could be different for "related" business because this form of commerce directly fosters the organizational mission as well as providing revenues. A hospital would not want to stop providing medical care simply because the incremental profits from medical care are smaller than the incremental decrease in donations resulting from the sale of medical services. However, if the goal of the organization were to provide free medical care to the indigent, and fee-for-service care were a source of revenues and not otherwise of value to the organization, then the shutdown rule above would apply here. Although the rule is stated in terms of the legal distinction "related" versus "unrelated," it is not the legal standards that govern here. Rather, the rule applies to any income source that does not directly contribute to the organization's central mission; it does not apply to income generated from activities that do foster that mission directly.

Given that the organization decides to keep its unrelated business open, should it adjust its production level and pricing to account for the interaction with donations? The answer depends on what aspect of commercial activities concerns the donors – is it the quantity sold, the price charged, or the profits generated from sales? To analyze these possibilities, we first need to decompose the marginal cost of producing an unrelated good or service into two components – marginal production cost (MC) and marginal donation cost (MDC). MC is the ordinary marginal cost of providing another unit of the unrelated good or service. MDC is the incremental change in donations resulting from producing an additional unit of unrelated output and can be positive or negative. *Full marginal cost* (FMC) is defined to equal MC – MDC, so FMC > MC when donations fall in response to marginal production. The general solution to this problem goes a little beyond this textbook[1] but we can approximate it by assuming that the amount spent on fund-raising is independent of the quantity of production. Then, when donors react to the quantity produced, the organization should solve the following equation for Q:

$$FMC(Q) = MR(Q) \qquad (9.3)$$

In particular, if donors react negatively to unrelated output production, FMC is higher than MC, so given an unchanged MR function, the organization should produce an incrementally lower quantity of the unrelated output. When donors react positively, the reverse is true.

The rule is similar, but more complex, when donors react to the price charged by the nonprofit organization or social enterprise rather than the quantity. If the organization is a price-taker in a perfectly competitive market, then quantity increases will have no effect on price, and hence no effect on donations. However, nonprofit organizations in such situations might want to charge a lower price than the market price – not to gain market share but rather to increase their donations. Starting from a competitive equilibrium, consider a marginal reduction in price, accompanied by a marginal increase in production that keeps $MC(Q)$ equal to the new lower price. This will decrease revenues from sales but increase donations and it is possible that the second effect would outweigh the first. If so, the organization should continue lowering its price until at the margin, the second effect exactly equals the first.

What if donors react to profits from sales, rather than to the quantity or price of sales? This would occur if the perceived need motivation were the only reason for crowd-out. If a dollar of added profits crowds out less than a dollar of donations, the organization can ignore the complications presented by crowd-out. Maximizing profits from sales will also maximize profits from sales plus fund-raising. It is hard to imagine a perceived need reason why a dollar of profit would crowd-out more than a dollar of donations, but were this the case, the organization should reduce sales profits below the maximum available.

The interaction between sales and donations is just one factor that will determine the best mixture of revenue sources for a nonprofit organization or social enterprise. In economic terms, the choice of revenue mix depends on two factors – the profits from investing in different types of revenue generation and the riskiness of the mixture of alternative revenue sources. The profits or net returns are the differences between gross revenues and the costs of producing those revenues: donations less fund-raising costs, grants less grant solicitation and administration costs, sales revenues less production costs, and so on. The costs of each revenue source should include "transaction costs" (discussed further in Chapter 13) such as the delayed payments, reporting, and other accountability requirements that eat up government grants (Grönbjerg, 1993). Kearns (2006) lists other considerations important to nonprofit CEOs and board chairs, such as catalyst potential (does the source open the door to other sources of valued outcomes?), mission alignment, and organizational expertise. Finally, some sources of revenue are riskier than others. Riskiness depends on the predictability of a revenue source, the nature of crowd-out, and the correlation between the net returns of each revenue source (e.g., Kingma, 1993; Frumkin and Keating, 2011; Young, 2017; Chang, Tuckman, and Chikoto-Schultz, 2018).

Multiple outputs

Many nonprofits market multiple services. Nonprofit hospitals sell parking services, hotel services, flowers, research, and medical services. Nonprofit theaters, dance companies, and symphony orchestras sell refreshments, souvenirs, and educational materials as well as performances. Nonprofit universities sell undergraduate education, graduate education, adult non-degree education, research services, housing services, medical services, recreational privileges, and parking. Religious organizations sell dining and other social experiences, books and videotapes, and rent their facilities for use by non-members. Some of these multiple outputs are mission-related (undergraduate and graduate education; appendectomies and brain surgery), and some may be "unrelated" commercial ventures (parking, dormitories).

There are important interactions to consider when an organization markets several outputs. First, there may be "cost complementarities" that make production of multiple products within one organization more efficient than production of each product by separate organizations. Second, there may be "demand complementarities" that make consumption of multiple products from one organization more efficient than consumption of those same products produced in separate organizations. These two kinds of complementarity are referred to collectively as economies of scope and are an important reason why multiple outputs are marketed by an organization. The detailed impacts of economies of scope on pricing and output decisions are complicated and left to more advanced texts (Graham, 2013). However, with some simplifying assumptions, we can develop an essential understanding of the rules for pricing of nonprofit services in this situation.

Suppose that economies of scope affect only fixed costs, so that there are no interactions among the marginal costs or among prices for the variety of products produced. With no such interactions, the multiproduct nonprofit social enterprise is free to use the appropriate pricing and output rules for each product separately. If the market for computers is competitive, then the university bookstore should sell computers at the going market rate and choose a quantity to offer for sale that makes marginal cost equal to this price. If the market for hospital parking services is monopolized, the hospital should determine the number of spaces that makes marginal cost equal to marginal revenue and charge the maximum price consistent with filling this lot (assuming the hospital only cares about the revenues generated, rather than the well-being of parkers). Similarly, pricing for mission-related activities will follow the organizational objective, rather than maximizing profit, as considered earlier. This classic case was analyzed by James (1983).

James considered three kinds of nonprofit output services: favored, neutral, and disfavored. Favored outputs are mission-related and neutral outputs are mission-unrelated. To this list, she adds disfavored outputs, which either actively impair attainment of the organizational mission or are otherwise distasteful to those in control of the organization. For example, the management of a nonprofit art museum may positively dislike the poor-quality reproductions of its paintings that it sells and the special exhibitions it puts on that attract vandalism-prone crowds. Nonetheless, the museum sells both outputs to generate revenues that help maintain its core collection.

In general, neutral outputs will be produced whenever they generate profits, and disfavored outputs will be marketed only if they generate sufficiently large profits. Profits from both of these outputs can then be dedicated to financing incremental output of the favored good or service, allowing this product to be marketed for a loss or even given away. This process of transferring profits from one output to support another is known as *cross-subsidization*. This practice is quite common. James cites evidence that universities profit from the sale of education to undergraduates and use this revenue to cross-subsidize graduate education. She also cites evidence that nonprofit hospitals use profits from appendectomies and other routine treatments to cross-subsidize research and prestige-generating but underutilized facilities such as open-heart surgery units.

As noted earlier, the income elasticity of supply is generally zero for for-profit firms. However, an increase in the fixed revenues received by a nonprofit firm will affect nonprofit supply. The income elasticity of supply is positive for favored outputs, zero for neutral outputs, and negative for disfavored outputs. Consider then the effect of a major donation. Such a gift would allow the organization to reduce distasteful but profitable activity and encourage further production of favored (mission-related) outputs.

What of the own-price and cross-price elasticities of supply? Suppose that the price of a disfavored output goes up. This means that a given quantity of the disfavored output will generate more profits, so that clearly the supply of the favored output will go up. However, we cannot say with any certainty whether the quantity supplied of the disfavored output will go up or down. This ambiguity occurs because of two opposing forces. On the one hand, the higher price enables the organization to obtain a given cross-subsidy while selling less of the disfavored output. On the other hand, the higher price implies that each unit of the disfavored output will support a larger number of units of the favored output. This increase in the efficiency of the cross-subsidy may encourage the organization to increase its disfavored activity.

The sign of the price-elasticity of supply for the disfavored output depends upon which of these two opposing forces is larger for the particular organization we are considering. If the first effect dominates, the price elasticity will be negative; if the second effect dominates, it will be positive.

Interpreting unrelated business income as a disfavored output, Schiff and Weisbrod (1991) applied the James model to the controversy over "unfair competition" between for-profit and nonprofit organizations. They found that the tax advantages of nonprofits allow them to cross-subsidize and hence better accomplish their missions, although this may not be the most efficient method of helping nonprofits. They also found that nonprofit organizations may respond to price changes in their commercial markets in the perverse manner explained above, decreasing the quantity they supply when the price goes up or costs go down.

Price discrimination

There are two types of price discrimination. One practice is to charge the same customer different per-unit prices depending upon the quantity bought, for example, by providing quantity discounts. The other type of price discrimination is charging different prices to different customers (e.g., sliding-scale fees, discounts for senior citizens, or lower tuitions for promising low-income students to attend college). It is the second type of price discrimination that is of special interest to nonprofits and social enterprises.

In order to consider price discrimination by nonprofit organizations and social enterprises, we need to understand two underlying factors. First, price discrimination is not always technically feasible. Second, even where such practice is technically feasible, for-profit firms face important informational and incentive limitations in their ability to price-discriminate. In particular, we will see how the profit imperative creates distrust among consumers, and how a nonprofit organization or social enterprise can overcome this distrust to accomplish two kinds of goals – income redistribution and provision of high fixed-cost services.

First it should be clear to the reader that price discrimination is only possible for organizations with some degree of market power. Under perfect competition, organizations are price takers and cannot set prices differently for different customers. Within this context, price discrimination is only feasible for goods and services that are not resalable. It would be difficult for a street vendor of hotdogs to offer a substantially lower price to indigent than wealthy customers because hotdogs can be resold. Indigent customers would buy extra hotdogs and resell them to the wealthy at a price higher than they paid but lower than the wealthy would be charged by the vendor. Soon the vendor would sell no hot dogs at the higher price. This process is known as *arbitrage*; it applies to any resalable good where transactions occur often enough to make it worthwhile for intermediaries to enter the market.

Arbitrage cannot occur for goods or services where the act of consumption is inextricably intertwined with the supply of the good to the consumer. For example, an appendectomy is not resalable. Job training programs provide another example. Here, the recipient may gain the skills to employ herself as a job trainer, but this "resale" does not use up the training she has received. In these cases, price discrimination is feasible.

Arbitrage possibilities should be carefully considered in charity ventures. For example, the distribution of free food to third-world governments may not end up helping needy residents, if the food can be resold for cash. Distribution of free cheese to homeless alcoholics may not improve their nutrition either, for recipients can sell the cheese to finance more alcohol. Provision of owner-occupied housing units at a subsidized price will certainly help those lucky enough to first occupy the units, but often the original occupants will resell their units to the highest bidders, presumably at the going market rate for real estate of this type. While the indigents receive higher income as a result, these units will not remain dedicated to the poor and even the initial occupants may not end up in better housing units than they occupied prior to the program.

Finally, resalability may itself be under the control of the original vendor. In the housing example, we could continue to dedicate housing units to the poor by renting units only to those certified as eligible and prohibiting leasers from subletting their apartments. Concert tickets provide another example. If tickets are sold in advance (with no limits on individual purchases or legal restrictions on scalping), price discrimination in ticket prices would clearly be impossible. However, if tickets are sold only at the door, and proof of eligibility is required for anyone seeking the lower price, it would be possible to effectively price discriminate.

Price discrimination is also impossible if competitors don't follow a compatible pattern of prices. A day-care center that charges a higher-than-cost price to well-off families in order to subsidize lower-than-cost prices for others will not be able to maintain this pricing pattern if equal-quality competitors offer their services to well-off families at a price equal to their cost. There are other complications here too: for example, some of the well-off might be willing to pay extra to place their children in a center with more diverse clientele. This issue has not yet been fully studied, but the essential point remains that in choosing a pattern of prices, an organization must consider the pricing practices of its competitors – current and potential. This is one reason why we discuss only price-discriminating monopolies below, leaving the complexities of imperfectly competitive situations for future research.

Let us first consider price discrimination by for-profit monopolies. Profit-maximizing monopolies would like to price according to the following rule – a practice called *perfect price discrimination*:

> *Charge each customer his or her maximum willingness to pay for each unit purchased. Produce a quantity that makes the price charged for the last customer equal to marginal cost.*

This rule is clearly anti-consumer since all the gains from trade accrue to the seller under this pricing pattern. Each buyer is asked to pay a price equal to what the product is worth to him or her. Thus, buyers just break-even and sellers receive maximal benefit. Nonetheless, this rule does have some social virtue. Perfectly price-discriminating monopolies do not limit production to a level less than that which is socially efficient, as single-price monopolies do. (Recall the discussion in Chapter 8.) This is because there is no need to lower anybody's price in order to sell an additional unit – the marginal revenue function for a discriminating monopolist is the same as the demand curve. In order to maximize profit, the discriminating monopolist will move down the demand curve, charging each successive customer less and less, until the level of price becomes equal to marginal cost. At this level the output Q is the same as it would be if the firm were a single price monopolist whose objective was to maximize social benefit (by setting P = MC) and the same as that resulting from a perfectly competitive market. This is illustrated in Figure 9.6 which shows that different prices are charged to each customer with the last customer charged a price P_n just equal to marginal cost MC.

In addition to producing at socially efficient levels, perfectly price-discriminating monopolies may also find it financially feasible to produce socially-valuable goods that have high fixed costs and low marginal costs which would be unprofitable if a single price were charged. This is made possible by the collection of all the extra revenue resulting from charging each customer as much as he or she is willing to pay.

Realistically, for-profit monopolies never have sufficient information to perfectly price-discriminate. At best, they may be able to distinguish customers on the basis of credit history, age, ethnicity, gender, zip code of residence,

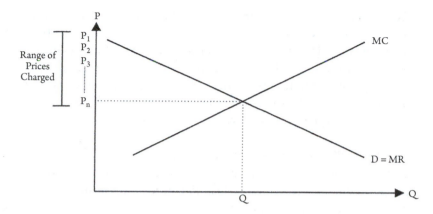

Figure 9.6 Production by a profit-maximizing price discriminating monopolist

and the like in order to guess which customers, on average, are willing to pay more than others. Discriminating on the basis of these imperfect indicators is sometimes illegal (as in ethnicity or gender), and in any case these indicators are not accurate enough to allow perfect price discrimination. Of course, if the monopoly tries to refine its estimates by asking individuals how much they would be willing to pay, consumers will have a strong incentive to lie. Anyone who truthfully reported a high willingness to pay would be rewarded with a correspondingly high price. Consumers that lie about their willingness to pay are billed for a lesser amount and it is unlikely that any one consumer's payment will make the firm shut down to avoid losses. Understanding these incentives, monopolies do not bother to ask and so do not obtain anything close to the revenues potentially available through perfect price-discrimination.

However, if consumers believe that they are purchasing from an organization that has no wish to exploit them, they may be more willing to reveal their true preferences. Nonprofit organizations may be perceived as trustworthy in this way. This idea led Hansmann (1981) to suggest that performing arts are non-profit because they need price discrimination to survive. The performing arts typically have very high fixed costs (rehearsal, set design and construction, and so on), and low marginal costs (an extra performance costs much less than the set-up costs). When a perfectly price-discriminating monopolist can cover fixed costs but a single-price monopoly cannot, we can conclude two things: first, it is socially desirable for the show to go on because, in the aggregate, consumers are willing to pay more than the show costs to produce. Second, the show cannot go on without price discrimination or some other source of supplementary financial support (Anheier and Ben-Ner, 2003).

Consumers will not trust for-profit performing arts organizations in this context, but they are willing to volunteer information about their willingness to pay by donating to nonprofit organizations. Thus, Hansmann views donations to arts organizations as a form of "voluntary price-discrimination." The implication for nonprofit pricing is that organizations can charge a lower than break-even ticket-price with the expectation that donors will step in and allow the organization to survive.

Ben-Ner (1986) observes another way in which nonprofit price discrimination can be helpful. If the organizational mission is to subsidize services for the poor, and fixed revenues are insufficient to accomplish this mission, price discrimination can help fill the gap. Such price discrimination can take the form of "overcharging" the better-off customers or asking them for a donation as well as a payment. In either case, patrons need assurance that the overpayment will be dedicated to subsidizing the poor, rather than enriching those who control the organization – hence the advantage of the nonprofit form in implementing this practice.

In some circumstances, however, nonprofit organizations or social enterprises may not be perceived as trustworthy, and their ability to price-discriminate is also impaired. This is particularly true for products that are unrelated to the organization's mission. Purchasers of these unrelated products (e.g., raffle tickets) may have no interest in helping the organization's target beneficiaries. Alternatively, donors may feel that these services are unseemly and may decrease their donations. There can be merit in these complaints, for nonprofit organizations and social enterprises have as much incentive as for-profit monopolies to perfectly price-discriminate in unrelated markets, even if the proceeds are dedicated to a nobler purpose.

As noted above, one common practice of price discrimination is to charge a high price to the better-off customers in order to give service away free to the deserving poor. Another pattern is to charge even the deserving poor some nominal fee. How should a nonprofit organization choose between these options? Social services and health care agencies face these issues regularly. If a fee is charged to all consumers, the extra revenue allows the organization to serve more customers. Hence, there is a difficult value trade-off to be made here: is it better to provide a smaller level of assistance to the neediest in order to assist an additional person who is a bit less needy? Each organization must decide for itself how it values quantity of service against the level of assistance it provides to particular individuals. But framing the question in the foregoing terms – pitting the value of serving one more client against the marginal loss of help to an existing client – again demonstrates how "thinking at the margin" can facilitate determination of the best policy in any given instance.

Finding the right niche

Perfectly competitive firms, in the long run with free entry, do not generate any surpluses from sales, whether they are for-profit or nonprofit. For unrelated businesses designed to support a nonprofit organization's primary mission, strategic managers must therefore plan to avoid this fate. Unrelated business can generate a short-run profit, but if there are no barriers to entry, it may not be worthwhile for the nonprofit to enter this market. Profits will be short-lived, and the present value of profits may not exceed the entry and exit costs. Staff hired for their ability to produce and market the unrelated good or service will need to be transferred into the mission-related part of the organization's operation (where they may have less ability) or released (with consequent severance and placement costs and losses in the morale of remaining workers). Nonprofit commercial ventures in competitive industries are only worthwhile if short-run profits are sufficiently high, entry by others is anticipated to be slow, and the costs of one's own entry and exit are sufficiently small.

Product differentiation is a common strategy that for-profit firms pursue to maintain profits in the face of competition. By developing a product with unique quality or stylistic characteristics and protecting this version through patents, reputation, and trademarks, an organization, in effect, becomes a monopolist in producing its version of the product. However, because there is competition from other versions of the product, the cross-price elasticity between versions will be high, and the monopoly profit potential from any one version will be low. If other organizations enter the market by designing their own special versions of the product, profits per supplier can be driven to zero even though each organization has some control over the price it charges. This is the "monopolistic competition" market structure mentioned in Chapter 8 and is seen in many portions of the nonprofit and social enterprise sectors, such as higher education, hospitals, and elder care.

Nonprofit organizations and social enterprises can adopt the same sort of strategy, with the same sorts of long-run considerations. The present value of the costs of developing a unique product, entering production of this product, and eventually exiting production must be smaller than the present value of net revenues generated from the sale of the product. Because many nonprofits and social enterprises are unique institutions in themselves, they have great potential for creating special versions of products. A sweatshirt from Yale is different from a sweatshirt from Stanford. And a calendar from the Cleveland Museum of Art distinguishes itself from one from the Museum of Modern Art in New York. (And what about the coffee mug sold in the gift shop of the Cleveland Clinic, famous for heart surgery, which says "I've been by-passed in Cleveland?") Nonetheless, nonprofit commercial ventures should be undertaken with an eye to the future and a careful analysis of long-run competition.

Pricing and the organization's mission

The price of a product determines how much the consumer will pay and how much the producer will receive, but the transfer of revenues is not the only function prices play. We have already discussed two aspects of how price discrimination is related to mission: discrimination can be used to finance a good with high fixed costs or to support redistribution through subsidized prices for those deemed worthy. There are several other mission-related facets of nonprofit and social enterprise pricing to consider as well. Prices also affect attainment of output, the effectiveness of educational and advocacy missions, client effort, and the types of consumers who get to consume a good.

Suppose that the nonprofit or social enterprise mission requires an increase in the consumption of some service beyond its market equilibrium level. For example, a community health organization may subsidize health care because it believes that consumers place too low a value on their own health and do not consider the external effects of contagious illnesses when they decide how much health care to purchase. A nonprofit university may subsidize adult learning, based on the belief that this is something adults undervalue until they experience it. A symphony orchestra may subsidize concerts for elementary school students in the hope that many of them will develop a lifelong taste for live classical music.

In all these cases, the market demand curve, which represents the marginal valuations consumers place on the service, lies below the marginal valuation the organization places on the service in question. We can think of the latter curve as a "beneficial demand curve" because it represents the organization's desired purchases on behalf of consumers at each possible price. As illustrated in Figure 9.7, consumers are willing to purchase only a fraction of beneficial demand at the market price. Hence, the organization must somehow reduce this price. In Panel A, the nonprofit reduces its price from P_1 to P_2 in order to achieve a level of consumption Q_2, in excess of market demand Q_1, that corresponds to beneficial demand at the original price P_1. In some cases, that

Figure 9.7 Pricing a mission-related service: general case

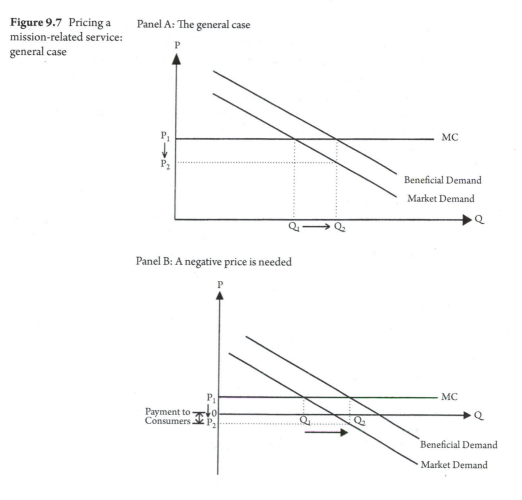

Panel A: The general case

Panel B: A negative price is needed

price may even need to be negative (Panel B), that is, consumers may need to be paid to induce sufficient consumption. For example, schools may have to reward recalcitrant students with valuable gifts in order to increase attendance. Or parents in some communities may have to be induced with payments before they have their children vaccinated. A nonprofit organization finances its price reduction using fixed revenues (donations, grants, asset income, etc.), but it may or may not have sufficient fixed revenues to fully accomplish its goal. Whether the goal is fully realizable depends upon the amount of fixed revenue, the price elasticity of demand (which tells the organization how much it must reduce the price to obtain the desired increment in consumption), and the magnitude of the difference between market and beneficial demand.

When consumption of a good or service has beneficial side effects contributing to the organizational mission, the analysis is identical. Two categories of side-effects are important here – public education and advocacy effects. If, say, a cancer society sells frisbees imprinted with the seven deadly warning signs of cancer, consumers learn something while playing and this advances the educational mission of the organization. Bumper stickers and buttons with slogans highlighting particular beliefs and social causes also foster the advocacy missions of various organizations. In these cases, the market demand curve represents consumer valuations that are lower than the value the organization places on the consumption of the good. Thus, nonprofits and social enterprises want to sell these items below their market value.

In many cases, an organization may require the active effort of consumers to attain its goals, and the price may affect the client's level of effort. Such an argument has long been championed by psychotherapists to justify their fees and has been applied by Habitat for Humanity to housing programs. The Habitat case highlights that the required payment need not be in the form of cash; they require recipients of housing assistance to provide "sweat equity" by working to build their houses. Twelve-step programs of recovery also require noncash payments, as those who are sufficiently recovered pledge to bring the message of hope to those still in need.

Requiring payments may lead a client to work harder towards recovery, but it can induce participation in a very different way as well. Those who would feel sufficiently stigmatized if they were to accept free care may be quite happy to accept aid if they are required to pay a "fair share" of the costs consistent with their ability to pay. Sweat equity has an advantage here over monetary payment, for although individuals are endowed with varying amounts of money, we are all endowed with the same amount of time (even if that time has differing economic value). In addition, payment through sweat equity, like payment of cash, helps finance care for others. The incentive effects of required payments must be weighed against the value trade-offs considered earlier. Organizations may want to charge a bit more than the price that would induce a desired level of effort because the added revenues allow them to help more of the almost-as-needy. Or they may prefer to provide aid at a lower but positive price, to the few most needy consumers.

Finally, price can serve a screening function, restricting the class of customers to those who are willing to pay. This effect can either promote or hinder organizational objectives. A social club that wishes to restrict its membership to the wealthy without being too blatant can simply charge enormous membership fees. University tuition and financial aid serves some screening functions as well. It is difficult for an admissions officer to determine on the basis of high school grades and standardized test scores alone, which applicants are truly talented and motivated, but the applicants have some idea where they stand on these dimensions. Oversimplifying for purposes of illustration, a university that wishes to reserve its spaces for talented and dedicated students might offer student loans instead of grants-in-aid. Those applicants who know that their grades are inflated, and those who do not intend to study hard, will not wish to take loans because they may calculate that their level of success in college education is unlikely to lead them to sufficiently lucrative jobs upon graduation to pay these loans.

In summary, there are several social issues that may require nonprofit organizations and social enterprises to adjust their prices beyond what market conditions would dictate. These organizations may decide that consumers on their own will not demand as much of a given service as they should, or that the service is associated with educational and advocacy benefits that justify lowering the price. Alternatively, prices may be seen to have a positive motivational effect on client effort or they may be used as a signal to attract certain customers and not others. These nuances make the pricing of nonprofit and social enterprise services an important and challenging exercise.

SUMMARY

The nonprofit and social enterprise sectors contain many examples of imperfect competition, as when one organization is the only one of its kind, or when as few as two similar organizations share a market for a similar product. Much of what is known from the study of the for-profit sector about monopoly, oligopoly and monopsony can shed light on the workings of such imperfectly competitive subsets of the nonprofit and social enterprise sectors, but many adjustments are needed when they are applied to mission-motivated organizations.

Labor markets can be analyzed in much the same way as the markets for output goods and services. Unlike output markets, however, the suppliers of labor are individuals and the demanders are organizations. The market for volunteer labor can be analyzed in much the same way as that for paid labor, although measures of supply and demand are more difficult to operationalize. The interactions between the paid and volunteer labor markets have important implications for the combinations of volunteer and paid labor that nonprofits choose to employ.

Pricing the commercial outputs of nonprofit organizations and social enterprises requires that managers assess a variety of market and nonmarket considerations and potential strategies. Basic relationships between price changes and revenue changes depend on the elasticity of demand, as in traditional economics, but also on interactions among various revenue sources. Sophisticated pricing and production strategies can increase revenues (price discrimination), maintain revenues against the forces of entry and exit (product differentiation), finance non-marketable activities related to the organizational mission (cross-subsidy), motivate consumers (adjustment of market prices to account for social benefits) and enhance client effort (institute fees to account for client self-worth). The basic analysis of competitive and monopolistic markets serves as the foundation to analyzing these various possibilities.

NOTE

1. The full solution requires the reader to set up a constrained optimization problem and simultaneously solve the first-order conditions of the Lagrangian. Adjustments to fund-raising depend on the cross-partials of the crowd-out function. See Andreoni and Payne (2003) for a very similar formulation.

SELECTED REFERENCES AND CITATIONS

Andreoni, J. and Payne, A.A. (2003). Do Government Grants to Private Charities Crowd Out Giving or Fund-Raising? *American Economic Review*, 93(3), 792–812.

Anheier, H.K. and Ben-Ner, A. (Eds.) (2003). *The Study of the Nonprofit Enterprise: Theories and Approaches*. New York: Kluwer Academic/Plenum Publishers.

Apgar, W.C. and Brown, H.C. (1987) *Microeconomics and Public Policy*. Glenview, IL: Scott, Foresman and Company.

Ben-Ner, A. (1986). Nonprofit Organizations: Why Do They Exist in Market Economies? In Rose-Ackerman, S. (Ed.), *The Economics of Nonprofit Institutions: Studies in Structure and Policy* (pp. 341–361). New York: Oxford University Press.

Brudney, J.L. (1990). *Fostering Volunteer Programs in the Public Sector*. San Francisco: Jossey-Bass.

Chang, C.F., Tuckman, H.P., and Chikoto-Schultz, G.L. (2018). Income Diversity and Nonprofit Financial Health. In Seaman, B.A. and Young, D.R. (Eds.), *Handbook of Research on Nonprofit Economics and Management* (2nd ed., pp. 11–34). Cheltenham, UK and Northampton, MA: Edward Elgar Publishing.

Duncombe, W.D. and Brudney, J.L. (1995). The Optimal Mix of Volunteer and Paid Staff in Local Governments: An Application to Municipal Fire Departments. *Public Finance Quarterly*, 23(3), 356–384.

Ehrenberg, R.G. and Smith, R.S. (2018). *Modern Labor Economics: Theory and Public Policy* (13th ed.). Florence, KY: Routledge.

Emanuele, R. (1996). Is There a (Downward Sloping) Demand Curve for Volunteer Labor? *Annals of Public and Cooperative Economics*, 67, 193–208.

Frumkin, P. and Keating, E.K. (2011). Diversification Reconsidered: The Risks and Rewards of Revenue Concentration. *Journal of Social Entrepreneurship*, 2(2), 151–164.

Graham, R. (2013). *Managerial Economics for Dummies*. Hoboken, NJ: John Wiley and Sons.

Grönbjerg, K. (1993). *Understanding Nonprofit Funding*. San Francisco: Jossey-Bass.

Handy, F. and Srinivasan, N. (2005). The Demand for Hospital Volunteers. *Nonprofit and Voluntary Sector Quarterly*, 34(4), 491–509.

Hansmann, H. (1981). Nonprofit Enterprise in the Performing Arts. *Bell Journal of Economics, 12,* 341–361.

Herzer, D. and Nunnenkamp, P. (2013). Private Donations, Government Grants, Commercial Activities, and Fundraising: Cointegration and Causality for NGOs in International Development Cooperation. *World Development, 46,* 234–251.

James, E. (1983). How Nonprofits Grow: A Model. *Journal of Policy Analysis and Management, 2,* 350–365.

Kearns, K.P. (2006). Income Portfolios in Nonprofit Organizations: Theory, Practice, and Research Questions. In Young, D.R. (Ed.), *Financing Nonprofits: Putting Theory into Practice* (pp. 291–310). Lanham, MD: AltaMira Press.

Kingma, B.R. (1993). Portfolio Theory and Nonprofit Financial Stability. *Nonprofit and Voluntary Sector Quarterly, 22(2),* 105–120.

Kingma, B.R. (1995). Do Profits "Crowd Out" Donations, or Vice Versa? The Impact of Revenues from Sales on Donations to Local Chapters of the American Red Cross. *Nonprofit Management and Leadership, 6(1),* 21–38.

Okten, C. and Weisbrod, B.A. (2000). Determinants of Donations in Private Nonprofit Markets. *Journal of Public Economics, 75(2),* 255–272.

Schiff, J. and Weisbrod, B. (1991). Competition between For-Profit and Nonprofit Organizations in Commercial Markets. *Annals of Public and Cooperative Economics, 62(4),* 619–640.

Segal, L. and Weisbrod, B.A. (1998). Interdependence of Commercial and Donative Revenues. In Weisbrod, B.A. (Ed.), *To Profit or Not to Profit: The Commercial Transformation of the Nonprofit Sector* (pp. 105–127). Cambridge, UK: Cambridge University Press.

Simmons, W. and Emanuele, R. (2010). Are Volunteers Substitutes for Paid Labor in Nonprofit Organizations? *Journal of Economics and Business, 62(1),* 65–77.

Steinberg, R. and Weisbrod, B.A. (1998). Pricing and Rationing by Nonprofit Organizations with Distributional Objectives. In Weisbrod, B.A. (Ed.), *To Profit or Not to Profit: The Commercial Transformation of the Nonprofit Sector* (pp. 64–82). Cambridge, UK: Cambridge University Press.

Yetman, M.H. and Yetman, R.J. (2003). The Effect of Nonprofits' Taxable Activities on the Supply of Private Donations. *National Tax Journal, 56(1),* 243–258.

Young, D.R. (2017), *Financing Nonprofits and Other Social Enterprises.* Cheltenham, UK and Northampton, MA: Edward Elgar Publishing.

REVIEW CONCEPTS

Ad Valorem Tax: Is based on the assessed value of an item such as real estate or personal property. It is a percentage markup of the price.

Arbitrage: Buying where a good or service is cheaper and reselling it where it has a higher price.

Crowd-out and Crowd-in: The relationship between two revenue sources. Crowd-out means an increase in the first source causes a decrease in the second, and crowd-in means an increase in the first source causes an increase in the second. Commonly applied to the relationship between commercial revenue and donations, or between donations and government funding.

Economies of Scope: Decreases in average total cost made possible by increasing the number of different goods produced.

Excise Tax: A tax on use or consumption of certain products. Excise taxes (also called "duties") are sometimes included in the price of a product, such as motor fuels, cigarettes, and alcohol.

Full Marginal Cost: When there are revenue interactions, the full marginal cost of producing an output is the sum of the marginal production cost and marginal reduction in donations.

Labor: A factor of production when human effort is rented and directed to produce goods or services.

Marginal Product of Labor: The additional output when labor is increased by one unit and all other factors of production are held constant.

Market Demand for Labor: The relationship between the quantity of a particular kind of labor that employers would like to hire and the wage rate.

Minimum Wage: A legally specified minimum rate of pay for labor employed in covered occupations and industries.

Perfect Price Discrimination: A set of personalized prices for each unit of a good or service sold to each possible buyer. Prices are set equal to a person's willingness to pay for that unit.

Per-unit Sales or Excise Tax: A tax consisting of a fixed dollar amount for each unit purchased.

Per-unit Subsidy: A negative tax consisting of a fixed dollar amount for each unit purchased.

Price Discrimination: The practice of selling the same good/service at different prices to different customers and/or charging different prices for different units purchased by the same individual.

Tax Incidence: The manner in which the burden of the tax is shared among economic constituencies (consumers, employees, employers, etc.). The statutory tax incidence states who is responsible for collecting taxes and sending them to the government. The economic tax incidence states whose prices are changed because of the tax's effect on market equilibrium.

Value Marginal Product of Labor (VMPL): The extra value created by the employment of an additional unit of a factor of production. The VMPL for labor is the product of the marginal product of labor and the price (if the output market is competitive) or more generally, marginal revenue or marginal societal benefit, measured in dollars per unit of labor.

EXERCISES

1. Analyze the incidence of a hotel tax that is designed to raise revenues for local arts organizations by taxing city visitors who stay in downtown hotels. Graph the general shape of the demand and supply functions for hotel rooms, making a reasonable guess about slopes in the short run and the consequent incidence of the tax. What factors will determine how much revenue arts organizations will receive from the tax? Then conduct the same exercise using long-run supply and demand.

2. Suppose a nonprofit art museum opens a gift shop and sells commercial art supplies which it claims will encourage amateur artists. Analyze what you think will be the impact on sales if the government decides that these sales constitute "unrelated income" and collects unrelated business income tax on profits from the sale of commercial art supplies.

3. A community health clinic operates in a heterogeneous neighborhood with families having a wide range of incomes. It offers a variety of services from urgent care to elective cosmetic procedures. If the clinic depends mostly on fees and wishes to ensure that all community residents are well served, how can a strategy of price discrimination be designed to foster this objective? How can the strategy of cross-subsidization also be usefully employed in this case?

4. Suppose a nonprofit nursing home is dependent on private donations for a major portion of its revenues but is considering various ways of increasing earned income to strengthen its financial base. Which of the following possibilities are likely to have a significant effect on donations and which ones are not? Explain your reasoning in each case:

(a)   Charging extra for meals and snacks;
(b)   Putting in a cappuccino bar and selling gourmet coffee to residents;
(c)   Selling crafts made by elderly residents;
(d)   Developing and marketing a new line of sports clothing for senior citizens;
(e)   Raising prices for basic residential care.

5. Consider a specific organization you have worked for or volunteered at. What are the advantages and disadvantages of starting a new commercial operation within that organization? Apply the tools of this chapter where appropriate and your own knowledge of the particulars where the tools are not quite appropriate.

6. Suppose that a mental health clinic decides that in order to make its services more affordable, it will lower its prices. How would this affect the clinic's demand for labor if it follows the conventional logic of choosing its labor input based on maximizing its financial surplus (profit)? Do you think this approach to calculating the clinic's demand for labor is appropriate in light of the organization's likely mission? Why or why not?

10
Economic decision making under risk

I should have checked my certainty equivalent before this!

10.1 Introduction

In the first nine chapters of this book, we analyzed economic decision making as a "deterministic" process. That is, we assumed that if we could estimate certain things, such as the elasticity of demand, or the marginal costs and benefits of a particular program, then we could determine an efficient course of action, for example, setting a particular price or choosing a new programmatic alternative. In the Methodological Appendix in the Online Companion (https://www.e-elgar.com/textbooks/young) we indeed show how such estimates can often be made with some precision, using available data and statistical techniques of econometric analysis.

In this chapter, however, and in the next one, we take a different tack, recognizing that often there is a substantial distinction between a "good decision" and a "good outcome." That is, decisions are frequently cloaked in sufficient uncertainty that even if we use the correct techniques and the best available information for analyzing and implementing efficient decisions, the ultimate outcomes of those decisions remain uncertain. There are two generic sources of such uncertainty. The first is intrinsic in nature. Certain variables that affect the outcomes of decisions, like the weather or the economy at large are, to a substantial extent, random in nature and hence can be predicted only to within an estimate of probability. Decisions of this kind are considered in the present chapter. Another source of uncertainty is that which derives from the reciprocal or reactive behavior of other decision makers. Recall from our discussion of concentrated markets in Chapter 8 that oligopolies present a special problem because pricing decisions are dependent not on gauging general market conditions but rather the reactions by a small handful of other firms. In such circumstances of a few, interdependent decision makers, the source of uncertainty for any given decision maker is the reaction of other identifiable decision makers. This situation is analyzed in the next chapter using the methodology of game theory.

Decision making under uncertainty involves *risk* because decisions become gambles or *lotteries* in which actions are chosen, as if dice were thrown in a particular way, and outcomes are manifest as a result of the way the dice land. Risk presents some special issues for economic decision making because different decision makers may feel differently about risk. That is, the willingness and ability to bear risk differs from person to person and organization to organization. So, as we will see below, we will need some way of characterizing and accounting for risk tolerance as well as measuring risk itself. The concept of the "certainty equivalent" as expressed by the parachutist in the cartoon above is one such way of doing this, as we will see.

Needless to say, the nonprofit and social enterprise world is fraught with situations of economic decision making under risk. Many significant, discrete actions, such as hiring a new person, undertaking a new program, making an investment or starting a fund-raising campaign, or outsourcing a particular organizational activity, all may involve substantial uncertainty and a range of possible outcomes. Indeed, analysis of many of the kinds of decisions considered in earlier chapters – such as pricing or choosing among alternative service programs – can also be usefully cast within the framework of decision making under risk that we will consider here.

10.2 Gambling against nature

The outcomes of many nonprofit economic decisions are, to a substantial degree, beyond the full control of decision makers. In these situations, non-profit and social enterprise managers and leaders can take their best shot by choosing a course of action that offers the best chance of success. But other variables beyond their control will set the parameters for the lotteries associated with the actions they choose: the state of the economy, the weather, the political or social circumstances, the vagaries of the particular markets in which they do business, the internal environment of the organization, or simply the serendipity of everyday life. Consider the following common situations:

- The success of a nonprofit commercial venture, such as a lawn service that employs ex-offenders, will depend on the state of the local economy, the weather, the ability to attract local capital, and other hard to predict factors that could create either a favorable or unfavorable situation in which to launch the program.
- The decision on whether to replace an existing fund-raising software package depends on how well potential donors will respond to the new package, what other packages come onto the market in the coming months, what new fund-raising approaches are undertaken by nonprof-its competing for the same donors, and what unanticipated technical glitches may occur in converting to a new software package.
- The decision on whether to charge for access to a "members only" sec-tion of an organization's website depends on how existing users react, e.g., by becoming members or dropping out, and on donors' willingness to continue to support the organization's public service mission after part of its website has been restricted to paying customers.
- The decision to conduct a national search to replace a social enterprise's retiring CEO depends on the vagaries of the national job market as well as the likelihood of finding an internal candidate with appropriate talents and support of the staff.

In each of these common situations, decision makers are faced with choosing among discrete alternatives, each of which could result in a particular gain or loss, depending on how the wheel of fortune turns. In order to analyze any such decision, we need first to answer the following questions:

- What are the alternative courses of action?
- What are the different possible outcomes associated with each alternative?

- What is the likelihood of each possible outcome, given that a particular alternative is chosen?

The nature of the answers to the first two of these questions is clear, as we are already familiar with alternatives and outcomes from previous chapters. Alternatives describe the different choices open to the decision maker. Outcomes actually can be broken down into two parts – what actually results as a consequence of the choice, and the value that we put on that result. Here we will call the latter the "payoffs" associated with particular outcomes. So, in the first example above, a nonprofit can choose, or not choose, to undertake the lawn service venture. Suppose it does choose to undertake the venture. Then it may be successful or unsuccessful (outcome), and the payoffs associated with these possible outcomes may be estimated in such terms as net revenue or net social benefit.

How then do we answer the third question, that is, the likelihood that a given outcome will result from a particular alternative? This is where we enter the world of *probability*. Probability is a way of characterizing the uncertainty associated with what we will call "risky decisions," that is, choices where the outcomes result in part from random influences and where the best we can do is estimate the chances of different outcomes occurring. Below, we consider the mathematical rules of probability. For more detail, see the Methodological Appendix (https://www.e-elgar.com/textbooks/young).

10.3   Rules of probability

Probability is a number that describes the likelihood of a particular occurrence. For example, if we flip a coin, we can assign probability estimates to the chances of the coin landing on "heads" or "tails." There are two main schools of thought on the meaning of probability. The "frequentists" regard probabilities as something objective that can be determined by observing the frequency of outcomes, whereas the "Bayesians" consider probability to be a subjective quantity representing the decision maker's best judgment based on experience and any current information that he or she may have that can be used to logically update that judgment. For instance, all of us have substantial experience with coins, and so we would be fairly comfortable saying that the chance of a flipped coin landing on "heads" is roughly 50 percent. A frequentist would be willing to adjust the probability of heads on a given flip if given laboratory testing information on a particular coin which showed that it was unbalanced and tended to favor tails. A Bayesian would start with an initial belief (say, that the coin is fair) and adjust that belief after a large departure from a 50–50 split. Either way, the same mathematical rules apply when working with probabilities.

Before turning to those rules, we need to distinguish an *event* from an outcome. There are two outcomes of a coin toss – heads or tails, but many possible events. One event would be "three heads in a row occurred;" another event would be "a head outcome was followed by a tail and then another head." An event, therefore, is a combination of outcomes that has a particular probability. Outcomes can be made into events: "we tossed the coin once and heads occurred," but there are many more events than there are outcomes. The laws of probability concern events:

1. The probability of any event is a number between 0 and 1.
2. The sum of probabilities of all possible, mutually exclusive events must add up to 1.

In the case of our coin flip, these two rules play out as follows, assuming a fair and balanced coin:

Probability of head = 0.5
Probability of tail = 0.5
Probability of head or tail = 1.0

Now suppose there are two events that are "independent" of one another in the sense that the outcome of one has no bearing on the outcome of the other. Here's the next rule:

3. The probability of a joint occurrence of independent events is the product of the probabilities of these events.

This is also a fairly intuitive rule, as our coin example demonstrates. Suppose we flip a coin twice in a row. The result of the first flip should have no influence on the second flip, so the two flips are independent events. Thus:

Probability of 2 heads = $0.5 \times 0.5 = 0.25$
Probability of 2 tails = $0.5 \times 0.5 = 0.25$
Probability of head then tail = $0.5 \times 0.5 = 0.25$
Probability of tail then head = $0.5 \times 0.5 = 0.25$

Note that the four events are mutually exclusive, that is, if one event happens, the other events cannot happen at the same time. In addition, together they constitute all possible outcomes of two flips of the coin. Therefore, the sum of their probabilities must add up to 1, as they do.

Finally, we need a rule for calculating the probability of an event that is dependent on the occurrence of another event (unlike the coin flip where the outcome of the second flip was independent of the result of the first flip). Here we need to introduce the concept of "conditional probability" through the following rule:

4. The probability of an event E that is dependent on the occurrence of one of several possible other events F or G, is calculated as follows:

$$p(E) = p(E|F)\,p(F) + p(E|G)\,p(G) \qquad (10.1)$$

where: $p(E)$ is simply the probability of event E;

$\quad$ $p(F)$ and $p(G)$ are the probabilities of events F and G respectively.

$\quad$ $p(E|F)$ is the "conditional probability" of E occurring, given that F occurs; and

$\quad$ $p(E|G)$ is the conditional probability of E occurring, given that G occurs.

Note that the probabilities of the conditioning events F and G must add up to 1 since they constitute all the possibilities for conditioning E.

Let's illustrate this rule with a simple example. Suppose candidate A is running for board president of her professional society, the Internet Surfers of America. A's chances depend on the voter turnout. She knows she has a better chance if the turnout is high (H) than if it is low (L) because she has broad recognition but does not have a large core of loyal fans. Turnout depends on the weather and other random factors rather than A's campaign style. Based on her best information about past elections and her best judgment of her chances in different circumstances, she makes the following estimates:

$$p(H) = 0.6;\ p(L) = 0.4;\ p(A|H) = 0.7;\ \text{and}\ p(A|L) = 0.2 \qquad (10.2)$$

That is, she judges that there is a 60 percent chance of a high turnout and 40 percent of a low turnout, and that she has a 70 percent chance of winning if the turnout is high, but only a 20 percent chance if the turnout is low. What is her chance of winning overall? Applying rule number 4, we compute this as follows:

$$p(A) = 0.7 \times 0.6 + 0.2 \times 0.4 = 0.5 \tag{10.3}$$

This same type of calculation can easily be illustrated with a construction called a "probability tree," which for this example is shown in Figure 10.1.

Figure 10.1
Probability tree analysis
of election to board
presidency

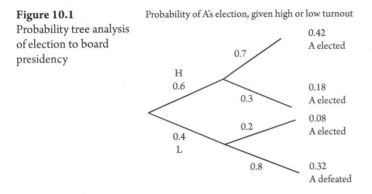

Probability of A's election, given high or low turnout

Note the following attributes of this tree: The numbers on the four outer branches represent the conditional probabilities, given the occurrences in the first stage of the tree (H or L). The probability of any particular combination of events is found by multiplying the probability numbers on successive branches. For example, the probability that the voter turnout will be high (H) and A will be elected is $0.6 \times 0.7 = 0.42$. The overall probability that A is elected is the sum of the probabilities of all the circumstances under which this can occur, namely when the turnout is high and when the turnout is low. So, we add 0.08, the probability that A wins and the turnout is low, to 0.42, the probability that A wins and the turnout is high, to obtain the overall estimate of 0.5 that A will win. Finally, note that the sum of the probabilities at the (right hand) end of the tree must add up to 1 because these represent all the possible outcomes of the compound (two stage) random process that characterizes this election.

Before proceeding further, we need to define a *lottery*. A *simple lottery* is a complete set of (mutually exclusive and collectively exhaustive) payoffs to available outcomes, with a probability assigned to each payoff. A *compound lottery* is a lottery of lotteries, that is, a complete set of lotteries and the associated probabilities of playing each lottery in that set. The probability tree in Figure 10.1 is a compound lottery, with payoffs in the form of winning or losing the election. A very useful result is that compound lotteries can always be reduced to simple lotteries using the rules of probability. In particular, the compound lottery in Figure 10.1 is equivalent (in terms of payoffs) to the simple lottery shown in Figure 10.2.

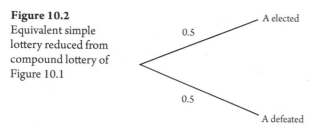

Figure 10.2 Equivalent simple lottery reduced from compound lottery of Figure 10.1

10.4 Decision trees

A decision tree is a graphical construct that represents both the choices and the contingencies associated with making a particular risky decision. Such a tree has two types of "nodes" – places where the tree divides into branches. There are *decision nodes* representing a choice the decision maker must make, with branches for each possible choice, and *probability nodes* or *chance points* with branches indicating the probability of each possible outcome. By working backwards through the tree, from outer branches to the root, decision makers can calculate their best choices. Figure 10.3 illustrates a very simple but highly useful decision tree. This tree represents a single choice, with one alternative involving risk. The X is a decision node, and the circle is a chance point. The generic question captured in this tree is whether one should pick the certain course of action (no change) with a sure payoff of C or another alternative (action) whose outcome might be better (A) or worse (B) than C.

Lots of important nonprofit and social enterprise decisions can be analyzed with this tree, for example whether to undertake a commercial venture or invest the funds in a fixed interest account; whether to merge with another organization or remain independent; whether to outsource a newsletter or continue to publish it in-house; whether to move to a new location or stay put; and so on. In each of these instances, there is a known alternative born of long experience, and a new alternative, the results of which are uncertain.

Figure 10.3 A simple and useful decision tree

Simple decision tree: action with uncertain outcome vs. known status quo

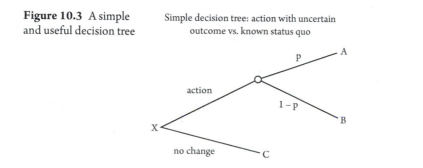

To analyze such a choice using a decision tree, we need to explain the statistical concept of *expected value*. Expected value is what one would logically expect to receive from a lottery on any given play. Intuitively, this expectation reflects what the outcome would be "on average" if we played the lottery many times. We calculate expected value using our probability estimates of different outcomes. For example, suppose the flip of a coin yielded us $10 if the coin landed on heads and zero if it came up tails. Then the expected value of flipping the coin would be $5 because we believe there's a 50/50 chance that the coin will come up heads. In formal terms then, for the simple lottery pictured in the upper branch of Figure 10.3, the expected value of making the risky (action) choice is:

$$E(V) = pA + (1 - p)B \qquad (10.4)$$

A reasonable way to decide what to do, if you don't care about risk, is to compare the expected value of payoffs for the risky option with the payoff for the safe option and select the larger of the two. We will modify this statement below to take into account different attitudes toward risk, but let's stick with this story for now. An illustrative example should help make things clear. Suppose we put the following numbers in the tree in Figure 10.3, to represent the Natural History Museum's decision of whether or not to undertake a new commercial venture, selling chocolate dinosaurs in supermarkets:

A = $1 million profit
B = −$0.5 million (loss)
C = $0.05 million return on an alternative safe investment (e.g., a U.S. bond)
p = 0.4
1 − p = 0.6

This risky venture promises a very sweet payoff if successful, and a substantial loss if it fails. Its chance of success (p) is only 40 percent, but the alternative safe investment has a very modest payoff.

The expected value of the venture in this case is 0.4 × $1million + 0.6 × (−$0.5 million) = $0.1 million. Since $0.1 million is greater than $0.05 million, it would appear that the risky venture is a superior choice. However, as with so many other things in life, this answer "depends" – in this case on one's "risk preference" or attitude towards risk. In this case, for example, the museum directors might worry excessively about their organization following their chocolate dinosaurs towards extinction!

10.5 Risk preference

Any time a sure thing is compared with a lottery, there might be trade-offs between the benefits (higher expected wealth) and costs (possibility of lower wealth) and so the decision maker's preferences become relevant. Attitudes towards risk fall in three ranges:

- *Risk-averse* decision makers prefer a lower level of risk. They are therefore willing to give up some amount of expected return from the risky alternative in order to have the higher safety of the sure thing. A mildly risk-averse person is only willing to sacrifice a small amount of expected wealth in order to gain the safety of the sure thing, but more risk-averse people are willing to give up a lot. Risk aversion leads people to buy insurance.
- *Risk-neutral* decision makers neither like nor dislike risk. They therefore select the alternative with the higher expected value.
- *Risk-loving* decision makers enjoy taking risk. They are willing to give up a portion of the return from the safe alternative in order to consume more risk. In other words, a risk lover will pick some risky alternatives that, on average pay less than the sure thing. Risk lovers buy tickets in the state lottery competition.

Like preferences for all other goods and services, risk preference applies at the margin. The same person may buy insurance (because she is risk averse at the margin for big losses) and lottery tickets (because she is risk preferring at the margin for small losses). Risk preferences can be quantified using the concepts of *certainty equivalence* and *risk premiums*. Suppose, like contestants on Monty Hall's old television show *Let's Make a Deal*, decision makers have a choice between "what's behind door number 2" (a lottery) and $10,000. The certainty equivalent of the lottery would be $10,000 if the decision maker would take the sure money had it been a penny greater than $10,000 and take the lottery if the sure money had been a penny less than $10,000. In other words:

> *The* certainty equivalent *of a lottery is that sum of money that makes the decision maker indifferent between the lottery and the value of the sure outcome.*

The decision maker is risk averse if the certainty equivalent is less than the expected value of a lottery, risk neutral if the certainty equivalent is the same as the expected value, and risk loving if the certainty equivalent is greater than the expected value of the lottery. We measure risk preferences by the *risk premium*, defined as the expected value minus the certainty equivalent. The risk premium is a positive number for the risk averse, zero for the risk neutral, and negative for risk lovers.

Now reconsider the simple decision situation represented in Figure 10.3. Any decision maker can specify his own certainty equivalent (CE) such that he is indifferent to the opportunity of receiving CE for sure or undertaking the risky (action) choice that could result in A or B. If the CE is greater than C (the payoff of the status quo), then it is best to undertake the risky alternative. If CE is less than C, then the riskless "no change" option is best.

Let's apply this model to a few cases, first revisiting the earlier example of the chocolate dinosaur venture. We saw earlier that a risk-neutral museum director would go ahead with this venture, given that its expected value exceeds the certain payoff of the riskless investment. Suppose, however, that the museum director is risk-averse with a certainty equivalent for the venture of CE = $0.04 million. That is, the museum director would just accept $40,000 in exchange for undertaking the venture. Since, the certain payment of the riskless option is C = $0.05 million, the director would logically choose the riskless investment and decide not to undertake the venture (since C > CE). So, we see from this example that two decision makers, each with different attitudes towards risk, can logically make different risk choices.

Again, using the simple decision tree of Figure 10.3, consider the following decision situation. HELP, a nonprofit social service organization is contemplating the purchase of new fund-raising software (*Tin Cup for Windows*). If the software is successful, it will yield a net gain in revenue from donations of $50,000 (outcome A). If the software works poorly, it will cause a loss of $10,000 (outcome B). If the funds are not used to purchase new software, the current software will be upgraded, yielding a net gain of $5,000 with certainty. The estimated probability of success of the new software is p = 0.7, and the probability of failure is 1 − p = 0.3. The expected value of the new software option is therefore:

$$E(V) = 0.7 \times \$50,000 + 0.3 \times (-\$10,000) = \$32,000$$

However, the executive director is risk averse and states her certainty equivalent to be CE = $25,000 for the option of undertaking the risky new software option. Because the CE is greater than the yield (C) of $5,000 with certainty if *Tin Cup* is not purchased, *Tin Cup* should be purchased.

Consider a third example, this time using a 10-point scale to rate the possible outcomes. An all-volunteer association, *World Humvee Owners of America*

(*WHOA*) is considering whether to hire its first paid executive director. The organization is getting along but has minimal potential for growth because the volunteers have too little time to devote to it. They believe that *WHOA* could potentially be much more successful and dynamic if the right paid director were in the driver's seat. On the other hand, hiring the wrong person could drive the association off the road. On a scale from 1 to 10 they rate the potential success associated with hiring the right candidate at 10, but failure of such a director would rate a 2. They rate the status quo at 3, a bit better than hiring a bad director. After a difficult search, the board has found a candidate, Tanker Jones, whom they think can do the job, but they're not sure. They assess Tanker's probability of success at 50/50; that is, p = 0.5 and 1 – p = 0.5. Finally, the board is risk averse (that's why they drive Humvees). While the expected value of hiring Tanker is E(V) = 6, their certainty equivalent for this lottery is only 4. Nonetheless, 4 is greater than C = 3 so they decide to go ahead with the appointment.

These various examples show that with some very simple logic, systematic subjective judgments, and a very simple decision tree model, managers can make rational decisions in the face of risk. Of course, they would prefer their decisions to have more predictable consequences, and they might find it worthwhile to gather additional information that would reduce uncertainty. Now we consider whether it is best to decide using our current level of information or to incur costs to gather more information before deciding. But what is such information worth? We address this question next.

10.6 The value of (perfect) information

Consider again the simple decision tree of Figure 10.3 and suppose that, as before, outcome A is better than the "no change" alternative resulting in C, but outcome B is worse than C. How would better information aid us in making the decision and improving the result? That depends, of course, on the quality of information available. Suppose, however, we could obtain "perfect information," that is, information that would tell us for sure whether the outcome of the "action" alternative was going to be A or B. Such information is as good as it gets, and its value would represent an upper limit to what we should be willing to pay for any information that purports to predict the outcome of that choice.

If we had perfect information, what would we do? This depends on what the information tells us. If we learn that the payoff to the risky choice would be A, we would pick the risky choice (because we have assumed that A is greater than C) and receive A as our payoff. If, instead, we learn that the payoff to

Figure 10.4 New lottery if perfect information can be obtained

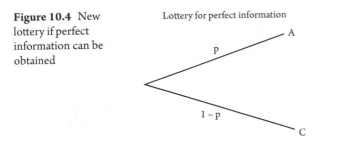

Lottery for perfect information

the risky choice would be B, then we would pick the safe choice (because we have assumed that C is greater than B) and receive C as our payoff. However, since we don't know in advance what the information will be, we must consider what the chances are of receiving each of these messages. But we already have those estimates: with probability p the information source will predict A and with probability (1 − p) the information source will predict B. So, if we expect to gain access to perfect information but do not yet know what that information will be, we have the new lottery shown in Figure 10.4.

The expected value of this lottery is:

$$E(V|PI) = pA + (1 - p)C \qquad (10.5)$$

So, the increased value to a risk-neutral decision maker as a result of perfect information is the difference between $E(V|PI)$ and the expected payoff $E(V)$ in the original decision situation of Figure 10.3. The latter, as we have seen, in turn depends on whether the decision maker would have originally chosen the *action* alternative or the *no change* alternative. Similarly, for the risk-averse or risk-preferring decision maker, the value of perfect information will be the difference between the certainty equivalent in the original situation of Figure 10.3 (CE^O), if the risky alternative were chosen, or the certain payment C if the riskless alternative were selected, and the certainty equivalent of the perfect information lottery of Figure 10.4 (CE^{PI}). Table 10.1 sets forth the various possibilities for risk-neutral and risk-averse decision makers.

Table 10.1 Value of perfect information for risk-neutral and risk-averse decision makers

	Would choose risky alternative without perfect information	Would choose riskless alternative without perfect information
Risk Neutral	$(1 - p)(C - B)$	$p(A - C)$
Risk Averse	$CE^{PI} - CE^O$	$CE^{PI} - C$

Figure 10.5 Perfect information lottery for the commercial venture decision

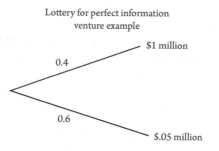

Lottery for perfect information venture example

0.4 — $1 million

0.6 — $.05 million

In essence, what Table 10.1 says is that if the decision maker were originally going to choose the risky action alternative, the value of perfect information is the difference between expected value (or certainty equivalent) of that lottery and that of the perfect information lottery. However, if the decision maker would have originally chosen the no-change alternative, the value of perfect information is the difference between the expected value or certainty equivalent of the perfect information lottery and the certain pay off C of the no-change alternative in the original decision tree.

Let's revisit our original example of the Natural History Museum considering whether it should launch a new chocolate dinosaur commercial venture. In this case, we computed that a risk-neutral director would undertake the venture, given that its expected value was $0.1 million compared to the $0.05 million value of C, the safe alternative investment. And we determined that if a risk-averse director's certainty equivalent for the venture alternative were only $0.04 million, he would decide not to undertake the venture. Figure 10.5 displays the perfect information lottery for this example.

The expected value of this lottery $E(V|PI) = \$0.43$ million. However, the risk-averse director will have a certainty equivalent less than this because there is a positive risk premium required for the director to choose the risky alternative. Suppose, therefore, that the risk-averse director's certainty equivalent for the perfect information lottery is $CE^{PI} = \$0.25$ million. This is all the information we need to calculate the value of perfect information (or the maximum possible value of any information) in this example. The various contingencies are displayed in Table 10.2.

Note that only two cells in this table are relevant because we know what the risk-neutral and risk-averse directors would do in the absence of perfect information. We can see from these calculations that perfect information is worth more to the risk-neutral director, because it is more likely to change her original decision than it is to change the decision of the risk-averse director. Still, perfect information would be worth quite a lot to either decision maker

Table 10.2 Value of perfect information for the commercial venture decision

	Would choose risky alternative without perfect information	Would choose riskless alternative without perfect information
Risk Neutral	$(1 - p)(C - B)$ $= 0.6 \times (\$50K + \$500K)$ $= \$330K$	NA
Risk Averse	NA	$CE^{PI} - C$ $= \$250K - \$50K$ $= \$200,000$

and this calculation certainly suggests the value of additional research which might contribute to greater certainty about the outcome of the venture. Real (imperfect) information is likely to be worth substantially less than these upper bound estimates, however, depending on the anticipated reliability of the information. Calculations of the value of imperfect information are also possible, given probability estimates of the likelihood that the information provided is right or wrong. Other texts on decision theory offer this more detailed analysis for the interested reader (see Behn and Vaupel, 1982).

10.7 Variations on the theme

The previous sections of this chapter cover the basic elements for analyzing risky decisions. While the single-stage, simple decision-tree model of Figure 10.3 is useful for a wide range of such decisions, real world decisions can often be more complex in many ways. Certainly, decisions may involve more than one risky option. In addition, the outcomes of particular alternatives may involve several random events (compound lotteries) rather than a single stage lottery, and indeed more than two contingencies at any given stage (chance point). However, we have already discussed the tools necessary to deal with such complications. To help illustrate this point, let us consider one final example, that of a choice between two risky ventures, as depicted in Figure 10.6.

In this case Preppy High is considering two possible new initiatives to help raise funds for the school. Venture 1 is a travel program for alumni that would take graduates to exotic world ports for two-week educational seminars on local wildlife (human and otherwise). Venture 2 is a new yoga program for alumni and local community residents designed to bring participants peace in mind and body.

Figure 10.6 Choice between two risky ventures

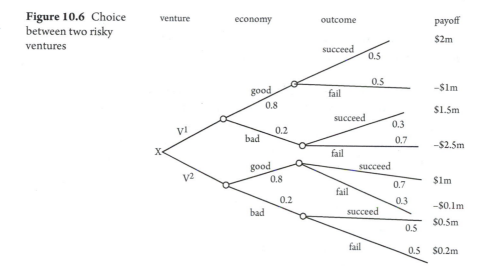

As described in the decision tree, venture 1 (the travel program) is the riskier venture with the higher potential payoff and the greater potential loss. Venture 2 is less risky with a greater chance of success and lower potential payoffs and losses. The success of each venture depends on the performance of the economy in the immediate future. Venture 2 is better able to weather a bad economy and in fact will do reasonably well in a bad economy (when people really need peace of mind) while potentially running a small loss in a good economy. Figure 10.6 indicates the school development director's best estimates of the probabilities of a good or bad economy, and the *conditional* probabilities that each of the ventures will succeed or fail, given the state of the economy. The dollar figures on the right side of the tree indicate the payoffs associated with each contingency of success or failure in a good or bad economy, for each venture alternative.

By multiplying the probabilities along the branches of the tree with the payoffs at the ends of the branches we can calculate the expected payoff value of each venture as follows:

$$E(V^1) = 0.8 \times 0.5 \times \$2m + 0.8 \times 0.5 \times (-\$1m) + 0.2 \times 0.3 \times \$1.5m$$
$$+ 0.2 \times 0.7 (-\$1m) = \$0.14m$$

$$E(V^2) = 0.8 \times 0.7 \times \$1m + 0.8 \times 0.3 \times (-\$0.1m) + 0.2 \times 0.5 \times \$0.5m$$
$$+ 0.2 \times 0.5 \times \$0.2m = \$0.606m$$

Based on this calculation a risk-neutral school principal would choose venture 2. Interestingly, a risk-averse principal would do the same since her certainty equivalent for venture 2 (CE^2) (the less risky venture with the higher expected value) would be greater than that for venture 1 (CE^1). Only a risk-loving principal with his eye on the potentially higher payoff of venture 1 in a good economy might gamble on venture 1.

Finally, what about the value of information in this case? A source of perfect information would be able to tell the principal when the negative contingencies were going to occur. In these cases, the principal would refrain from investing in that venture. Replacing the negative outcomes with zeros in the decision tree of Figure 10.6 (since these contingencies would be avoided with perfect information) yields the following expected values:

$$E(V^1|PI) = \$0.89 \text{ million and } E(V^2|PI) = \$0.63 \text{ million}$$

Thus, with perfect information, the risk-neutral principal would change his mind and undertake venture 1 rather than venture 2. The difference in expected values with and without such information is $E(V^1|PI) - E(V^2) = \$0.89\text{million} - \$0.606\text{million} = \$0.284$ million, representing the very most this decision maker should pay for information that would predict the outcomes of the two ventures.

A risk-averse principal in this case may or may not reverse her decision, depending on how conservative she really is. If, with the prospect of perfect information, the travel program (venture 1) becomes sufficiently attractive, she may indeed switch as well. A risk-loving principal would most certainly switch from the yoga program to the travel venture (V^2 to V^1) with the prospect of perfect information, if he hadn't already preferred V^1. In general, (subjective) estimates of the certainty equivalents before and after the prospect of perfect information will yield the upper bounds for the value of information in each of these cases.

10.8 Extensions and refinements

Research on economic decision making suggests that people tend to be risk averse and prefer to avoid big losses more than they seek to secure large net gains. (For a full exposition see Kahneman and Tversky, 2000 for the original idea and Tversky and Kahneman, 1992 for the extension of the original idea that was cited when Kahneman won the Nobel Prize in Economics). The present text employs the simple concept of certainty equivalents to capture an individual's risk preference in a particular decision situation. A more general treatment is to characterize a decision maker's risk preference over a range of possible gains and losses by constructing a "utility" function that translates those gains and losses into a curvilinear index that reflects both the subjective increases in well-being as gains increase and the perceived reduction of well-being as actual losses become greater (see Frank, 2010). With such an index one can carry through the analyses described above by calculating expected utilities (which incorporate risk preference) rather than expected values of payoffs (which do not).

A further nuance is that assessment of risk may itself be uncertain. That is, we may not have a very precise idea about the value of the probabilities we assign in analyzing risky decisions such as those described above. For example, we may be unsure of the probability of "heads" in the coin flip of an unfamiliar or suspect coin. In this case of general "uncertainty" rather than simple risk, the mathematics of probability distributions must be applied to the analysis of decisions and decision trees. The principles behind the calculations illustrated in this chapter remain the same, but the mathematics is more complex. (For further study, see Howard and Abbas, 2016; also see the Methodological Appendix (https://www.e-elgar.com/textbooks/young) for explanation of probability distributions.)

An important application of decision making under risk in the nonprofit sector is the shaping of a nonprofit's mix of different sources of income. An organization's combination of income from fees, gifts, government contracts and investments, and the particular sources of income within these broad categories, may be understood as an "income portfolio." As such, the problem of specifying this portfolio may be viewed as an exercise in portfolio management, similar to managing a portfolio of stocks, bonds and real estate (see Kingma, 1993). The objective of a securities portfolio manager is to maximize financial return subject to a given level of risk tolerance or equivalently to minimize risk subject to achieving a minimum desired level of income return. The mathematical methodology of portfolio optimization allows the portfolio manager to identify the various combinations of risk and return that are achievable and efficient. For these efficient combinations, greater return entails greater risk and lower risk entails lower return. The same logic can be applied to nonprofit income portfolios once each prospective source of income is identified and understood in terms of its intrinsic volatility (risk), fund development costs and income yield. The key insight from finance theory is that the volatility of the income portfolio depends not just on the volatility of each income source, but also on the correlation between returns for each pair of income sources. Thus, diversification strategy is more complicated than just adding a source of income to the mix in case the other sources come up short. (For a fuller discussion of nonprofit income portfolios, see Young, 2017).

SUMMARY

Many of the resource-related decisions that confront managers of nonprofit organizations and social enterprises engender risk because the outcomes of those decisions cannot be predicted with certainty. While managers may proceed to make these decisions using their best single guesses and estimates of the costs and benefits of alternative actions, it is often worthwhile to bring risk more directly into their calculations. There are several ways of doing this, depending on the circumstances. For example, in accounting for opportunity costs through discounting of costs and benefits over time (see Chapter 6) one can include "risk premiums" directly into the discount rate to account, in *ad hoc* fashion, for the fact that the future is difficult to predict. And, as discussed in Chapters 8 and 11, if uncertainty derives from the countermoves of other decision makers, game theory analysis can help the nonprofit decision maker or social entrepreneur think through her risky decisions, in part, by trying to anticipate the strategies of others.

In the present chapter, we have demonstrated the usefulness of another fairly general decision analysis framework for analyzing economic (and other) nonprofit organization and social enterprise decisions, where the outcomes of alternative courses of action may vary widely and occur with substantially different likelihoods due to (impersonal) environmental influences beyond the manager's control. In such cases, the selection of a particular course of action can be characterized as a "lottery" in which potential outcomes and their payoffs are specified, and the chances of alternative outcomes can be estimated using subjective probabilities that represent the decision maker's best judgment, given her experience and available information.

With this model, the laws of probability can help the decision maker to distinguish alternatives with greater expected payoffs from those with lower expected payoffs. In addition, this model allows the decision maker to take into account his own, or his organization's, tolerance of risk, by subjectively evaluating lotteries against the prospects of payoffs that are certain. Finally, this decision analysis model enables a decision maker to consider the value of information that may be purchased to reduce risk. In this connection, we showed how the "value of perfect information" can be computed as an upper bound to what the decision maker should be willing to pay for any such information.

It has been argued in some quarters that nonprofit decision makers often overemphasize risk and make untenably conservative decisions based

implicitly on unrealistic assumptions about the likelihood of various contingencies (Scanlan and Dillon-Merrill, 2006). One strength of the decision analysis framework offered here is that it forces the decision maker to
think explicitly about the likelihood of possible outcomes, as well as his or
her tolerance of risk per se. Even crude estimates of these parameters have
the potential for substantially improving the efficiency of nonprofit and
social enterprise decision making in situations involving risk.

SELECTED REFERENCES AND CITATIONS

Behn, R.D. and Vaupel, J.W. (1982). *Quick Analysis for Busy Decision Makers*. New York: Basic Books.

Frank, R.H. (2010). *Microeconomics and Behavior*. New York: McGraw-Hill.

Howard, R.H. and Abbas, A.E. (2016). *Foundations of Decision Analysis*. New York: Pearson North America.

Kahneman, D. and Tversky, A. (Eds.) (2000). *Choices, Values and Frames* Cambridge UK: Cambridge University Press and New York: Russell Sage Foundation.

Kingma, B.R. (1993). Portfolio Theory and Nonprofit Financial Stability. *Nonprofit and Voluntary Sector Quarterly*, 22(2), 105–119.

Lee, W. (1971). *Decision Theory and Human Behavior*. New York: John Wiley & Sons.

Scanlan, E.A. and Dillon-Merrill, R. (2006). Risky Business: Understanding and Managing Risk in the Nonprofit Sector. In Young, D.R. (Ed.), *Wise Decision-Making in Uncertain Times* (Chapter 4, pp. 55–73). New York: The Foundation Center and the National Center on Nonprofit Enterprise.

Tversky, A. and Kahneman, D. (1992). Advances in Prospect Theory: Cumulative Representation of Uncertainty. *Journal of Risk and Uncertainty*, 5(4), 297–323.

Young, D.R. (2017). *Financing Nonprofit and Other Social Enterprises*. Cheltenham, UK and Northampton, MA: Edward Elgar Publishing.

REVIEW CONCEPTS

Certainty Equivalent: The payment in-hand that a decision maker would accept as equivalent to the value of the opportunity to choose a given risky alternative. A certainty equivalent less than expected value indicates risk aversion.

Conditional Probability: The probability of an event, given that another event has already taken place.

Decision Node: A point in a decision tree where the branches represent alternative choices available to the decision maker at that stage in the decision process.

Decision Tree: A representation of a risky decision in the form of a tree with a sequence of choice points and probability nodes, useful for analyzing decisions when the results of alternative choices differ in their likelihoods and payoffs.

Event: A combination of outcomes that has a particular probability. Each complete path, from start to finish in a decision tree, is an event.

Expected Value: The probability-weighted sum of possible payoffs from a given choice. The average value one expects to see when an event is repeated many times.

Game Theory: A methodology for analyzing decisions when the payoffs depend on the choices of others.

Independent Events: Two events whose individual occurrences do not affect the likelihood of the other occurring. When events A and B are independent, $p(A) = p(A|B)$ and $p(B) = p(B|A)$.

Lottery: A set of mutually exclusive and collectively exhaustive payoffs and their probabilities. A simple lottery is a choice between payoff A with probability p and payoff B with probability (1 – p). A compound lottery is a lottery between lotteries.

Probability: A number between 0 and 1 that represents the likelihood that a given event will occur. Probabilities may be gauged by subjective beliefs or objective frequencies of occurrence.

Probability Node: A point in a decision tree where the branches represent probabilities, but the choice is not made by the decision maker. This can be thought of as a decision node for Mother Nature.

Risk: A situation in which more than one possible payoff of a choice can occur with non-zero probability.

Risk-averse: The preference of a decision maker who values a risky choice at less than its expected payoff value.

Risk-neutral: The preference of a decision maker who values a risky choice by its expected payoff value.

Risk-preferring: The preference of a decision maker who values a risky choice at more than its expected payoff value.

Risk Premium: The amount of money needed to compensate the decision maker for bearing risk in a lottery; equal to the expected value minus the certainty equivalent of the lottery.

Value of Perfect Information: The maximum amount a decision maker should pay for information that would tell her with certainty what payoffs will result from each available option.

EXERCISES

1. Ruff Barker, a dogged social entrepreneur is undertaking a new venture PainlessPaws that would ease the lives of aging dogs and cats with arthritis by supplying them with special supportive shoes. The success of the new venture depends on whether Ruff can raise external investment capital. If he can, he estimates PainlessPaws' chances of success at 90 percent; if he cannot he will finance the venture from his own limited savings but estimates the chance of success at only 50 percent. Moreover, he assesses the chance of attracting an external investor at 60 percent. What is the overall probability that PainlessPaws will succeed?

2. Back to Bach (BTB), an early music group, offers its concerts in local venues such as churches, high schools and community centers. Demand for its programs has grown and it is considering the purchase of its own performance facility. With its own venue BTB can offer more concerts and have greater control over the scheduling of performances. The executive director Flyoff DeHandel (FD) estimates that without a new space, BTB will continue to break-even and hold its attendance steady. With a new venue, there is risk of running an operating deficit but also a good possibility that profits will be generated, allowing further expansion. FD thinks that BTB has a 75 percent chance of running a $100,000 surplus and a 25 percent chance of running a $100,000 deficit in the new venue, depending on how much the general public likes the new facility and scheduling. If BTB is indifferent to risk, should it choose the new venue or stay put? If BTB can hire a consultant to determine whether the new venue will be successful, what is the most that BTB should be willing to pay for the consultant's report?

3. The Community Foundation of North Fork (CFNF) is approached by the North Fork Food Bank (NFFB) with a proposal to fund an investment in its new environmentally sensitive

utensil disposal business. NFFB is asking for a Program-Related Investment (PRI) in the form of a one-year 6 percent, $100,000 loan whose principal will be repaid to CFNF along with a modest financial return if the venture succeeds; otherwise the loan would convert to a grant that does not have to be paid back. The loan would be made from CFNF's general investment fund in which the $100,000 would normally earn $5000 annually. As a PRI, the $100,000 would earn $6000 if the utensil disposal business succeeds but nothing if it fails. Staff of CFNF and NFFB agree that the venture has a 90 percent chance of succeeding. If the leadership of CFNF is risk-neutral should it fund the PRI? If it is risk-averse, what value of its certainty equivalent for the PRI would lead CFNF to reject the proposal?

4. Consider an issue in your organization, or your personal life, where a specific change in the status quo is being considered. On a scale from 1 to 10, assign a value to continuing the status quo. Now consider two or more possible outcomes of the contemplated decision to change the status quo. Assign a value of 1 to 10 to each possible outcome as well as a probability between 0 and 1 to represent the likelihood of that outcome if you decide on the change. (Be sure the probabilities of all of these outcomes add up to 1.) Chart your decision with a decision tree and use it to consider what you or your organization should do. How does your attitude towards risk affect your choice? What further information would you like before making the choice and what would that information be worth to you?

11

Games of collaboration and competition

Now would be a good time to use our dominant strategy!

11.1 Introduction

numbers of buyers and sellers whose behavior, in the aggregate, could be characterized by impersonal demand and supply functions. Thus, any individual economic decision maker, buyer or seller, could purchase or sell a good or service without provoking any specific counter-reaction from other actors in the marketplace. However, as Chapter 8 explains, in "small-number situations" with few buyers or sellers, actors have substantial *market power*. Market participants know that the behavior of others matters and must account for the way others react to their decision making. Hence decision makers will try to anticipate each others moves and take positions that will allow them to defend against untoward contingencies or improve their own positions. Chapter 8 reviews some of the classical and mathematical models that economists have developed to understand oligopolistic markets characterized by these conditions. Some of these models are based on the tools of "game theory," which is a way of conceptualizing and "solving" interactive decision-making situations involving two or more decision makers. In this chapter, we apply game theory to a variety of such resource-related decision-making situations commonly encountered by nonprofit organizations and social enterprises. We also examine games among donors to capture the essence of the free-rider problem.

Clearly, decision makers in small number situations face considerable uncertainty of a different kind than we considered in the previous chapter. Rather than making choices whose outcomes are contingent on the impersonal vagaries of nature, decision makers in these circumstances are perplexed by the whims and scheming of other decision makers. Just like the football team in the cartoon above, they try to anticipate what their adversaries will do in reaction to their own choices. It is to this realm of decision making that game theory specifically applies.

Nonprofit managers meet many such game situations. Here are a few examples:

- Two universities are applying for the same research grant. Should they collaborate or compete? If they compete, should they propose different projects or go head-to-head on similar projects?
- A few hospitals systems dominate the local market for health care. One is trying to decide whether to raise its rates for elective plastic surgery. Should it do so? How will its competitors react?
- A social service organization is negotiating with its employees union. What benefits should it propose for the next contract? What will the union propose or agree to? Will a strike result?
- A local United Way invites a major youth-serving organization to join its ranks and confine its local fund-raising to the collective campaign. Under what terms should this offer be made, and under what terms will it be accepted?
- An environmental advocacy organization wants to stop a corporate polluter from fouling the wetlands in its metropolitan area. The corporation in turn wants to improve its public image but protect its economic interests. Should the organization employ confrontational or collaborative tactics and how can the corporation be expected to react?

In each of these and many other cases, the outcomes depend simultaneously on the decisions taken by each participating economic actor who in turn must try to take account of another's choices. Thus, each decision maker retains only partial control over the consequences of his or her choices, and even the best intentions by all parties can lead to undesirable results. For example, the corporate polluter and the environmental organization may each decide to take aggressive positions to protect themselves in the absence of understanding the other's flexibility, whereas mutual compromise might have led to a better situation for both.

11.2 The elements and vocabulary of game theory

Game theory has a long and distinguished history, the brainchild of geniuses including John von Neumann, Oskar Morgenstern and John Nash, and it has become quite sophisticated in its mathematical development and application to complex situations. But its rudiments are relatively simple and intuitive, and easy for a practicing manager to understand and apply. There are many kinds of games in game theory. Abstractly, a game consists of a set of *players* and player preferences over outcomes of the game, a set of choices available to each player, the outcome resulting from each combination of choices made by players, and rules that cover the order of player moves and the information available to each player at the time each choice is made by that player. For example, we could have two players, Fred and Wanda. They can each choose between applying for a high-paying job at a Starbucks, applying for a lower-paying job at Buckstars, and not applying for a job (available choices). If they both apply for the same job, a coin is tossed to decide who gets it (outcomes). They choose simultaneously without knowing the choice of the other player (rules of the game). They each like the Starbucks job best, the Buckstars job second-best, and no job least. However, they hate uncertainty so much that they prefer not applying over applying for the same job that the other player applies for (preferences). These are the elements of any game.

We will start our analysis of behavior in games with a simple, but useful kind of game:

- There are exactly two players. The basic approach described here works for any finite number of players greater than two, so we stick with the simplest case.
- Each player has a small set of alternative choices ("discrete choice"). For example, we could simplify the duopoly game to say that each firm could choose one of two prices – the perfectly competitive equilibrium price (low), or the price that would be picked by a monopoly firm (high).

The actual Bertrand duopoly game described in Chapter 8 presents each firm with an infinity of alternatives ("continuous choice") – any price on the positive real number line can be selected. Restricting attention to discrete choice games allows us to work with *payoff matrices* that specify the *payoffs* to each player resulting from each combination of choices by both players.

- Payoffs measure preferences in that whenever a player likes alternative 'A' better than alternative 'B,' 'A' will have a larger numerical payoff. If the players play for money, a player's payoff is simply the amount of money he or she receives. But payoff scales can be developed for whatever the player cares about. For example, Fred's payoffs in the example above could be 2 for the Starbucks job, 1 for the Buckstars job, and 0 for unemployment. We need not worry about the arbitrariness of the exact numbers chosen, as long as the higher numbers are assigned to the preferred alternatives.

- Every player knows the payoff matrix and knows that the other players also know the payoff matrix (the payoff matrix is *common knowledge*) before making any decisions. This assumption is called *complete information*, and dramatically simplifies games. Unfortunately, many management decisions are better described as games of incomplete information, which is a more advanced topic beyond the scope of this introductory text.

- Initially, we will look at "simultaneous-moves" games, where each player chooses an action without knowing what the other player has chosen. So even though we are assuming that there is complete information, players do not know everything.

- Finally, we assume that the players cannot make a binding agreement prior to making their choices. Games where binding pre-play agreements are possible are called *cooperative games*, but we are looking at *competitive games* (also known as "non-cooperative games") where those agreements are not enforceable.

With these assumptions, the set of available actions for a player is called the "strategy set" and a player's "strategy" is the choice of an action in that player's strategy set (e.g., the player might select the strategy "high price" in the Bertrand duopoly game). The payoff matrix lists the payoff to each player resulting from each combination of strategies that could be chosen by the players. The generic two-person, two-strategies-each game is shown as Figure 11.1.

Here, each player has two possible strategies or choices, s_1 and s_2 for player A and S_1 and S_2 for player B. The four boxes indicate the payoffs to each player for each combination of strategies, with the payoff to the row player (A)

Note: Each cell contains the payoff to the row player followed by the payoff to the column player.

Figure 11.1 A two-player game in matrix form

		Player B (column player)	
		S_1	S_2
Player A s_1		A_{11}, B_{11}	A_{12}, B_{12}
(row player) s_2		A_{21}, B_{21}	A_{22}, B_{22}

listed first by convention. Thus, if player A chooses her first strategy, s_1 and player B chooses her second strategy, S_2 then the payoffs are A_{12} for player A and B_{12} for player B.

An *equilibrium* in economics is a balancing of forces, where further movement of economic variables ceases. For example, in competitive markets, when price is too high, the quantity demanded is more than the quantity supplied causing the price to move downward. In competitive equilibrium, prices allow markets to clear, so prices stop moving. In games, we have different kinds of equilibria applicable to different games. We start with the most compelling kind of equilibrium, a dominant strategy equilibrium, where we understand how players get to equilibrium from any starting point and why their equilibrium strategies are stable. Dominant strategy equilibria are compelling because we can confidently predict that most players will play their dominant strategies, but there are also many games where no dominant strategy equilibrium exists. We then turn to John Nash's beautiful breakthrough, the Nash equilibrium for competitive games. This will prove less compelling as a prediction, because we know that once reached, Nash equilibrium is stable, but we don't know why players move to a Nash equilibrium (Klarreich, 2017). Thus, there are many experiments in behavioral economics that test when Nash equilibrium gives accurate predictions of human behavior.

There are two important classes of games – "zero-sum" games and "non-zero-sum" games. Zero-sum games are those games where the sum of the payoffs across players add up to the same constant number, no matter what the choices of strategies. We call these zero-sum games because the constant number is usually zero, although this is really immaterial to the solution of the game. The basic point is that zero-sum games are games of *direct conflict* such that one player's winnings directly reflect the other player's losses and vice versa. If the game in Figure 11.1 were zero sum, then $A_{11} + B_{11} = A_{12} + B_{12} = A_{21} + B_{21} = A_{22} + B_{22} =$ a constant number, often zero.

The second kind of game is, not surprisingly, one in which the sum of payoffs to each player does not add up to the same constant number regardless of strategy choices. This means that certain combinations of strategy choices can be better or worse for both players. These *non-zero-sum games* are in many ways more interesting because they include opportunities for cooperation, deception, threats, information sharing, and other nuances of strategic human behavior and decision making.

11.3 Examples of games played once and equilibria

We begin this section with a discussion of the easier cases, where a dominant-strategy equilibrium exists because this is the most compelling kind of equilibrium. We illustrate dominant-strategy equilibria for zero-sum and non-zero-sum games. We then consider solving some games that do not have a dominant-strategy equilibrium, using a slightly broader concept to make reliable predictions: iterated-dominant-strategy equilibrium. Then we move to the harder cases, where no such equilibrium exists. There is always at least one Nash equilibrium, so we define and illustrate Nash equilibria with two examples.

Easier (dominance-solvable) games

We start with the most straightforward example, a marketing game between two local hospital systems. This is shown as a "constant sum" game, with market shares in each case adding up to 100 percent, where we assume that the two players want to maximize market share, rather than profits. Figure 11.2 is the payoff matrix for this game.

To analyze this game, we can use the concept of *dominant strategies* (what the team in our cartoon was looking for). A player's dominant strategy is a single strategy which is best regardless of which strategies are selected by other players. Notice that Community Clinic is better off using aggressive marketing when University Systems chooses aggressive marketing (the payoff is 50 percent, the first number in the top left cell – versus 25 percent, the first number in the bottom left cell) and when University Systems chooses normal

Figure 11.2 Market share game – two local hospital systems

		University Systems	
		Aggressive Marketing	*Normal Marketing*
Community Clinic	*Aggressive Marketing*	50%, 50%	75%, 25%
	Normal Marketing	25%, 75%	50%, 50%

marketing (75 percent versus 50 percent). Thus, aggressive marketing is a dominant strategy for Community Clinic. Aggressive marketing is also a dominant strategy for University Systems because it is the best response to aggressive marketing by Community Clinic (50 percent, the second number in the top left cell – versus 25 percent, the second number in the top right cell) and also the best response to normal marketing by Community Clinic (75 percent versus 50 percent).

When each player has a dominant strategy it is natural to assume that each will play its dominant strategy, and we call the result a *dominant-strategy equilibrium*. Note that in this game, both players have dominant strategies – aggressive marketing. So, the strategy combination (Aggressive, Aggressive) is a dominant strategy equilibrium and we confidently predict that when real players play this game, they will split the market fifty-fifty.

The prisoner's dilemma

What if the two hospitals cared about profits instead of market shares? Then we need to display payoffs in dollars. Figure 11.3 displays this kind of payoff.

This is not a zero-sum game since the payoffs do not add to the same number in each cell. But the numbers are such that we have the same dominant-strategy equilibrium, (Aggressive, Aggressive). Still, these are very different games. In the profits game, equilibrium payoffs are (−$1 million, −$1 million), despite the fact that both players prefer the bottom-right outcome of (+$1 million, +$1 million). This example illustrates two differences between results of zero-sum and non-zero-sum games:

- Unlike zero-sum games, there can be "win–win" strategies.
- Unlike zero-sum games, there can be outcomes that both players prefer but are not supported by equilibrium strategies.

Figure 11.3 Two local hospital systems competing for profits

| | | University Systems | |
		Aggressive Marketing	*Normal Marketing*
Community Clinic	*Aggressive Marketing*	–$1M, –$1M	$3M, –$3M
	Normal Marketing	–$3M, $3M	$1M, $1M

Figure 11.4 A prisoner's dilemma for universities

		Private U	
		Next Year	*This Year*
State U	*Next Year*	2, 2	0, 3
	This Year	3, 0	1, 1

When there is a dominant-strategy equilibrium but both players would be better off moving to a non-equilibrium outcome, the game is called a *prisoner's dilemma*. The name of this game derives from the original example – two prisoners held in separate cells, each with an individual incentive to inform on the other but jointly better off if they both keep quiet (e.g., see Hargreaves Heap and Varoufakis, 1995). Another example of a prisoner's dilemma game is depicted in Figure 11.4. In this game, two universities in the same city are considering launching a new certificate program in social enterprise management. The problem here is two-fold. First, there is a "first-mover" advantage to the institution that launches its program first and consequently comes to dominate the market. Second, these programs would generate a larger market overall if they had another year to develop their messages and materials.

Once again, there is a dominant-strategy equilibrium (this year, this year) that is inferior to the outcome (next year, next year). Why don't the universities reach this Pareto-preferred outcome? The answer is that if one player chooses "next year," the best response of the other player is "this year." Pre-play communication would not change these basic incentives. Both players would agree to wait and hope that the other player honored that agreement. But when they simultaneously decide what to do, it is better to break the agreement. Game theorists call communication without enforceable commitment "cheap talk," and predict it should have no effect if the payoffs are accurately described in this matrix. In the next chapter, we will consider behavioral economics and find that even cheap talk has real effects on outcomes. The likely explanation is that talk is a social interaction, and social interaction makes the players care about more than financial payoffs. The strictly monetary payoffs listed in our payoff matrix become inaccurate after talking.

Some games do not have a dominant-strategy equilibrium. Consider the UBIT game (Figure 11.5), which depicts the decision of a nonprofit museum of whether to declare taxable unrelated business income from its gift shop sales and thus pay the UBIT, and the decision of the Internal Revenue Service (IRS) of whether to audit that organization:

Figure 11.5 The UBIT
game

		IRS	
		Audit	*Don't Audit*
Museum	*Pay UBIT*	−5, 5	−4, 4
	Evade UBIT	−9, 9	0, 0

If the museum evades the UBIT and the IRS audits the museum, the IRS will require tax payments plus a penalty. If the museum pays the UBIT and gets audited, it bears the additional cost of preparing for the audit. If the IRS doesn't audit the museum and the museum evades taxes, the museum does quite well. If the IRS doesn't audit, and the museum pays taxes, at least the museum saves on audit-preparation costs.

The IRS has a dominant strategy in this game, but the museum does not, so no dominant-strategy equilibrium exists for this game. Audit is a dominant strategy for the IRS because auditing is better both when the museum pays UBIT (the payoff is 5 versus 4) and when the museum evades UBIT (9 versus 0). The museum does not have a dominant strategy, because its best response to Audit is to Pay (-5 versus -9) but its best response to Don't Audit is Don't Pay (0 versus -4).

So, can we predict behavior in this game, and if so, how would we define equilibrium? Recall that we have been restricting attention to games of complete information, where each player knows the payoff matrix. When the museum looks at this payoff matrix, it can see that the IRS will never fail to audit because auditing is a dominant strategy. The museum can then cross out the "don't audit" column, and there is a dominant strategy for the remaining column – pay the UBIT. This kind of equilibrium, where dominated strategies are eliminated from consideration until each player has a dominant strategy, is called an *iterated-dominant-strategy equilibrium*. Games that have either a dominant- or iterated-dominant-strategy equilibrium are called "dominance solvable."

Unfortunately, many simple games are not dominance solvable. Before turning to these games, we should discuss where the payoff numbers come from, as game theory is not practical without accurate payoffs. In the above examples, we just made the numbers up; sometimes assumed payoffs are reasonable and sometimes fanciful. In the UBIT game, we assumed that the museum cares about its financial condition, and that there is no problem calculating financial positions in each cell in practice. But we also assumed that the nonprofit museum has no moral qualms about violating tax law, which may or may not be true for real-world museums. The problem of calculating payoffs is even worse for the IRS. As a bureaucratic entity, it is not clear what makes the IRS better off or worse off. The IRS is acting on behalf of the U.S. government, which is acting on behalf of the citizenry, and IRS decision makers are subject to review at many levels. The next chapter describes the experimental method and behavioral economics, tools that can help uncover what each player really cares about in practice. What seems like a footnote in this chapter is worthy of careful thought in each practical application.

Harder (Nash equilibrium) games

Consider next the *coordination game* presented in Figure 11.6. The coordination game is one in which both parties have a real incentive to get together on a common solution, but where coordinated action may be difficult to achieve and certain coordination solutions may be better than others. In this coordination game, a local Opera and Ballet want to schedule fund-raising events in either August or March. Both understand that they would be better off working together on a joint event than going it alone. Otherwise donors will be upset and contribute to neither. March is a better month in terms of potential contributions since many potential donors are on vacation in August. However, communication between the two organizations isn't very good and both have boards and staff that tend to follow their own muses.

This game has no dominant strategies and no dominated strategies to eliminate, and so is not dominance solvable. Nash's beautiful insight was that for games like this, we should focus on the stability of solutions. (March, March) is stable, because if the Opera picks March, Ballet's best response is also to pick March. Ballet would never unilaterally deviate from this strategy. At the same time, Opera would never unilaterally deviate from March because this is the best response to Ballet choosing March. We call (March, March) a *Nash equilibrium* because if we start in this cell, no player wishes to unilaterally deviate. A Nash equilibrium is a strategy combination that is a best response for every player to the best-response strategies of other players.

Figure 11.6 The coordination game – scheduling a fund-raising event

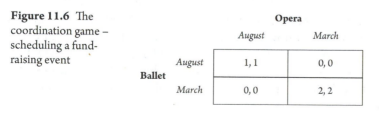

		Opera	
		August	*March*
Ballet	*August*	1, 1	0, 0
	March	0, 0	2, 2

All games have at least one Nash equilibrium. If there is a dominant strategy or iterated dominant strategy equilibrium in a game, that outcome is also a Nash equilibrium. To confirm this for the hospitals game presented as Figure 11.3, where (Aggressive Marketing, Aggressive Marketing) is the dominant strategy equilibrium, the row player (Community Clinic) does not want to unilaterally move because its payoff would fall from -$1 million (first number in top left) to -$3 million (first number in bottom left) if it did so. The column player (University Systems) also does not want to move (same numbers but now looking at the second number in top left versus the second number in top right). Hence, (Aggressive Marketing, Aggressive Marketing) is a Nash equilibrium. In the three other cells, one or both players would want to unilaterally move, so the dominant-strategy equilibrium is the only Nash equilibrium. For practice, the reader can confirm that the same is true in the games described by Figures 11.4 and 11.5.

Nash equilibria present solutions for games that are not dominance-solvable, but there is no guarantee that there is only one Nash equilibrium. In this coordination game, Figure 11.6, (August, August) is also a Nash equilibrium, but the other two strategy combinations are not, so we have exactly two pure Nash equilibria. We call games like this coordination games because if, say, the Opera chooses one Nash equilibrium and the Ballet chooses the other, the result is not an equilibrium.

How do we predict behavior when there are multiple Nash equilibria? It is not always so simple, but for this game March is clearly the better equilibrium, as both players prefer this outcome, know the payoff matrix, and so know that the other player also prefers this outcome. To avoid miscalculation, it is best that the players talk this over and come to a mutual understanding before playing the game. Unlike the game where hospitals compete for profits where talk is cheap, talk is useful here because neither player has an incentive to deviate from the agreed-upon date. Communication can take the form of talking, but there are other ways to send coordinating signals when, as we have assumed, the players don't talk. If the Opera stated clearly and publicly that it would hold its fund-raiser in March, the Ballet would have the incentive to follow suit.

Sometimes, there is a hidden Nash equilibrium. Consider the cocktail party game described in Figure 11.7, between a nonprofit CEO and a potential donor she is trying to pin down. The donor and the CEO have both been invited to the same cocktail party. The donor would like to attend if the CEO sends regrets but would prefer not to be there if the CEO is attending. On the contrary, the CEO doesn't really want to go unless the potential donor is going to be there.

Figure 11.7 The cocktail party game

		CEO	
		Attend	*Stay Home*
Potential Donor	*Attend*	−1, 1	1, −1
	Stay Home	1, −1	−1, 1

In this game, neither player has a dominant strategy. Worse yet, none of the strategy combinations are stable; if one player knew what the other player was going to do, she would change strategy. For example, if the donor and the CEO had both decided to attend, and knew the other's intention, each would have an incentive to change her mind. So, it looks like there are no Nash equilibria, but what if coin flips determined the strategy of each player? Specifically, we call the action "attend" or the action "stay home" *pure strategies*, meaning they are chosen with 100 per-cent probability. There are also *mixed strategies*, where players consciously choose probabilities of actions instead of actions that are implemented for sure. For example, a mixed strategy for the CEO would be to attend with a probability of 40 percent and stay home with a probability of 60 percent. A Nash equilibrium in mixed strategies is a set of probabilities for each player such that neither player wants to unilaterally deviate by changing these probabilities. Mixed-strategy equilibria are beyond the scope of this book but are covered in many game theory textbooks (e.g., Davis, 2003). Every game has at least one Nash equilibrium, sometimes easy to find (pure-strategy equilibria) and sometimes less obvious (mixed-strategy equilibria).

11.4 Repeated games

Many games are repeated on an ongoing basis. The cocktail game is not over after one party, as any major-gift solicitor knows. The two hospitals make their marketing choice every year. Strategies in repeated games are more complex, more interesting, and can achieve equilibrium outcomes that are not possible when the game is played only once. Bad behavior by one player can be punished in future rounds of the game, and good behavior rewarded. In games of incomplete information, strategy must incorporate learning about the other players as well as short run gains. Sometimes, it is best to use strategies that keep your opponent from learning about your true payoffs, other times a player wants to speed learning to build trust.

Vocabulary for repeated games

Before we turn to specific examples of repeated games, some definitions are in order. A game played once and only once is called a *single-shot game*. Repetition means that the same payoff matrix applies to a sequence of player choices. We call the series of choice opportunities the "repeated game" and the payoff matrix that is repeated the "constituent game" or *stage game*. Repeated games fall into three categories:

- Finitely repeated games: The game is repeated a specified number of times, and the number of repetitions is common knowledge.
- Infinitely repeated games: The game is repeated without limit, and that fact is common knowledge.
- Indefinitely repeated games: After each round is completed, there is a probability that the game will end and a complementary probability that there will be at least one more round. Repetition is finite, but players never know when the game will end when they select their stage action.

The payoff to any player in a repeated game consists of the sum of the payoffs realized in each stage game. Usually, stage payoffs are discounted so the game payoff expected at the beginning of the game is the present value of the stream of future payoffs (see Chapter 6 on present value calculation).

In a single-shot game, a strategy is an action chosen from a list of alternatives, but things are more complicated in repeated games. In standard game theory, players are forward-looking and hyper-rational, calculating decisions or contingent decisions for each round of the game before starting play. So, in a repeated game, a strategy has two components:

- An action for the first round of the game.
- A rule specifying what action the player will take in each future round in response to each history of the game to that point.

Examples of repeated games

Consider first the repeated prisoner's dilemma. When this game is played only once, as in the university example discussed above, the only equilibrium has lower payoffs than those in another cell. Here we consider two churches in neighboring parishes competing for donations to their annual campaigns. Figure 11.8 depicts the stage game of this repeated prisoner's dilemma:

Figure 11.8 A repeated prisoner's dilemma

		Church of the Holy Cow	
		Stick to Own Parish	Solicit in Both Parishes
Church of the Holy Mackerel	Stick to Own Parish	3, 3	1, 4
	Solicit in Both Parishes	4, 1	2, 2

Every year, these churches choose whether to confine their appeal to potential donors in their own parish or to also reach out to people in the neighboring parish. If they both reach out, then considerable friction is generated, and both churches do poorly. If they both confine themselves to local appeals, they each do well. But if one church reaches out while the other stays home, the aggressive church reaps large rewards by cutting into the other's donor base. If this were a single-shot game, the dominant-strategy equilibrium has both churches soliciting in both parishes, even though both players would prefer to be in the top left cell. But this is a repeated game that takes place every year, which opens up new possibilities for equilibrium.

A strategy in repeated games is a first-period action and a rule for selecting actions in future periods. The Church of the Holy Cow ("Cow") has a very useful strategy in mind – it will stick to its own parish in the first year and continue to do so every future year unless the Church of the Holy Mackerel ("Mackerel") has solicited in both parishes in any previous year. If Mackerel has ever solicited in both parishes, Cow will also solicit in both parishes forever after. This serves to punish Mackerel from taking advantage of Cow's strategy. Gun-crazy game theorists (remember "single-shot") call these punishments *trigger strategies*, which in turn are classified by the severity of the punishment. Cow punishes forever for a single transgression by Mackerel, so this is called the *grim trigger strategy*. If instead, Cow punished for one period, then tried again and solicited only in its own parish unless Mackerel had a second transgression, this forgiving punishment is called the *tit-for-tat strategy*.

The grim trigger strategy is useful in this game because if both players use this strategy, we have a Nash equilibrium that is better than anything we could get in the single-shot game. To show that this is a Nash equilibrium we have to show that Mackerel would never deviate from the grim trigger when Cow plays the grim trigger strategy and vice versa. What would happen if Mackerel deviated from the strategy by soliciting in both parishes in some period? Cow would solicit in both parishes in every future period. Mackerel

Year	Mackerel's Action	Cow's Action	Mackerel's Payoff	Mackerel's Payoff if he Hadn't Deviated	Change in Payoff due to Deviation
2003	Solicit Own	Solicit Own	3	3	0
2004	Solicit Both	Solicit Own	4	3	+1
2005	Solicit Both	Solicit Both	2	3	−1
2006	Solicit Both	Solicit Both	2	3	−1
Each Year After	Solicit Both	Solicit Both	2	3	−1

Figure 11.9 It doesn't pay to deviate

would profit in the first period after deviating, increasing its payoff by 1 (from 3 to 4). Then Cow would punish according to the rule, and in response to that punishment, Mackerel is better off choosing to solicit in both parishes every period because that is the best response to Cow's punishment. Figure 11.9 illustrates the consequences when Mackerel deviates in 2004.

Mackerel gains the first year it deviates but loses each year after that, and provided the interest rate isn't so high that the future barely matters, Mackerel will not want to deviate. The game is perfectly symmetrical, so if Mackerel uses a grim trigger strategy, Cow will not want to deviate either and we have a Nash equilibrium in which each player's payoff is three in every round.

Why does the interest rate matter? Because this determines the present value of the change in payoffs resulting from Mackerel's deviation in 2004. Letting r denote the interest rate, the present value in 2004 of the deviation, using the formula for the present value of a perpetuity (see Chapter 6), is:

$$\text{PDV(Deviation)} = 1 - \frac{1}{1+r} - \frac{1}{(1+r)^2} - \frac{1}{(1+r)^3} - \cdots = 1 - \frac{1}{r}$$

When the interest rate is 10 percent (0.10), the present value is a loss of 9. The deviation generates a loss whenever the interest rate is less than 90 percent.

If the game is repeated indefinitely, the probability that there will be another round also enters the calculation. Say that the probability of a succeeding round is 90 percent. Once Mackerel deviates in 2004, there is only a 90 percent chance that Cow can punish him in 2005, and with an interest rate of 10 percent, the expected present value of the 2005 punishment is -0.9/1.1 which is about 0.82; and so on in 2006 and future years. There is a smaller punishment each year than the punishment in the infinitely-repeated game, but the punishment suffices to deter deviation. A lower probability that there will be a succeeding round makes it harder to deter deviation. For example, when that probability is 50 percent and if the interest rate stays at 10 percent, Mackerel will gain from deviating despite the ensuing punishment.

However, this argument falls apart when the game is played a definite finite number of times. Say that the game is played 10 times. Mackerel thinks about the whole game before deciding what to do in each round, and in particular, it understands that nobody can punish it for its choice in the last round. Therefore, Mackerel will behave opportunistically in the last round by deviating from the trigger strategy. Cow, thinking the same way, also solicits in both parishes in the last round, and Mackerel can figure this fact out from the complete information it has about the game. In effect, Cow has the incentive to take the punishment action and further punishment is not possible.

Mackerel next considers the ninth round. It knows that it will get "punished" in the tenth round no matter what it does in the ninth round, so there is no reason to cooperate in the ninth round either. Thinking about the eighth round, Mackerel knows that it will get punished in the ninth and tenth rounds, and so on, until we find that Mackerel will solicit in both parishes in every round. This logical process is called "backwards induction," and backwards induction implies that players will play the bad single-shot equilibrium in every round provided that there is only one equilibrium to the stage game, as is the case here.

Our next game is a repeated donation game played by two wealthy donors (who, for no particular reason, are named Warren and Bill). Both players care about total donations to a particular charity and they are the only donors to this charity. Petty cash and pocket change are of no concern to Bill and Warren, so their choices are to give nothing or $1 billion. Figure 11.10 presents their payoff matrix for the *constituent game*.

Figure 11.10 The donations game

		Bill	
		Give $0	Give $1 Billion
Warren	Give $0	0, 0	175, 75
	Give $1 Billion	75, 175	150, 150

Here, the payoffs are not received in monetary form, but in the warm glow of giving and enjoyment of the charitable output. These are free-rider payoffs, that is, payoffs that make people give less than they otherwise would because they hope that the other player will make up the difference. To see this, note that if Warren gives nothing, Bill likes seeing the charity spend $1 billion more than he likes keeping that billion for himself and so he donates. But donations to the charity have diminishing marginal value to Bill, so if Warren donates $1 billion, the added value to Bill of the second $billion donated is less than the value of keeping the $1 billion for himself. The same is true for Warren. What is the equilibrium of the stage game? There is no dominant strategy for either player, so no dominant-strategy equilibrium exists. There are two pure-strategy Nash equilibria – bottom left, and top right. To see this, suppose we start in the bottom left cell. Warren does not want to move to top left (he would lose 75 if he did) and Bill does not want to move to bottom right (he would lose 25 if he did). For symmetric reasons, neither player wishes to deviate from top right, so both are Nash equilibria.

The two players disagree on which Nash equilibrium is better, with Warren preferring top right and Bill preferring bottom left. That is why the outcome in the single-shot game with these payoffs would be difficult to predict. But there is a sense in which neither of these outcomes is best for the players when the game is repeated. If both players each give $1 billion in every repetition, they would each receive a payoff of 150 times the number of rounds played (possible discounting for the future, aside). If instead the players both agreed to play one of their single-shot equilibria in each round, they would alternate between the two equilibria, receiving a payoff of 175 in half the rounds and 75 in the other half. If there were an even number of repetitions, each player would get 125 times the number of rounds played, which is lower than the payoffs they would achieve if they always gave $1 billion apiece.

The single-shot game has no equilibrium in which each player gets 150, but in the repeated game, there is a strategy that obtains those payoffs in almost every round, regardless of whether the game is finitely, indefinitely, or infinitely repeated. The strategies that lead to this equilibrium involve punishment, but the punishment action is the single-shot Nash equilibrium that the deviator likes least. In this game, if Bill deviated in 2004 (resulting in payoffs that year of 75 for Warren and 175 for Bill), Warren could give zero in 2005 and every future year. Bill's best response would be to give $1 billion in 2005 and beyond, and deviation would not pay.

In finitely-repeated donation games like this, the strategy that works best is to play a grim trigger except in the last two rounds. The last two rounds have play-

Year	Bill's Action	Warren's Action	Bill's Payoff	Bill's Payoff if he Hadn't Deviated	Change in Payoff due to Deviation
2002	Donate $1B	Donate $1B	150	150	0
2003	Donate $1B	Donate $1B	150	150	0
2004	Donate $0	Donate $1B	175	150	+25
2005	Donate $1B	Donate $0	75	150	−75
2006	Donate $1B	Donate $0	75	150	−75
2007	Donate $1B	Donate $0	75	150	−75
2008	Donate $1B	Donate $0	75	150	−75
2009	Donate $0	Donate $1B	175	175	0
2010	Donate $1B	Donate $0	75	75	0

Figure 11.11 It doesn't pay to deviate in finite repetitions if the stage game has two Nash equilibria

ers first coordinating on one of the two Nash equilibria in the stage game, then on the other Nash equilibrium. Backward induction does not eliminate the resulting equilibrium in most games like this (the exceptions are technical and beyond the scope of this book). Figure 11.11 illustrates this point if the game is held every year from 2002 to 2010 and Bill considers deviating in 2004.

It doesn't pay to deviate in 2004 for any reasonable interest rate, using the present value formula. It pays to deviate starting in 2008 because this strategy says that in the last two years, players must choose one Nash equilibrium in 2009 and then the other Nash equilibrium in 2010, with no time left for punishment. It might pay to deviate in 2007 (see exercise 11.6 at the end of this chapter), so this strategy achieves the better outcome in all years except a few at the end.

Our next example is the *battle-of-the-sexes game*, named after the original example where a husband and wife must decide individually whether to go to a boxing match or a night at the opera. The husband likes boxing more, the wife likes opera more, but they are each happier if they attend the same event. There are two Nash equilibria to the single-shot battle-of-the-sexes game, when they both go to the opera or when they both go to the boxing match, and the players disagree about which Nash equilibrium is better. In our example two private foundations have received the same two grant applications. One asks for funding for an addiction treatment program, the other seeks funding for a job training program. The Block Foundation and the Slab Foundation are small and can only afford to make one moderate grant per year. Figure 11.12 shows the payoffs in the stage game.

Figure 11.12 The foundation grants game

		Block Foundation	
		Fund Addiction Treatment	Fund Job Training
Slab Foundation	Fund Addiction Treatment	3, 4	0, 2
	Fund Job Training	2, 0	4, 3

These payoffs reflect two considerations. First, assuming both foundations can agree on one strategy, the Block Foundation would rather fund addiction treatment than job training, and the Slab Foundation would rather fund job training. Second, there are assumed economies of scale in each of these program areas. The economies of scale are such that the limited funding provided by a single moderate grant will not accomplish very much, but many times more charitable output is produced if either grantee receives two grants. Like the original battle-of-the-sexes game, there are two Nash equilibria in pure strategies: both foundations fund addiction treatment or both fund job training. The two players disagree on which Nash equilibrium is better, and if they cannot coordinate on one or the other, both will suffer.

As a repeated game, the players have several ways to achieve one or the other stage-game Nash equilibrium in almost every round. They could agree to alternate, with both funding addiction treatment in even years and both funding job training in odd years. If they cannot agree on which foundation gets its way first, they could agree to decide by a coin toss. This strategy would yield a Nash equilibrium with average payoffs per round of 3.5 even if the game is finitely repeated. Backward induction does not rule out this outcome because the punishment strategy is another Nash equilibrium of the stage game. Alternatively, they could agree to use some random external event (coin toss, whether the temperature is above or below average on the decision day) to decide their action in any particular round. A coin toss would work here, because it gives an equal probability of either equilibrium, resulting in the fairest outcome where each receives an average payoff of 3.5.

Our final example is the game of *chicken*. The original example of the game of chicken involved two drivers, racing at full speed towards a direct head-on collision. Whoever swerves first is the loser, but if nobody swerves, both drivers lose their life. Chicken is an anti-coordination game – the worst outcomes occur when the two players pick the same action. There are two Nash

Figure 11.13 Labor relations as a game of chicken

		Management (CSST)	
		Insist	*Request*
The Union (UCW)	*Insist*	0, 0	90, 10
	Request	10, 90	50, 50

equilibria to the single-shot game of chicken – either the row player swerves, and the column player drives straight, or the row player drives straight, and the column player swerves. The column player prefers the first equilibrium, the row player prefers the second, and there is a good chance that if they fight over who gets to win, they will end up in the worst case (drive straight, drive straight). There is also a third Nash equilibrium in mixed strategies, but obviously tossing a coin to decide whether to swerve will result in a lot of crashes.

In our example of a game of chicken, Community Service of Small Town (CSST) is engaged in a labor dispute with the Union of Case Workers (UCW) on over-time pay. CSST is asking its case workers to add two hours to their work week while UCW insists that such an addition be paid at over-time rates. If both parties aggressively insist on their positions, a strike occurs and both sides lose. If one party insists and the other merely asks that its position be considered, the more aggressive party will prevail in the negotiation. If both parties approach the negotiation by asking that their positions be considered, an equitable solution will be reached. The numbers in the game matrix reflect these various possibilities (Figure 11.13).

In the single-shot game there are no dominant strategies. Once again, there are two pure-strategy Nash equilibria, (insist, request) and (request, insist). In addition, the players disagree on which Nash equilibrium is better and so may end up in the top left cell. There seems to be no way to get to the better solution (request, request) as a stable equilibrium. If CSST knows that UCW is choosing the request strategy, it has a unilateral incentive to change from request to insist. What then is the solution? One solution is to convert this game from a competitive game (meaning the players cannot enforce any pre-play agreements) to a cooperative game (with binding enforcement of pre-play agreements). Cooperative game theory is a technical subject beyond the scope of this book, but the gist of it here is just common sense. If the players recognize that the (request, request) outcome is the best they can bargain for, they could sign a contract with stipulated penalties for contract violations, enforceable in a court of law. Or they could hire some third party like a mutually agreed-upon arbitrator and agree to resolve all disputes through arbitration.

As a repeated game, punishment strategies can be very effective, although there are credibility issues. Players are only deterred by the threat of punishment if the threat is credible, that is, if the player who contemplates violating the agreement believes that the threatened action would actually occur following a violation. Real players of this game might seek to change the game itself, adding new actions or deleting allowed actions from the choices in any round. For example, in the original game of chicken, one driver might lock his steering wheel and throw away the key to make the threat of never swerving fully credible. In this game, UCW might call for a walkout or CSST might impose a lockout to gain more bargaining power. These are called "precommitment devices," and obviously (as any fan of the movie *Dr. Strangelove or: How I Learned to Stop Worrying and Love the Bomb* would know), it is important to tell the other players that you have used a pre-commitment device.

11.5 Donation games

As we saw in the donations game above, fund-raising is a game. First, it is a game among the potential donors the gifts of others affect both one's own behavior and one's payoffs from each strategy a donor might pursue. Second, it is a game between the social enterprise or nonprofit organization and its donors. Different organizational strategies regarding solicitation, transparency, commercial activity, acceptance of government grants and contracts, executive compensation, and a host of other factors can affect the psychic, social, and financial payoffs to donors. Third, it is a game played between organizations, which, as shown in the repeated prisoner's dilemma above, may choose overlapping donor pools or differentiation strategies to stand out in the choices made by donors. Donation games sometimes involve simultaneous choices, and sometimes involve sequences of choices. For example, university capital campaigns are usually conducted in two stages, with players moving in a particular order. In the first, "silent", phase, wealthy donors are asked to commit to major gifts. When total silent-phase gifts exceed some threshold (perhaps 40 percent to 60 percent of the campaign goal), the second, "campaign" phase is announced to the public, along with the silent-phase total. The general public is then asked to add to that pot. We discuss many of these factors in the next chapter on behavioral economics. Here we lay out the main games that are used to analyze donor behavior.

The most important such game is the "public goods game". Earlier in this text (starting with Chapter 3) we discussed collective goods – goods that are collectively consumed such that the marginal cost of letting an additional person consume the good is zero. We also distinguished excludable collective goods from nonexcludable collective goods based on the practicality of excluding nonpayers. For many years, economists used a different label for goods consumed in this nonrival way – "public goods." Public goods were divided into excludable public goods and "pure" (meaning nonexcludable) public goods. Game theorists never moved on to the newer labels, so the public goods game concerns voluntary donations in support of a pure public good.

The example of the donations game discussed above is a simplified public goods game, with two players who each choose one of two amounts to give. In general, public goods games can have any number of players greater than or equal to 2, and each player can choose to donate any non-negative amount of their available wealth. This means that we would need an infinite number of rows and columns to display the payoff matrix, and since nobody has that much time, the game is described by equations instead of a matrix. We won't consider the details here, but all the tools discussed in this chapter still apply to the problem. Some public goods games have a dominant-strategy equilibrium, where now a strategy is dominant if the same level of giving is the best response to any level of giving by other players. All public goods games have at least one Nash equilibrium, meaning that no one wants to unilaterally deviate from his or her Nash equilibrium strategy. Usually, all the Nash equilibria involve free-riding in just the same way that was described in our simplified donations game example. All players would prefer an outcome where more is given, but that outcome is not an equilibrium in the single-shot game. Variations on this game include repetition (finite or indefinite repetition), anonymity (giving to an anonymous other versus giving to a named charity), giving versus taking (allowing players to add to or subtract from the pool of others' giving), introduction of costly punishment and/or reward actions to the available strategies, and simultaneous versus sequential contributions. All these variations, and many more, have formed the framework for experiments designed to test whether game theory predicts the behavior of real people.

Three additional games are designed to distinguish different motivations for giving, and test whether donors with different motivations behave differently as predicted by traditional game theory. The "dictator game" is so simple it hardly qualifies as a game. This game has two players, one labeled the dictator and the other the receiver. The dictator is given a sum of money and told that she can keep all or any part of that sum and give the rest to the receiver. If the dictator has self-regarding preferences, caring only about her own monetary payoff, the dominant-strategy equilibrium is to keep all the money. If people play the dictator game and depart from this dominant-strategy equilibrium, this counts as evidence that the dictator cares about something beyond her own monetary payoff – fairness, inequality, helping others, and so on. If so, payoff matrices that include only monetary payoffs do not accurately capture the real payoffs of the game.

When dictators share their winnings with receivers, it is not clear which of the alternative motivations explains their altruistic behavior. Additional games are played with the same players in order to sort this out. The "ultimatum game" works this way. There are two players, a sender and a receiver. The sender is offered a sum of money and asked to propose a way to divide that sum between himself and the receiver. The receiver has two possible responses to the sender's proposal – accept or reject. If the receiver accepts the proposal, the money is given to the sender, who then divides it as proposed. If the receiver rejects the proposal, the money is not given to the sender and both players receive a monetary payoff of zero. If both players care only about their own monetary payoff, then the equilibrium reflects dominant strategies – the sender should propose a penny for the receiver and keep the rest for himself, and the receiver should accept the proposal. The penny is necessary to break a tie in the receiver's response. If the sender proposes nothing for the receiver, the receiver is indifferent between accepting or rejecting. If any positive amount is proposed for the receiver, the dominant response is to accept the proposal. Again, departures from this dominant strategy equilibrium indicate that non-monetary factors enter into the motivations of either givers or receivers or both. Hence, we learn more about the role social norms play and about the difference between self-interested giving and altruism.

The last game we discuss is the "trust game" Again, there are two players – a sender and a responder. The sender is given a sum of money to divide with the responder but understands that any money he sends is tripled before it is received by the responder. The responder then divides this tripled sum between herself and the sender. This game explores obligation, reciprocity, and trust. If players care only about their own money, both realize that the responder will not send any money back to the receiver. Knowing this, the sender would send nothing to the responder. But real people care about things in addition to their own money. For example, suppose the sender had $10 to give and cared about the responder. He might give $6 to the responder, so the responder receives $18. If the responder feels morally obligated to repay the sender, she would send $6 back and the final allocation would be $10 to the sender and $12 to the receiver. If the sender trusts that the responder believes in repaying generosity with generosity (reciprocity) he would instead send $10, and the responder would receive $30. If that trust were warranted and the responder believes in reciprocity, the responder would send $15 of that back and the final allocation would be that both players get $15. The patterns of play in these four games reveal a lot about motivations and behaviors of donors.

SUMMARY

Game theory offers a helpful conceptual framework for understanding economic and other strategic decision situations. Game theory is particularly useful when there are a small number of players, where risk to any one decision maker derives from the potential countermoves of other identifiable decision makers. In this chapter we have examined several generic types of games involving two players. Several equilibrium concepts are used to predict behavior in games – dominant strategy, iterated dominant strategy, and Nash equilibria (in both pure and mixed strategies). Sometimes we have confidence in the predictions of game theory (when a dominant strategy equilibrium exists), sometimes little confidence (as in the single-shot battle-of-the-sexes game, where there are multiple equilibria and no reason to expect any one equilibrium is more likely than any other).

The simple games discussed here represent the tip of a game theory iceberg. We have made many simplifying assumptions in order to present the basic tools of game theory and develop some intuitions about how games are played. More advanced courses in game theory present tools to understand what happens when these assumptions don't hold. For example:

- When there are more than two players in a repeated game, how do punishments work? Punishment provides a collective benefit, and perhaps there is some free-riding in that provision.
- What happens when games are played with incomplete information? We need new equilibrium concepts to cover the fact that players do not know the entire payoff matrix. These concepts introduce learning and concealment strategies and the value of developing a reputation. For example, in the repeated prisoner's dilemma game, one player has little idea whether the other player's threat to play the grim trigger strategy is credible, and it might be rational to provoke that player to see if the threat is carried out. Simulations reveal that more forgiving trigger strategies like tit-for-tat should be used, to recover less painfully from "call-my-bluff" actions.
- What differences occur when games are played sequentially rather than simultaneously, and how do outcomes vary between first-movers

and others? We hinted at some of this complexity when we mentioned university capital campaigns, but there is much more.

- What difference does pre-play communication make? We hinted at some of this analysis, illustrating a game where talk is cheap and another where talk can help solve the coordination problem, but there is much more.
- How do the results of one-shot games differ from those that involve repeated plays of the game? We provided an introduction to this topic, suggesting that punishment and reward options open up new and superior equilibrium outcomes in indefinitely or infinitely repeated games. Punishment strategies are useless in definitely repeated games where the stage game has a unique equilibrium due to backward induction, but when the stage game has multiple equilibria, cooperation can be sustained in most periods (as in the foundation grants game above).
- How do ideas about reciprocity, fairness, altruism and cultural norms influence play in games? How can we write payoff matrices when these things matter? When do different motivations predict different behaviors? We hinted at answers here when we discussed the public goods, dictator, ultimatum, and trust games.

In recent decades, the study of game theory has bled into the burgeoning sub-disciplines of experimental and behavioral economics, wherein game situations are simulated in laboratories or in controlled field experiments. These experiments test and modify the strict assumptions made for *homo economicus* players, comparing *homo sapiens* behavior with that predicted in traditional game theory for *homo economicus*. Some of the papers, with titles like "kindness or confusion," test whether real people have the incentives, intelligence, and information necessary to figure out their equilibrium behavior. Others examine whether monetary payments or fairness, empathy, sympathy, reciprocity, social information, cultural norms, envy, retribution, and other such factors are important motivators of real-world game players. The next chapter discusses the experimental method and summarizes the results of selected experiments relevant to nonprofit and social enterprise managers.

SELECTED REFERENCES AND CITATIONS

Camerer, C.F. (2003). *Behavioral Game Theory: Experiments in Strategic Interaction*. Princeton, NJ: Princeton University Press.

Davis, M.D. (2003). *Game Theory: A Nontechnical Introduction*. Mineola, NY: Dover Publications.

Dutta, P.K. (1999). *Strategies and Games: Theory and Practice*. Cambridge, MA: The MIT Press.

Hargreaves Heap, S.P. and Varoufakis, Y. (1995). *Game Theory: A Critical Introduction*. London and New York: Routledge.

Klarreich, E. (2017). In Game Theory, No Clear Path to Equilibrium. *Quanta Magazine* July 18, 2017. Retrieved from https://www.quantamagazine.org/in-game-theory-no-clear-path-to-equilibrium-20170718/ (accessed November 14, 2018).

McMillan, J. (1992). *Games, Strategies and Managers.* New York: Oxford University Press.

Spaniel, W. (2011). *Game Theory 101: The Complete Textbook.* CreateSpace Independent Publishing Platform.

Stanton, A.A. (2006). Evolving Economics: Synthesis. *MPRA Paper No. 767,* November 10. http://mpra.ub.uni-muenchen.de/767/.

Zagare, F.C. (1984). *Game Theory: Concepts and Applications,* Sage University Papers. Beverly Hills, CA: Sage Publications.

REVIEW CONCEPTS

Battle-of-the-Sexes Game: A coordination game in which it is better for each player to choose the same strategy; but there are two Nash equilibria and players disagree about which one is better.

Chicken Game: A game in which the two players face a direct confrontation in which both could be severely damaged. An anti-coordination game in which, when both players select the same action, both are harmed.

Common Knowledge: The assumption that something is known by all players and that all players know that other players know this thing as well.

Competitive Game Theory: The branch of game theory that assumes that players cannot make pre-play agreements that are enforceable. Also known as non-cooperative game theory.

Complete Information Games: Games where all players know the payoff matrix and also know that other players know the payoff matrix.

Cooperative Game Theory: The branch of game theory that assumes that groups of players can make enforceable agreements before playing the game.

Coordination Game: A game in which both parties have a real incentive to get together on a common solution, but where coordinated action may be difficult to achieve. Coordination games have multiple Nash equilibria, and unless players all select the same Nash equilibrium, disequilibrium results.

Dominant Strategy: A strategy where the player's best response to a choice by other players is the same for all possible choices by other players.

Dominant-Strategy Equilibrium: The strategy choices and payoffs that result when each player has a dominant strategy and plays that strategy.

Equilibrium: The resolution of a game resulting from the choice of strategies by each of the players.

Grim Trigger Strategy: The strategy that punishes a player forever for deviating from cooperation.

Iterated-Dominant-Strategy Equilibrium: The strategy choices and payoffs that result when there is no dominant strategy equilibrium to the full game, but elimination of dominated strategies leads to a dominant strategy for each player.

Market Power: The ability of an organization to significantly influence market prices.

Mixed Strategy: A strategy that specifies the probability a player will choose each available action, rather than specifying choice of a single action.

Nash Equilibrium: The solution to a game from which neither player has incentive to deviate unilaterally.

Non-Zero-Sum Game: A game in which the sum of payoffs to each of the players varies with their choices of strategies.

Payoff: The reward or penalty a player receives from the outcome of a game.

Payoff Matrix: A table showing the payoff to each player from each combination of actions.

Player: A participant in a game who makes decisions and obtains payoffs from the game's outcome.

Prisoner's Dilemma: A game in which both players can benefit from cooperation but face incentives to improve their own welfare at the other's expense.

Pure Strategy: A strategy containing only actions that are chosen for sure when called for, and no actions are chosen by random probability.

Single-Shot Game: A game that is not repeated.

Stage Game: The game that is repeated in a repeated game.

Tit-for-Tat Strategy: A trigger strategy that punishes deviations by the other players for one period, then initiates another try at cooperation.

Trigger Strategy: A strategy that punishes deviations by the other players.

Zero-Sum Game: A game in which the sum of the payoffs to each of the players is a constant number no matter what their strategy choices.

EXERCISES

1. United Way of River City (UWRC) is considering inviting River City General (RCG), a major medical center, to join its annual federated fund-raising campaign. To do so, RCG must discontinue its own campaign but is assured a fair share of the proceeds from the UWRC campaign. The expectation is that the joint campaign will raise more funds than the sum of two separate campaigns. However, if UWRC decides to invite RCG but RCG declines, UWRC will gain a public relations benefit (and raise more funds than otherwise) and RCG will suffer from damaged community relations and be less successful in its own campaign than it would have been were it not invited. If RCG expresses a wish to join the campaign but UWRC does not extend the invitation, then RCG will be viewed favorably but UWRC will suffer a public relations problem that will make its campaign less successful than if the issue had never come up. The payoff matrix is:

		River City General (RCG)	
		Accept Invitation	*Decline Invitation*
United Way of River City (UWRC)	*Extend Invitation*	10, 10	9, 7
	Don't Invite	7, 9	8, 8

(a) Is this a zero-sum or non-zero-sum game?
(b) Are there dominant strategies for either player?
(c) Are there any Nash equilibria?
(d) What will each player decide to do?
(e) How sensitive is this result to the sizes of the estimated payoffs to each party? Experiment with the numbers in the matrix to determine the circumstances under which the solution would be different.

2. The board and the musician's union of the Decibel Symphony Orchestra (DSO) are in a dispute about overtime pay. The union can try to get its way, or it can negotiate to

reach a voluntary agreement. Similarly, the board can refuse to consider overtime pay and lock out the musicians or it can negotiate with the union. At issue is a sum of $100,000 from an unrestricted fund that will remain unexpended if agreement is not reached. The payoff matrix is:

		Board	
		Lockout	Negotiate
Union	Strike	0, 0	90, 10
	Negotiate	10, 90	50, 50

(a) Is there a dominant strategy for either the Union or the Board?

(b) Are there any Nash equilibria for this game when it is not repeated?

(c) Can you confidently predict what will happen when the game is played exactly once? Explain.

(d) If this game were repeated indefinitely, what do you think will happen and why?

(e) If this game were repeated exactly ten times, and the board and the union both understood that there would be ten repetitions, what do you think will happen and why?

3. Lake Fishy is shared by two nonprofit summer camps, Camp Tumult and Camp Krazykids. Both organizations promote their fishing programs, but the fish population of the lake is depleted and needs restocking, which is expensive. Both camps will suffer in attendance and revenues if families of fishing enthusiasts stop sending their children to Lake Fishy. If either camp restocks Lake Fishy both camps will benefit because the fish don't discriminate between Tumult and Krazykids campers. So, each camp must decide whether to restock the lake themselves at a modest level that they can afford. But if both camps decide to do so, both camps will receive bigger benefits than either could achieve for their individual efforts. This situation can be modeled as follows, where the payoffs represent revenues net of restocking costs:

		Camp Tumult	
		Restock	Do Nothing
Camp Krazykids	Restock	15, 15	5, 10
	Do Nothing	10, 5	7, 7

(a) In the absence of any agreement between the two camps, what will each camp decide? How sure are you of your prediction, in light of the nature of this game?

(b) What do you expect would happen if Camp Krazykids announced its decision before Camp Tumult decided? How sure are you of your prediction, in light of the nature of this game?

(c) If the camps talked before deciding and made an agreement that would not be binding in a court of law, what would they agree to? Would both Camps stick with the agreement?

4. Phil Anthropy is an alumnus of Wiseacre University and a potential major donor to WU. Phil is a sci-fi fan and also a music buff and would like to endow a professorship in extra-terrestrial sound. WU's cosmology and music departments have no interest in the subject and the university would much prefer an unrestricted gift. Phil and WU are at logger-heads and Phil threatens to give nothing if his preference is not accommodated.

   Model this situation as a game of *Chicken*. What are the likely choices of strategy by Phil and WU? What is the expected outcome of the game? How might the situation be improved (e.g., the game be modified with additional strategies) so that both parties are happier with the result?

5. Jane Goodshoes has a great idea for a social enterprise: collecting donated used foot-wear and sending it to leather craftsmen in less developed countries who can refurbish the shoes and resell them at modest prices in local markets. This venture would help develop entrepreneurs, boost local economies and also address the health issues of local people who suffer from foot injuries for lack of shoes. Jane has applied to the Podiatric Healthcare Foundation (PHF) for a Program-Related Investment (PRI) loan to finance her capital needs for this project. Jane's organization, GoodyTwoShoes (GTS) which is an L3C (low profit, limited liability company) would repay the loan to PHF at below market rates. PHF would take a small loss in terms of return on its investments but it would benefit in terms of advancing its mission to improve foot health. The problem is that PHF is unsure whether the PRI would jeopardize its charitable tax status, given the lack of clear guidelines by the Internal Revenue Service on loans to L3Cs. GTS needs a loan and must decide whether to apply for the PRI or seek funds at a less favorable rate from a bank, but Jane doesn't have the time to do both. Meanwhile, PHF must decide, as a matter of policy, whether or not to accept and fund such an application if it were received. The game can be described as follows:

<table>
<tr><td></td><td></td><td colspan="2" align="center">**Podiatric Healthcare
Foundation (PHF)**</td></tr>
<tr><td></td><td></td><td align="center">*Accept PRIs*</td><td align="center">*Exclude PRIs*</td></tr>
<tr><td rowspan="2">**Goody Two Shoes
(GTS)**</td><td>*Apply for
PRI*</td><td align="center">10, 7</td><td align="center">0, 5</td></tr>
<tr><td>*Seek bank
loan*</td><td align="center">8, 8</td><td align="center">8, 6</td></tr>
</table>

The payoff numbers are estimates of the relative levels of benefits, on a scale from 1 to 10, for each outcome to each party. The best outcome for GTS is to receive the PRI; if it applies and is rejected it is out in the cold. If GTS seeks a bank loan, it benefits less and doesn't care what PHF decides. The best outcome for PHF is to accept PRIs as policy but not have GTS apply; in this case it still gets credit for a forward looking, beneficent policy but minimizes its risk. If PHF decides to exclude PRIs as a policy decision, it looks bad if GTS applies and is rejected, but less bad if GTS decides not to apply.

(a) Do GTS and PHF have dominant strategies?

(b) Is there an equilibrium for this game? If so, what kind(s): Dominant Strategy, Iterated Dominant Strategy, or Nash?

6. Recall the donations game illustrated in Figure 11.10. In the text, Figure 11.11 was used to show that it does not pay Bill to deviate from the grim trigger strategy by giving nothing in 2004 when Warren uses the grim trigger strategy. We asserted that the story would be different if Bill deviated from the grim trigger strategy by giving nothing in 2008. Demonstrate that the text is correct by illustrating this case with a table like that in Figure 11.11. Then, create a similar table for the cases when, instead, Bill deviates by giving nothing in 2007. What do you learn from this last deviation?

12

Behavioral research in economics

I think we need a new default option!

12.1 Introduction

For a long time, economists made a set of simplifying assumptions that did not seem to interfere with the validity of their analyses. These included the hyper-rational *homo economicus* assumptions and the assumption that preferences are self-regarding (that is, individuals care only about their own consumption and labor). But before mathematics became central to economics, economists questioned these assumptions. Adam Smith, widely regarded as the father of modern economics, wrote (1759/1976, vol. 1, page i.1.1):

> However selfish man may be supposed, there are evidently some principles in his nature, which interest him in the fortune of others, and render their happiness necessary to him, though they derive nothing from it except the pleasure of seeing it.

Now we are in the midst of the rapidly evolving behavioral economics upheaval, in which the limits of the old assumptions are challenged. Some of the new findings are immediately applicable to nonprofit and social enterprise management, others suggest future applications are near. No revolution comes without critics and defenders of the old guard, so we begin this chapter with a discussion of methodology focused on what kinds of evidence are convincing. We compare analysis of *happenstance data* – data that is naturally generated in the real world, with analysis of experimental data. Behavioral economics uses both but relies more heavily on *experiments* with human subjects. The next section discusses donations, providing evidence for some innovative approaches to fund-raising. Then we discuss some findings on motivating managers, workers, and volunteers, particularly when they work in nonprofit and social enterprise settings.

12.2 What makes empirical evidence convincing?

Behavioral researchers use a variety of methods to draw conclusions from data. Often, the most useful conclusions concern cause and effect, because these are the conclusions that a manager can use to guide practice. For example, if we observe that Republican donors have made larger donations than Democratic donors, we might be tempted to target our fund-raising efforts only on Republicans. But first, we should see whether it was registration as a Republican that *caused* them to give more. Maybe the Republicans in our donor pool were simply wealthier than the Democrats, and it was wealth rather than political party that made them give more. If so, we should target the wealthy of either disposition.

We may observe that those who go to hospitals are more likely to die than those who do not, but it would be foolish to refuse to go to hospitals on the basis of this observed correlation in happenstance data. The researcher needs to uncover how much of this correlation results from the fact that hospitals actually kill people (through the spread of infections, medical mistakes, or the use of high-risk high-return procedures), as opposed to the fact that people who are sick (and therefore more likely to die) go to hospitals. Experts in econometrics (the combination of economics and statistics) and experimental design know how to sort those things out, but no one study is conclusive. Rather, better-designed studies offer more persuasive evidence on causality. When multiple studies, using different data and/or methodologies, come to the same conclusion, the causal interpretation becomes more persuasive.

Econometrics and experimental design are separate courses in themselves, and beyond the scope of this book. But an introduction to the topic is useful.

It will help managers assess the strength of recommendations to change practice based on new research in the field. Hence, we provide an intuitive introduction to the evaluation of research designed to uncover cause and effect relationships. The Methodological Appendix in the Online Companion (https://www.e-elgar.com/textbooks/young) goes further than the text but gives only a taste of what the reader could learn from fuller treatments of the material. Increasingly, managers are conducting behavioral experiments on the job with their own donors, clients, or workers to improve their decision making. Microsoft began using experiments in 2000 under the name A/B testing because they were testing some alternative (B) against their current practice (A), conducting over 7000 A/B tests in 2011 (Hanington, 2012). Nonprofit managers and social entrepreneurs might want to test what persuasion strategy or market segmentation works best with their donors, or what compensation approach best motivates their workers and volunteers.

First, let us provide a working definition of *causality*. What does it mean, say, to conclude that cigarettes cause cancer? The first requirement for causality is that there is a joint pattern linking the purported cause to the purported effect (those who smoke are more likely to get cancer, and those who smoke a lot have a higher incidence of cancer than those who smoke a little). Second, there should be no *reverse causality* (having cancer doesn't cause the victim to smoke more). To tell whether there is reverse causality, we can look at the order in time (did smoking occur before cancer was detected or was cancer detected before smoking began?), or we can manipulate the data (for real with experiments, virtually with statistical techniques) to see whether a change in one factor causes a change in the other. (If we increase the amount of smoking, does the cancer risk go up? If we increase the amount of cancer, does smoking go up?) Finally, we want to be sure that the joint pattern between the purported cause and purported effect isn't explainable in other ways. Here the concern is that some third factor may cause the "cause variable" and the "effect variable" to move together. In our smoking example, it might be that people who don't take health advice are more likely to smoke, and people who don't take health advice are more likely to get cancer for other reasons. Then, the observed pattern of correlation could be due to differences across people in whether they listen to health advice, rather than smoking causing cancer. In such case we would say "the correlation between smoking and cancer is *spurious*" meaning not necessarily an indicator of causality.

The first problem with happenstance data is that everything changes at once, but we want to know the independent effect of one variable on another. Regression analysis (see the Methodological Appendix in the Online Companion (https://www.e-elgar.com/textbooks/young)) solves this by distinguishing the independent part of each cause-variable's variation and correlating that with the effect variable. The quality of the answers produced by regression analysis depends on the sample size (number of observations used for analysis) and the hidden processes that generate happenstance data (in particular, whether the various cause variables all move together, or move independently within the sample of available data).

The second problem with happenstance data is figuring out whether the joint pattern of cause and effect variables is causal. This is much harder to solve than the first problem, and the answers produced have more limited persuasive appeal. The solutions are beyond the scope of this discussion, but some rely on the combination of traditional economics theory with statistical techniques. However, strict rationality imposes a structure on the data that is often inconsistent with behavioral economics.

In particular, happenstance data contains choices made by humans – whether to donate or not; among donors, deciding how much to give; or, in our other examples, deciding whether and how much to smoke or deciding whether to go to the hospital. The analyst rarely knows the reason why the humans in the happenstance sample made their choices, and this omission greatly complicates causal inference. In the hospital example, we are unable to tell whether those in the hospital have a higher mortality rate because of pre-existing illness or the hospital itself is responsible. Now, it is pretty easy to obtain data on the health status of hospitalized patients before they enter the hospital, and so we can use multiple regression methods to control for health status. Some sick people do not go to the hospital; some healthy people go; so, regression exploits the difference between mortality rates of healthy and sick people going to the hospital and the difference between the mortality rates of healthy and sick people that do not go to the hospital to determine whether hospitals kill. But there are many other factors that determine whether someone goes to the hospital, some difficult or impossible to observe. It is this "unobserved heterogeneity" that casts doubt on our causal inference.

Experimental methods address both these limitations. In an experiment, we use human subjects and divide them (randomly) into two or more groups. The experimenter has the power to administer the "causal" variable to one group (the *treatment group*) and to make sure the other group is not exposed to the "causal" variable (the *control group*). After the treatment, outcome measures are obtained for each subject (subject died or lived). The difference between the average outcomes in the treatment group and the control group is called the *treatment effect*. For example, instead of looking at happenstance data of people who chose whether to smoke, the researcher could force *randomly-*

assigned treatment group members to smoke and prohibit randomly-assigned control group members from smoking. Or, the experimenter could take a sample of sick people and randomly assign treatment group members to hospitals while not allowing control group members to go there. Obviously, there are ethical and practical concerns with these examples, and these experiments should not be done on humans (white mice are often used).

But continuing with these examples, we can clearly see what we gain from the use of experiments. The experimental design changes one thing at a time. There are no unobserved variables explaining why a subject chooses a treatment, because the subject does not choose. Still, there are unobserved variables that may affect the outcome. For example, suppose for the sake of argument that women are more likely than men to develop fatal infections in the hospital. If all our women were assigned to the treatment group and all our men assigned to the control group, this would cause us to over-estimate the average hospital treatment effect (all else held equal). If subjects were assigned the opposite way, we would under-estimate the average treatment effect. Randomizing assignment to the two groups reduces this bias, but sometimes a coin does come up heads five times in a row and five women could be assigned to the same group. It is far less likely that a fair coin would turn up heads 40 times in a row, so experimentalists use a large sample of people in each group to make the expected differences in all unobserved variables small. In conclusion, experimental methods greatly reduce the number of rival explanations for the observed effect, so that the claim that treatment effects are causal effects is very persuasive.

Let's turn now to an example of an ethical and practical experiment designed to determine the effect of executive compensation on donations to a particular charity. As an experiment, we could expose subjects to different information about executive compensation and ask them to make donations. Specifically, subjects would be given a small sum of money (say $10) and told they could keep all that money for themselves or donate any part of it to a specified charity. Subjects would read some information about that charity, and then decide how much to give, and the experimenter would make sure that real money goes to that charity as specified. One way to design the experiment would be to set up four groups – three treatment groups and one control group. The control group subjects would be told about the charity's mission, but not told anything about executive compensation. The first treatment group would be told about the charity's mission and that the executive compensation was fairly low. The second and third treatment groups would be told that executive compensation was average and above average, respectively. We would calculate two kinds of treatment effects: whether a

Table 12.1 Results from a fictional experiment

	Control	Executive Compensation Treatment		
		Low	Medium	High
% Making Donation	30%	43%	31%	20%
Average Donation[a]	$4.23	$5.01	$3.98	$4.01
Number of Subjects	100	100	100	100

Note: [a] This is the average for donors only, and nondonors are excluded from the calculation.

gift was made and if so, how much was given. For the first sort of treatment effect, we would compare the percentage of subjects making a donation in the control group versus one of the treatment groups. Suppose we ran this experiment and got the results shown in Table 12.1.

(These numbers are made up for illustration, as we haven't conducted this experiment.) The results show that 30 percent of those assigned to the control group made a donation, whereas 43 percent of those in the low-compensation treatment group donated. Thus, the average treatment effect of low executive compensation on the percent making a donation was 13 percentage points (43 percent to 30 percent). The corresponding treatment effect on average donations is $0.78, and both treatment effects increase total donations. In the control group, 30 people donated an average of $4.23 so total donations were $126.90. Similarly, 43 people donated an average of $5.01 in the low-compensation treatment, for a total of $220.01. Comparing low, medium, and high compensation reveals that each increase causes a substantial decrease in donor participation, whereas the difference in amount donated is substantial when compensation is raised from low to medium and tiny when raised from medium to high.

How persuasive would these results be? They would be pretty persuasive for the populations from which participants were drawn for the experiment (*internally valid*), probably providing a good estimate of the causal effect we were looking for.[1] But there are questions about whether these results generalize to other groups of people (particularly if the subjects were all undergraduate students), or charities with different missions than the one included in this experiment. The latter are questions about *external validity*.

We could also analyze happenstance data using multiple regression analysis. Suppose we have data on CEO compensation from a large and nationally-representative sample of nonprofit organizations and we also know how much was donated to each organization. We may be able to include each CEO's exact compensation, but let's assume that the survey only collected categorical data on whether that compensation was low, medium, or high. If we entered this data into a statistical software package and ran the appropriate multiple-regression analysis, we would learn the difference in treatment effects between low, medium, and high. There is no control group in happenstance data, so we cannot estimate the treatment effect of each category, but from the differences in average donations after adjusting for other variables, we can estimate the effects of medium versus low, medium versus high, and high versus low executive compensation treatments.

How persuasive are results from happenstance data? We can solve the two listed challenges to external validity if our data allows us to estimate separate regressions for each kind of charity because our data are nationally representative. But we have a harder time with internal validity because of the happenstance nature of our data. First, we do not know whether any of the real-world donors knew what executive compensation was when they made their decisions. Second, we don't know the direction of causality – perhaps donations under the previous CEO were especially low, and the charity hired a new more expensive CEO to fix the problem. Because each kind of study has different validity challenges, the strongest case for identifying a causal treatment effect can be made when the results of both kinds of studies are in agreement.

12.3   The behavioral economics of giving

The economics of giving is one of the central areas of active current research in behavioral economics; we can only touch on some highlights here. A more complete picture is provided by one of the survey articles cited in the references, and doubtless by the time the reader reads this, more important and usable knowledge will have appeared. Here, we introduce the empirical literature on free-riding behavior, a central problem in fund-raising described in Chapter 11. The consensus finding is that real people are, on average, more generous than predicted in the *homo economicus* model of free riding, but there is still an undersupply of donations. Economists have developed alternative ways of collecting money that result in higher giving levels even from those concerned only with their narrow self-interest. We summarize studies of the effectiveness of these approaches, which are ready for use by practitioners. Next, we discuss other behavioral factors that affect donations, including the nature and framing of the ask, gender differences, and racial differences. We conclude this section with a discussion of donor motivation and the implications of different motivations for behavior.

Free and easy riding

Voluntary donations support nonprofit provision of collective goods. We learned in Chapter 11 about "public good games" and described how to find equilibrium in these games. We showed that the equilibrium levels of giving are suboptimal – less than the socially efficient amount – when donors care only about their own well-being.

Recall from Chapter 11, these key points required to follow this discussion. In a public goods game, the players are asked to individually decide whether to invest any part of their money in a project that benefits everyone playing the game or to keep it all for themselves. This is like a popular way of collecting donations called the *voluntary contribution mechanism* – everyone is asked to part with some of their money for a charitable activity that benefits everyone who cares about that activity. After all the money is collected, it is all spent on that charitable activity.

Once we specify what the players care about, game theory allows us to predict how people will behave, and that prediction is called an "equilibrium." We can also calculate the amount of donations that will be needed to obtain social efficiency, called the "optimum." If we make the assumption that people care only about their own consumption (self-regarding preferences) then in almost all cases, the total amount donated is less than the optimal amount. In part, this is because the player cares only about the total amount donated, hoping that everyone else will donate enough that he can enjoy the benefits for free. This is called *free-riding behavior*. But the deeper reason for this result is that players in this game operate on the wrong margin. Each player gets a small fraction of the value produced by her gift and weighs that fractional benefit against the full-cost loss of donated money. Setting marginal private benefit against marginal costs, the two are equal at a low or zero level of giving because fractional social benefits are smaller than full social benefits. The right margin from a social efficiency standpoint is to set marginal social benefit equal to marginal costs, which happens for a higher level of giving. (This intuition is useful and almost technically correct, but full understanding requires that we also discuss the game-theoretic nature of human interaction, which we cannot do here.)

That's the theory. How does it work out in reality? Economists, psychologists, sociologists, political scientists, and anthropologists have all conducted experiments on free riding, sometimes under the names of "social dilemma" or "collective decision" experiments. Subjects in these experiments behave in a variety of ways, with average giving that is 40 to 60 percent of the amount available to give. This "excess generosity" finding has been replicated hundreds of times using many methodological variations, and we regard the conclusion as convincing. Cornes and Sandler (1984) called this "easy riding" because people give something but still hope that other group members will cover more than their shares.

A class can easily replicate the finding using classmates as subjects in a pedagogical experiment.[2] Here is how to do this experiment in class:

1. The instructor (experimenter) splits the class up into "investment" groups of three or four people, labeling each group with a letter of the alphabet.
2. The instructor announces that if this were a real experiment, each subject would receive an envelope with five hundred-dollar bills in it. No real money is involved in today's experiment (unless the instructor wants to make a very large donation), but subjects should try to act as they would if real money were involved.
3. The instructor announces the rules.

   (a) Each subject can keep all five hundred-dollar bills or secretly put one, two, three, four, or five hundred-dollar bills in the envelope labeled "group investment." (The instructor can use counterfeit money for this purpose, or simply ask students to write down on a slip of paper without their names on it which group they are in and how many bills they choose to place into the group investment).
   (b) The instructor explains that the group investment fund will be invested in a way that guarantees the money will be doubled. The proceeds from that fund will be divided equally among the players.
   (c) Group members are not allowed to communicate with each other during the experiment.
   (d) At the end of the experiment, each subject is paid in cash. The amount will be the sum of the money left in the first envelope plus a share of the returns from the group investment account.

4. The instructor works through an example like this:
   Suppose the members of a group of three invest the following amounts: $200, $0, and $500. Thus, the total amount invested is $700. Doubling this produces $1400. Split three ways, each person gets $466.67 in investment returns. The first player invested $200, so has $300 left in his first envelope. His total payment is $300 + $466.67 = $766.67. Similarly, the second player's total payment is $966.67, and the third player's is $466.67. Are there any questions?

5. The subjects make their decisions, which are collected, displayed for each group (without names), and payoffs are calculated.

Here are a few suggested variations:

- Experience and learning: Keeping subjects in the same groups, give them a fresh $500 and repeat the experiment as many times as you like.
- Experience: Randomly change who is in each group by passing out private information sheets that say, for example "You are in group A." This way, a subject does not know who is in their own group, so has little ability to learn from what was done in past rounds of the experiment.
- *Cheap talk*: Allow subjects to meet and discuss the experiment before they make their decisions. But the decisions are still made secretly, so if any agreements were reached pre-play, there is no ability to find out who broke the agreement.
- Salient rewards: Rather than paying subjects with imaginary money, pay them something they care about that isn't too expensive, like chocolate.
- Inequality: Put different amounts in the first envelope for members of the same group.

These versions of the experiment don't quite meet the standards of a scientific study. In particular, no real money is paid to participants, so if some subjects just want to mess with the results, they can do so at no cost and ruin the experiment. But you can learn a lot from this experiment. First, what is the self-regarding equilibrium of this game? If people care only about the money they will receive, they will invest $0 in the group account. Why? Although the money players will receive depends on the amount given by other members of their groups, they are always wealthier by giving zero than by giving any positive amount. If, in a group of four, everyone else gives $500, and I also give $500, then I will receive ¼ (2 × ($500 + $500 + $500 + $500)) = $1000. However, if I give $400 and everyone else gives $500, I will be paid $1050. Better still, if I give $0 and everyone else gives $500, I will be paid $1250. My other group members are hurt by my opportunism (they would each receive $750), but if I am self-regarding, I don't care about that.

The same story is true no matter what amount the other group members give. For example, if they each gave $0 and I did the same, I would be paid $500. Giving zero is my best response to zero giving by other players, as, for example, if I gave $500, I would only be paid $250 (although other group members would receive $750 each). Giving zero is the best response to any level of giving by others, and I cannot affect what other people do when I give, so the equilibrium is to give zero (in game-theoretic terms, the dominant strategy equilibrium has each player giving zero).

Students will probably find that every group puts at least some money in the group account, but several class members will give zero, and several will give $500. From this, we conclude that the average class member did not act like they had self-regarding preferences. How does this compare with the optimum? In this experiment, it is socially optimal for each group member to give $500. Then (with group size of four), each receives $1000 so that total payments are $4000, versus the $2000 they would be in self-regarding equilibrium or the $3500 when three group members give $500 apiece and the fourth gives nothing.

In scientifically-conducted studies like this, average gifts are around $300. Socially optimal behavior is very rare in this experiment, even when subjects are all enrolled in philanthropic studies or nonprofit management programs. Contrary to early experimenter expectations, group size does not seem to have much of an effect – large groups are just as generous as small groups.[3] Results are also not very sensitive to the stakes – subjects given $5 give the same 40 to 60 percent as subjects given $500.

When subjects can talk with other group members, average giving goes up a bit. This is surprising to some economists, but not other social scientists, because talk is cheap. Group members may all agree to invest $500, but when they actually invest, they do so in secret and there is nothing to hold members to that agreement. Apparently, social and psychological factors matter here. This suggests that donors should be broken into smaller groups and encouraged to talk about how to divide up the burden of paying for good works.

In the classroom experiment, subjects made their decisions in secret. When anonymity is removed, so that group members know who else gave and how much they gave, giving goes up. Being observed matters, but even subtle hints that donors might be observed seem to matter as well. In a set of fascinating experiments, a poster containing artistic renderings of a pair of human eyes was placed in the room where the decisions were made, and average gifts went up substantially. For example, Bateson, Nettle, and Roberts (2006) put an eyes poster above the coffee pot for an academic department and found that payments to the honor box tripled.

We can learn more about free riding in the real world from experiments that repeat the public goods game with the same subjects. First, repetition increases average donations when group members stay the same across rounds, but not otherwise. This is especially true when the subjects who repeatedly interact are like-minded, perhaps explaining why fraternal societies and religious congregations are so successful at raising money. Second, giving tends to decline in the later rounds, with a larger drop-off in the final round. If group members are allowed to communicate, this helps to prevent the decline over time in average donations.

Getting self-regarding people to donate more

Fund-raisers are in a powerful position in a game with potential donors. They set the rules of the game regarding who gets to play, who moves first, and what information is shared with participants at each point in time. Economists have focused on sets of rules (called *mechanisms*) designed to reduce or eliminate the free-rider problem. The first mechanism, discussed above, is the voluntary contributions mechanism, where donations are submitted simultaneously and only the final total is announced. Although people donate more than they would if purely self-regarding when the voluntary contribution mechanism is used, they do not donate the optimal quantity and self-regarding donors give little or nothing. The *provision point mechanism* is superior, few fund-raisers know about it, but it is something that will become increasingly common in the future. How does this work?

In the provision point mechanism, the fund-raiser announces a campaign goal (the "provision point"), collects pledges, and if the pledges are greater than or equal to the provision point, asks that the pledges be paid. If the pledges are less than the provision point, the campaign is ended, and donors are told that they need not honor their pledge. This reduces free riding in theory, and as we shall see, in practice as well. In theory, under the voluntary contribution mechanism, each donor realizes that his or her own gift is a small part of the total. Thinking at the margin, the donor asks, "is it worth giving up, say, $100 of my money to get total spending on the collective good to increase from, say, $1,000,000 to $1,000,100?" Many will conclude it is not worth the cost to make such a small difference. In contrast, under the provision point mechanism, if the provision point is set to $1,000,000, the donor thinks "my $100 donation might make the difference between spending $0 (if the goal isn't reached) and spending $1,000,000 (if my donation pushes the total over the top);" this is a big motivation for self-regarding donors to give something.

In practice, the effectiveness of the provision point mechanism depends on what happens if total pledges exceed the provision point. If the excess is given back to donors, this is called a *rebate rule*, and the natural rebate rule works best – return the excess in proportion to pledges. Thus, if the provision point is $1,000,000 and $2,000,000 is pledged, each donor would be asked to pay half of her pledge. Some donors will pay their full pledge anyway but telling donors "we don't need that for this campaign" is the key that makes them willing to give so much.

The provision point mechanism also addresses the *assurance problem* that total donations will be enough to make personal donations worthwhile. Psychologically, the provision point mechanism addresses a donor's need to feel essential, but not taken advantage of by other donors. A recent paper by Hudik and Chovanculiak (2018) summarizes evidence on the effectiveness of the provision point mechanism from laboratory and field experiments, then discusses combining the mechanism with crowdfunding. They mention several current crowdfunding platforms that make charitable fund-raising using the provision point mechanism easy and inexpensive by automating rebate payments. This remains an area of very active research and implementation, so readers of this text should look for additional progress in the literature in future years.

Another mechanism is a *raffle*. Donors purchase raffle tickets that give them a chance of winning a valuable prize. In a raffle, the size of the prize is set before any tickets are sold, so that marginal ticket sales provide net resources to the fund-raiser dollar for dollar. That is, if the prize is $500 and more than 500 $1 raffle tickets are sold, the 501st ticket is pure profit. John Morgan (2000) proved a surprising result: the chance to win a prize reduces free riding by self-regarding individuals, so that by choosing a sufficiently large prize, the fund-raiser can come close to the socially-optimal level of spending on a collective good. In contrast, in a *lottery* where the size of the prize depends on how many lottery tickets are sold, self-regarding individuals free ride just as much as they do in the voluntary contributions mechanism. These results have been confirmed through laboratory (Morgan and Sefton, 2000) and field (Landry et al., 2006; Carpenter and Matthews, 2017) experiments. Charitable auctions are another mechanism that helps with free riding (Goeree et al., 2005; Carpenter, Holmes, and Matthews, 2008).

University capital campaigns are often conducted in two phases. A *silent phase* asks major donors for large gifts before the campaign and the campaign goal are announced. After 40 to 50 percent of the campaign goal is reached, the campaign enters a *public phase*, where potential donors are told on the announcement day about funds raised previously. This practice is a little puzzling to economists, who worry about whether the announcement will increase free riding in the public phase because donors feel that their contributions are not necessary, but there are game theoretic and behavioral reasons why the approach can be productive. The seed money from the silent phase solves the assurance problem and future donors recognize that the large seed donations reflect well on the quality of the organization. Finally, donors like to support a winner in a kind of bandwagon effect. In any case, List and Lucking-Reiley (2002) conducted a field experiment with a capital campaign for a research center at a university. They found that increasing the seed money from 10 percent to 67 percent of the campaign goal resulted in a nearly sixfold increase in donations. They also used a rebate rule for one of the treatment groups and that increased donations by about 20 percent.

12.4 Appealing to stakeholders and decision makers

Hyper-rational members of the species *homo economicus* are swayed solely by facts when they judge or decide things. Persuasive rhetoric and the ways that facts are presented play no role. But managers and other stakeholders are *homo sapiens*, affected by rhetoric, framing, and a reluctance to make difficult decisions. In this section, we selectively review findings from the experimental literature on valence framing and on the importance of the "default option".

> Imagine that the U.S. is preparing for the outbreak of an unusual Asian disease, which is expected to kill 600 people. Two alternative programs to combat the disease have been proposed. . . . If Program A is adopted, 200 people will be saved. If Program B is adopted, there is a 1/3 probability that 600 people will be saved, and a 2/3 probability that no people will be saved. Which of the two programs would you favor?

Which would you pick? Tversky and Kahneman (1981, p. 453) put this question to subjects, and 72 percent picked Program A, and the rest picked Program B. Then they asked another group of subjects the same question, with identical wording except for the descriptions of the two programs:

> If Program C is adopted, 400 people will die. If Program D is adopted, there is a 1/3 probability that nobody will die, and a 2/3 probability that 600 people will die.

This time, only 22 percent of subjects picked Program C, even though this program is objectively identical to Program A. The only difference is that the description of Programs C and D emphasize the potential loss from picking the risky and safe programs, whereas Programs A and B emphasize the potential gains from the two programs. This was the first study of loss-gain framing (or, as some authors prefer, "positive versus negative framing") and led to hundreds of studies on variations of loss-gain framing effects.

(Collectively, these variations are called *valence framing effects*.) Early studies seemed to be producing conflicting results, but Levin, Schneider, and Gaeth (1998) concluded that this is because there are three distinct types of valence framing (risky-choice framing, attribute framing, and goal framing) and the framing effect depends on which type is used. Tversky and Kahneman's experiment was on *risky-choice framing*, where subjects choose between a sure thing and a risky thing and the choices are framed as gains achievable versus losses avoided. The evidence is strong and reasonably consistent that people prefer the safer option when both are framed as gains and the riskier option when both are framed as losses. This result can be used by nonprofit or social enterprises that seek to change behavior through *social marketing*.

A second kind of valence framing cited by Levin, Schneider, and Gaeth (1998) is called *attribute framing*. This is about evaluating success or failure, rather than making risky choices. An organization that says, "We have successfully treated 90 percent of our clients" (positive frame) will be regarded more highly than one that says, "only 10 percent of our clients failed to complete the treatment" (negative frame). Attribute framing studies consistently find that positive framing leads to a higher evaluation, whether describing hamburger (75 percent lean versus 25 percent fat), surgery outcomes (survival rate versus mortality rate), or basketball players (percentage of shots made versus missed). Although nonprofit and social enterprise managers want to make rational decisions at all times, they should be aware of this persistent bias that may cloud the judgments of those they serve.

The third kind of valence framing is *goal framing*, in which the organization's mission or service-program goal is described by the potential to provide a benefit or gain (positive frame) or to avoid a loss (negative frame). In goal framing, the question is whether positive or negative frames better motivate stakeholders and their commitment to the organization. Unlike the other kinds of valence framing, most experiments find that negative goal framing has a stronger effect on behavior. This is one reason why politicians in competitive races often go negative ("if my opponent wins, the world will end") rather than positive ("if I win, unicorns will sing to fair maidens throughout the land"). The research suggests that nonprofit advocacy groups should stress the harms if the program they support is not adopted, rather than the benefits if the program is adopted.

If you are sure that you like something, and sure that you don't like the alternative, framing plays little role. Whether this author is told that a cup of coffee will make him cheerful and alert (positive framing) or that failure to drink a cup of coffee will result in headaches, bad textbook writing, and a feeling of hopelessness (negative framing), this author wants a cup of coffee. But even professional economists are not sure of which health plan offered by their employers to sign on to. When decisions are hard to make, and preferences are fuzzy, simple manipulations of the default option affect behavior. This was first shown by Samuelson and Zeckhauser (1988), who, in a series of experiments, found that a health care plan, or a retirement plan, was much more likely to be chosen under status quo framing ("here is your choice unless you choose otherwise") than under neutral framing ("here is a list of choices, pick one"). The same is true for organ donations (Johnson and Goldstein, 2003). The United States has an opt-in policy, where anyone who wants to donate their organs after passing away can give permission by checking a box on their driver's license application. Most European countries have a similar policy on an opt-out basis, where it is presumed you give permission unless you check a box on your driver's license application that says "I do not want to be an organ donor." This is a very difficult decision, so most drivers stick with the default option – no permission (U.S.) and permission (Europe). The effect was confirmed by Johnson and Goldstein (2003) and others.

How can nonprofit and social enterprise managers use the default option? Membership organizations could make renewal the default (along with a statement, "You will be billed . . .") unless the member opts out by checking a box. Continuing program enrollment (such as free lunch at child day care, weekly shopping trips for the elderly, season tickets for the theater) could also work on an opt-out basis. More controversially, instead of including a box that says, "I would like to increase my donation by XX dollars" on an annual appeal, the organization could make a small increase the default. These options should be considered, but there are practical, marketing, and ethical issues whenever the default option is (or is perceived to be) too pushy, so caution is advised.

12.5 The behavioral economics of incentives

One prominent topic from standard economics is the *principal–agent problem*, when one or more people (principals) employ others (agents) to complete a task. This is a problem because the principal wants the agent to work hard and complete the task in particular ways but it is costly or impossible for the principal to verify compliance. If the principal and agent have identical goals, there is no problem (this is called a stewardship relation), but when the agent has her own interests, particular forms of noncompliance are expected. Principal–agent problems abound in nonprofit organizations and social enterprises: between the Board (whose members want the organization's mission to be efficiently pursued) and the CEO (who wants to advance his career and compensation); between organizations (which want current and future donations) and their fund-raisers (who want to job hop and so may be willing to increase short-term donations at a cost to long-term performance); and between donors (who want their donations to be used in particular ways) and Boards (with different mission priorities) (Steinberg, 2010).

When it is difficult to observe actual behavior, traditional economists suggest using monetary incentives that better align the interests of the agent and the principal. For example, to deal with the for-profit agency problem between shareholders (principals) and top managers (agents), a profit-sharing contract may be offered to the managers. This way, it pays for the managers to work harder and smarter to maximize shareholder value. In traditional economics, a financial bonus counts as an incentive. But behavioral economics paints a more complex picture, where sometimes financial bonuses act as disincentives. These findings are particularly applicable to the nonprofit and social enterprise sectors, where paying volunteers a little something can be counterproductive. Here we summarize recent findings on what works as an incentive, with a focus on social organizations.[4]

In the aptly titled paper, "Pay enough or don't pay at all," Gneezy and Rustichini (2000) report two experiments where financial bonuses were counterproductive. In the first, high school students conducted a door-to-door campaign for charity after random assignment to three groups. All three groups were told that raising as much as possible was important, and that was the only motivation provided to the control group. The "small payments" treatment group also received a bonus (paid by a third party) equaling one percent of the money they collected, and the "large payments" treatment group received a ten percent bonus. Consistent with the title, the control group raised the most money, the small-payments group the least money, and the large-payments group in between. In the second experiment, parents often showed up late to pick up their children at a day-care center, so the center imposed a small fine. The fine was counterproductive, both in the short term and after the fine system was abolished.

But sometimes fiscal incentives work well. For example, an organization with a social marketing mission might provide incentives for people to exercise more. If the incentive is high enough, people will exercise, and many of those who do will find that they like the way regular exercise makes them feel. This positive reinforcement will lead some to make a habit of exercising even after the incentives are discontinued. Opera, live theater, and ballet are other goods provided by nonprofit organizations in the "Try it, you'll like it" category, where we expect fiscal incentives to work well.

Behavioral theory helps us make sense of these conflicting results. Building on early work by psychologists, Benabou and Tirole's (2003) behavioral-economic model asserts that people care about three things: extrinsic rewards, engaging in an activity, and their *image* (both self-image and public reputation). *Extrinsic* rewards are those supplied by others, like incentive payments, and *intrinsic* rewards are provided by the satisfaction of engaging in an activity you like. Traditional principal–agent theory asserts that extrinsic rewards combine with intrinsic rewards to determine behavior, but things are more complicated in the behavioral model. Agents react not only to extrinsic rewards, but they also try to figure out why those rewards are being given and react to the reason for the reward as well. For example, the agent might infer that larger rewards reflect the fact that the principal feels the task is difficult or costly to accomplish. Or the agent might infer that the principal believes the agent is unmotivated or incompetent. So, if a student is paid for improvement in classroom tests, that student may conclude that he is regarded as having low skills, or being asked to perform an unpleasant task, or being asked to do something that is hard and success is unlikely. This negative information can lower the student's intrinsic motivation for completing the task. These inferences lead to *motivational crowd-out* – a reduction in intrinsic motivation caused by extrinsic rewards. Negative information like this doesn't disappear, even if the financial rewards are canceled, so there can be a permanent reduction in agent motivation.

The reputational channel produces more behavioral effects. A volunteer naturally feels good about himself because volunteering self-signals that he is a good socially-responsible person. Volunteering also conveys the impression to others that the volunteer is pro-social and a good guy, enhancing the volunteer's public reputation. How does this change if the volunteer is paid a little something? Self-image and public reputation concerns no longer motivate the volunteer because nobody is sure if the volunteering signals goodness or greed. If self-image is the chief concern, volunteering and other acts by agents are unaffected by observability. But if public reputation motivates behavior, then extrinsic incentives are productive when payment is made privately but counterproductive when the payment is made publicly and the agent's activity and performance are observed by people the agent wants to impress. This was confirmed in experiments by Ariely, Bracha, and Meier (2009). In one experiment, subjects completed a computer task for charity, with effort measured by the number of mouse clicks. They found that when the task was performed in private, monetary incentives increased clicks by

241, but when the task and payment were public, clicks fell by 330, so public incentive payments were counterproductive. A second experiment involving bicycling for charity came to the same conclusion.

Some people do not want either an outstanding reputation or a terrible reputation because they just don't want to stand out. Jones and Linardi (2014) found that some of their subjects were "wallflowers." Wallflowers will move to average levels of volunteering when their efforts are made visible, which, for some, is lower than the effort they make when not observed. The wallflower effect was particularly strong for women subjects.

Agents are more productive, innovative, and dedicated when they feel trusted and in control. Trust is particularly important for the types of agents a social sector organization wants to employ, those with intrinsic pro-social motivations. When the principal provides extrinsic incentives, the agent may feel untrusted, particularly if monitoring is pervasive. Even if trust remains, there is the danger that the agent will feel manipulated and controlled, particularly if the requirements for earning incentive payments are minutely detailed and tied to specific procedures rather than outcomes. It also matters whether the agent feels penalized for bad behavior rather than rewarded for good behavior because these frames make the agent assume that the principal is hostile rather than kind.

Fiscal incentives in social interactions send information about appropriate social norms for behavior. In the day-care study of Gneezy and Rustichini (2000), the authors argue that parents felt that showing up late would violate norms of appropriate social behavior and inconvenience the day-care worker. So, parents tried hard to show up on time. When the system changed to impose fines on late parents, the perception changed to that of a business norm. Under the business norm, it is perfectly OK to show up late if you are willing to pay for the added costs. Heyman and Ariely (2004) surveyed students and found that monetary incentives reduced the perception that an interaction is social. In an experiment, when they substituted incentive payments of candy (viewed as social) for payments of money (viewed as business), subjects performed better on a computer task.

This framing effect of monetary rewards is captured by the following thought experiment (Gneezy, Meier, and Rey-Biel, 2011, p. 201):

> You meet an attractive person, and in due time you tell that person, "I like you very much and would like to have sex with you." Alternatively, consider the same situation, but now you say, "I like you very much and would like to have sex with

you, *and*, to sweeten the deal, I'm also willing to pay you $20!" Only a certain kind of economist would expect your partner to be happier in the second scenario. However, offering $20 worth of (unconditional) flowers might indeed make the desired partner happier.

SUMMARY

Behavioral economics has greatly enriched the power of economics to predict and interpret real-world behavior. In this chapter, we began by introducing the main tool of behavioral economics, experiments with human subjects. The opportunity to conduct such experiments is not limited to academic researchers – experiments can be conducted by nonprofit and social enterprise managers on the job, so we devoted some attention to the methodology of experiments. We showed that experiments and statistical analyses of natural data both produce persuasive evidence, but the two have different strengths and weaknesses.

It is difficult to keep up with the rapid progress being made in behavioral economics, but we highlighted some applications to fund-raising and management. The basic problem in fund-raising is the tendency of donors to give too little while enjoying the fruits produced by the donations of others. Free riding is most severe for self-regarding donors but is present even when donors are altruistic. A variety of mechanisms – rules for gathering donations – reduce free riding, so we discussed evidence supporting some of these mechanisms – the provision-point mechanism, charitable raffles and lotteries, charitable auctions, and the silent phase/public phase approach to capital campaigns.

Next, we discussed the behavioral economics of appealing to stakeholders and decision makers. Valence framing, the decision to describe programs and decision outcomes positively, as a gain, or negatively, as a loss, can change decisions and evaluations. Positive framing increases choice of the safer option when risk-choice framing applies and increases the assessment of programs and organizations in cases of attribute framing. However, it is frequently better to use negative goal framing to increase stakeholder support. We also pointed out the power of the default option to affect difficult choices. A simple opt-out treatment makes drivers more willing to donate organs than an opt-in treatment.

In the last section, we discussed principal–agent problems and the use of incentives to minimize these problems. We found complex behavioral factors affect whether an extrinsic incentive will crowd-out intrinsic motivations, so that sometimes fiscal incentives are counterproductive and other times fiscal incentives have their intended positive effects. This completes our tour of the current state of behavioral economics for nonprofit and social enterprise managers.

NOTES

1 The discussion in the text assumes that most treatment effects and differences in treatment effects are statistically significant, with the lone exception being the difference between the effect of medium versus high on amount given. The Methodological Appendix in the Online Companion (https://www.e-elgar.com/textbooks/young) defines this term more precisely, but the idea is that we want to distinguish differences due to the composition of each group from differences due to the treatment.

2 This version of the public good experiment is based on the pioneering experiments of Marwell and Ames (1979).

3 For the remainder of this section, we follow Gächter and Herrmann (2009), which contains the appropriate citations to studies.

4 For the remainder of this section, we follow Gneezy, Meier, and Rey-Biel (2011), which contains additional details and citations to studies.

SELECTED REFERENCES AND CITATIONS

Andreoni, J. and Payne, A.A. (2013). Charitable Giving. In Auerbach, A.J., Chetty, R., Feldstein, M., and Saez, E. (Eds.), *Handbook of Public Economics* (Vol. 5, pp. 1–50). London: Elsevier.

Ariely, D., Bracha, A., and Meier, S. (2009). Doing Good or Doing Well? Image Motivation and Monetary Incentives in Behaving Prosocially. *American Economic Review, 99(1)*, 544–555.

Bateson, M., Nettle, D., and Roberts, G. (2006). Cues of Being Watched Enhance Cooperation in a Real-World Setting. *Biology Letters, 2(3)*, 412–414.

Bekkers, R. and Wiepking, P. (2007). Generosity and Philanthropy: A Literature Review. Retrieved from https://pdfs.semanticscholar.org/d308/359cced588576a062a1dc4ffe68ccbf70147.pdf (accessed November 14, 2018).

Bekkers, R. and Wiepking, P. (2011). A Literature Review of Empirical Studies of Philanthropy: Eight Mechanisms that Drive Charitable Giving. *Nonprofit and Voluntary Sector Quarterly, 40(5)*, 924–973.

Bekkers, R. and Wiepking, P. (2011). Who Gives? A Literature Review of Predictors of Charitable Giving Part One: Religion, Education, Age and Socialisation. *Voluntary Sector Review, 2(3)*, 337–365.

Benabou, R. and Tirole, J. (2003). Intrinsic and Extrinsic Motivation. *The Review of Economic Studies, 70(3)*, 489–520.

Carpenter, J., Holmes, J., and Matthews, P.H. (2008). Charity Auctions: A Field Experiment. *The Economic Journal, 118(525)*, 92–113.

Carpenter, J. and Matthews, P.H. (2017). Using Raffles to Fund Public Goods: Lessons From a Field Experiment. *Journal of Public Economics, 150*, 30–38.

Cornes, R. and Sandler, T. (1984). Easy Riders, Joint Production, and Public Goods. *The Economic Journal, 94(375)*, 580–598.

Gächter, S. and Herrmann, B. (2009). Reciprocity, Culture and Human Cooperation: Previous Insights and a New Cross-Cultural Experiment. *Philosophical Transactions of the Royal Society of London B: Biological Sciences, 364(1518)*, 791–806.

Gächter, S. and Thöni, C. (2005). Social Learning and Voluntary Cooperation among Like-Minded People. *Journal of the European Economic Association, 3(2–3),* 303–314.

Gneezy, U. and Rustichini, A. (2000). Pay Enough or Don't Pay at All. *Quarterly Journal of Economics, 115,* 791–810.

Gneezy, U., Meier, S., and Rey-Biel, P. (2011). When and Why Incentives (Don't) Work to Modify Behavior. *Journal of Economic Perspectives, 25(4),* 191–210.

Goeree, J.K., Maasland, E., Onderstal, S., and Turner, J.L. (2005). How (Not) to Raise Money. *Journal of Political Economy, 113(4),* 897–918.

Hanington, J. (2012). The ABCs of A/B Testing. Blogpost July 12, 2012. Retrieved from https://www.pardot.com/blog/abcs-ab-testing/ (accessed April 29, 2018).

Heyman, J. and Ariely, D. (2004). Effort for Payment: A Tale of Two Markets. *Psychological Science, 15(11),* 787–793.

Hudik, M. and Chovanculiak, R. (2018). Private Provision of Public Goods via Crowdfunding. *Journal of Institutional Economics, 14(1),* 23–44.

Johnson, E. and Goldstein, D. (2003). Do Defaults Save Lives? *Science, 302(5649),* 1338–1339.

Jones, D. and Linardi, S. (2014). Wallflowers: Experimental Evidence of an Aversion to Standing Out. *Management Science, 60(7),* 1757–1771.

Landry, C.E., Lange, A., List, J.A., Price, M.K., and Rupp, N.G. (2006). Toward an Understanding of the Economics of Charity: Evidence from a Field Experiment. *The Quarterly Journal of Economics, 121(2),* 747–782.

Levin, I.P., Schneider, S.L., and Gaeth, G.J. (1998). All Frames are not Created Equal: A Typology and Critical Analysis of Framing Effects. *Organizational Behavior and Human Decision Processes, 76(2),* 149–188.

List, J.A. and Lucking-Reiley, D. (2002). The Effects of Seed Money and Refunds on Charitable Giving: Experimental Evidence from a University Capital Campaign. *Journal of Political Economy, 110(1),* 215–233.

Marwell, G. and Ames, R.E. (1979). Experiments on the Provision of Public Goods. I. Resources, Interest, Group Size, and the Free-rider Problem. *American Journal of Sociology, 84(6),* 1335–1360.

Morgan, J. (2000). Financing Public Goods by Means of Lotteries. *The Review of Economic Studies, 67(4),* 761–784.

Morgan, J. and Sefton, M. (2000). Funding Public Goods with Lotteries: Experimental Evidence. *The Review of Economic Studies, 67(4),* 785–810.

Samuelson, W. and Zeckhauser, R. (1988). Status Quo Bias in Decision Making. *Journal of Risk and Uncertainty, 1(1),* 7–59.

Smith, A. (1759/1976). *The Theory of Moral Sentiments.* Oxford: Clarendon Press.

Spencer, M.A., Swallow, S.K., Shogren, J.F., and List, J.A. (2009). Rebate Rules in Threshold Public Good Provision. *Journal of Public Economics, 93(5–6),* 798–806.

Steinberg, R. (2010). Principal–Agent Theory and Nonprofit Accountability. In Hopt, K.J. and von Hippel, T. (Eds.), *Comparative Corporate Governance of Non-Profit Organizations* (pp. 73–125). Cambridge, UK: Cambridge University Press.

Tversky, A. and Kahneman, D. (1981). The Framing of Decisions and the Psychology of Choice. *Science, 211(4481),* 453–458.

Vesterlund, L. (2016). Using Experimental Methods to Understand Why and How We Give to Charity. In Kagel. J.H. and Roth, A.E. (Eds.), *The Handbook of Experimental Economics* (Volume 2, pp. 91–151). Princeton, NJ: Princeton University Press.

Wiepking, P. and Bekkers, R. (2012). Who Gives? A Literature Review of Predictors of Charitable Giving. Part Two: Gender, Family Composition and Income. *Voluntary Sector Review, 3(2),* 217–245.

🗨 **REVIEW CONCEPTS**

Assurance Problem: The reluctance of individuals to donate because they are unsure whether a sufficient amount of giving by others will occur to make the charitable effort worthwhile.

Attribute Framing: The choice to describe an evaluation of a person, organization, or program in terms of success achieved versus failures remaining. A form of valence framing.

Causality: The relationship between two variables where manipulation of one (the cause) yields a change in the other (the effect). Causality is established by a pattern of relationship, absence of reverse causality, and rejection of alternative explanations for the pattern.

Cheap Talk: Pre-play communication in a game that results in agreements that cannot be enforced.

Control Group: A group of subjects used as the benchmark who do not receive the experimental treatment.

Experiment: A scientific method where the researcher intentionally applies one or more treatments to randomly assigned subjects and withholds those treatments from other randomly assigned subjects, then measures differences in outcomes.

External Validity: The extent to which causal conclusions of a study generalize to real-life situations, other groups of people or organizations, and other times, places, and cultures.

Extrinsic Motivation: Motivation arising from factors outside an individual, such as monetary incentives, pressure, or prestige.

Free Riding: The tendency of self-regarding individuals to donate little or nothing towards a collective good despite appreciating the donations of others.

Goal Framing: The choice to describe an organization's mission or specific goals in terms of benefits sought versus harm avoided. A form of valence framing.

Happenstance Data: Data generated by natural processes and obtained through measurement and surveys.

Image Motivation: Motivation to do something in order to maintain a good self-image and/or external reputation.

Internal Validity: The extent to which a causal conclusion based on a study is warranted for those being studied.

Intrinsic Motivation: Motivation to do something because it is fun or satisfying. The reward is the behavior itself.

Lottery Mechanism: An approach to fund-raising where lottery tickets are sold to people who know that a collective good is financed by the lottery's profits. The lottery prize increases with the number of tickets sold.

Mechanism: A set of rules that one player can impose on a game to produce desirable outcomes.

Motivational Crowd-out: Reduction in intrinsic motivation caused by extrinsic rewards.

Principal–Agent Problem: How one individual, the principal, can design a contract or reward structure that motivates others (agents) to act in the principal's interests.

Provision Point Mechanism: An approach to fund-raising where a campaign goal (provision point) is announced, and donors are told they will only have to honor their pledge if the campaign goal is met.

Public Phase: The second phase of a typical capital campaign, in which there is a general call for giving. Occurs after announcement of seed gifts that constitute a large share of the campaign goal.

Raffle Mechanism: Like a lottery mechanism, but the size of the prize is fixed in advance of ticket sales.

Random Assignment: The experimental procedure that gives each subject an equal chance of assignment to a control or treatment group.

Rebate Rule: A rule for determining what is done with the excess of pledges over the provision point in the provision point mechanism.

Reverse Causality: A challenge to internal validity, where manipulating what was thought to be the effect variable causes a change in what was thought to be the cause variable.

Risky-Choice Framing: The choice to describe a decision that compares a definite outcome with a risky outcome in terms of gains that could be achieved (positive framing) or losses that could be avoided (negative framing). One form of valence framing.

Salient Rewards: Meaningful benefits provided to subjects based on their behavior in the experiment. An attempt to mimic the real-world consequences of behavior in a laboratory setting.

Silent Phase: The first stage of a typical capital campaign, in which a few major prospects are asked to contribute a large sum prior to announcement of the campaign and the campaign goal.

Social Marketing: Activities designed to change behavior for the benefit of target-group members and society as a whole.

Spurious Correlation: A pattern of association between two measured variables that is not due to either variable causing the other. Usually results from an unmeasured variable that causes both measured variables to change, as when prior health status is unobserved and mortality and hospital usage are measured.

Treatment: An intentional intervention applied to one group in an experiment. The goal of the experiment is to determine whether this intervention causes an independent change in some outcome.

Treatment Effect: The average difference in an experimental outcome between the treatment and control groups.

Valence Framing: Formulating a message either in positive terms or negative terms.

Voluntary Contribution Mechanism: A method of fund-raising in which donors simultaneously decide how much to contribute to a collective good, after which the sum donated is applied to provision of that collective good.

EXERCISES

1. Are you a fully rational donor? What are some choices you have made regarding who you give to and/or how much you give that are difficult to describe as the outcome of a rational calculation based on facts? Why do you think you made those decisions?

2. Wossamotta U. began offering online education and wanted to evaluate it. They asked Professor Peabody to design an experiment to do so, and he decided to evaluate the Russian Espionage Class taught by Professor Badenov. Badenov taught two sections of this course, one online, with 20 students, and the other traditional, with 43 students. Both sections took the same exams, and class average grades were almost the same, so Peabody concluded that online education is just as effective as live instruction.

   (a) Was Peabody's study an experiment? Why or why not?
   (b) Was Peabody's conclusion scientifically persuasive? Are there problems with internal validity? External validity?

3. If you have experience in fund-raising, have you encountered behavioral, rather than traditional economic, reactions to a direct mail campaign? To a fund-raising special event? To telemarketing? To major donor solicitation? Explain and discuss the implications.

4. Americorps enrolls "stipended volunteers," but pays them just enough to get by. What do you think would happen to the number of Americorps volunteers if pay was

increased to allow members to enjoy a middle-class lifestyle? What do you think would happen to volunteer effort if pay were increased? Why?

5. Oxfam's mission statement is "To create lasting solutions to poverty, hunger, and social justice." American Red Cross "Prevents and alleviates human suffering in the face of emergencies by mobilizing the power of volunteers and the generosity of donors." The American Heart Association seeks "To build healthier lives, free of cardiovascular diseases and stroke." Comment on any valence framing in these missions.

   (a) What kinds of valence framing are illustrated here?

   (b) Which (if any) of these mission statements would create the highest stakeholder evaluation of the organization according to experimental findings summarized in this chapter?

   (c) Undoubtedly, valence framing was not the top priority of the mission-statement writers, so it may be difficult to fit these mission statements into positive or negative frames and you may think that some mission statements mix both kinds of frames. Discuss these complications as well.

13
Market failure

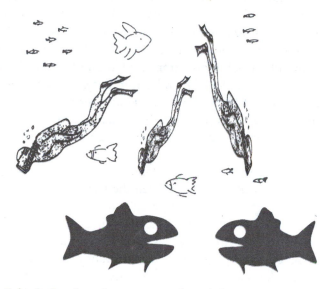

I think the idea of common pool goods has gotten out of hand!*

13.1 Introduction

In Chapter 7, we looked closely at the market structure called "perfect competition." There we analyzed how markets work to bring demand and supply into balance by establishing market-clearing prices at which goods and services are exchanged without leaving consumers wanting more or producers having more to sell than consumers will buy. This is the way that markets help to put economic resources to their best uses, that is, to allocate resources efficiently according to the Pareto criterion discussed in Chapter 1. This is the "invisible hand" that Adam Smith described when he argued that maximum efficiency is achieved when many consumers and producers inter-act in the marketplace, each individually pursuing his or her self-interest. In

---

* Parts of this cartoon were taken from open source artwork. Images were taken from "open art", accessed on February 21, 2018, drawn by Last-Dino (the two large fish) and j4p4n (the scuba divers).

Chapter 8, we examined market structures featuring imperfect competition where one or more participants exert market power, and therefore are able to influence the going price of a good or service in ways not possible under perfect competition. This led to inefficiency.

However, even highly competitive markets do not always work perfectly. There are some conditions of *market failure* in which markets do not allocate resources efficiently. We have already seen examples of this. In Chapter 3, we cited conditions of information asymmetry wherein producers are more informed about the quality of services than are consumers (or vice versa), and where the utilization of nonprofit organizations may be a more efficient means of service provision than commercial service. (Further analysis of conditions of partial information is offered in Chapter 10 which discusses decision making under risk and uncertainty.) And in earlier chapters we noted that market transactions may ignore certain social benefits and costs that do not directly impact those who make (private) supply and demand decisions, a phenomenon called *externalities* in this chapter.

It is important for us to understand the foregoing conditions for several reasons. First, market failure is often the basis on which government intervenes in markets, by imposing regulations, taxes, or subsidies to address unintended social costs or benefits. Second, market failure helps explain why we choose in some circumstances to utilize institutions other than for-profit businesses operating through markets to allocate resources. Market failure is one of three keys in "three failures theory" explaining the role and presence of the different sectors in different activities (Steinberg, 2006).

Third, we will find that some concepts of market failure are usefully applied within the internal context of managing organizations. Indeed, we can even help explain why organizations exist by referring to situations of market failure where it is more efficient to allocate resources within the rules and confines of an organization than through open market exchange. However, replacing markets with organizations does not eliminate market-failure conditions – these conditions merely become management problems (see Williamson, 1975, 2008).

There is an additional complication when private nonprofit organizations address market failures. Organizational objectives vary and may or may not coincide with broader notions of social efficiency. Thus, in Chapter 9, we spoke of pricing using "beneficial demand" to correct market failures as seen by a particular nonprofit organization with particular objectives, rather than using a "marginal social benefit curve" (as we will describe below) to represent societal benefits more generally.

In this chapter, we explore the sources of market failure in more detail and then illustrate how nonprofit organizations have addressed these problems in the markets for day care, blood, and the performing arts. We then illustrate the power of market-failure analysis to provide insights on more general non-profit management dilemmas – fund-raising, volunteers, contracting versus internal production, pricing, and joining trade associations. As the leadoff cartoon suggests, some of these situations resemble common pools wherein competition by economic actors for the same resources is inefficient, to the detriment of all parties.

13.2 Circumstances that lead to market failure

The invisible hand theorem essentially states that equilibrium is efficient when all goods, bads, and services are traded in perfectly competitive mar-kets. If we lived in such a world, there would be no efficiency rationale for either a government or a nonprofit sector. However, many goods are not traded at all or are traded in imperfectly competitive markets, and these market failures lead to inefficiency. In some circumstances, either govern-ments, nonprofit organizations, social enterprises or some combination of these can reduce these inefficiencies, but in order to understand how, we need to know more about the sources of market failure.

We have already seen how for-profit monopolies control prices, resulting in market failure when all customers are charged the same price. There is no market failure, but possible inequity, when monopolies use perfect price discrimination. We have also seen how nonprofit monopolies may use one market failure (monopoly) to finance remedies for other market failures; thus, the efficiency consequences of nonprofit monopolies are ambiguous. Governments can correct market failures by enforcing anti-trust regulations, nationalizing the monopolized industry, or regulating the affected firm. Note that we say governments *can* correct the failures, not that they will necessarily do so. Limitations on government stem from political considerations and transactions costs within this form of organiza-tion; however, we leave more detailed study of the subject of "government failure" within the "three failures model," to other texts (Douglas, 1983; Steinberg, 2006).

In this chapter, we focus on four interrelated sources of market failure – *transactions costs*, *nonappropriability*, *externality*, and *informational asymme-try*. Like monopoly, these sources of market failure undermine the efficiency of market provision. Sometimes they may even preclude the existence of markets for certain goods and services, requiring different institutional arrangements involving government, nonprofits, social enterprises and other organizational forms.

Cost of transactions

In order for markets to work well, it must be relatively inexpensive to arrange contracts and to buy and sell goods and services. In the world of the Internet and social media, it is now almost costless to shop for a product online, as such purchases no longer require traveling to a store, and this is especially the case when shipping costs are included in the price. However, such minimal cost transactions are not universal. Transactions may be costly for a variety of reasons. Goods and services themselves may be complex, hard to measure, or inherently uncertain, thus difficult to specify in contracts. For example, the market for medical care suffers from these complications. Transactions costs may be high because of various physical, cultural or institutional barriers to trade, for example, currency or language problems, long distances between consumers and suppliers, or governmentally-imposed tariffs and regulations. Or, transactions costs may be high because markets are inherently difficult to police. For example, the market for hunting on private land is made costly by the difficulty of preventing poaching. Markets work most efficiently when transactions problems are minimal. Sometimes, the nonprofit institutional form helps to reduce transactions costs, as discussed below, and this provides one important role for the nonprofit sector.

Appropriability of goods or services

In order for markets to work, consumers must be able to appropriate the benefits of the good or service to themselves, and suppliers must be able to exclude would-be consumers who fail to pay. Lack of appropriability may be associated with the character of a particular good or service itself (for example, fresh air cannot normally be captured for sale to consumers in heavily polluted regions) or with the failure of government to define and enforce property rights (for example, where the ownership of mineral rights associated with real estate is left unclear in the law). Thus, an aspect of the appropriability requirement is that a governmental framework of laws and contract enforcement is necessary for the operation of efficient markets.

Externalities

Sometimes people are forced to consume items they do not want. No such problem applies when a neighbor buys ugly interior furnishing, because no one else needs to see those furnishings. However, when one resident lets his lawn and the exterior of his house deteriorate, neighbors are forced to view this unsightly mess. This is an example of an *external cost* (or, synonymously, a "negative externality" or an "external diseconomy"). Alternatively, sometimes people consume items that they need not purchase. If a group of teenagers band together to help an elderly couple in the neighborhood do home and yard maintenance, others in the neighborhood, who see the appearance of their street improve, also benefit from their generosity, perhaps even in the form of an increase in the value of their own homes. This is an example of a *positive externality* (or, synonymously, an "external benefit" or "external economy"). Finally, an externality is *reciprocal* if someone in a group purchases a good and the entire group benefits from that purchase (no matter who the purchaser). This special kind of externality is called a *public good*, which we will discuss further below. Reciprocal externalities can also occur when the entire group is harmed (when anyone enters a crowded highway, everyone else is slowed down), which may be termed a "public bad."

Externalities cause market failure for either or both of two reasons: first, the external cost or benefit may not be appropriable. There may be no way for consumers of external benefits to garner the level of benefits they desire, and there may be no way for producers to exclude those who do not pay for external benefits (or to include those who would pay). Second, even if a (secondary) market could be established for the external effect, this market may be quite "thin," that is, it may have few buyers or sellers, so that monopolistic or monopsonistic conditions may result. Organizing a market for helping street beggars would be quite difficult because it suffers these problems (e.g., all passers-by on the street would benefit but few could be induced to pay for those benefits). Nonprofit organizations sometimes address this kind of market failure.

Informational asymmetry

Markets fail where information is costly or lacking. In Chapter 3 we discussed the condition of *information asymmetry* under which consumers are disadvantaged relative to producers, leading consumers to prefer nonprofit organizations over for-profit providers. (See also Chapter 10 for ways decision makers can purchase better information in situations of risk.) The markets for child day-care or nursing-home services for the elderly provide examples where information asymmetry is a condition leading to market failure. Informational asymmetry combines elements of appropriability (there may be no way for someone to secure truthful information from a nursing-home operator about hidden aspects of the quality of care) with elements of market power (informational markets may be too thin for perfect competition to prevail). Information creation, as well as dissemination, may suffer from market failures. Research and the development of innovations some-times create nonappropriable external benefits, so market failure occurs here as well. (For example, everyone benefits from better information about the weather, but few would invest in climate research.) Nonprofit organizations may address both problems. However, before we can turn to the applications of market failure to nonprofits, we need to say more about externalities and public goods.

13.3 Externalities

We employ the following as our working definition of an externality:

> *An externality is a benefit or a cost received by third parties as a result of market transactions that are not controlled by the third party.*

Here are some examples of externality-creating market activities:

- *Inoculations for communicable diseases.* When an individual receives an inoculation, that individual benefits from the protection, but society at large (third parties) also benefits from the reduced risk of the spread of disease. This is a positive externality.
- *Musical performances.* An accomplished musician who practices Beethoven near an open window benefits not only himself but those (third parties) within earshot. Rappers and Hip-Hop fans may regard this as a negative externality, but others will regard this as a (positive) external benefit.
- *Traffic congestion.* When people drive on crowded roadways they impose additional delays on other (third party) drivers, a negative externality.
- *Smoking.* When people decide to smoke they may not take into account the health and aesthetic costs imposed on (third party) nonsmokers from secondary inhalation.
- *Pollution.* When people buy non-biodegradable products or when manu-facturers pollute the air or water they impose environmental costs on citizens (third parties) not accounted for in their decisions.
- *Education.* When people invest in their own education they become more productive, but this does not create *external* growth benefits because more productive workers receive higher salaries. If, however, as a result of those higher salaries, the educated worker abandons a life of crime, this has external benefits in his community.

There are two kinds of externalities, with differing effects on social welfare. A *technological externality* occurs when market activities of others affect the

third party's cost or well-being. All of the examples above illustrate technological externalities. Those who don't catch diseases because others were
vaccinated are happier. When a car enters a crowded highway, it increases
transportation costs for those caught in resulting traffic jams. The other kind
of externality is called a *pecuniary externality* and occurs when the third party
pays different prices for goods and services as a result of the market transactions of others. For example, if the U.S. government decides to purchase a
billion barrels of oil for its Strategic Petroleum Reserves, the price of gas will
go up for all Americans. Technological externalities generally create market
failures, but pecuniary externalities do not (although both kinds of externalities affect market equilibrium). For this reason, we pay no further attention
to pecuniary externalities.

How does a technological externality create market failure? To show this, we
need to distinguish private and social costs and to distinguish private and
social benefits. We learned in Chapter 6 about the distinction between private costs (borne by producers) and external costs (borne by third parties),
and we defined social costs as the sum of these two. The key equation here is
for marginal costs, and it is an identity:

$$MSC(Q) = MPC(Q) + MEC(Q) \qquad (13.1)$$

where: MSC is marginal social costs, a function of the quantity Q
MPC is marginal private costs, a function of Q, and
MEC is marginal external costs, also a function of Q.

We learned in Chapter 7 that the competitive market supply curve is the horizontal sum of firm supply curves consisting of marginal cost curves. We were
unconcerned with externalities in that chapter, but now we need to be more
precise – profit maximizing firms, at least, are using their MPC curves, rather
than the other cost curves, to make supply decisions. Therefore, MPC(Q) is
the same as the market supply curve for competitive markets. If there are no
externalities caused by producers, then MEC(Q) is zero for all values of Q,
and the MSC and MPC curves will coincide. If a market transaction creates
an increase in costs for third-party suppliers (for example, highway congestion causing increased transportation costs for trucking firms) MEC will be
positive, so the marginal social costs curve will lie above the supply curve.
If a market transaction reduces costs for third-party suppliers (for example,
beekeepers providing free pollination services for flower producers), MEC
will be negative, so the marginal social costs curve will lie below the supply
curve. There is some ambiguity in deciding which curve to shift, and in this
text, we call anything that raises the costs of third-party producers an external

cost and anything that lowers the costs of third-party producers a negative external cost (showing up as MEC with a negative sign) rather than calling this reduction in costs a "benefit."

The same sort of distinction can be made on the benefit side. We define *marginal private benefits* (MPB) as the benefits received by buyers. We measure these marginal benefits as the highest price buyers are willing to pay for an additional unit of a good. Recall that the height of the demand curve represents marginal willingness to pay, so the demand curve is identical with MPB(Q). If third-party consumers are helped by the market transaction (for example, community members facing lower risk of infection as a result of parents vaccinating their children), this shows up as a positive *marginal external benefit* (MEB), and the sum of the two, the *marginal social benefit* (MSB) curve, lies above the demand curve. Thus, we have a second identity:

$$MSB(Q) = MPB(Q) + MEB(Q) \tag{13.2}$$

where: MSB is marginal social benefits,
      MPB is marginal private benefits, and
      MEB is marginal external benefits, all as functions of Q.

If third-party consumers are hurt by this market transaction (for example, local residents suffering toxic effects of industry locating a toxic waste disposal site nearby), MEB will be negative and the MSB curve will be below the demand curve. Again, we are resolving the ambiguity between calling something a negative benefit or a cost by looking at whether the externality affected third-party consumers (in which case it affects the MEB term) or third-party producers (in which case it affects the MEC term).

Now we will show exactly where the market failure caused by externalities comes from. But first, we have a new tool to demonstrate the allocative efficiency part of the invisible hand theorem. Recall that allocative efficiency is about producing the right quantity of each good or service. Thinking at the margin, net social benefits (benefits minus costs) are maximized at a quantity where MSB(Q) = MSC(Q), because if the left-hand side were bigger, there would be a net gain if Q is increased, and if the right-hand side were bigger, there would be a net gain if Q is reduced. Here, in its entirety, is the proof of this part of the invisible hand theorem:

1. If there are no externalities on producers, the MSC(Q) is the same as supply.

2. If there are no externalities in consumption, the MSB(Q) curve is the same as demand.
3. MSB(Q) = MSC(Q) when supply crosses demand. So allocative efficiency is obtained.

Figure 13.1 illustrates a positive externality on consumers in panel A and a negative externality on consumers in panel B. We will use it to prove that there is a market failure in each case using the same logic as our proof of the invisible hand theorem. In both panels, MEB is not equal to zero because

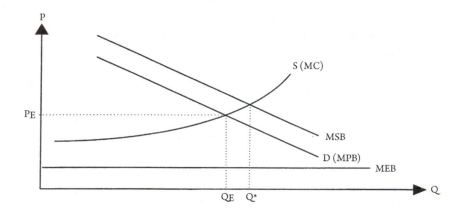

Figure 13.1 Panel A: The market equilibrium Q_E is too small when there is a positive externality on consumers

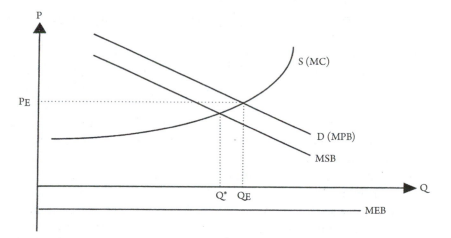

Figure 13.1 Panel B: The market equilibrium Q_E is too big when there is a negative externality on consumers

Figure 13.1A–B Externalities create inefficiency

third-party consumers are affected. In both panels, there is no externality on producers, so MSC(Q) and MPC(Q) are identical and simply labeled MC. In panel A, MSB lies above demand (MEB is positive), and in panel B, MSB lies below demand (MEB is negative). The market equilibrium quantity (Q_E) occurs where supply crosses demand, that is, where MC(Q) = MPB(Q); the socially efficient quantity (Q^*) is where MC(Q) crosses MSB(Q).

The same analysis applies to externalities in production as we did for externalities in consumption in Figure 13.1 (the reader should try it – its good practice) and come to the following important conclusion:

> Competitive markets overproduce goods that create external costs and underproduce goods that create external benefits.

There are many possible solutions to market failures resulting from positive externalities:

- *Mandates*: Government can mandate provision or consumption at a certain level. We do not allow young children or their parents to decide for themselves whether to attend schools, substituting compulsory attendance laws for consumer choice. This solves the potential underprovision of elementary and secondary education in a free market.
- *Subsidies*: Subsidies can be offered to induce higher levels of production and consumption. Subsidized student loans and work-study programs tied to good academic standing as a full-time student at an accredited university provide an example of the subsidy approach. So do need-based scholarships.
- *Social marketing*: Promotional advertising could increase demand, moving it closer to the MSB curve. A "go back to school" campaign is an illustration of this. We are not portraying efficiency accurately in this approach (strictly speaking, a change in personal preferences cannot be judged by the efficiency standard), but it is a plausible way to increase education and thereby increase the external benefits in equilibrium.
- *Taxation*: Alternatives to the desired behavior can be taxed. For example, recreational activities available during school hours can be made more expensive so that youth find it less desirable to cut classes. If movies are a relevant substitute for schooling (with a positive cross-price elasticity), then a tax on movies shown during school hours would help correct the market failure. Charitable donations are another good with external benefits, and taxes encourage charitable donations a different way. The charitable donation tax deduction reduces income taxes by a fraction of

the amount donated, which has the effect of reducing the price of giving, hence increasing giving.

- *Prizes*: Prizes can provide tangible rewards to those who most success-fully increase their consumption of the desired good. Thus, students can be given awards for exceptional attendance or educational achievement.

Similar kinds of remedies are available to address negative externalities:

- *Mandates*: Government can set limits or impose restrictions on behavior. For example, smoking can be prohibited in public places or pollution standards can be set and enforced.
- *Taxes*: Taxes can be imposed to discourage externality-producing behav-ior. For example, cigarettes or gasoline, or even effluents and emissions themselves (such as sulfur dioxide and carbon at power plants) can be taxed.
- *Social marketing*: Information campaigns, such as "quit smoking" or "take public transit" or "eat healthy and exercise" advertising, can be mounted to ask people to reduce their externality-producing behaviors.
- *Prizes*: Sanctions, such as publicly citing the worst industrial polluters, can be applied. Alternatively, a prize or public commendation can be offered to the firm that best reduces its pollution.
- *Subsidies*: Subsidies can be provided to encourage people to use substi-tutes for the externality-producing activity. For example, public transit or biodegradable packaging can be subsidized.
- *Tradeable permits*: A limited number of permits can be issued, and those without permits can be prohibited from engaging in the externality-generating activity. Permits can be bought and sold, so that those who would find it most costly to reduce the externality-generating activity will buy permits from those who find it somewhat easier. (So-called "cap and trade" programs to control air or water pollution work this way.)

Note that the various remedies for negative and positive externalities are basically the same and fall into three categories: (1) educating people and hoping that they will change their behavior voluntarily; (2) policing behavior through direct rules and regulations; or (3) providing incentives so that costs and benefits faced by individuals or organizations conform more closely with the social costs and benefits implied by their actions.

The last approach is, in principle, the one usually favored by economists because it does not try to change people's preferences or values, nor does it try to impose uniform standards on everyone. What economists basically try to do in cases of externalities is to find ways of "internalizing the externalities" by bringing the social benefits into the decision-making process of individual consumers or producers in the marketplace through taxes and subsidies. Examples of policies that internalize externalities are:

- Taxes based on the carbon content of fossil fuels to reduce global warming due from greenhouse effect;
- Tradeable permits permitting the emission of sulfur oxides by fossil-fuel power plants within a predetermined aggregate ceiling;
- Gasoline taxes that reflect the pollution and wear and tear on roadways imposed on others by driving;
- Highway tolls during peak hours that reflect the congestion costs imposed by commuters;
- Tuition scholarships that reflect the benefits to society of undertaking further education;
- Cigarette taxes that reflect health costs imposed on others from smoking.

Each of these solutions has unique advantages and disadvantages. For example, a tax on gasoline reduces driving and hence automobile pollution, but perhaps a more efficient way to reduce automobile pollution is to improve automobile technology by replacing internal combustion cars with hybrid or electric cars. Alternatively, a tax based on tail-pipe emissions would allow each driver to find the most efficient way to control pollution and thereby cut the tax. However, it would also create much larger transactions costs than a tax on gasoline because it would be very expensive to install equipment to measure tailpipe emissions on every car (Downing, 1984; Kilenthong and Townsend, 2014).

As we saw in earlier chapters, nonprofit or social enterprise organizations may depart from competitive or monopoly equilibria to promote their own missions. In so doing, they equate beneficial demand, rather than price or marginal revenue, with marginal cost. Does this promote social efficiency? Possibly. If there is a positive externality, using market demand to determine output creates a market failure. Loosely speaking, for example, if a nonprofit's beneficial demand curve lies above the market demand curve but below the marginal social benefit curve (described earlier), nonprofit production will enhance social efficiency by moving production closer to the optimum. If beneficial demand coincides with MSB, nonprofit production will entirely correct the market failure. However, a nonprofit organization could make things worse. Suppose, for example, that the Corvette Society believed that Corvettes were an underappreciated good (like opera) and subsidized rides by young children in Corvettes in the hopes that they would grow into aficionados. This organization's beneficial demand would be higher than the market demand, whereas the additional pollution produced by these cars suggests that marginal social benefits would be below market demand. The Corvette Society would worsen economic efficiency by moving production of Corvettes away from the social optimum.

In summary, externalities are a form of market failure wherein the costs or benefits of an activity are not fully taken into account by private decision making as reflected in unfettered markets. Economists' approach to externalities involves policies that attempt to internalize externalities, through subsidies, taxes, and other means. The concept of externality is an important one for nonprofit and social enterprise managers and policymakers for a number of reasons. First, nonprofits and social enterprises are often involved in addressing social problems and issues involving important externalities – both positive and negative – such as environmental issues, health issues, education, and the like. Second, nonprofit managers and social entrepreneurs may themselves be involved in producing or reducing important externalities. If they are to truly operate in the public interest, they must be aware of, and attend to, these externalities.

13.4 Public goods

Pure Public Goods are a special kind of reciprocal externality with two essential characteristics, *nonexcludability* and *nonrivalry*:

> *A good is nonexcludable, if once it is produced, consumers cannot be prevented from using or benefitting from it except at great cost.*
> *A good is nonrival if one person's use of it does not reduce the amount available for use by others.*

Examples of pure public goods are national defense, public art, light houses, and clean air. Radiation leaks from nuclear plant accidents such as Fukushima in 2011 and Chernobyl in 1986 produced "pure public bads" (the negative of public goods); their cleanups were a public good. In each case, once the good is produced it is difficult or impossible to prevent anyone from using (or being affected by) it, whether or not they pay for it; moreover, one person's use does not detract from another's use.

Notice that our definition of a public good is specific and technical and differs from the common usage of the words in English. A public good, by this definition, may or may not be a governmentally-provided good. Sometimes, governments provide goods with no externalities, and sometimes the private sector provides public goods. This is why some economists (including authors of this book) prefer to label these as "collective goods," which characterizes the collective consumption of nonrival goods. The term "public goods" reflects a history of two-sector thinking by economists – if the market fails, government was thought of as the only alternative, and the market certainly fails for collective consumption goods. We have kept the traditional name because it is still more prominent in the discipline.

From a market failure point of view, of course, if goods can be enjoyed without having to pay for them, then the benefits are nonappropriable and for-profit firms will not be able to sell them. Any payments for this good would be entirely voluntary, essentially equivalent to donations. However, consumers are not likely to trust for-profit firms with donations because of contract failure. That is, consumers could not tell which part of the public good is financed with their donation and which part is financed with someone else's donation, so incremental donations could be diverted to dividend payments to stockholders, with donors none the wiser.

Presumably, nonprofit organizations and some social enterprises can do better here because they have no stockholders that want to trick donors out of their funds. However, the externality problem remains to be addressed. Because any one donor's contribution in support of a pure public good benefits all other potential donors, donations have external benefits and therefore will be underprovided in equilibrium. This is the famous free-rider problem discussed in Chapter 11: each potential donor hopes that some other donor will supply the necessary funds and allow them to enjoy the good for free. As a result, aggregate donations will be inadequate to support an efficient level of public goods.

In reality, many goods and services have some but not all of the characteristics associated with public goods. The taxonomy in Table 13.1 maps the variety of goods and services that have both, one, or neither of the characteristics of pure public goods.

An excludable and rival good that generates no externalities is called a *pure private good*. Private goods are optimally provided by competitive markets, for all the relevant social costs and benefits are taken into account by buyers and sellers.

A *common-pool good* is rival but not excludable. The fish contained in a public pond constitute a common good because two consumers cannot catch and eat the same fish, but anyone is welcome to try. If any fisher catches a fish, it becomes harder for the others to secure their own catches, so there is a reciprocal negative externality. Fund-raising is a common-pool good, as too

Table 13.1 Varieties of public and private goods

	Excludable	Nonexcludable
Rival	**Pure Private Goods** clothing food	**Common-Pool Goods (Congestion Goods)** urban freeways underground oil
Nonrival	**Excludable Public Goods (Toll Goods)** symphonies open highways museums	**Pure Public Goods** defense lighthouses public art

many competing charities fish in the same donor pool. As with other negative externalities, we expect and see overfishing if the market is unregulated.

An *excludable public good* (also known as a *toll good*) is excludable, but not rival. An uncrowded museum gallery is an excludable public good because it is feasible to charge an admission fee, but visitors do not deplete the display nor significantly reduce the viewing pleasure of other visitors. An uncrowded highway is also an excludable public good, where tolls can serve as the excluding device.

Because at least some of the benefits of consumption of excludable public goods can be appropriated by the supplier, these goods will be supplied by for-profit firms. However, there are two problems with for-profit supply. First, the amount of the good supplied will be suboptimal. This is because nonrival goods produce beneficial externalities. Second, there will be over-exclusion unless the for-profit firm can perfectly price-discriminate. At any single price, there will be some consumers who would benefit from entering the facility and are willing to pay something to do so but are not willing to pay the going price. For-profit suppliers would not admit these customers because they wish to keep their price, hence profits, high. This exclusion is socially inefficient because there are no social opportunity costs from letting additional customers enjoy an excludable public good.

A perfectly-price-discriminating for-profit monopoly would optimally provide an excludable public good and would exclude nobody. Those willing to pay any price would be let in at a price equal to their maximum willingness to pay, because the firm values their revenue and suffers no added cost from letting additional customers in. However, in Chapter 8 we argued that perfect price discrimination is generally infeasible because the firm would need information from consumers to adopt its price structure, and consumers would not trust a for-profit firm with the necessary information. This is one reason why some nonprofit firms may come into existence (Ben-Ner, 1986; Studer, Stuhlinger, and Von Schnurbein, 2014). Consumers are more willing to trust a nonprofit firm with the information it needs to price discriminate to supply an excludable public good optimally.

13.5 Policy application: day care for young children

Day care for young children involves consumers who cannot fend for themselves and suffers from two sources of market failure (Young and Nelson, 1973; Mocan, 2002):

- *Asymmetric information*: Parents may have a difficult time assessing the quality of care delivered to their children, particularly those intangible aspects of care-giving that are more difficult to observe than the condition of physical facilities or the availability of toys and other equipment. Since young children cannot report these aspects to their parents very well and parents frequently have little time for direct observation, parents suffer an informational disadvantage relative to those who supply the day-care services. For-profit suppliers might take advantage of consumer ignorance by shortchanging on the promised quality level, training, and supervision of staff. This problem is becoming less severe due to modern technology. For example, installation of webcams at day-care centers allows for parental monitoring at any time.
- *Externalities*: The benefits of day care accrue to children, but the purchasing decision is made by parents. High-quality day care provides lifelong benefits for some children. If nutrition and health check-ups are offered, children may grow up to be healthier and more productive. If educational programs are included, children may learn more effectively as they grow up, becoming more productive citizens. Although parents are not generally self-regarding in these decisions and try to do what is right for the child, they may not always fully appreciate these benefits or be able to afford them and may thus purchase a lower quality or quantity of care on their own than would be efficient from the perspective of society.

What solutions are available to remedy these market failure problems? Two remedies have been widely discussed and applied, nonprofit supply and public subsidy and regulation:

- *Nonprofit supply*: Nonprofit suppliers are less likely to take advantage of their superior information because the nondistribution of profits constraint reduces their incentive to do so. In addition, it is easier to maintain consumer control over a nonprofit organization than over a for-profit organization facing constant threats of takeover bids. Nonprofit day-care facilities often place parents on the board of directors and encourage parents to visit the facility more often, thus reducing the information gap (see Ben-Ner and Van Hoomissen, 1993; Ben-Ner, 1994). Finally, nonprofit day-care facilities are often established and run by close-knit groups of consumers that interact repeatedly in other settings and so must maintain an atmosphere of mutual trust. Church-run and workplace facilities gain trust through this mechanism.

- *Public subsidy and regulation*: If the quality or quantity of day care supply is less than it should be because a center fails to account for positive externalities to society at large, this can be remedied by providing public subsidies to effectively increase the demand for quality care. Subsidies can be made available for day-care services meeting certain standards of quality and perhaps targeted to lower income groups for which the externalities are greatest.

    Regulation by government can help ensure that suppliers providing subsidized day-care services do indeed offer the standard of care required by public policy. Restricting the subsidy to nonprofit suppliers (or limited profit social enterprises) may be helpful in ensuring the desired quality level since these suppliers are less compelled to achieve profits at the expense of quality. However, such restriction may also create inefficiencies in nonprofit or limited profit organizations, because of their blunted profit incentives, are slow to expand to meet the increased demand for services that may be stimulated by a subsidy.

13.6 Policy application: selling blood

Several aspects of market failure are associated with a free market in the supply of transfused blood. A study of this issue is found in the classic piece by Nobel Prize winner, Kenneth Arrow, written in 1975, years before the world was aware of an illness known as HIV/AIDS. Some of the issues raised when examining this practice are typical issues of market failure:

- *Asymmetric information*: People who know that their blood is contaminated by serum hepatitis, the HIV virus, or some other pathogen may conceal this fact in order to receive money for their blood donation.

- *Externalities*: The transmission of infection from donors to recipients of blood is a market transaction with no externalities if the recipient is symmetrically-informed about blood quality. However, an uninformed blood recipient may receive pathogens as an unintended side-effect of his purchase, and this external cost can be retransmitted to others with whom the recipient interacts.
- *Transaction costs*: "Bad blood" can often be detected prior to transfusion through the use of biochemical tests, but these tests are expensive and not completely reliable. The lack of reliability is a sad fact of life but causes no market failure in itself because we lack the capability to do better with our current technology. Testing is a required transaction cost in the market for blood, not a source of market failure per se. However, if asymmetric information and externalities are present, more intensive and costly testing may be needed, and this additional transaction cost does reflect market failure.

What remedies can be employed to address these market failure issues? In this case, the key is to analyze the motivations of blood donors under alternative circumstances. While most potential donors are likely motivated by the desire to help others, some may be primarily motivated by the prospect of payment. It is unlikely that altruistic (potential) donors would try to conceal any knowledge that their own blood was bad. Their aim is to help, not to harm, the recipients of their donation. However, those who are in it for the money would be less concerned with harming others, and those among them with bad blood would be less likely to withhold the sale of their precious bodily fluids. If donors are paid for their blood, blood will be supplied by both tainted and untainted money-seekers. If instead, blood must be truly donated (that is, payments for blood are outlawed), only untainted altruists will contribute, and the average quality of blood supplies will improve. This is the solution proposed by Richard Titmuss (1971) and discussed by Healy (2006).

The limitation of the voluntary system is, of course, the free-rider problem. Despite the fact that blood donations create a public good, i.e., an inventory of untainted blood available in an emergency for whomever may be stricken, individuals will not voluntarily contribute to this good at the level that would be efficient for society as a whole. Thus, by solving the market failure problems through voluntary donation, we introduce additional problems of allocation that require further attention. How can the free-rider problem be addressed in the case of blood supply? Several alternatives suggest themselves, including supplementary profitmaking supply, selective incentives, social pressure, and coercion:

- *Supplementary profitmaking supply*: With intensive (costly) testing, a parallel system of paying for blood donations may be permitted to operate in order to ensure that an adequate supply is forthcoming. This may create a problem if those who might otherwise volunteer would then seek to be paid. However, assuming that altruistic donors find this alternative unappealing, the parallel systems can work in tandem.

- *Selective incentives*: Voluntary donors can be rewarded with recognition and tokens of appreciation, increasing the likelihood that they will continue to give and encourage others to give. However, if the reward is sufficiently attractive, it may risk bringing back donors with selfish motives into the system.

  A particularly interesting selective incentive is to test each donor's blood for the presence of pathogens. For example, suppose that a free test for AIDS is provided to blood donors. Individuals who suspect they may have AIDS may decide to give blood in order to take advantage of this test. This will have the beneficial effect of detecting HIV, but will draw more high-risk individuals into the donor pool. The HIV test is not perfect, and it is possible that this sort of test will be counterproductive if a large number of HIV-positive individuals are brought into the system, only some of whom are detected through testing. In addition, those at high risk for HIV are also at high risk for other diseases (such as type C hepatitis) for which, for many years, there were no available blood tests. Thus, free AIDS testing is probably not the best incentive to offer donors. Some have proposed that if these tests are to be offered for free, they should be offered regardless of blood donation in order to eliminate these perverse effects (Thompson, 1990).

- *Social pressure*: Campaigns to increase social awareness of the need for blood donations, and mobilizing smaller work and social groups through events to encourage donations, constitute additional strategies to overcome the free-rider problem in this case.

- *Coercion*: The government could require healthy individuals to give a certain amount of blood each year, as a matter of law. This solution to the free-rider problem would be problematic for a number reasons not the least of which would be the problem of certifying exemptions for health reasons. Obtaining exemption from giving would require costly medical certification. Thus, some people might decide to give blood even if they were unhealthy. Alternatively, the government could pay for such certification but that would add another high transaction cost to the arrangement. A second problem is that many would regard control of their own blood as an inviolable right. (Those who are already stuck for taxes would object to this additional needling by the government!)

13.7 Policy application: the fine and performing arts

Museums, symphony orchestras, opera, theater and ballet often operate outside the pure market system because they involve various manifestations of market failure that require alternative solutions (see Baumol and Bowen, 1966; Last and Wetzel, 2010):

- *Externalities*: The appreciation of art is one means through which citizens become educated about their culture, learn to be creative, and gain peace of mind. Healthier, more educated, and more creative citizens may contribute to the society at-large, not just earn higher salaries for themselves. Thus, there are positive external benefits from consumption of the arts. In addition, children who are encouraged, at an early age, to appreciate the arts may find more functional outlets for their creative drives, thereby reducing the quantity (or at least enhancing the quality) of graffiti and hence reducing the negative externalities accompanying these activities.
- *Public goods*: Public art beautifies a city. Art promotes free expression and arguably cultivates democratic values. Promotion of quality in art symbolizes a society's values of achievement and excellence. Preserving great works of art maintains a society's cultural heritage. These are all goods which can be consumed jointly (i.e., they are nonrival) and without exclusion.
- *Toll goods*: Symphonies, theater performances, and museums are toll goods. Once admitted to a museum or theater, individuals enjoy the same paintings or performances without imposing additional costs or detracting from the enjoyment of others. Although for-profit firms may provide toll goods, they necessarily exclude nonpayers and those who can pay very little, which is inefficient (Feldstein, 1991; Rushton, 2017).

What are the remedies for these various manifestations of market failure in the arts?

- *Public subsidy*: If performing arts are underprovided because of market neglect of external benefits, then public subsidy can help. Subsidies targeted to children and other key populations may be especially efficient here. Subsidies devoted to particular forms of artistic creation that may ultimately have commercial application may also be helpful if these innovations cannot be copyrighted or patented.
- *Public provision*: Pure public goods (e.g., publicly-displayed sculpture or classical artistic performances on over-the-air radio and television) would not be provided at all by for-profit firms without some form of advertising. Rather than inducing entry of private providers with adver-

tising rights or by subsidizing them (as in the early years of National Public Radio), there may be lower transactions costs when government produces the goods directly. The British Broadcasting Corporation (BBC) provides an example of this approach.

- *Voluntary provision*: Given the limits to government or for-profit provision of the fine and performing arts, another approach is to support public goods and external benefits of the arts through voluntary contributions (Hansmann, 1981; Ben-Ner, 1986; Ivey, 2010; Kearns et al., 2012). Since it is unlikely that such voluntary support would be offered to for-profit providers or even governmental institutions, this solution implies organizing artistic institutions as nonprofit organizations. The reason is that donors are concerned that their donations actually go towards support of the programs they want to help. If they give to for-profits, they fear that contributions will simply enrich the owners of the business. If they give to government, they may fear that contributions will simply replace tax dollars that otherwise might have been allocated to the service. If they give to nonprofits these reservations are reduced or eliminated.

  However, nonprofit provision and voluntary support again raise the problem of free riders, where people benefit from the output of an organization but do nothing to contribute to the creation of its output. For example, members of a religious congregation may attend services and benefit from activities sponsored by the organization, while not contributing to its upkeep. Parents may benefit from the work of members of a parent–teacher organization while not spending any of their own time on activities related to enhancing the experience of students at that school. In such cases, it is possible for some to benefit from the donative activities of others, while not contributing themselves. Here, exploiting social mechanisms such as peer pressure among board members of a prestigious cultural institution, or using selective incentives, such as recognition of contributors through token gifts or listing of names in programs for performances, are means to help overcome free-rider problems.

Public subsidies in support of toll goods can be markedly helpful. Because museums, symphony orchestras, and other such toll goods have high fixed costs and low variable costs, average costs fall, and marginal costs remain very low over a wide range of output (see Figure 13.2). This makes it impossible for any supplier, for-profit or nonprofit, to provide the socially efficient quantity (where price equals marginal cost), charge a single price, and at least break-even (see the loss rectangle in Figure 13.2). A price greater than or equal to average cost at the optimal quantity is necessary to avoid bankruptcy, but this would exclude those consumers who are willing to pay more than it costs to increase production from Q_1 to Q_2.

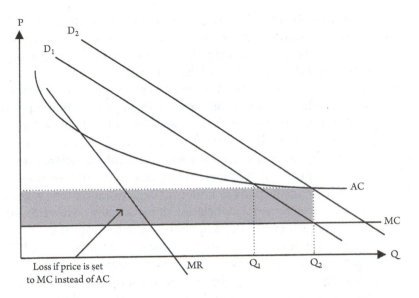

Figure 13.2 When fixed costs are high and marginal costs low, a subsidy is required

This problem could be solved using either a per-unit or a lump-sum subsidy. Viewed from the perspective of producer price, a per-unit subsidy of the right size would raise demand to D_2, allowing efficient provision to proceed. Alternatively, the organization could be provided with a lump-sum subsidy equal to the area of the loss rectangle in Figure 13.2 on the condition that it provide the optimal quantity and charge consumers a price equal to marginal cost at this quantity.

13.8 Management applications

A variety of concerns facing nonprofit managers and social entrepreneurs may be usefully analyzed within the framework of market failure. Here we consider fund-raising, volunteer recruitment, teamwork, contracting-out for services, pricing of services, and the decision to join a trade association.

Fund-raising

The task of inducing donors to contribute funds to support a nonprofit organization or social enterprise requires overcoming the free-rider problem. As suggested above, this task may be addressed through approaches that employ social pressure (in small groups such as boards, work groups, or small associations) or through selective incentives (e.g., prizes awarded with membership support of a public radio station). Behavioral economics suggests additional approaches (Chapter 12), as do game theoretic approaches like the provision point mechanism (Chapter 11). Alternatively, organizations may turn to the marketplace, undertaking profitmaking enterprise in market niches where they may enjoy some advantage over business competitors. For example, a nonprofit or social venture may have some monopoly power such as use of its logo on clothing, or a special location such as a bookstore on a university campus. By entering into such monopolistically-competitive industries, the organization can generate profits to cross-subsidize its public goals.

Recruiting volunteers

This is another area of management which suffers from free riders. Volunteering has both private and external benefits. There is no market failure with respect to the private benefits – someone seeking training, companion-ship, or volunteer amenities need not be subsidized to contribute. However, there is no assurance that private benefits will suffice to overcome the free-rider problem associated with the public-good benefits of volunteering. Again, the social pressure strategy can be utilized. Personalized solicitation, friend-to-friend, is thought to be the most effective means of getting people to volunteer or to give money (Freeman, 1997; Simmons and Emanuele, 2007). Thus, a nonprofit organization can tweak the social conscience of its volunteers. It can also provide more private benefits to these individuals, for example, training, volunteer recognition awards, free family use of the facili-ties, and the like. Properly done, the external benefits of recruiting additional volunteers can outweigh the added costs of mobilizing social pressure and providing these private rewards. Finally, behavioral economics suggests that making volunteer effort more visible increases volunteer effort (e.g., Ariely, Bracha, and Meier, 2009).

Teamwork

Many kinds of organizational work, such as care for a group of clients or patients requiring custodial care, or the performing of a musical ensemble, are carried out in teams. The functioning of boards and committees also requires teamwork. In such cases, the output of the team is like a public good. Credit for the output goes to all team members without excluding the slackers. Thus, there is an incentive for team members to free-ride on the efforts of their colleagues. This free-rider problem can also be addressed through social pressure: the smaller the team, the more likely it is that other team members will identify the laggards and embarrass or cajole them into higher performance. If the group is expected to interact in team efforts many times in the future, cooperation is even more likely because low performing team members can be held accountable in future rounds of activity.

One of the problems with teams is that they involve difficulty in measuring individual contributions. Thus, one strategy is to divide work in such a way that the members' tasks are more differentiated and hence more easily attributable to individuals. This is one reason that musical ensembles are broken into physically-separated sections playing different parts. Imagine the first violin's difficulty in leading a violin section scattered at random throughout the orchestra. This strategy of work differentiation is like transforming a public good into a private good so that potential free riders can be identified and individually penalized or excluded.

Subcontracting versus in-house work

Brochures can be printed in-house or contracted out. Fund-raising events can be planned, advertised, and managed by staff or by external fund-raising counsel. Lawyers, accountants, conference planners, layout artists, and financial and benefit managers can be employees of nonprofit organizations and social enterprises or they can serve these organizations on a contract basis. Market-failure analysis provides important insights into this category of choices.

Obviously, the quality and cost of work available in-house versus outside is a prime consideration in this decision. This, in turn, will depend on whether there is sufficient competition in the market to induce competing suppliers to minimize costs and maintain quality while obtaining low economic profits. If so, external quality and cost are likely to be superior to what can be mounted in-house. In addition, an organization's own demand for service will matter. If that demand is large, then it can afford to devote specialized resources to it, to develop special expertise, and to exploit potential economies of scale in order to achieve efficiency. If internal demand is very limited, an organization is unlikely to develop the internal capacity to compete well with outside suppliers.

But how is an organization to know if outside contractors are superior, and how does an organization ensure that a contractor does the job properly? These are even more fundamental questions in the decision to contract out or to undertake an activity internally. In short, the decision to contract out depends on the relative *transaction costs* of the two alternatives.

In the case of contracting, transactions costs include the cost of obtaining information about prices and quality, the costs of bargaining and negotiating a contract, the costs of monitoring quality as the goods or services are delivered and the costs of enforcing a contract if something goes wrong. These transactions costs differ for different kinds of goods and services. Contracting for a printed brochure may be relatively simple and inexpensive. One draws up some specifications on what is needed and solicits proposals – including prices and proposed designs – from alternative suppliers. Choice is made based on the proposals, contracts can be made clear as to what is to be delivered by when and for how much, and contract enforcement is fairly straightforward.

Transactions costs also depend upon the type of organization one is contracting with. If the contractee is trustworthy, less effort is needed to write, negotiate, and enforce the contract (handshakes are cheaper than lawyers). Nonprofit contractors and some for-profits are more likely to be trustworthy in this fashion. A large for-profit firm providing a fairly standardized product and enjoying substantial brand-name loyalty would have much to lose from its opportunistic reading of contract loopholes, and this makes them more trustworthy as well.

The costs associated with this market process can be compared to the in-house capacity for printing and the greater control one may have over an employee's work compared to an outside contractor. If the organization has a strong in-house capability it may choose to stay in-house. Otherwise, it is likely to go outside.

The case of organizing a fund-raising event may be different because it is more complex and less easy to monitor than printing procurement. It is difficult to compare the quality and effectiveness of alternative fund-raising consultants on the basis of their success with other clients, as each campaign or event is, to some extent, unique. One never knows the extent to which previous campaign successes are due to fund-raising counsel's expertise rather than a favorable fund-raising environment for the particular organizations and campaigns involved. Once an event is over, one cannot easily prove the contractee is at fault even if the net returns are disappointing.

Nonetheless, there are advantages to contracting with an external fund-raising consultant. Fund-raising has become a highly technical and skilled profession, and few nonprofit boards of directors and chief executive officers have sufficient expertise to keep their campaigns at the forefront of fund-raising proficiency. Developing such expertise internally would distract board and executive attention from the charitable mission, which involves the provision of services and not the raising of funds. In addition, there is much "learning-by-doing" in fund-raising – an outside fund-raising consultant with experience conducting a variety of campaigns for a variety of organizations will do a better job than an in-house campaign conducted by those with more limited experience. Finally, there are economies of scale. Outside consultants that work for many charities can spread the organizational overheads (costs of interviewing and recruiting the best people, development and implementation of software, etc.), resulting in lower average costs to every client than if the clients conducted separate in-house campaigns.

Pricing

Sometimes the transactions costs of pricing nonprofit and social enterprise outputs can exceed the expected revenue. This is particularly true for toll goods, where in order to collect a fee one has to erect a fence or other structure for keeping out nonpayers. In such cases, it may be better to simply give the goods away. More commonly, transactions costs enter into the design of fee structures. If one provides discounts for children and senior citizens (or otherwise differentiates fees by demographic characteristics, ability-to-pay, and the like), more customers can be served and more revenue collected. However, it is more complicated and expensive to administer a multipart fee structure, so one might not want to distinguish too many groups.

A sliding-scale fee based on ability to pay has many of the same characteristics as a toll good. In order to keep out those falsely claiming eligibility for low rates, one needs to collect and verify information on the income or wealth of each customer. This cost will be particularly important under three conditions: (1) if there is high turnover of customers/clients, so that a sense of community is not able to overwhelm incentives for opportunistic behavior; (2) if the organization bears the search costs, as opposed to letting a government agency bear all the costs of verifying eligibility; and (3) if the difference between the highest and lowest price charged is great, so that the payoff to false claims is large. Managers will need to be aware of these issues when designing pay structures for their consumers.

13.9 Joining a trade association

Trade associations provide pure public goods for member organizations and others in the same industry. Some lobby their legislatures on matters that affect organizations directly (such as tax exemption, eligibility for receipt of deductible donations) or that affect attainment of their mission (e.g., refining spousal-abuse statutes to deter domestic violence). Others educate the public about the need for, and availability of, member-organization services (for example, a campaign to alert the public to the ten signs of depression and where to get help). Should an individual organization do its own lobbying and public education? Should it join or organize a trade association? Because non-members benefit from these services whether or not they join the trade association, the free-rider problem appears once again. If the industry is small, subtle social pressure may be enough to induce industry members to provide support. In addition, in a small industry, the advantages of a unified effort may be less than the transaction costs (i.e., bargaining and maintenance of an organizational infrastructure) associated with establishing a trade association.

Some trade associations solve the free-rider problem by linking private or toll goods to their mix of services. If a trade association obtains supplies for its members through a buying collaborative or organizes professional conferences, it is supplying toll goods. Technical assistance, information services, and training are private goods offered at a better price to members than non-members can obtain from alternative suppliers. Still, it may be more efficient for a manager to do his or her own lobbying or to free-ride on the efforts of others. In any case, the ideas of market failure are helpful in thinking through these kinds of decisions.

SUMMARY

Competitive market outcomes are sometimes inefficient for four reasons: transactions costs, the nonappropriability of costs or benefits, externalities, and informational asymmetries. These problems can be at least partly addressed by government, the nonprofit sector, social enterprises, or all of these together. Market failure is a rationale for nonprofit provision in a variety of industries; we have discussed three of these – day care, blood supply, and the arts – in some detail. We have hinted at the many ways that government, nonprofits and social enterprises can seek to correct market failures – social pressure, linking private-good rewards to activities that provide external benefits, education, taxes, subsidies, and mandates, but all these approaches require us to estimate the costs and benefits of nontraded goods. How, precisely, does one locate a marginal social benefit curve in the real world or decide on the proper emission standard? We turn to this question in our next chapter.

SELECTED REFERENCES AND CITATIONS

Apgar, W.C. and Brown, H.J. (1987). *Microeconomics and Public Policy.* Glenview, IL: Scott, Foresman and Company.

Ariely, D., Bracha, A., and Meier, S. (2009). Doing Good or Doing Well? Image Motivation and Monetary Incentives in Behaving Prosocially. *American Economic Review, 99(1),* 544–555.

Arrow, K.J. (1975). Gifts and Exchanges. In Phelps, E.S. (Ed.), *Altruism, Morality, and Economic Theory* (pp. 13–28). New York: Russell Sage Foundation.

Baumol, W.J. and Bowen, W.G. (1966). *Performing Arts: The Economic Dilemma.* New York: Basic Books.

Ben-Ner, A. (1986). Why do Nonprofit Organizations Exist in Market Economies? In Rose-Ackerman, S. (Ed.), *The Economics of Nonprofit Institutions: Studies in Structure and Policy* (pp. 94–113). New York: Oxford University Press.

Ben-Ner, A. (1994). The Governance of Nonprofit Organizations: Law and Public Policy. *Nonprofit Management and Leadership, 4(4),* 393–414.

Ben-Ner, A. and Van Hoomissen, T. (1993). Nonprofit Organizations in the Mixed Economy. In Ben-Ner, A. and Gui, B. (Eds.), *The Nonprofit Sector in the Mixed Economy* (pp. 27–58). Ann Arbor: The University of Michigan Press.

Douglas, J. (1983). *Why Charity?* Beverly Hills: Sage Publications.

Downing, P.B (1984). *Environmental Economics and Policy.* Boston: Little Brown and Company.

Feldstein, M. (Ed.) (1991). *The Economics of Art Museums.* Chicago: University of Chicago Press.

Freeman, R.B. (1997). Working for Nothing: The Supply of Volunteer Labor. *Journal of Labor Economics, 15(1, Part 2),* S140-S166.

Gill, R.T. (1993). *Economics.* Mountain View, CA: Mayfield Publishing Company.

Gramlich, E.M. (1981). *Benefit–Cost Analysis of Government Programs.* Englewood Cliffs, NJ: Prentice Hall.

Gwartney, J.D, Stroup, R., Sobel, R., and MacPherson, D. (2015). *Economics: Private and Public Choice.* Stamford, CT: Cengage Learning.

Hansmann, H. (1981). Nonprofit Enterprise in the Performing Arts. *Bell Journal of Economics 12,* 341–361.

Hart, O. (1989). An Economist's Perspective on the Theory of the Firm. *Columbia Law Review, 89,* 1757–1774.

Healy, K.J. (2006). *Last Best Gifts.* Chicago: University of Chicago Press.

Independent Sector. (1992). *Giving and Volunteering in the U.S. 1991.* Washington, DC: Independent Sector.

Ivey, B. (2010). *Arts, Inc.* Berkeley, CA: University of California Press.

Kearns, K.P., Bell, D., Deem, B., and McShane, L. (2012). How Nonprofit Leaders Evaluate Funding Sources, An Exploratory Study of Nonprofit Leaders. *Nonprofit and Voluntary Sector Quarterly, 43(1),* 121–143.

Kilenthong, W.T. and Townsend, R.M. (2014). A Market Based Solution to Price Externalities: A Generalized Framework. NBER Working Paper # 20275.

Last, A.K. and Wetzel, H. (2010). Baumol's Cost-Disease, Efficiency, and Productivity in the Performing Arts: An Analysis of German Public Theaters. University of Lüneburg. Working Paper Series in Economics.

Mocan, H.N. (2002). The Market for Child Care. *NBER Reporter Online,* Spring, pp. 12–15.

Olson, M. (1965). *The Logic of Collective Action.* Cambridge, MA: Harvard University Press.

Ostrom, E. (1990). *Governing the Commons.* New York: Cambridge University Press.

Rushton, M. (2017). Should Public and Nonprofit Museums have Free Admission? A Defense of the Membership Model. *Museum Membership and Curatorship, 32(3),* 200–209.

Simmons, W. and Emanuele, R. (2007). Male-female Giving Differentials: Are Women More Altruistic? *Journal of Economic Studies, 34(6)*, 534–550.

Smith, A. (1776/1950). *An Inquiry into the Nature and Causes of the Wealth of Nations.* London: Methuen Publishing.

Steinberg, R. (2006). Economic Theories of Nonprofit Organizations. In Powell, W.W. and Steinberg, R. (Eds.), *The Nonprofit Sector, A Research Handbook* (2nd ed., pp. 117–139). New Haven, CT: Yale University Press.

Studer, S., Stuhlinger, S., and Von Schnurbein, G. (2014). Why Nonprofit? – Nonprofit Support Organizations for NPOs in Mixed Industries. Center for Philanthropy Studies (CEPS) Working Paper Series, No. 3.

Thompson, A.C. (1990). The Problem of High Risk Individuals Donating Blood. In *Economic Incentives in the Nonprofit Sector: Student Essays.* Cleveland, OH: Mandel Center Discussion Paper, Case Western Reserve University.

Titmuss, R. (1971). *The Gift Relationship: From Human Blood to Social Policy.* London: Georgy, Allyn & Unwin.

Williamson, O. (1975). *Markets and Hierarchies.* New York: Free Press.

Williamson, O. (2008). Transaction Cost Economics: The Precursors. *Institute of Economic Affairs*, pp. 7–14, September 11.

Young, D.R. and Nelson, R.R. (Eds.) (1973). *Public Policy for Day Care of Young Children.* Lexington, MA: D.C. Heath.

REVIEW CONCEPTS

Common Pool Good: A good or service that is rival but not excludable, such as water from an underground pool.

Externalities: The side effects of market transactions that affect the well-being, costs, or prices of third parties that have no voice in the transaction.

External Benefits: An increase in third-party well-being or a reduction in third-party costs resulting from a market transaction between other parties. Synonyms are positive externality and external economy.

External Costs: A decrease in third-party well-being or an increase in third-party costs resulting from a market transaction between other parties. Synonyms are negative externality and external diseconomy.

Free Rider: One who receives the benefit of a good/service without contributing to its costs. Public goods that generate external benefits offer people the opportunity to become free riders.

Informational Asymmetry: A situation in which buyers or sellers have important information about the product/service that is not possessed by the other side in a potential transaction. Generally this causes a market failure.

Marginal Social Benefit (MSB): The gain to society from a one-unit increase in some market activity. MSB is the total of marginal benefits to buyers of the good (marginal private benefits, MPB) and marginal benefits to third party consumers (marginal external benefits, MEB).

Marginal Social Cost (MSC): The value to society of what is given up to get a one-unit increase in some market activity. MSC is the total of marginal costs to producers of the good (MPC or simply MC) and marginal external costs on third-party producers (MEC).

Market Failure: The failure of the market system to attain allocative efficiency. This means that potential gain exists from adjusting the quantity of some goods and services, but that this gain is not realized in equilibrium.

Nonexcludable: Describes a good with characteristics such that it is impossible or prohibitively expensive to limit its consumption to a select group of consumers, for example, clean air.

Nonrival: Describes a good whose consumption by one person does not affect the consumption of the same good by another person, for example, an uncrowded highway. A good is nonrival if the marginal cost of letting another person consume it, given that it has been produced, is zero.

Pecuniary Externality: Occurs when a market transaction affects the prices at which third parties trade. Pecuniary externalities do not cause market failure.

Public Goods: Collectively consumed goods. When produced by anyone, a group of individuals can simultaneously enjoy the quantity produced. Divided into Pure Public Goods (nonexcludable and nonrival) and Excludable Public Goods (nonrival). National defense, poetry, and national parks are all public goods.

Technological Externality: Occurs when a market transaction affects the well-being of third-party consumers or the costs of third-party producers. Technological externalities generally cause market failure.

Toll Good: A good or service that is non-rival but excludable, such as an uncongested highway.

Transactions Costs: The costs of doing business through a particular institutional arrangement, for example, through contracting out versus in-house provision of services.

EXERCISES

1. Identify positive or negative externalities associated with the following services that might be provided by a nonprofit organization or social enterprise. In each case, indicate what financing and organizational arrangements you would prescribe to increase efficiency:

   (a) Books for children in low income families.
   (b) Prenatal health care.
   (c) Emergency relief after natural disasters such as storms and earthquakes.
   (d) Shelters for the homeless.
   (e) Low-cost wireless coverage in low-income communities.
   (f) Language education for refugees.

2. Analyze the following nonprofit and social enterprise management functions in terms of the "free-rider" concept and describe a strategy for dealing with the problem in each case:

   (a) Organizing a board of trustees for a new organization.
   (b) Mobilizing start-up capital for a new social venture.
   (c) Carrying out a membership drive for public radio.
   (d) Managing a team project involving staff from different departments of an organization.
   (e) Establishing a "community watch" crime-prevention program in an urban neighborhood.

3. Classify the following goods and services as Private Goods, Common Pool Goods, Toll Goods, or Pure Public Goods. In each case, indicate what this classification implies for how the good or service is most efficiently organized or financed. Which ones are best provided by private, nonprofit organizations or social enterprises, and which ones are not? Why?

(a) Bagels.
(b) The Internet.
(c) Major league baseball.
(d) Protecting whales.
(e) An open-air concert on Public Square.
(f) Prevention of terrorism.

4. A museum employs an "honor system" to charge visitors. In this system, visitors are asked (by a sign at the door) to put a specific fee into a locked box at the entrance. Use the ideas of transactions costs and free riders to compare the efficiency of such a system to each of the following alternatives:

(a) A conventional system in which payments are enforced through a toll collector or controlled-access ticket machine.
(b) A system that simply asks for donations.
(c) A system with a toll collector who asks each visitor to pay what he or she thinks is right.

5. The board of a small volunteer-based nonprofit environmental advocacy organization is contemplating contracting out for its financial management services rather than hiring a regular permanent staff member or continuing to rely solely on volunteer effort. Identify and discuss the considerations that the members of the board should weigh in this decision.

6. The director of the Association of Stamp-Collecting Clubs would like to induce member clubs to authorize more funds to lobby against pending legislation that would reduce government support for the Post Office. The director sees this as a long-term threat to the members of the association. Member clubs agree in principle but seem indifferent to taking action and are more interested in getting the latest information on the new stamps that will be coming out this year. Analyze the director's concerns as a market-failure problem and make a recommendation to address the issue. How can the director stamp out this problem without going postal?

7. Modern medicine requires the supply of various bodily organs for transplantation. In what ways is the "market" for vital organs similar to, and different from, the donation of blood? What are the issues in organizing this market and what institutional arrangements seem preferable?

8. In what ways are the market failure issues associated with nursing homes for the elderly similar to those associated with day care for children? How are they different? What recommendations would you make in deciding on a market structure in each case, and why do you offer this advice?

14
Cost–benefit analysis

Sigh, I hope, someday, my externalities will be positive

14.1 Introduction

Cost–benefit analysis (CBA) is a decision-making tool that combines all that we have learned from Chapters 4 through 13. Every social entrepreneur and nonprofit manager should know something about it. It is also a misunderstood tool, often applied incorrectly; even some textbooks make basic mistakes. Finally, it is a tool that applies to social enterprise and nonprofit managers but needs to be tweaked for appropriate use in cases of private action for the public good. In this chapter we will start by defining cost–benefit analysis more carefully, explaining where the tool can be used, and comparing cost–benefit analysis to other social decision-making tools. We will then circle through the details at multiple levels of analysis. First, we explain the accounting framework used in cost–benefit analysis and the basic way to combine numbers for social decisions. Next, we take a deeper look at the normative underpinnings of the concept, detailing the differing value judgments when CBA is used for economic efficiency versus social welfare. The next section discusses practical matters, followed by an example of cost–benefit analysis. We conclude with a discussion of the challenge of accounting for the private notions of the public good embedded in mission statements.

14.2   What is cost–benefit analysis?

A social entrepreneur or nonprofit manager faces long-term choices about what areas to work in, which projects to build, and which service programs to use or rework. Each of these choices involves implicit and explicit costs, benefits to trading partners and others, losses in some years and gains in others, and unintended side effects (such as the impact that the violinist in the above cartoon is having on passersby). Some of these costs and benefits occur in markets where quantification is relatively easy, but others occur outside markets and are harder to measure. Cost–benefit analysis provides a framework to reconcile all the trade-offs involved in order to make a decision.

In its simplest application, a profit-maximizing firm compares alternative ways to invest available capital. Should it build a new factory, employ a hub-and-spoke distribution system, expand the scope of its profit line? Here, it is a simple matter to calculate the impact of decisions on long-term profits, where the only benefit that matters is total revenues produced and the only cost that matters is a market-based opportunity cost:

- Calculate the incremental profits each year that the program remains in effect. Incremental profits are the difference between the expected profits with the program and without the program. The profits represent the net benefit (benefits minus costs) of the project to the firm.
- Determine an appropriate risk-adjusted interest rate for discounting future expected profits into present value.
- A project is worth doing if the present value of these net benefits is positive.
- If there is a choice between several rival alternatives, the project with the largest net benefits should be selected. Rival alternatives means choice of one alternative precludes doing any of the others.
- If there are multiple projects that can be undertaken simultaneously, every program with positive net benefits should be adopted. If, in addition, available capital does not cover all the programs, the program with the largest net benefits should be selected first, then the second largest net benefits, and so on until available capital is exhausted.

- This application of the cost–benefit analysis framework is called "capital budgeting."

French civil engineer and economist Jules Dupuit pioneered cost–benefit analysis in 1844 as a better way for governments to evaluate potential public works projects. Rather than simply choosing the projects that had the lowest cost to taxpayers, he urged that all costs imposed on the public be quantified and entered into the calculation. In other words, he went beyond the capital budgeting framework to a more general social-cost framework. The modern definition of cost–benefit analysis follows this development.

There is no point in a project that replicates what the private sector would otherwise do, so the cost–benefit framework is useful in cases of market failure. More recently, the growth of mission-motivated nonprofit organizations and other forms of social enterprise brought the recognition that the framework used to decide on public action for the public good can also be used to decide on private action for the public good. With this background we offer the following general definition of cost–benefit analysis:

> Cost–benefit analysis is a framework for decision making and evaluation of organizational programs, activities, and initiatives, for governments and private-sector social enterprises and nonprofit organizations operating in an environment of market failure. It is analogous to the profit criterion used for making decisions and evaluating performance in the commercial business sector.

Various approaches have moved nonprofit and social enterprise managers in the direction of full cost–benefit analysis. Specifically:

- Social enterprises and the new hybrid organizations are urged to report a double bottom-line (financial profits and social benefits) or a triple bottom-line (adding environmental benefits to the list). Cost–benefit analysis incorporates all these bottom-lines but goes beyond separate enumeration to produce a single number useful for social decisions and investments.
- Grantees of the Roberts Enterprise Development Fund (since renamed REDF) have been asked to report a Social Return on Investment (SROI) since 2000. The idea has spread to other funders, and the details on how to calculate an SROI continue to evolve. In spirit, the SROI is quite similar to cost–benefit analysis, but there are some differences we will discuss later in this chapter.

- In order to avoid the need to quantify all the benefits of a project, *cost-effectiveness analysis* is sometimes used. In cost-effectiveness analysis, there is some standardized output (like number of lives saved) produced by alternative programs. Cost-effectiveness analysis calculates the (opportunity or explicit) cost of producing that output (e.g., cost per life saved) and recommends that the lowest cost program be used. However, cost-effectiveness analysis does not tell us how much we should use the lowest cost program (e.g., how many lives we should save) – we need full cost–benefit analysis to make that decision rationally. In addition, cost-effectiveness cannot be used when there are several desirable outputs and the analyst must choose between alternatives with different objectives. Thus, cost–benefit analysis is much more general than cost-effectiveness analysis.

- United Way of America requires local affiliates to distinguish between *outputs* and *outcomes* when evaluating the effectiveness of funded programs. Output measures, like the number of clients served, do not adequately capture the social value created by these programs. Outcome measures, like the number of clients who stayed sober or lasted on a job for one year, better capture social value. This is a small step in the right direction, and cost–benefit analysis quantifies the outcomes and their social benefits as well.

14.3 A first pass: the accounting framework of cost–benefit analysis

Essentially, cost–benefit analysis mimics profit-analysis in the business sector by substituting "social benefits" for "revenues" and "social costs" for "private costs" to compute the net gain from a given alternative course of action. Thus, in its most basic (if inadequate) form, CBA tries to account for all the gains and losses of a given action, no matter whom they fall upon, rather than compute gains and losses solely from the financial viewpoint of the organization itself.

The accounting framework is one of aggregation – adding up over people, adding up over the goods and services that affect people, adding up the value of what is gained and the value of what is given up, and aggregating over time. Many shortcuts will be discussed presently, but in theory, here are all the steps:

- Calculate all the effects of the program in question, including both intended and unintended effects. This means, for example, that when we evaluate the impact of electric cars on air pollution, we include not only the reduction at the automotive source, but also the air pollution effects of shifting from gas and hybrid to electric, the air pollution effects of generating power to recharge the batteries, a host of impacts on other aspects of the environment (such as those relating to the disposal or recycling of lithium batteries), and a host of nonenvironmental effects (on lithium miners, on pedestrians who didn't hear the car that hit them, on petroleum workers that need to be retrained for some other employment, etc.).

- Calculate the benefits and costs of all these impacts for each person affected in each year in which they are affected (aggregate the effects).
- Calculate the present value of expected future benefits and costs for each person affected (aggregate over time).
- Add the present value of costs across those who give up something of value and add the present value of benefits across those who receive something of positive or negative value (aggregate across individuals).
- Compute 'Net Social Benefit' for society as the aggregated benefits minus the aggregated costs.

If we don't care about distributional effects, who wins and who loses, the calculation is much simpler. We don't have to assign effects to individual people. For traded goods with no externalities, single demand and supply curves suffice to get the totals we need. Calculating the costs and benefits of untraded goods, externalities, collective goods, and informational market failures is more complicated, but there is no need to look at any individual information here either. Transfer payments resulting from the program cancel out – one person's loss is another person's gain (see Chapter 6).

In either case, the calculation should compute the net social benefit of the program or project and use this number for decision making in all the ways that the present value of the expected change in profits is used in capital-budgeting decisions. Projects should be selected in order of net social benefits: if they are rival, select the project with the largest net social benefits; if they are nonrival, select projects in order of net social benefits until available capital is exhausted.

Many textbooks, and the protocol used in calculating SROI, incorrectly state that decision makers should select projects or programs in order of their *benefit–cost ratios*. The confusion is understandable – wouldn't a project that "returned $5 for every dollar spent" be a better one than a project that "returned $3 for every dollar spent?" The first project is indeed better if both programs have the same cost because, in that case, the program with the highest cost–benefit ratio also has the highest net social benefit. But when

Table 14.1 Use net social benefits, not benefit–cost ratios

	In School	Home Delivery
Costs	$1,000,000	$2,500,000
Benefits	$4,000,000	$7,000,000
Benefit–cost Ratio	4	2.8
Net Social Benefits	$3,000,000	$4,500,000

the programs have different costs, the two approaches provide conflicting advice. For example, suppose there are two rival programs for feeding hungry children – an in-school free breakfast program or a service that delivers free meals to the child's house. We will talk more about how to calculate the benefits of each program shortly, but for now consider these numbers as given in Table 14.1.

In this example, in-school breakfasts are less expensive to deliver, but fewer kids are reached because there are hungry children who are not of school age or able to attend school. The benefit–cost ratio is higher for the in-school program, but clearly home delivery is better for society. (Note: these numbers are made up and we do not know which program would be better in the real world.) The lesson is clear: *do not use benefit–cost ratios*. At best, they produce the same (correct) answers as net social benefit, but net social benefit always gives the correct answers.

To summarize, it is important to work within an organizing framework that brings everything together into a structure that is useful for decision-making purposes. The basic elements to include in this framework are:

- *The alternatives*: What are the different projects or program options that we wish to evaluate? If two alternatives are mutually exclusive, the opportunity costs of pursuing one option should include the benefits foregone by not undertaking the other. For example, if a nonprofit art museum is considering whether to set up a Picasso exhibit in one of its galleries and the alternative is to use that gallery for an exhibition by local artists, the costs of the Picasso initiative should include net benefits foregone by not undertaking the local exhibition.
- *Costs*: What are the different elements of opportunity cost that must be accounted for?
- *Benefits*: What are the different elements of gain that must be considered?
- *Beneficiaries and cost-bearers*: Who are the different societal groups that receive benefits and/or bear costs?

- *Transfer payments*: What transfers of resources take place between beneficiary and cost-bearing groups?
- *Timing of costs, benefits, and transfers*: What is the pattern of incidence of costs, benefits, and transfer payments over time?
- *Bottom lines*: What is the net present value of benefits and costs to each group, and what is the net difference between benefits and costs for society as a whole.

Table 14.2 Cost–benefit matrix framework

	Group 1	Group 2	Group 3	All Society
PV of Benefits				
Benefit a	+			+
Benefit b			+	+
Benefit c		+		+
PV of Costs				
Cost d		+		+
Cost e			+	+
Cost f			+	+
PV of Transfers				
Transfer g	+		-	0
Transfer h		−	+	0
Net Benefits				
(a + b + c)–(d + e + h)	+	+ or −	+ or −	+ or −

Note: PV = Present Value.

Source: Adapted from Long, Mallar, and Thornton (1981).

A matrix format that brings together the relevant dimensions of CBA is displayed in Table 14.2. This matrix is similar to that utilized in Long, Mallar, and Thornton's (1981) analysis of the Job Corps program. The important groups on whom the program under assessment might have impact are listed across the top, and each type of benefit, cost, and transfer payment labels a row of the matrix. All entries are calculated in present value terms so that the effects of different patterns of incidence over time are taken into consideration. The last row adds together these benefits, costs, and transfers to yield the net effect of the alternative on each relevant group and on society as a whole. Three important aspects of this matrix should be understood:

- Define groups that do not overlap and together include everyone affected by the program. For example, in a program for training unemployed workers with new skills, the groups could be the workers, workers' families, employers, and taxpayers. These groups do not overlap and collectively account for all of the significant benefits, costs, and transfers accompanying the program.

- Net transfer payments to any group may be positive or negative, but the sum of transfers across all groups must be zero.
- Some benefits, costs, or transfers are difficult to estimate in quantitative terms. These should appear in the matrix qualitatively by using +'s and –'s to indicate the likely direction of impact. Although these items cannot be included in the quantitative totals displayed in the last row, they explicitly show the limits of the calculation and signal where additional effort would refine the analysis. (Note, in Table 14.2, all entries are shown as +'s or –'s, but most of these would be replaced by quantitative estimates in any actual application.)

14.4 Second pass: the normative framework of cost–benefit analysis

When Dupuit invented modern CBA in 1844, he wanted an operational way for the State to reverse the economic inefficiencies caused by market failures. But social welfare depends on the distribution of costs and benefits, and not just the size of the pie, so that the best practice today is to use CBA to maximize social welfare by taking distribution into account. In this section we first make the best case for focusing only on efficiency and we describe how to measure efficiency by various kinds of "surplus." Then we discuss the mechanics of introducing concerns about the distribution of well-being.

The norm of efficiency

Economic efficiency occurs when resources are put to their most highly valued uses so that the total value produced by the economy is maximized. At first, this appears to be an uncontroversial notion. Everyone should be concerned about minimizing waste and making the best use of limited resources. However, as we saw in the introductory chapter, economic efficiency by itself ignores the question of "who gets what?"

Recall that the concept of economic efficiency is based on unanimous consent to an economic change. An economic state is efficient or "Pareto optimal" if it is feasible and no alternative feasible economic state receives unanimous consent. Any time market failures are fixed, the economy becomes more efficient but that does not mean that everyone benefits from the change. Real-world policies have winners and losers. To deal with these complications, economists developed a modification of efficiency, the *Kaldor-Hicks criterion*, named after the two economists who invented it:

A project or program improves Kaldor-Hicks efficiency if it produces benefits in excess of costs such that the beneficiaries could, in principle, compensate the cost-bearers and still be better off.

The Kaldor-Hicks criterion is one way to make CBA practical in situations where full compensation of cost-bearers is unlikely, that is, when the new situation does not obtain the unanimous consent of those affected. But as a normative standard, it is at best questionable. If compensation of cost-bearers does not actually take place, who is to say if society as a whole is actually better off when some gain and some lose? How do we compare the welfare of one person with that of another? Is society really better off because I gain $20 while you lose only $10? Even in situations where no individual incurs a net loss, unquestioning application of the Kaldor-Hicks principle is controversial because we might care about improving the lot of the least fortunate in society or making the distribution of society's wealth more fair. Unadorned, cost–benefit analysis is not geared to take these considerations into account.

Measuring efficiency gains: benefits

The price of a diamond is far higher than the price of water, but clearly water, essential to life, is more valuable to consumers. Price is an exchange value – it tells us how much we must pay to obtain one unit of a good or how much we can sell that unit for. For cost–benefit analysis, we must somehow monetize the use value to the buyer, rather than the exchange value. We use 'willingness to pay' to do so, where willingness to pay is the highest price at which a consumer is willing to buy a unit of the good. A thirsty traveler crossing the desert is willing to pay a very high price for water (say $10,000) and a somewhat lower price for a small diamond, reflecting the difference in use value. Now, if that thirsty traveler can buy a liter of water for $2, he comes out ahead by $9,998, the difference between what he is willing to pay and what he must pay, and this is his *consumer surplus* from a liter of water. If that consumer was willing to pay up to $300 for a small diamond, but even the smallest diamond costs more than that (say $700), he would not buy the diamond and would receive no consumer surplus. You only get consumer surplus when your willingness to pay exceeds the price and you obtain a unit of the good. Next, what if that thirsty traveler bought his first liter of water, but wants more? We simply need to know the willingness to pay for each additional liter. If he were willing to pay $10 for a second liter, $3 for a third liter, and only $1 for a fourth liter, he would buy three liters and his consumer surplus would be ($10,000 − $2) + ($10 − $2) + ($3 − $2) = $10,007.

Figure 14.1
Consumer surplus

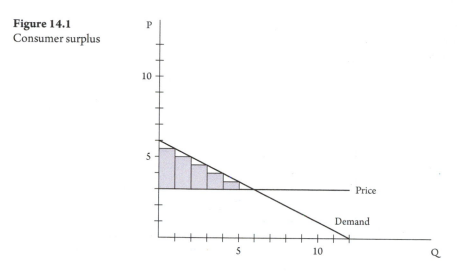

Recall from Chapter 4 that we defined (inverse) demand functions – reading from quantity to price instead of vice versa – and showed that the height of the curve is the highest price anyone is willing to pay to buy an additional unit of a good or service, given the consumption of previous units. In the water example, we were in effect describing the thirsty traveler's demand curve and calculating his consumer surplus by subtracting the height of a horizontal price line (at $2) from the height of the demand curve for each unit purchased. This idea generalizes to multiple consumers if we don't care about the distribution of income (see Figure 14.1).

This figure illustrates a typical demand curve with the price set at $3. The curve indicates that someone is willing to pay $5.50 for the first unit of this good. That person receives $2.50 of consumer surplus from the first unit. By no coincidence, the area of the first shaded rectangle is $2.50 because area is length times width, the length is willingness to pay minus the price, and the width is one unit. Someone – perhaps the same person or perhaps someone else – is willing to pay $5 for the second unit, has to pay $3, and obtains $2 in consumer surplus, the area of the second rectangle. Add $1.50 in consumer surplus from the third unit, $1 from the fourth, $0.50 from the fifth, while the sixth unit provides no gain and no loss if it is purchased. Therefore, adding the areas of the rectangles together, this market is producing a surplus of $7.50 for consumers of this good.

But what if people can buy a half unit of this good? Then there are twice as many rectangles, each half as wide to add up. If they can buy quarter units, the rectangles become more numerous and half again as wide; here, we are moving through a series of progressively better estimates of consumer surplus, so that in the limit, the infinitesimally wide rectangles fill in the entire

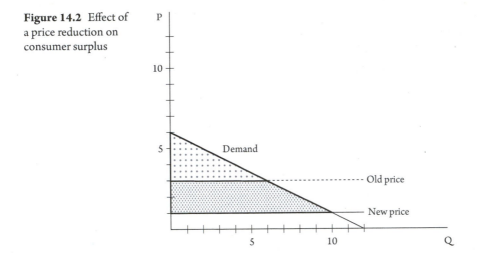

Figure 14.2 Effect of a price reduction on consumer surplus

triangle bounded by the demand curve and the price. This limit is the right way to approach consumer surplus because it is always possible to buy fractional levels of output. (Demand gives the quantity you want to buy per unit of time, so if you buy 1 cup of coffee a year, you are buying 1/52nd of a cup per week or 1/365th of a cup per day.) In conclusion: *consumer surplus equals the area below demand and above the price up to the quantity consumed.* If the demand curve is a straight line, this area is a triangle whose area is ½ base times the height. Consumer surplus here is exactly ½ × 6 × $3 = $9.00, the area of the dotted triangle (see Figure 14.2).

Suppose the project we were evaluating lowered the price of this good from $3 to $1. Then, the consumer surplus triangle would become bigger, incorporating all the area down to the lower price and higher quantity. The gain in consumer surplus is given by the darker filled trapezoid, which you could calculate directly if you remember the formula for area of a trapezoid. However, it is far easier to calculate the area of the new triangle (½ × 10 × $5 = $25) and subtract the area in the smaller triangle ($9) from this to compute a gain of $16. CBA would count the change in consumer surplus as a benefit. This is how we monetize that benefit.

A second kind of surplus is that obtained through production and distribution of goods and services. Producer surplus is defined as payments beyond those necessary to make the seller want to sell. Thinking at the margin, the seller adds to profits whenever the price exceeds marginal cost, so any payment in excess of marginal cost contributes to *producer surplus.* Using the logic of adding rectangles, then taking the limit, we conclude that for a firm: *producer surplus is the area above the marginal cost curve and below the price*

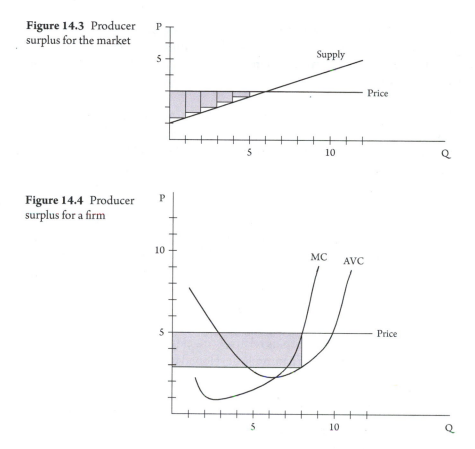

Figure 14.3 Producer surplus for the market

Figure 14.4 Producer surplus for a firm

line, up to the quantity sold. If we are looking at the competitive market level: *producer surplus is the area above the supply curve and below the price, up to the quantity sold* (see Figure 14.3).

In the long run, producer surplus is equal to economic profits, but in the short run, the two differ by fixed costs. Fixed costs are sunk costs and so should be ignored in subsequent decision making. The benefit from selling is a reduction in losses due to fixed costs. This allows us to use a shortcut for seeing producer surplus at the firm level – instead of calculating the area above a curved MC function (which requires integral calculus or approximations like Simpson's rule), we can calculate the area of the rectangle above AVC and below the price up to the quantity sold (i.e., variable profits, see Figure 14.4). This rule works in the short run, when AVC is below ATC, and in the long run where fixed costs become variable and the AVC rises to overlap ATC.

A third kind of surplus is that created by transfer payments to governments or private organizations, such as taxes and donations. The transfer payment itself does not matter if we use the Kaldor-Hicks approach – one person's gain is exactly equal to another's loss. For distributional analysis, it is trivial to monetize the value of a transfer payment because the payment itself is in the form of money.

Many of the goods and services valued in CBA are not bought and sold. Charity care, offered for free to the needy, is one of those goods, as are other nonexcludable collective goods. Traders create externalities that are consumed without purchase by third parties. Even though these goods are not purchased, those affected have a willingness to pay for good effects and a willingness to pay to reduce bad effects. Charity care, like that provided by a soup kitchen, has two impacts on consumer surplus. First, some people get free soup, and the value of this soup is calculated the ordinary way, as an area under the demand curve and above the price of zero. Second, the soup is a collective good to all those who care about the fact that the hungry are being fed and to all those who care about the people receiving the food. However, we calculate the surplus from collective goods differently.

We can calculate collective surplus relatively quickly if we don't care about the distribution of income, using a formula developed by Paul Samuelson (1954). The formula applies either when we have a nonexcludable collective good or we have an excludable collective good for which the power to exclude is not being used. Samuelson noted that there is a different relationship between the individual and the market when we are dealing with collective goods rather than private goods. For private goods, different people buy different quantities and each buyer is unaffected by the quantity bought by others. All consumers face the same price, so market demand is the sum of the quantities demanded by each consumer at each possible price (horizontal addition). However, for collective goods, each buyer (or donor) consumes the total quantity available, as consumption is nonrival. So, Samuelson showed that the marginal benefit of a collective good is the sum across all consumers of their willingness to pay for one more unit. We construct a "marginal social benefit curve" (MSB) as the vertical sum of individual demand curves, and this substitutes for the market demand curve for calculating social surplus. The social surplus from supplying any quantity is the area under this MSB curve up to the quantity provided. Figure 14.5 illustrates this when there are only two consumers, Fred and Barney, who are willing to pay for the collective good in question. The MSB curve is kinked because Barney does not want to consume more than five units, but Fred will consume up to twelve units of the collective good. The height of MSB is ten dollars per unit when $Q = 0$ because we add the Y-intercepts (seven and three) of the two demand curves here. The shaded area represents the social surplus from two units of the collective good.

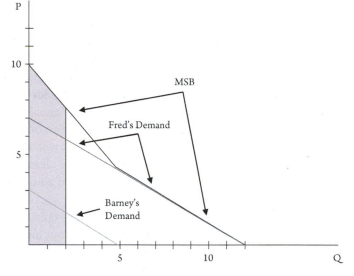

Figure 14.5 Social surplus when Fred and Barney consume two units of a collective good

Suppose, for example, a consortium of multi-billionaires decides to give $10,000 to every poor family in America. If we don't care about the distribution of income, this is simply a transfer payment, where the gains to the poor exactly balance the loss to the rich, and efficiency is unchanged. But everyone outside the consortium who cares about the poor in this country will receive a benefit they did not pay for, so the transfer payment jointly produces a nonexcludable collective good. The value of that good can be obtained from each third-party beneficiary as the area under the vertical sum of willingness-to-pay curves for poverty relief. The change in consumer surplus resulting from the gift of the billionaires is simply the area under this vertical sum curve between the amount of poverty relief with and without that gift. Consortium members also receive surplus if the amount they donate is less than the maximum amount they are willing to donate, and this adds to the surplus of non-members.

Nonexcludable collective goods are a special case of the more general market failure of externalities. As we pointed out in Chapter 13, a collective good is a reciprocal external benefit and a collective bad is a reciprocal external cost. This means that we calculate surplus measures for externalities in a similar fashion, but with some added complications. In either case, we are likely talking about goods and services that are not bought or sold by most of the people affected, so we cannot construct a demand curve directly from market data. Instead, we construct 'shadow' demand curves, representing what each affected person would be willing to spend if the good, bad, or service could be separately purchased. We use these to construct the Samuelsonian MSB curve by vertically adding the shadow demand curves of everyone that is affected by the program. If the program improves air quality, we add vertically across everyone who breathes or otherwise values cleaner air. The social benefit of an increase in air quality is the change in the area under this MSB curve, that is, the area under MSB at the higher level of air quality minus the area under MSB at the original air quality level. A step can be saved in the calculation, because if you calculate two areas where the smaller area is entirely within the larger area and subtract one from the other, you will get the same answer as if you just looked at what is in the larger area but not the smaller one. This means the social benefit of cleaner air is equal to the area under MSB between the new and old levels of air quality.

What if the program being evaluated by CBA creates harmful externalities as an unintended side-effect? Continuing with our air pollution example, if the program harms air quality, we want to subtract the area under the MSB curve at the new, lower air quality level from the area under the MSB curve at the old, higher level of air quality. Numerically, this is still equal to the area under MSB between the two quantities of clean air, but now it is a negative number rather than a positive number. Some CBA practitioners would move this to the cost side of the cost–benefit equation, but we suggest instead it should count as a negative benefit, subtracting from the other positive benefits of the program and kept on the benefits side. It doesn't really matter where you put it as long as you are consistent.

What if the program creates consumer, producer, and social surpluses in multiple years? Then we want to calculate present values, of course, but should that be done before or after we aggregate over people? The answer depends on whether we are including distributional concerns in our analysis. If we only care about efficiency, the order of aggregation doesn't matter, but if we incorporate distributional concerns, discounting should be done for each person before we add across people.

Consider briefly the benefit side of a program to develop job skills for unemployed teenagers. Trainees might produce marketable goods and services such as basic automobile repairs or office work which employers or the general public are willing to purchase at a competitive price. These benefits are properly calculated as changes in consumer and producer surplus in the markets for these goods and services.

However, the principal benefits of such a program might be the enhanced productivity of trainees in future years, perhaps a reduction in crime, and other benefits for which there are no direct markets. In such cases, indirect estimates must be made of what citizens are, or at least should be, willing to pay for these benefits. To a first approximation, the trainee would like to pay nothing but would be willing to pay up to the present value of the change in future wages due to training. But we have to be careful about that approximation in light of the unclear counterfactual. Perhaps if teenagers did not participate in this program, they would participate in some other program that would also raise their wages. So, we want to estimate the gain in present value of future wages from this program against the gain in present value of future wages minus the opportunity costs of participating in the next best training opportunity that a teenager could take. Such increased earnings represent direct gains to the recipients, for which they are (or should be) willing to pay – hence, such a calculation serves to estimate part of the benefit of the program. Estimating the benefit or reductions in future crimes by trainees is harder because there is a collective good involved. The private benefit is that victims do not suffer from as much crime. The collective benefit is that everyone in the community can feel safer and are willing to pay for that feeling of safety when the crime rate is lower.

The grand total on the benefits side is the present value of all consumer surpluses plus producer surpluses plus social surpluses from nontraded and collectively-consumed goods created by the program.

Measuring efficiency gains: costs and the bottom line

We covered measurement of costs extensively in Chapter 6. CBA requires the use of opportunity costs – the value of everything that must be given up if a program is adopted, rather than accounting costs. As a reminder and to expand on the points made previously, consider a program to train unemployed teenagers in job skills. The direct costs include paid staff, supplies, and capital equipment. If these resources are purchased in competitive markets and there are no externalities from their use, the prices or wages attached to these resources times the change in quantity of goods or workers is an accurate measure of opportunity cost. This measure of costs would not have to account for an induced change in the price of these resources in most cases, because the program uses a tiny portion of the resources available. However, if the program causes the price of one or more resources to change, we would instead look for program-related change in the area under the marginal cost curve for that resource.

If a program uses donated resources such as in-kind gifts or volunteer labor, market prices do not provide reliable measures of resource cost. In Chapter 6, we discussed the cost of volunteering to the volunteer as the net benefits he could obtain from his next-best use of time. The next best use of time is found by selecting the alternative with the highest net benefits from a list including volunteering elsewhere, devoting more time to paid work, spending more time with the children, spending more time in educational opportunities, or simply relaxing. There are also direct costs to the employing organization from recruiting, training, supervising, and providing supplies and facilities to the volunteer, and these costs are properly valued by market prices in most cases. We also discussed donated goods or services, noting transactions costs (processing the donation and sending proper thank you notes), tax deductions that affect the costs to the donor but not the total cost to society (when distribution matters, these must be distinguished), and the value foregone because donated resources are not available for their next best use. The list price of, say, a donated computer is not an accurate valuation of opportunity costs because computers are often donated when they are obsolete, making the list price a fiction.

Finally, the costs of any program include the external costs of activities involved in the program. These might occur because an activity (say, nocturnal marching bands) raises the costs of production at a neighboring facility (say, a residential facility for nervous insomniacs), or because an activity (say, limburger cheese production) reduces the enjoyment one can get from neighboring activities (say, at a pickup bar). In the latter case, we recommended counting the cost as a negative benefit, but it is somewhat arbitrary whether it is classified as a negative benefit or a positive cost provided it is not included in both places. Mechanically, this can be calculated as the change in total variable costs in the first case, and the area under a shadow demand curve in the second.

In sum, we monetize efficiency gains by changes in total surplus: consumer plus producer plus external surplus plus social surplus. Consumer and producer surpluses measure benefits minus private costs, whereas costs must be subtracted from social benefits (the area under the MSB or shadow demand curves) to produce social surplus. Changes in total surplus are changes in net social benefits.

14.5 From efficiency to social welfare: distribution matters

Using CBA to obtain economic efficiency is not easy, but the calculation becomes even harder when the program changes the distributions of income and well-being, for two reasons. The first is the question of how to mechanically introduce distributional concerns into the calculation of net social benefits. The second is more fundamental – there is no consensus on the ideal distribution of income or the importance of fixing various departures from that ideal. That said, if we ignore distribution, we are making an implicit assumption that the current distribution of income is ideal, an assumption that few would agree with. There are many clever and complicated ways to address these difficulties, as reviewed in Adler (2016), Boadway (2016) or the textbook by Boardman et al. (2018). Here we highlight some themes without including all the details and alternatives.

Weights: the basic idea

Mechanically, we can produce weighted sums of changes in individual net social benefits, where the weights are chosen to reflect the social importance of adding to that person's well-being. For example, if there are only two kinds of people – rich and poor – and the social judgment is made that a gain to a poor person is three times as important as a gain to a rich person, we would compute:

$$\Delta \text{Social Benefit} = 3 \times \Delta \text{NSB}_{poor} + \Delta \text{NSB}_{rich} \qquad (14.1)$$

where Δ is shorthand for 'the change in' and NSB is the social benefit provided to the subscripted class of people, and the weights applied to each class are 3 and 1. Sometimes the weights are rescaled to sum to 1; in this case, the weight on benefits to the poor would be ¾ and the weight on benefits to the rich would be ¼. Such rescaling would never affect decisions made through CBA as long as there is consistency across programs

When distributional weights are used we cannot use the total market demand curve to compute the change in consumer surplus. Instead, we need class-specific demand curves. Continuing our example, the demand curve for the poor would be the horizontal sum of individual demand curves across all poor people affected by the program, and the demand curve for the rich is the horizontal sum across all rich people affected by the program. We calculate the change in consumer surplus separately for each class using class-specific demand curves and then apply the weights. When the number of classes is small this adds a manageable amount of work to the calculation. Moreover, it is unlikely that there is sufficient information to include a large number of classes, narrowly defined. There is a trade-off, and practical CBA analysts will accept a small number of classes as an approximation to finer-grained distributional concerns. It is better to make an imperfect correction for distributional concerns than to make no correction at all.

Distributional weights are needed throughout the cost–benefit calculations. We must weight total costs and that requires us to calculate who bears each cost or part of a cost. We need weights for the benefits from nontraded goods, and class-specific shadow demand curves to calculate the benefits to each class. Finally, we must weight transfer payments. Suppose we were evaluating a transfer payment of $1000 from a rich person to a poor person. If we were only concerned with efficiency, there would be no change in net social benefit because the rich person's loss is equal to the poor person's gain. If instead we counted gains to the poor as three times more important than gains to the rich, net social benefits would increase by $2000.

Comparing the well-being of one person to another

Suppose Fred is confined to a wheelchair, Barney is not, and both have the same income and wealth. Does a $100 increase in Fred's consumer surplus represent the same gain as a $100 increase in Barney's consumer surplus? Or suppose Virginia is married with three children and a spouse in the household, and Sue is single and lives alone, but both have the same income and wealth. Would a $100 increase in consumer surplus mean the same thing to Virginia and Sue? For such circumstances, a more sophisticated approach to individual net benefits is needed.

Individual net benefits are frequently calculated by assuming that individual well-being is a function of consumption and non-consumption attributes. Some of the important non-consumption attributes are health status, family size and composition, age, and leisure time. After making technical and substantive simplifying assumptions, we can come up with a way of measuring individual well-being that is fully comparable across individuals. The method involves adjusting consumption expenditures using 'equivalent income' to adjust for non-consumption attributes and then use something related to the certainty equivalent of a lottery (see Chapter 10) called a Von-Neumann/Morgenstern utility function to attach numerical values. (See Fleurbaey (2016) for details.)

What weights should we use?

Traditional cost–benefit analysis, using the Kaldor-Hicks criterion, can be thought of as a weighted sum of individuals' well-being in which all the weights are the same. So, the threshold question is: "Should weights be uniform?" Our answer is "probably not," but some economists disagree so we start by summarizing this controversy. Then, accepting the need for non-uniform weights, we discuss whether there is a defensible basis for picking the weights assigned to each class.

The arguments made in support of uniform weights are:

- The current distribution of income is optimal. If all people have the income they deserve according to some philosophical criterion, then a gain to any person should count the same as a gain to any other person.
- Governmental tax and welfare programs can compensate for any maldistribution caused by the program under scrutiny.
- By maximizing (uniformly-weighted) total surplus, we can, with suitable payments from winners to losers, make everyone better off. The analyst's job is to create the potential for everyone to gain, and if the politicians fail to ensure that these payments are made, it is not the analyst's fault.
- The choice of non-uniform weights is arbitrary, allowing the analyst to manipulate results for political or personal benefit.

However:

- The value judgment that the distribution of income is already optimal is offensive to many in our society (such as single parents working two jobs who cannot afford basic necessities) and controversial at best to others.
- Government can adjust the distribution of income, but governments are guided by political forces rather than abstract notions of distributional justice.
- The winners might not want to compensate the losers. They might not even know who the losers are. If the analyst recommends a policy that predictably worsens the distribution of income, the "not-my-job" claim is hollow.
- Proper CBA requires that all decisions regarding weights or other aspects of methodology be explicitly discussed in the report. It is therefore easy to see through attempts to manipulate the results. In addition, standards of good practice require that the analyst conduct sensitivity analyses to see whether the bottom line judgment would change if plausible alternative assumptions (including assumptions about proper weighting) were made. Finally, the choice of uniform weights is arbitrary and represents a growth-at-all-costs mentality.

So, what non-uniform weights should be used? There are two major approaches in the literature – "utilitarian" and "social justice" weighting. Utilitarian weighting builds on the idea of diminishing marginal utility – the idea that the first ice cream you consume adds more personal value than the second ice cream, the second adds more than the third, and so on. Diminishing marginal utility might not set in from the get-go – maybe the first beer isn't very good, but by the third beer you stop noticing the peculiar taste and enjoy it a lot – but past some point (11 beers?) an additional beer does not add as much to your happiness. If there is diminishing marginal utility for all goods, then there is diminishing marginal utility to income. The gain I get when my income goes up from $0 to $100,000 is huge, but when my income increases in the future by the same amount, from $1,200,000 to $1,300,000, my additional enjoyment is somewhat smaller.

Early utilitarians argued that redistribution from the rich to the poor will add to total value, because the loss of utility when a rich person gives up $10,000 is smaller than the gain in utility when a poor person receives $10,000. The problem with this argument is that we are comparing gains across people. Who is to say that a gain to a money-loving millionaire is less important to him than a gain to, say, a cleric who has taken a vow of poverty? But modern CBA offers some rebuttal to this point, as we have devised methods to make utility more comparable across individuals. Thus, the utilitarian approach to weighting picks weights equal to each person's marginal utility of income.

The other approach, which we call "social justice," is usually called "Atkinson isoelastic weighting" in the literature, a label that is not very helpful when you are first learning the concept. This weighting scheme came from a review by Nobel prize-winning economist Kenneth Arrow (1973) of a book by Harvard philosopher John Rawls, *A Theory of Justice* (1971) . Both took the position that distributional justice should be judged from an "original position," a hypothetical place where real humans get to choose principles for a good society without knowing what role they would play in that society. This "veil of ignorance" assures that principles of justice are derived in a way that is not self-serving. Rich people might argue that the current distribution of income is socially just when they know that they will be among the rich, but might disagree from an original position where they are as likely to be rich as poor. Arrow interpreted and extended his argument to the risk preferences of a person in an original position. Someone who was very risk averse would care about the well-being of the worst-off in society almost exclusively; someone who was risk neutral would care about average well-being.

Atkinson used this insight to develop a formula to select distributional weights in CBA. His simplifying assumption ("isoelastic") means that all the analyst must do is select a single number that captures risk preferences, and a full set of weights emerges from that number. The only time a person in the original position would select uniform weights is when she is risk neutral; otherwise varying degrees of extra emphasis are applied to the disadvantaged. The Atkinson approach makes conducting sensitivity analysis easy. If there is doubt regarding whether we have picked the right risk preference, we can recalculate net social benefits by changing a single number. One can show that this approach produces weights that are the product of the marginal utility of income and the "marginal moral value of utility" for people in each class.

Losing weight(s)

If you find traditional CBA unsatisfactory, but object to all the assumptions necessary to calculate weighted benefits and costs, what should you do? A compromise position is to conduct traditional CBA and a distributional impact analysis in parallel. The distributional impact analysis should provide details on who the winners and losers are, as in the cost–benefit matrix framework discussed above. Consider the two cases presented in Table 14.3 regarding the proposal to pass the Baggins Act in The Shire. Panel A shows a CBA for this proposal, which affects the urban residents in Hobbiton and Buckland differently than the rural residents in Barrow Downs. The Baggins Act has a positive net social benefit of $5million but is perhaps a bit unfair because the net benefit to rural residents is four times as large as that to urban dwellers. Still, both groups benefit, so the Baggins Act should probably be passed.

Table 14.3 Equity versus efficiency without using weights

Panel A: Relatively easy case: the Baggins Act

	Urban Residents	Rural Residents	Total
Benefits	$4 million	$6 million	$10 million
Costs	$3 million	$2 million	$5 million
Net Social Benefit	$1 million	$4 million	$5 million

Panel B: Harder case: the Underhill Act

	Urban Residents	Rural Residents	Total
Benefits	$4 million	$7 million	$11 million
Costs	$5 million	$1 million	$6 million
Net Social Benefit	–($1 million)	$6 million	$5 million

Panel B shows the effects of a different proposal, the Underhill Act. This Act harms urban residents but helps rural residents far more than it hurts urban residents so that the net social benefit is $5 million, the same as the Baggins Act. Using the Kaldor-Hicks criterion, the Underhill Act should be passed, but with winners and losers it is a hard case to decide. Is the $6 million gain to rural residents worth the $1 million loss to urban residents? Using distributional weights for the two groups would mechanically answer that question, but choosing the weights is just as much a moral decision as expressing an opinion without weights. Weights have the advantage that if we make many difficult decisions using the same set of weights, we will make a consistent moral judgment, but if we are just making a few difficult decisions, we can decide case-by-case.

14.6 Practical matters

Here, we discuss three questions that arise in practice. First, how do we deal with prices in cases of market failure? Second, how should we incorporate secondary effects? And finally, how can we estimate shadow demand curves for nontraded goods?

Corrections to market prices

When private goods are traded in competitive markets, equilibrium prices are the same as marginal social cost and marginal social benefits, so they reflect the costs and benefits appropriate for CBA when small changes are made to quantities (where a small change is one that does not affect the price). But we saw in Chapter 8 that single-price monopolies charge a price on the demand curve that is above their marginal cost (and, assuming no externalities, above marginal social cost). We can use that price to evaluate the benefits of small changes in quantities to consumers, but we need to use marginal cost to evaluate the cost of a small change. For large changes, we use the change in consumer and producer surplus as the benefit, and the area under the marginal cost curve between the two quantities for the cost.

Taxes and subsidies can cause a market failure or fix a market failure, and if this were a textbook for government managers conducting CBA, we would have to address these effects. But we need not worry about them here because nonprofit and social enterprise managers lack the power to set taxes (unless they are such powerful advocates that they can change government policies). Still, taxes change prices, and that is relevant for calculating costs and benefits. In Chapter 9, we saw how a sales tax creates a wedge between the price paid by the consumer (including the tax) and the price received by the producer (not including tax). To account for this, we should use the consumer price to evaluate the benefits to consumers of a small change in the quantity of a taxed good, and the producer price to evaluate the costs to producers. Nonprofit exemption from sales taxes varies across the states, but an exempt nonprofit does not face this complication on its own purchases.

Wedges like this arise in other kinds of taxes as well. A payroll tax creates two wage rates – one for the worker and one for the firm; property taxes create two implicit rental rates on purchased property, and so on. In all these cases, one price is used for small changes to evaluate costs and another price to evaluate benefits. For large changes, consumer and producer surplus already distinguish the two prices by using supply and demand curves.

Finally, price regulations, like the minimum wage or rent control, break the connection between price and the corresponding marginal costs and values when these regulations bind (that is, when the regulation forces the market to pay a higher wage or charge a lower rent than the free-market equilibrium). We discussed the minimum wage in Chapter 9 and Figure 9.3. When the minimum wage binds, the quantity of labor demanded (by employers) is less than the quantity of labor supplied (by workers). A small increase in the quantity of labor has costs per unit equal to the minimum wage, but benefits per unit that are lower and equal to the height of the labor supply curve at the regulated-equilibrium quantity of labor. Similarly, rent control constitutes a price ceiling – a maximum legal price. When the maximum legal price is lower than the free market price, there is a shortage of rental units as the number of units supplied at the lower price is less than the number of units demanded. The regulated price will equal marginal social costs but will be below marginal social benefits. We get the proper price for calculating benefits from the height of the rental demand curve at the regulated-equilibrium quantity (Figure 14.6).

Secondary effects

Secondary effects are the ripples created in the economy by changes in the prices of resources used by the program under consideration. Since the owners of resources may gain or lose from such ripples, and consumers of other products produced with these resources gain or lose from resulting product-price changes, these effects can be important determinants of the distribution of costs and benefits. However, such effects are merely reflections of the primary benefits and costs to society as a whole. Adding these effects to the primary ones would be double counting.

To illustrate, suppose that a university decides to build a new facility at some distant site. The value of that facility would be accounted for by the primary

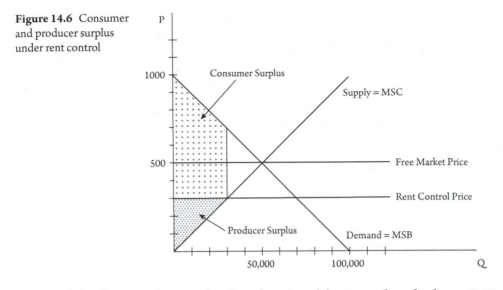

Figure 14.6 Consumer and producer surplus under rent control

benefits to students and to beneficiaries of the research and other activities that would be carried on via new programs at the facility. Having the facility nearby might also make local businesses, government agencies, or other nonprofits more productive by giving them access to new knowledge or information that was not previously accessible. These would all be primary benefits.

At the same time, land prices and wage rates might rise in the vicinity of the new facility because additional businesses would compete for nearby locations, providing gains to local land owners and workers. However, many of these gains might be offset by losses (lower land prices or lower wage rates) in other locations which experience losses of economic activity as a result of business moving to the new site. The gains in land prices or wages at the new site would only be reflections or partial captures of the primary benefits by resource owners who capitalized on these gains by charging higher prices to the primary beneficiaries for their land or labor. These secondary benefits to local resource owners at the new site do not add to the primary benefits, just as the losses at other sites do not subtract from those benefits. Secondary effects change the distribution of winners and losers, but not the efficiency of a project and if we care about the former, we should include secondary effects like we include transfers.

Estimating shadow demand curves

There are no demand or supply curves for goods that are not bought and sold, but we still need to calculate the change in net social benefits resulting from changes in the quantities of nontraded goods of the program in question. We do so with cost functions and shadow demand curves, as discussed above. But how can we get information on the shape and location of these shadow demand curves?

The literature provides three major approaches to estimate shadow demand: *contingent valuation, hedonic regressions,* and *the travel-cost method.* There are pros and cons to each approach so ideally we should combine estimates from all three, but the analyst rarely has the time and money to do so and in any case the gain in accuracy might not be worth the cost. We will describe each method applied to CBA of a project that would increase safety in a public park. Because we are evaluating the benefit of a single program, we do not need to know the whole shadow demand curve – we only need to know the area under shadow demand for safety between the current quantity of safety and that expected following completion of the project. Safety is a benefit for anyone who might use the park, so we need to add up willingness to pay across everyone who might do so. Finally, we assume that the park does not get too crowded to enjoy as a result of the program. Had we not assumed this, we would have to incorporate congestion costs into our calculation.

Contingent valuation is a sophisticated approach to simply asking beneficiaries about willingness to pay for some change. We begin by asking a sample of park users and nonusers what they would be willing to pay for enhanced safety in this park. The method calls for personal interviews, and respondents should receive detailed information on the attribute they are asked to value. For our example, respondents would be told how many people use the park, what the park is like, how many muggings, rapes, and other crimes are committed in the park each year, and the likely reduction in these crimes if the project is put in place. The method is "contingent" because the stated value depends on the quality of the information presented to the survey respondent. Respondents are asked to reflect on their answers in ways that mimic the thinking process for a purchase. Here, the interviewer might say "You've said that you are willing to pay $200 a year for this project. You've told me your budget is tight. What are some things you might cut in your spending in order to pay $200? Do you want to revise your answer after thinking about this?"

Many nontraded goods can be bought and sold as part of a package. Those living just outside the park presumably pay more to buy or rent their homes because the park makes the neighborhood better. But property values vary for many other reasons as well. Hedonic regression analysis uses statistical methods to sort out how much of the variation in property values is due to proximity to the park, how much is due to the number of square feet of built space and acreage of the property, how much is due to the number of bathrooms, and so on. In order to estimate the shadow demand for the safe parks that we want, our sample must include some properties occupied by people living near safe parks and some properties near dangerous parks. After removing the effect of other variables, this difference in property values reflects willingness to pay for safe parks. In effect, hedonic regression identifies the benefits of nontraded goods using secondary effects of programs like the one being evaluated.

The travel cost method is another way of estimating willingness to pay from market behavior. When people travel from far away to visit the park, they incur costs and reveal that their willingness to pay for the park experience exceeds those costs. If we have information on visitors to safe and dangerous parks, we can use the difference in willingness to incur travel costs to estimate the value of park safety, after statistically controlling for other factors that make the parks different.

14.7 An example

In a collaborative effort supported by the Music Foundation of America, the Philharmonic Orchestra of Viola, Kansas works with the Viola School District to identify children with outstanding musical talent who are from underprivileged families. The program offers special musical instruction provided by volunteer orchestra members. Instrumental rentals and lessons are provided without charge to selected children. The foundation grant pays for staff support and instrument rentals. The grant also offers modest stipends to participating students and their families to ease the financial pressures they face while participating in the program. The school district makes its facilities available for practices and performances. Several times a year, the participating children give free public concerts. The program is scheduled to continue for a period of three years.

The first question we might ask is: which groups stand to gain from this program and which groups bear the costs of this fictional program? Consider the following:

- The selected children receive special instruction in music.
- Donors to the Music Foundation pay for staff and instrument costs and receive satisfaction from helping out.
- Orchestra members bear the costs of volunteering and receive the special satisfactions provided by acting generously.
- Citizens/taxpayers bear the costs of using the school facility. They also pay the policing and clean-up costs associated with the concerts. On the benefit side, citizens/taxpayers receive free concerts; they are spared

antisocial behavior that might have occurred if the participating children were not in the program; and they might receive increased future tax payments from children who go on to pursue productive careers in music.

Thus, it appears sensible in this case to calculate benefits and costs for the following distinct groups:

- participating children and families;
- music foundation donors;
- orchestra volunteers; and
- citizens/taxpayers.

This set of groups meets the criterion of minimal overlap between group members while including all relevant beneficiaries and cost bearers. While there may be some overlap between taxpayers and orchestra volunteers, foundation donors, or the families of participating children, for analytical purposes such overlap is small enough to be ignored. Note that we are also making no distinctions between the local citizens/taxpayers of Viola and citizens/taxpayers elsewhere. It is probably reasonable to assume that most of the citizen/taxpayer benefits and costs associated with the program are confined to Viola. Exceptions will occur when participating children grow up and move away, thereby imposing costs or benefits on other jurisdictions. If such effects are anticipated to be significant, then the analysis can be expanded to include an additional group of "citizen/taxpayers elsewhere."

To fill out the rest of the prototype matrix of Table 14.2 we need to identify relevant costs, benefits, and transfer payments:

Costs are the most straightforward items to identify. They include:

- *salaries and benefits* for project staff;
- *supplies and services*, including office supplies, computers, photocopying, telephones, postage, etc. used to carry out the program, as well as the cost of providing and maintaining instruments;
- *facility costs*, including maintenance and repair expenses, clean-up after concerts, and foregone benefits from alternative uses of the school space during hours when the program is in session;
- *volunteer time* reflected in the opportunity value of the time donated by orchestra members; and
- *user costs*, including travel costs and the opportunity value of lost time borne by parents who carpool their children to practices and concerts.

Note two key characteristics of these items. First, they all represent real uses of resources, not just financial transactions. Second, the social cost of salaries and benefits, supplies and services, and maintenance and repair can be well-approximated by the necessary expenditures in markets. It takes more work to estimate other costs. We might want to approximate facility costs by the average rental rate for commercial space in the Viola area. Here are some problems with that approach (see the discussion of facility costs in Chapter 6 for more detail):

- If it is known that the space would otherwise go unused, the value of the foregone opportunity is zero.
- If the space is known to have other demands on it and commands a specific usage fee, that fee would provide a better estimate of the opportunity cost.
- If the space would have been used for another school program, then the opportunity cost would be what the school is willing to pay to secure those other uses.

Evaluating the cost of time volunteered by orchestra members poses other challenges. As discussed in Chapter 6, there are costs borne by the volunteer and costs borne by the orchestra and foundation. If the next best alternative for the volunteer is working more hours for pay, the cost to the volunteer is the after-tax wage rate times the number of volunteer hours, but if the volunteer cannot add to her paid work, the cost is probably lower than that.

Estimating user costs also requires some investigation. The out-of-pocket costs of driving children to and from the school or using a school bus for the same purpose may be estimated in a straightforward manner by multiplying distance traveled by appropriate mileage-cost estimates. In addition, parents may incur significant opportunity costs associated with the use of their time, especially if they must take time off from work to carpool their children. (On the other hand, parents might have to take care of their kids at home if they weren't at practice, which might be a cost or a benefit depending on parental preferences and the quality of parent–child interactions). In addition, selected children may incur opportunity costs from participating in the program. Specifically, some of these children might have to forgo working at part-time jobs or pass up team sports or other school-related activities to participate in the music program. In the former case, the opportunity cost to the student is the after-tax wages they would have earned if not for the program. In the latter case, willingness to pay for participating in the alternative activity is the appropriate measure.

Note that all the foregoing costs are incurred on a regular basis throughout the three years of the program. The present value of these costs is calculated by discounting over the three-year period.

Benefits are not as easily identified or estimated as costs. In this case, we have the following benefit items:

- *Direct benefits to participants* can be of two kinds. Some of the children may go on to become professional musicians; hence, the program potentially increases their future economic welfare. Many of the children will also be able to enjoy music to a greater degree because of the program, whether or not they pursue music as a career.
- *Benefits of satisfaction* accrue to donors and volunteers as a result of their support of the program.
- *Benefits of enjoyment* accrue to the citizens of Viola who take advantage of the free concerts.
- *Collective benefits* accrue to citizens insofar as they enjoy reductions in antisocial behavior resulting from engaging the children in a constructive cultural experience rather than leaving them on their own to get into trouble.

Unlike costs, most of the program's benefits are difficult to estimate by simply observing salient market prices. Some of these benefits may not be estimable at all in quantitative terms; in other cases, however, we can obtain approximate estimates by asking the basic question – what should the beneficiaries be willing to pay for these benefits?

In the case of participant benefits, we might try to estimate how many of the children will go onto professional music careers and what earnings they would command over those careers compared to an estimate of what they would otherwise earn. For example, we might assume the children would earn an average blue-collar salary if they did not become musicians. The present value of future earned income above (or below) what would otherwise be earned would estimate what the participants should be willing to pay to participate in the program. This estimate would be constructed from existing market data on the wages of people in music-related careers compared to the alternative baseline career.

Another participant benefit would be the "consumption value" of enjoying music to a greater degree due to the program. This benefit would be difficult to estimate in quantitative terms but could be identified qualitatively as a benefit of the program. Alternatively, graduates of similar programs could be asked to value their enhanced enjoyment of music through a contingent valuation survey.

Benefits to donors and volunteers would also be difficult to estimate quantitatively. Some volunteers might obtain valuable training that would enable them to earn extra income later on as music teachers. Others might gain from the social contacts they make in this program. These contacts might have economic value in later employment. In such cases, the value of additional future income can serve as a partial estimate of value to volunteers. Because the transactions are voluntary, we know that these benefits exceed the value of their forgone time, and if we find otherwise, we have underestimated the benefits. Contingent valuation could also be used here.

The benefits from free concerts might be estimated by noting the prices of tickets to similar events. Or we could use contingent valuation or the travel-cost method to construct the appropriate shadow-demand curve.

We need two things to value the collective benefits of reduced antisocial behavior. First, we need a careful scientific study of the effect of programs like this one on the amount and nature of antisocial behavior. Ideally, a field experiment has been conducted elsewhere and published and we can use that supplemental information. But if no such experiment exists, we should consider modifying the proposal to include such a study. This means we will have to guess at the treatment effect of the program on antisocial behavior for your CBA. However, we can add to the list of program benefits those that stem from learning the true treatment effect and sharing that knowledge with other potential adopters. The second thing that is needed is an appropriate shadow demand curve, or at least the area under such a curve between the quantity of antisocial behavior with and without the program. If pursued in full detail, evaluation of these benefits will be costly and difficult, but if we expect that the treatment effect will be small, we might settle for the best estimate we can get through internal reflection.

Unlike its costs, several of the program's benefits extend well beyond the three-year operation of the program. Immediate donor and volunteer satisfactions as well as enjoyment of the free concerts are limited to the three-year period, but participant benefits (enhanced future earnings, increased enjoyment of music, career-related benefits to volunteers, and social benefits of reduced antisocial behavior) may extend over long periods of time, even over participants' lifetimes. Clearly, the stream of future benefits must be appropriately discounted to estimate present values that are comparable to the cost estimates.

Transfer payments are relatively unimportant in this example because virtually all resource transactions (payments) are associated with the consumption of real resources or creation of new economic value. There are two exceptions:

- The stipends to participating students and families represent a transfer from the foundation donors to the participants.
- Any incremental income tax payments resulting from the additional future income earned by program participants represent a transfer from the participants to other citizen/taxpayers.

Like benefits and costs, transfer payments must also be discounted over time to provide figures that are comparable to the costs and benefits. Note that the stipends are paid over the three-year duration of the program, while the additional income tax payments would likely take place far (ten or more years) into the future.

The scope of this book does not permit detailed calculations of all estimated items in the cost–benefit matrix. However, Table 14.4 gives an idea of which items can be approximately quantified at reasonable cost, which items can be identified simply in terms of direction and incidence on particular groups, and what the magnitudes of the quantifiable benefits and costs might look like. A few explanatory notes are in order here to understand the numbers in this exhibit:

- A nominal discount rate of 5 percent is assumed.
- The costs of salaries, benefits, services and supplies are assumed to be specified in the project budget to be $50,000 per year for salaries and benefits and $10,000 per year for services and supplies. The table shows the present values of these numbers, calculated over the three-year period of the program.
- The facility cost is approximated by the rental value of equivalent space in commercial buildings nearby. This is estimated at $500 per month or $6000 per year. The present value in the table is calculated over the three-year period of the program.
- The cost of orchestra members' volunteer time is estimated by assuming that these individuals would otherwise be giving music lessons at $20/hour after taxes. If five volunteers each work two hours per week over a 40-week period per year, the total annual cost is $8000. The present value of this figure, calculated over the three years of the program, is shown in the table.
- User costs are estimated by assuming that, in order to transport their children to and from the program, the parents of the 20 participating

Table 14.4 Cost–benefit analysis for the Viola music program (for a 5 percent discount rate)

	Participants	Donors	Volunteers	Other Citizens	All Society
Costs					
Salaries and benefits		$136,162			$136,162
Supplies and services		$27,232			$27,232
Facility use				$16,339	$16,339
Volunteer time			$21,786		$21,786
User cost	$4357				$4357
Opportunity cost of time	+				+
Benefits					
Participant income	$471,868				$471,868
Concerts				$8170	$8170
Social benefit				$153,725	$153,725
Enjoyment	+				+
Satisfaction		+	+		+
Transfers					
Stipends	$10,893	($10,893)			$0
Tax payments	($94,374)			$94,374	$0
Total Benefit	$482,761	$0	$0	$256,269	$633,763
Total Cost	$98,731	$152,501	$21,786	$16,339	$205,876
Net Social Benefit	$384,030	($152,501)	($21,786)	$239,930	$427,887
Net Qualitative Benefit	+ or -?	+	+		+ or -?

children drive 10 miles per week at 20 cents per mile over a 40-week period. This totals $1600 per year. The table shows the discounted present value of this figure over the three-year period of program operation.

- The opportunity costs of the time children spend in the program and the time parents spend in transporting and assisting their children are assumed to be positive, but difficult to estimate with existing data.
- Benefits to participating children are estimated by assuming that five of the 20 participating children go on to music-related careers that they would not have pursued otherwise. (This estimate might come from an initial assessment of talents and motivations of the participants.) It is further assumed that in such careers these participants would earn approximately $10,000 more per year during their 30-year working careers, beginning 10 years after the program starts, than they otherwise

would have. The present value of this increment over the careers of the participants is shown in the table.

- The benefits to participants of enjoying music to a greater degree because of the program are assumed to be positive but not easily quantifiable.
- The benefits of satisfaction for orchestra volunteers and for foundation donors are also assumed to be positive but not easily quantifiable.
- The benefits to citizens who enjoy the free concerts are estimated by assuming that there are three concerts per year, each attended by 200 people, and that these attendees would, if necessary, be willing to pay $5 each, the minimum cost of concerts given elsewhere in town. The present value of this total annual benefit of $3000 over three years is shown in the table.
- The social benefits of the program are estimated by assuming (again based on initial assessments of participants) that one child is diverted from a life of crime and drug abuse because of the program. The value of this benefit is estimated by assuming that $10,000 per year is saved in treatment and damage costs over the next 30 years of that child's life. The discounted present value of that figure is shown in the table.
- Stipends to children and their families are $200 per family or a total of $4000 per year for the families of the 20 participating children. The present value of this figure over the three-year period of the program is displayed in the table as a transfer payment between donors and families.
- Additional tax payments by participants are calculated by assuming that the additional income earned by the five students that go on to music-related careers is taxed at the rate of 20 percent. Thus, a total of $10,000 per year represents transfer payments between participants and the rest of society. The present value of this figure over the 30-year earning period of the participants beginning 10 years after the program begins, is displayed in the table.

Given the foregoing estimates, one can see that on the basis of the quantifiable costs and benefits, the program benefits exceed program costs by a margin of more than $400,000. Hence it seems reasonable to characterize the program as efficient according to the Kaldor-Hicks criterion. In addition to this overall assessment, it may be observed that certain groups, specifically the participants and other citizens, benefit on balance, while other groups, such as the donors and volunteers, bear the principal costs. However, since donations and volunteering are voluntary, it must be true that the (intangible) benefits to these groups exceed the costs they bear.

In addition to "best-guess" estimates of benefits and costs, we carry out "sensitivity analyses" to see whether we would get a different answer if

Table 14.5 Sensitivity of net benefits to discount rate (quantified benefits less cost)

Discount Rate	Participants	Donors	Volunteers	Other Citizens	All Society
5%	$384,030	($152,501)	($21,786)	$239,930	$427,887
10%	$151,347	($139,265)	($19,895)	$123,154	$95,447
15%	$70,400	($127,860)	($18,266)	$75,041	($18,951)

some of our assumptions were wrong. Because some effects extend over 40 years, the assumed discount rate is a critical determinant of the net benefits. Table 14.5 compares net benefits using different plausible discount rates. At a rate of 10 percent, quantified benefits still exceed quantified costs by more than $95,000 but this represents a fourfold reduction in the net-benefit estimate because the bulk of the benefits occur much later than the costs. At a rate of 15 percent, the present value of costs exceeds that of benefits. Neglecting those intangibles where the costs or benefits were not estimated, the project should be rejected if the opportunity cost of capital is 15 percent.

It is also interesting to observe the effect of changes in the discount rate on the distribution of benefits and costs. Note that as the rate rises, the beneficiaries (participants and citizen/taxpayers) are most adversely affected: their benefits shrink dramatically while the costs borne by donors and volunteers do not shrink significantly. In the case of a 15 percent rate the program might thus be justified in terms of its distributional consequences (taking resources from wealthier donors and volunteers and creating benefits for less wealthy participants and average citizens) but not necessarily in terms of creating net economic value (depending on what one assumes about the non-quantified benefits).

14.8 Third pass: towards a cost–benefit framework for nonprofits and other social enterprises

Most of the literature on CBA takes the standpoint of a government agency trying to make sure its policies are efficient and fair. So far, we have suggested that CBA should be done the same way for nonprofits and other social enterprises. However, private notions of the public good are different from public notions of the public good. Perhaps private CBA should be modified to account for these differences. Academics have written very little on the subject, but here we speculate on the kind of changes that should be made.

Whether we take account of the distribution of income or not, CBA is justified by several relatively noncontroversial value judgments:

- *Consumer sovereignty*: Social judgments respect self-assessed well-being. A person is better off for the purpose of social judgments if she experiences the outcome she prefers.
- *Universality*: When judging a policy, everyone affected by that policy counts in the calculation.
- *Pareto dominance*: If a policy makes at least one person better off and harms nobody, it is a good policy. If a policy makes at least one person worse off and helps nobody, it is a bad policy.

Governments usually incorporate these value judgments into their cost–benefit analyses. But there are exceptions. Consumer sovereignty might be overruled if the affected party is a child, with the assessments of parents replacing self-assessed well-being. Consumer sovereignty might be overruled for addicts, the mentally incapacitated, or the lawfully incarcerated. Sometimes universality is challenged, as when the analysis ignores the effect of policy on foreign citizens, or a local government agency ignores the effect of local policies on other communities. Sometimes Pareto dominance is ignored, as when government evaluates programs designed to reduce victimless crimes. But a strong case is needed to justify these exceptions.

Private agencies with social missions are obligated to pursue their missions, and many missions are themselves inconsistent with the value judgments underlying traditional CBA. Specifically:

- Missions might violate consumer sovereignty. Religious organizations might ignore consumer surplus from sinful acts when they use CBA. Drug-addiction treatment centers serving court-ordered clients do not want to calculate and include the client's consumer surplus from obtaining forbidden drugs at a price that is less than willingness to pay. Even for those who voluntarily commit themselves to a treatment program, it is difficult to say whether consumer sovereignty should be respected because it is difficult to define the self-assessed preference of someone who pays an agency to prevent them from consuming something they value (Steinberg, 1992). Perhaps managers should conduct analyses that respect consumer sovereignty from time to time to check whether the mission should be modified, but otherwise CBA should respect organizational mission whenever it conflicts with consumer sovereignty. Which is not to say that the State or broader society will respect that mission, as the Church of Jesus Christ of Latter-day Saints (Mormon) found out in its early battles over polygamy.

- Missions might violate universality. Many social organizations have a particular focus on specified groups – co-religionists, the disadvantaged, immigrant communities, the tragically unhip, alumni, members, and the like. Should these organizations ignore the interests of affected parties outside their groups when they conduct CBA? How "social" must a social enterprise be to qualify as a "legitimate" organization pursuing a legitimate mission?

- Missions might violate Pareto-dominance. The whole point of a group advocating for a particular public policy is to make those advocating against that policy worse off. Human rights organizations might count costs borne by corrupt and dictatorial administrations as benefits in their private notion of the public good. Animal rights groups might not count the costs imposed on inconvenienced humans as relevant in their CBAs. Some religious organizations might regard imposing costs on sinners as a benefit, substituting their understanding of God's will for other notions of what makes a person better off in social judgments. Environmental groups might prioritize future generations over the present-value judgment that a program is not worth the costs.

Like governmental CBA, mission-based CBA can use weights to assess class costs and benefits. But some missions conflict with distribution-of-income weights. For example, post-graduate educators might want to select the most talented students, rather than the neediest, where the economically privileged may be more likely to develop and signal their academic talents. In other cases, mission-based weights are different but not clearly in conflict with need-based weights. Human organ allocation programs might prioritize the young, rather than the poor, reasoning that they can make better use of scarce organs than people with one foot in the grave.

Cost–benefit analysis in its current form is quite useful for managerial decision making and program evaluation. But there are some issues that need to be addressed for both government and private applications of CBA. First, CBA is incapable of dealing with missions designed to change personal preferences. For government, this might arise when evaluating programs designed to improve race relations or promote civil discourse. For religious nonprofits, this arises when programs designed to convert nonbelievers are assessed. Social marketing programs are designed to change preferences as the best way to change behavior. Cultural institutions wish to cultivate a taste for the arts and an appreciation of history. When we apply CBA to any of these programs, we might be stuck with conflicting advice – the program has negative net social benefits based on the pre-existing preferences, but positive net social benefits under the new preferences, , there is no easy solution to this problem. Second, evaluators may wish to incorporate more than efficiency and distributional judgments into CBA. Should we incorporate values for changes in the attainability of human rights, or does any human rights advantage outweigh all the costs and surpluses? If we are willing to make trade-offs, how can we monetize human rights? How should we handle program effects that enhance the legitimacy of institutions?

SELECTED REFERENCES AND CITATIONS

Adler, M.D. (2016). Benefit–Cost Analysis and Distributional Weights: An Overview. *Review of Environmental Economics and Policy*, *10(2)*, 264–285.

Apgar, W.C. and Brown, H.C. (1987) *Microeconomics and Public Policy*. Glenview, IL: Scott, Foresman and Company.

Arrow, K.J. (1973). Some Ordinalist-Utilitarian Notes on Rawls's Theory of Justice. *The Journal of Philosophy*, *70(9)*, 245–263.

Boadway, R. (2016). Cost-benefit analysis. In Adler, M.D. and Fleurbaey, M. (Eds.), *The Oxford Handbook of Well-being and Public Policy* (pp. 47–81). New York: Oxford University Press.

Boardman, A.E., Greenberg, D.H., Vining, A.R., and Weimer, D.L. (2018). *Cost-benefit analysis: Concepts and Practice* (5th ed.). New York and Cambridge, UK: Cambridge University Press.

Dupuit, J. (1844). De la mesure de l'utilité des travaux publics. *Annales des ponts et chaussées*, *8*, 332–375. [English trans. 'On the Measurement of the Utility of Public Works.']

Fleurbaey, M. (2016). Equivalent income. In Adler, M.D. and Fleurbaey, M. (Eds.), *The Oxford Handbook of Well-being and Public Policy* (pp. 453–475). Oxford: Oxford University Press.

Gramlich, E.M. (1981). *Benefit–Cost Analysis of Government Programs*. Englewood Cliffs, NJ: Prentice Hall.

Long, D.A., Mallar, C.D., and Thornton, C.V.D. (1981). Evaluating the Benefits and Costs of the Job Corps. *Journal of Policy Analysis and Management*, *1(1)*, 55–76.

Rawls, J. (1971). *A Theory of Justice*. Cambridge, MA: Harvard University Press.

Samuelson, P. (1954). The Pure Theory of Public Expenditure. *The Review of Economics and Statistics*, *36(4)*, 387–389. doi:10.2307/1925895.

Steinberg, R. (1992). The Market for Drug Treatment. In Gerstein, D.R. and Harwood, H.J. (Eds.), *Treating Drug Problems. Vol. 2: Commissioned Papers on Historical, Institutional, and Economic Contexts of Drug Treatment* (pp. 245–288). Washington, DC: National Academy Press.

REVIEW CONCEPTS

Benefit–Cost Ratio: Benefits divided by costs. An incorrect way to choose the best program using CBA.

Capital Budgeting: A procedure used to determine which investments should be selected. Includes private costs and private benefits but not factors that affect other members of society.

Consumer Surplus: The net gain from consumption calculated as the sum across units consumed of willingness to pay minus price.

Contingent Valuation: An interview procedure designed to produce valid estimates of the benefits of nontraded goods.

Cost–benefit analysis: A systematic process to choose the best alternative program that involves calculating the money equivalent of all opportunity costs and benefits and calculating (weighted or unweighted) net social benefits.

Cost-Effectiveness Analysis: A systematic way to decide between programs that have the same kind of benefit, based on social efficiency.

Equivalent Income: A method of adjusting income for differences in non-consumption attributes like family size or health status.

Hedonic Regression: A technique for estimating shadow demand curves for goods that are not separately traded but are traded in varying mixtures as part of a package of attributes. Hedonic regression calculates marginal willingness to pay for each attribute in those packages.

Kaldor-Hicks Criterion: An extension of the Pareto standard to situations in which some people are made better off and others are made worse off. A program should be adopted if the sum of the net benefits enjoyed by the winners exceeds the sum of the net losses incurred by the losers, so that it would be possible for the winners to compensate the losers and still come out ahead. The basic measure of efficiency in CBA.

Net Social Benefit: Total social benefits minus total social costs. Picking the project with the greatest net social benefit (weighted or unweighted) is the correct way to use CBA.

Outcome: The result of a program to further an organization's mission. Outcomes measure the impact of the program and are produced from organizational outputs and other inputs such as client effort.

Output: The products produced by a program that may help it to have impact on achieving its mission.

Producer Surplus: The net gain from production and distribution, calculated as the sum of price minus marginal cost of the units produced or distributed.

Secondary Effects: Spillover effects of a program due to changes in the prices of goods or factors of production. These would constitute double counting if changes in surplus from markets directly affected by the program are included.

Sensitivity Analysis: Testing the sensitivity of net social benefits to the assumptions made, by repeating CBA with different assumptions.

Shadow Demand Curve: The curve that shows what consumers would be willing to pay for each additional unit of a nontraded good.

Social Justice Weighting: An approach to counting net benefits accruing to some groups differently than other groups based on notions of social justice. Most commonly, the weights are based on the risk aversion of a person in Rawls' original position.

Social Return on Investment: A variation on CBA developed for social enterprises by the Roberts Enterprise Development Fund. Unfortunately, the wrong criterion is recommended in SROI: using at cost–benefit ratio instead of net social benefit.

Travel Cost Method: A technique for estimating shadow demand curves for goods that are not separately traded by calculating willingness to pay travel costs to use a facility.

Utilitarian Weighting: An approach to counting net benefits accruing to some groups differently than other groups based on adding a numerical measure of individual well-being. Utilitarian weights equal the average marginal utility of income in each group.

EXERCISES

1. For each of the following cases, specify:

   - What are the benefits?
   - What are the costs?
   - How can the benefits and costs be estimated using observable data?
   - What is the timing of benefits and costs? How sensitive is the calculation of present values likely to be to the assumed discount rate?
   - Who are the affected groups? What benefits and costs accrue to each group?
   - What are the important transfers and secondary effects among these groups?

   Construct a matrix for adding up the benefits and costs and identifying the distribution of benefits and costs among affected groups.

   Case 1: Flu Prevention
   A community foundation is considering whether to support an influenza prevention program that would inoculate vulnerable groups (young children, the elderly) in the region against the expected outbreak of the Liechtenstein flu this winter. The program involves publicizing the availability of flu shots and reimbursing doctors and clinics at a fixed price for the flu shots they administer to qualified recipients.

   Case 2: Upward Bound Program
   The Winding Creek School District is a low-income community concerned with the success of its student population. It is considering undertaking an Upward Bound Program that would send underprivileged high school students to a special college pre-paratory course in order to increase their chances of getting into, and succeeding in, college. The program would be paid for with tax dollars and a grant from the local community foundation and would be administered by a local private nonprofit school that specializes in compensatory college preparatory work. The program would use volunteer tutors from the community as well as paid staff and teachers.

2. For each of the cases above, would you want to use weights in your calculation of net benefits? Outline the pros and cons of using weights in each setting. If you used weights, what would you base them on?

3. Suppose you work for the charity Help for Homeless Munchkins, which has a program to help homeless munchkins find safe and dependable residences throughout Munchkin Country in the Land of Oz. Munchkin communities are much like human communities now that the Witch has found a permanent home under Dorothy's house. Thus, you can evaluate the charitable programs of HHM the same way as you would evaluate programs that help humans in Kansas. What are some likely benefits of the program to the community and to homeless munchkins? How would you measure these benefits in monetary terms? What tool would you use (choose between market demand curves, contingent valuation, hedonic regression, and the travel method) and how would you use that tool to calculate the money-equivalent benefit?

15

Using economics in practice

We must ignore our sunk costs and rebuild for the future!

15.1 Introduction

The manager of a nonprofit organization or a social enterprise is a generalist who must be aware of all the special functions and activities of his or her organization – marketing, finance, human resources, legal issues, and the like. The same may be said of social entrepreneurs who must assess the markets for their products, assemble financial and human resources, and set strategy for the future. While not experts in these diverse areas of practice, these leaders must be sufficiently familiar with them to effectively communicate with the experts and specialists, to evaluate what they are saying, and to work effectively with them. The nonprofit manager or social entrepreneur need not, for example, be an accountant to cope effectively with the issues of financial development and control, or an attorney in order to deal with statutory requirements or legal challenges. But she or he does need to have a general sense of accounting and legal principles, and how accountants and lawyers think, to know when to call them in, and to evaluate and act on their advice.

The case for understanding economic principles, as developed in this book, is similar. It has not been the purpose here to make nonprofit managers or social entrepreneurs into economists. That would be impossible and perhaps unfortunate, although economists aren't really such bad folk once you get to know them! (Any earlier attempts the reader may have made to earn an economics degree may be considered sunk costs, but like the characters in the above cartoon, the idea is to move forward without regret!) As the perceptive reader will have seen, the application of the methods of economic analysis to the problems and issues affecting nonprofit organizations and other social enterprises can be complex and highly technical, often fraught with nuance and sometimes requiring mathematical agility and sophisticated analysis of data. Nonetheless, the ability of managers or entrepreneurs to speak the economist's language and to frame and articulate issues in economic terms allows them to understand where economic consultants could help and to place their advice into proper overall perspective.

However, this book would be of very limited (and self-serving) value if all it did was to help nonprofit managers and social entrepreneurs determine when and how to employ the services of economists. The larger contribution of this book is to argue that the basic concepts which economists use to analyze issues involving the allocation of valuable resources are simple and intuitive, and that with some study, non-economist managers and leaders can use them to help their own thinking about the problems and decisions they face. Thus, the emphasis here is not on the technical details of economic analysis, but on the fundamental ideas that structure economists' thinking. If the lay reader comes away from this book with a basic understanding of opportunity costs; thinking at the margin; demand, supply, and competitive equilibrium; the effect of taxes or subsidies; decision making when there is risk and uncertainty; testing managerial ideas with experiments; strategy formulation; and cost–benefit analysis; then this book will have done its job. For in this case, the reader/manager/entrepreneur will have considerably enhanced his or her intellectual tool kit for addressing many of the challenges of managing nonprofit organizations and other social enterprises.

To see this point more dramatically, let us return to some of the short vignettes sketched in Chapter 1. How, in these cases, can the concepts developed in later pages help the managers and leaders of these various nonprofit organizations and social enterprises structure their thinking to effectively address the issues they face? Although we go into some depth, the discussion is not definitive, and we hope that the reader will find it of interest to elaborate on, and extend, what we say here. We have selected some vignettes for discussion here and leave the rest as a gift to the reader, encouraging you to analyze them in terms of what you have learned here.

15.2 Analyzing the vignettes

We select two cases from each of the categories discussed in Chapter 1: health care, education, the arts, social services, other subsectors, and social enterprises.

Health care

- A small hospital wishes to provide home health services. Should it do so on its own or in partnership with other hospitals?

This is a hard problem to analyze, and there are many tools and insights we have discussed that can help. The threshold question – does it make sense to provide home health services in either form, lurks in the background. The question is complicated by the special structure of health-care markets, reliant as they are on third-party payers. Therefore, the manager should consult economists to estimate the local demand for home health services by self and third-party payers, and also consult an expert on health policy to provide the background on how Medicaid, Medicare, Affordable Care Act providers and private insurers handle home health care: is it fully reimbursable? are costly supplemental services required? And so on.

Cost–benefit analysis takes time and is costly, but this decision is complicated enough that the cost–benefit matrix developed in Chapter 14 will be quite helpful. If we proceed this way, we should first check whether each alternative is consistent with the organizational mission. Does home health care directly benefit our mission, or is it something we want to do to generate profits that will cross-subsidize other missions? Does our mission encompass all that might benefit from home health care, or only certain groups? A partnership may reach a broader spectrum of the public than going it alone. If the hospital has a religious mission, it might or might not regard help provided to co-religionists the same as help provided to others. Does the mission require the organization to focus on certain kinds of treatments (e.g., either favoring or disfavoring hospice care) or certain kinds of costs and benefits? If so, would entering into a partnership necessitate compromising the hospital's position on, say, aggressive versus palliative care for the terminally ill?

We will have to resolve additional questions when we finalize the framework for analysis. Do we need to quantify all the benefits in monetary terms, or can we decide confidently using some qualitative evidence? Can we avoid monetizing the benefits and use cost-effectiveness analysis instead of CBA? Cost-effectiveness analysis is sufficient if the alternatives produce the same benefit. Do we care about distributional impacts? If so, what goes into the weights – income, medical need, or some combination of the two?

There are strategic considerations that may be answered informally or using game theory. How will other relevant actors respond to each choice? If there are economies of scale in home health care, then market forces lead to a natural monopoly, because the larger provider can always out-compete the smaller provider. If the partnership agreement uses multiple sites to provide services, some of these economies of scale would be lost, and this counts as an opportunity cost. Economies of scale might endanger the sustainability of either alternative, as perhaps a competitor will enter the market on a sufficient scale that both go-it-alone and partnership strategies will lead to bankruptcy.

Economies of scale may arise from the production side, but diseconomies of scale are likely due to the higher transportation costs of serving distant patients. If these outweigh production economies of scale, the partnership with multiple delivery sights is likely to be the better option. However, there are substantial transactions costs in arranging and maintaining a partnership. Lawyers are needed, managers of different organizations must trade organizational loyalties against loyalty to the partnership, and each partner will want mechanisms in place to assure that no partner embarrasses others in the partnership. There are also transactions costs in starting a go-it-alone program, particularly if employees lack training and experience in home health care. A more knowledgeable partner could help reduce these costs.

Finally, suppose that the hospital's competition is an existing monopolist for-profit provider. What leverage might the hospital have for securing home health care for its patients at the best possible price? If entry barriers are not too high and the hospital can mobilize charitable revenues to subsidize its price of services, it might use this leverage to negotiate a good price in lieu of entering the competition. Alternatively, it might enter the home health market at a price below that which the for-profit could sustain, in order to wrest the monopoly from the for-profit provider or induce it to negotiate a partnership arrangement or a lower price for consumers.

- A nonprofit mental health agency is considering raising money by selling employee benefit plans to local businesses, but it could lose money if donors react adversely or not enough businesses sign up. Should it go ahead with this initiative?

The wording suggests that the only reason for selling these plans is to raise money, so the main issue is profit calculation. There might be other reasons why these plans advance the organizational mission but put them aside for the moment. Managers should start with a market analysis: What is the demand for such services? What other providers are in the market now? Is there a threat of entry by other competitors?

Next, managers need to analyze three aspects of cost. First is the cost of entry. Does the current management have enough knowledge and experience to take on this project? Would new facilities, new managers, and new employees be necessary to enter this market? Are there licensing and certification fees or other costly regulatory measures to pay for? Next is the initial opportunity cost of production. Explicit costs include salaries of sales people, claims processors, and actuaries; expected benefit payments to employees of the contracting firm; taxes (if exemption does not extend to every source of income as in the case of unrelated business income); insurance and legal fees; and supplies. Implicit costs include an allocation of managerial salaries to reflect the fact that top managers are diverted from their other duties, the implicit cost of capital for reserves maintained to make payments to covered employees, and the implicit rental rate on any added facilities needed for the new program. Finally, we have the reduction in future costs stemming from learning by doing – experienced workers are more productive – and from reduced costs of finding clients as loyal clients renew their contracts.

If donors react adversely to the commercial venture, this would subtract from profits. First, the manager would need to find out what donors object to – the fact of the commercial operation, the price charged, or the profits generated, and then calculate the likely magnitude of decreased donations. There are published studies on the matter, but the context may differ from that in the published work, so it is probably best to conduct a new laboratory experiment to find out. The experimental context would also allow decision makers to try out different ways to market the commercial venture and see whether donor objections can be overcome by proper marketing. Another strategy the agency could pursue would be to spend more on fund-raising. If so, the relevant cost is not the fall in gross donations, but in net donations (donations minus the cost of fund-raising). Yet another strategy is to structure the commercial venture as a wholly-owned for-profit subsidiary. This veil might eliminate donor reactions to the commercial venture and protect the parent nonprofit from the worst of the worst-case scenarios. Additionally, if the organization would otherwise have to pay unrelated business income taxes on the profits generated from the business, the corporate income tax burden is often lower than the unrelated business income tax burden. However, there are additional transactions costs working across rather than within organizations, and the subsidiary approach might reduce economies of scope.

The organization must account for risks due to uncertain and fluctuating costs of employee benefits for covered workers, unexpected regulatory changes, unexpected changes in competition, and uncertain donor response. One way to approach this is to hire a financial analyst to calculate a risk premium for adjusting profits, using market data or organizational risk preferences to make this calculation. But the organization should also calculate a worst-case scenario to see how a disastrous commercial venture would affect other mission-related outcomes.

What if the organizational mission is directly advanced by promoting employee benefit plans? Then, to the extent it can afford the program, the organization should be willing to subsidize employee benefit plans with donations and profits from other activities and should sell more than the profit-maximizing quantity of plans. In addition, it will not be liable for unrelated business income tax payments because now the service relates to its tax-exempt mission. Everything else above also matters for this decision. Finally, if the organization views the venture in terms of general social benefits rather than as simply a means of increasing net income, it should recast the foregoing analysis in terms of net social benefits rather than profits per se.

Education

- A private college wishes to raise money to build a new wing on its library. Should it undertake a direct mail campaign, seek funds through personal solicitation, or some combination of the two? And how much money should the college invest in these fund-raising efforts?

Fund-raising is a component of nonprofit operations with a profitmaking objective. Thus, the college president and trustees can look at this issue as a traditional business problem. What combination of these alternatives will yield the most net revenue for the college? As considered in Chapter 5, the issue may be thought of in two parts. For a given budget allocated to fund-raising for the library, how much should be allocated to direct mail versus personal solicitation? Here the manager can apply the principle of equating the marginal revenue contributions of the last dollar allocated to each method. Next, one can ask, how large should the fund-raising budget be overall? Here, the guiding principle is that the budget should be expanded until a dollar more spending yields a dollar in return.

Some of the complications result from the timing of campaign returns. For example, direct mail may yield results faster than personal solicitation, but over time, personal solicitation may yield more money. Thus, the college's leaders must also ask themselves about the appropriate discount rate. If the personal solicitation route takes too much time it could jeopardize the financing of the library project. Also, if the campaign attracts new donors, it will have effects on future donations and costs of donations which must be transformed into their present-value equivalents. For these reasons the time streams of all revenues and costs must be understood and properly aggregated according to the present value principle before an efficient decision can be reached.

Where do we get the numbers needed to make these marginal revenue calculations? With lots of data, time, and expertise, we could estimate revenue functions econometrically. But a simple intuitive rule provides a starting point: from the records of the organization, calculate the change in fund-raising expenditures between two years ago and last year (or the last two years for which we have final totals). Then calculate the change in donations between these two years. The difference ratio is the change in donations divided by the change in fund-raising expenditures. This ratio is a simple, if imprecise, estimate of the marginal returns from the last dollars spent soliciting donations. If the differencing ratio is greater than one, too little is spent on fund-raising, to a first approximation. If the differencing ratio is less than one, then too much is spent, to a first approximation. The differencing ratio is an accurate measure of marginal revenues from fund-raising when the only reason donations change from one year to the next is that fund-raising expenditures change, but otherwise can be very inaccurate. A second approximation comes from the subjective evaluation of the manager as to how much of the change in donations is due to other factors (like an end to a recession or a scandal involving the organization). Thus, arithmetic is combined with experience-based intuition to obtain an adjusted differencing ratio.

The same logic leads to a differencing test to see whether the fund-raising budget is efficiently divided between direct mail and personal solicitation. The marginal revenue from direct mail is approximated by the change in those donations that are a response to the mailing divided by the change in costs of the mailing. The marginal revenue from personal solicitation is calculated the same way. If the estimated marginal revenue from direct mail exceeds the estimated marginal revenue from personal solicitation, more of the budget should be devoted to direct mail and less to personal solicitation. To use this approach, a second estimate that adjusts for other factors affecting donations may not be required because many of these other factors (recession, scandals) affect the marginal revenue estimates equally.

- A nonprofit research institute is considering a performance compensation system whereby its staff would receive salary bonuses tied to the level of research contracts they bring in. Should it go ahead with this proposal?

This proposal addresses the most basic concept of economic analysis – the use of incentives to make key economic actors (agents) work for the same goal as the principal. Management cannot directly observe the effort level of staff members, nor can it indirectly calculate the effort involved in bringing in research contracts. Contracts result from effort combined with luck and many other variables, so if a worker doesn't bring in a contract, management cannot tell whether that is because the worker was unlucky or did not try hard enough. Performance compensation seems to solve the principal–agent problem because higher effort leads to higher bonuses regardless of luck.

But we learn from behavioral economics that multiple motivations are in play, and that the provision of extrinsic rewards crowds out the intrinsic rewards staff may receive from their self-image and reputation as responsible workers. Unless the bonuses are substantial, they might be counterproductive.

Further, the focus on the quantity of contract dollars versus the quality and importance of the research might have costs to employees and the organizational mission. With incentives, the organization gets what is paid for (contract dollars) but not what may truly be wanted. Many of the research contracts that could be identified may be for very applied work that is not very interesting to the most talented researchers and not very valuable in terms of advancement of knowledge. Intrinsically-motivated researchers might share an organizational mission to secure contracts for the most important and interesting projects, projects that will increase the research institute's prestige and reputation. When they see others rewarded for bringing in lots of unimportant research, they might feel that their efforts are no longer valued and may quit (Nelsen, 1991). The organization too would suffer if it became known as the think-tank equivalent of an ambulance-chasing lawyer instead of a place where serious high-quality research is done. There might be social costs as well. Pure research, and research that has a longer-term payoff are collective goods, but it may prove easier to seek contracts for applied research with immediate practical applications. Careful design and implementation of the bonus system could reduce these unintended side-effects. For example, bonuses could be partly based on dollars brought in and partly based on importance of the contract to the organizational mission.

Compensation schemes may also affect donor willingness to give, and this cost could outweigh productivity gains in some cases. An organization that is seen as too aggressively pursuing contracts may look less worthy of donative support. Of course, this only matters if the research institute relies on donations for a substantive part of its budget and donors are aware of the structure of compensation.

The arts

- A museum sells art reproductions in its gift shop. At what quality and price should these items be offered for sale?

The sale of art reproductions by a museum may have dual objectives – generating profits that support the operations of the institution and promoting art appreciation through the dissemination of knowledge about cultural treasures. Neglecting the second objective for the moment, we still have a complicated problem – pick two variables (quality and quantity) to maximize profits. Further simplifying by assuming the museum has a monopoly on this market, we have two marginal conditions to solve. The first is the familiar one for monopolies – pick the quantity that makes MR = MC. The logic of the second equation comes straight out of thinking on the margin – pick the quality that makes the marginal revenue stemming from a one unit increase in quality equal to the marginal cost of quality. With two equations in two unknowns, we should have enough information to solve for the optimal quality and quantity, but the calculation is complicated by interdependencies. Each level of quality has a different demand curve associated with it, hence a different marginal revenue curve associated with the quantity of production, and a different price corresponding to the optimal quantity on the demand curve. To make the problem manageable, treat quality as a discrete variable that can take on two or three values (high/low or high/medium/low). Then calculate the optimal price and quantity for each quality level, calculate profits, and pick the quality level with the highest profits.

Now suppose that the museum has both objectives for art reproductions. James (1983) offers a mathematical appendix that shows how to trade off positive effects of an activity on revenues against positive, negative, or neutral effects on the organization's mission. The full treatment of James's approach is beyond the scope of this book, but intuitively we are buying mission attainment by spending some potential profits on selling more, or higher quality, reproductions. Another complication, beyond the scope of this book, is that it might make sense to produce several quality levels – a low-quality print sold to help profits and a high-quality reproduction sold to educate the public and help people to appreciate the cultural artifacts in the museum. Finally, if the museum faces competition, it still has some market power for reproductions of unique objects in its collection. Reproductions of a Van Gogh painting on display in the Musee d'Orsay will be more profitable than the same reproductions sold elsewhere. Still, there are all the game theoretic complications of duopoly to worry about (as discussed in Chapters 8 and 11).

● An orchestra requires major repairs to its concert hall. Should it dip into its endowment to undertake these repairs?

First, we have to be clear about the definition of *endowment* as used in this question. Federal laws in the United States such as UPMIFA (the Uniform Prudent Management of Institutional Funds Act) define endowment as a fund permanently restricted by the donor. The donor restriction may conform with the popular conception of an endowment: a fund whose principal (initial sum of money) must remain invested and unavailable for current use, whereas any earnings from those investments (dividends, interest, and capital gains) can be spent annually. Or the donor restriction may be that the principal can only be used to fund student financial aid or some other specific purpose. Funds that are treated according to the popular conception because the board has decided to treat them that way are, technically, called *quasi-endowments*. They are not "real" endowments because the board could end those restrictions whenever it wants to. So, the legally-correct answer to this question is absolutely not, unless the donor has permanently restricted the fund to pay for repairs and maintenance and has not imposed a restriction on spending the corpus.

Really, this is a question about the economics of quasi-endowment spending – whether the board should relax the don't-spend-the-principal restriction to make essential repairs. This leads to questions about why the quasi-endowment was restricted in the first place. If the endowment was set up merely to take advantage of growth through investments, the decision is simply financial.

Orchestra managers must ask "what is the opportunity cost of using these funds and what benefits are produced by spending on the repairs?" The opportunity costs involve lost investment returns on the endowment funds, a proxy for lost future benefits from the programs of the orchestra those funds would have supported. The benefits include reduced future maintenance costs because the hall is not allowed to deteriorate further, and perhaps more net revenues from performances if the hall were otherwise unusable or uncomfortable to patrons and performers. (Debussy's "Clouds" takes on a whole new meaning if the concert hall's roof leaks!)

There might be other reasons for establishing the quasi-endowment, and these complicate the decision. It might be that the spending restriction is designed to enforce fiscal discipline. Behavioral economics teaches us that rational long-run behavior is difficult to achieve in the face of short-run temptations. Quasi-endowments might be established as a nudge to make it harder for the board to spend prematurely. Because quasi-endowment restrictions can be reversed by the board, this is a soft nudge rather than a hard requirement. In order to reverse the decision to hold funds from current use, the board members are first reminded that it must reverse its previous decision, and this might make the board more reluctant to do so. Or it might be that the quasi-endowment fund was established because donors want assurances that their unrestricted gifts be treated like permanently restricted ones. If the orchestra maintains a reputation for preserving the corpus of the quasi-endowment, donors do not have to employ lawyers to insure their desired restrictions (Hansmann, 1990). In these two cases, it may be preferable to secure a bank loan even if the interest rate is higher than the rate of return on the quasi-endowment, provided that the difference is not too great. Another alternative to tapping quasi-endowment is to conduct a capital campaign for the building fund, but these take time that might not be available in the face of rapid decay of the building.

Social services

- A community agency for the elderly runs a day-care program and a Meals on Wheels program. How should it assign its limited staff and allocate its budget between the two programs?

The manager of this organization needs to think at the margin. How many added meals can be served by shifting a staff position from the day-care program to the Meals on Wheels program and what will be the loss in terms of output in the day-care program? What is the value of these changes in outputs at the margin? Is marginal revenue the proper measure of value or should the changes in outputs be gauged in terms of a more comprehensive measure of social benefits for each service like weighted or unweighted consumer, producer, and social surpluses? Thus, the manager must ask what the organization's objectives are before she can make the appropriate trade-offs.

Once the appropriate measure of value is selected, we have a familiar choice between two ways of achieving the same goal. The rule for such cases is that whenever the returns of a dollar spent on one program exceed the returns of a dollar spent on the second program, you should spend more on the first and less on the second. This rule can be applied at the program level or at the level of individual resources available to either program like staff, supplies, and equipment. The marginal worker assigned to the day-care program produces marginal day-care output and hence marginal day-care value. If day care is unrelated to the organizational mission, and day care is sold in a competitive market, then this marginal value is $MPL_{daycare} \times P_{daycare}$. If this is greater than $MPL_{meals} \times P_{meals}$ and the worker's wage does not have to be adjusted when he is transferred, he should be shifted from Meals on Wheels to day care. If instead wage changes must accompany the internal transfer (say, because hazard pay is needed before the worker is willing to drive the Meals on Wheels van in dangerous neighborhoods), then we want to compare the value of a dollar spent on staff in one program against the value of a dollar spent on staff in the other. Thus, we want to compare $(MPL_{daycare} \times P_{daycare})/wage_{daycare}$ with the corresponding figure for Meals on Wheels.

Alternatively, it is possible that the manager sees the two services as addressing different objectives. Meals on Wheels might be a "cash cow," the value of which is to produce profits that can be used to subsidize the day-care program. Then the agency should maximize its profits from Meals on Wheels (setting MR equal to MC) and use those profits to increase the quantity of day care. If so, the MR from day care would be much smaller than the MC of day care. If both activities advance the organizational mission, or if one of the two activities hurts the mission but is so profitable that when it is used as a cash cow the mission gain from cross-subsidizing the mission-advancing activity outweighs the cost, then the James (1983) model of nonprofits with multiple activities provides complete guidance.

- An international relief agency receives a grant to assist war refugees who are scattered among several countries. How can it target the expenditure of those funds to have the greatest impact?

Assuming that the agency has programs in each of the countries where refugees are congregating, the question here is where contributions at the margin in these countries will have the largest impact. The definition of impact is not an easy one here, but the agency must choose an appropriate metric, such as the number of refugees resettled, or the number of refugees brought into minimally acceptable living conditions. Then the problem is again familiar: divide up resettlement efforts so that they produce equal marginal value in terms of the organization's preferences. The costs of operating in the various countries may differ, governments may hinder NGO operations in some countries and assist NGO operations in others, some refugees will be easy to resettle, and others will be blocked because available relocation sites restrict immigration. All these factors enter into the targeting calculation.

If possible, the relief agency should consider the *counterfactual* when making its decisions. This requires it to assess how the current situation in the various migrant camps will change if the relief agency does not act. Will governments take care of refugees, exile them, or make camp conditions so bad that the refugees will leave of their own accord? Will other charitable or quasi-governmental agencies address resettlement issues if this relief agency does not? Benefits and costs should be weighed against the counterfactual.

But now, with human lives at stake, some may have ethical qualms about assigning finite values to saving people. If so, cost-effectiveness analysis provides an end run, focusing as it does on the cost per life saved or cost per refugee appropriately resettled. To use cost-effectiveness analysis, we have to assume that all the alternatives considered produce the same outcome. However, that assumption may well be violated here. War refugees may have problems specific to their temporary homes – in one camp, a lack of water; in another, no shelter from the elements; in a third, a cholera epidemic. If so, economic efficiency can only be obtained if we overcome our ethical qualms and establish dollar-equivalent values to outcomes.

Note that this logic does not account for considerations of equity – is it "fair" and "just" to favor refugees in certain countries or from certain religious, ethnic, or cultural groups over others? Nor does it account for geopolitical strategic concerns – where is it most important to help refugees in order to maintain societal stability or world peace? If those concerns are paramount, the measure of impact would change but the logic of thinking at the margin would still apply.

Other subsectors

- An environmental advocacy group is mounting a campaign advocating hazardous waste clean-up in its community. Should it hire a paid public relations staff or continue to rely exclusively on volunteer efforts?

The answer depends on relative costs and effectiveness. If the organization hires a paid staff member, it must bear the costs of her salary and benefits and the necessary supplies and services to support her work. It makes little sense to hire someone for a short project, so that unless the campaign requires continuous tinkering over an extended period of time, the firm should sub-contract the task to a self-employed public relations consultant. There are, in any case, transactions costs associated with hiring for a new position. If volunteers are utilized, the organization must consider both the opportunity cost of that volunteer time (in terms of its value to the advocacy group in the next best alternative use of volunteers) as well as the costs of recruiting, organizing and supervising volunteers. In either case, there could be *agency costs* if the employees or volunteers' interests do not align with the advocacy group in a way that ensures the success of the campaign.

The leaders of the environmental group will, naturally, also want to consider differences in effectiveness between employees and volunteers. Sometimes volunteers are more committed to the cause and the use of volunteers, if known by the public, signals a level of sincerity that may raise the effectiveness of the campaign. However, outsiders are unlikely to know whether volunteers or paid professionals are being used. Thus, the paid professional is likely to be more effective because of training and experience. Low quality public relations professionals are not likely to make a career in the business, so survival in the market is also an indicator that the professional is effective. There are no such signals for volunteers.

If the opportunity costs of employing paid professionals are lower than those for volunteers, and paid professionals are more effective, then the decision is obvious. If instead paid professionals cost more, the advocacy group will have to judge whether the added effectiveness is worth the added cost – a willingness-to-pay decision for the group.

- A community foundation administers a system of "donor-advised funds" (DAFs) through which local donors can make gifts to the foundation and then advise the foundation on how to allocate those funds to selected charities. DAFs offer a convenient and inexpensive way for major donors to oversee their philanthropies without having to administer their own foundations. What minimum level of donation should the community foundation require for establishing such a fund?

Each additional DAF entails a cost to the foundation consisting of the staff time associated with setting up the fund, investing the principal of the fund, overseeing expenditures made from it, and advising the donor about alternative charitable investments. At the same time, the lower the minimum investment required, the more donors will want to establish such funds, although the size of such funds is likely to diminish as additional (less wealthy) donors join the program.

Some DAFs charge administrative fees to cover the transactions costs of setting up the account and investment fees to cover the costs of investing the principal. Usually, there are no separate fees for operating costs, like making a disbursement from the fund to an eligible charity, so the other fees must cover these costs. Therefore, the foundation has to establish a fee structure before we can determine the answer to the question. If fees are set high enough, there is no need for a minimum level of donation. But the community foundation faces competition from other for-profit and nonprofit DAF sponsors, and this limits their ability to raise fees. For example, Fidelity Charitable charges an administrative fee of $100 or 0.6 percent of the initial donation, whichever is greater, for those selecting investment in their Conservative Income pool (as of the writing of this book. See Fidelity Investments, 2018). If the community foundation matches this rate, it will be paid $100 in administrative fees unless the initial donation is greater than $16,666.67. Fidelity offers a range of investment fees but using the 0.54 percent illustrated in the example they post online, an initial donation of $5000 would have an annual investment fee of $26.50.

Transactions costs are the same for big and small initial donations. If the community foundation matches Fidelity rates, the question is: does $100 cover all the costs of establishing and managing a $1 fund? If so, there is no need for a minimum investment. If not, the foundation would only break-even if $100 + 0.0054 × *minimum investment* is greater than or equal to foundation costs. Solving this equation gives a minimum investment that would be competitive and cover costs.

Community foundations typically offer two options. Donations can be made to the general fund, in which case the community foundation decides which nonprofits receive grants from those donations, or to a DAF, where the donor advises on those decisions. Foundations should be mindful that their policies on DAFs will affect donations to the general fund, and weigh these changes according to its mission.

Social enterprises

- A social justice nonprofit seeks to enhance the prospects of ex-felons in the labor force. Should it employ such individuals directly by running a business such as a landscaping company, or should it invest in advocacy programs to reduce legal barriers to employment of individuals with prison records in the general labor force?

This is a difficult decision, as it requires a mix of perspectives and evidence from economics, other business disciplines, and criminology. A full discussion would be lengthy because social enterprises can be for-profit, nonprofit, or some kind of hybrid, and sector matters here. Regardless of sector, the operation must be financially viable, and there are questions here about both alternatives. Businesses that employ ex-felons have higher insurance costs and may have greater agency costs, although this could go either way. The fact that ex-felons have few alternative employment prospects means that should they shirk or otherwise perform at less than their best and get caught, the penalty would be more severe than it is for most people. This deters workers from shirking and so the principal–agent problem is smaller for businesses employing ex-felons. On the other hand, if some workers retain their criminal ways, there is money to be made from pilfering valuable plants and equipment, making the principal–agent problem larger. We are only speculating here, and these issues have doubtless been the subject of previous studies, so our first task would be to hire an expert in the criminology research literature to advise on business viability. And, of course, a market analysis is necessary to see whether another landscape company can prosper in the local competitive market. That said, if the business loses money, it may still be viable. Nonprofit social enterprises can cross-subsidize the business with earnings from other commercial activities, grants, donations, and government contracts that reward the vendor for employing ex-felons. (For-profit social enterprises can also cross-subsidize a negative profit activity using earnings from other products, but grant or donor funding is unlikely.)

Advocacy must also be financially viable. Advocacy itself generates no revenue to cover the costs, so once again the activity must be cross-subsidized. Sector matters because it determines which sources are available to fund the subsidy and because advocacy is regulated and has tax consequences that are different across the sectors. The nonprofit should investigate whether advocacy can be effectively promoted in ways that do not endanger the organization's tax-exempt status and eligibility to receive tax deductible donations.

A more general comparison of the two alternatives requires cost–benefit analysis. There are no new complexities on the cost side, but in order to monetize the benefits, we first have to understand the effect of the employment and advocacy outputs on the outcomes that the social enterprise cares about. There is already a vast literature containing theory and empirical results on the effects of various employment programs and public policy reforms on employment prospects, and this literature might help assess the size and direction of the link from outputs to outcomes. An expert on this literature should be consulted to help the manager efficiently find comprehensible digests of the most relevant findings. This literature might also help the manager or analyst to understand the necessary counterfactual assumptions – assumptions about employment prospects if neither the landscaping business nor advocacy effort is in place. Benefits are always gains against counterfactuals. Perhaps, absent the landscaping business, some of those who would be employed as landscapers instead return to school. This would enable the ex-felons to gain higher-paying employment prospects; in this case the benefit of the landscaping employment would be negative. Or perhaps absent the advocacy effort, the efforts of other advocacy groups would suffice to change policy in the desired direction. If so, there would be no benefit to this organization's advocacy program. Because it may be unclear what the relevant counterfactual assumptions should be for each program, the cost–benefit analysis should conduct sensitivity analyses to see how the net social benefits of each program would compare under various plausible counterfactual assumptions.

Finally, there are differences in timing and scale and scope between the two programs. The costs and benefits of the landscaping business occur every year into the indefinite future, but the costs of advocacy end when the advocacy succeeds in changing laws and regulations and the benefits of advocacy occur only after the advocacy succeeds. Present value calculations account for these differences in timing. The landscaping venture is restricted in scale and can hire no more ex-felons than the local market allows (although perhaps the venture can be replicated in other communities). The venture is also restricted to employing those ex-felons who regard a job in landscaping as the best available alternative. In contrast, legal and regulatory reforms at the state government level resulting from advocacy efforts affect the employment prospects of every ex-felon in the state. This scale and scope difference might swamp other elements of the cost–benefit calculation, allowing the analyst to be less attentive to these other elements.

- A for-profit social business seeks to promote literacy by buying or receiving donated used books, selling some of them and distributing others free of charge to schools in low-income neighborhoods. How can it best decide how much to sell and how much to give away?

As a social business, this organization has two bottom lines – profit and social impact. The politically hard part would be for the management team to agree on how they would make trade-offs between the two goals. How much profit is the firm willing to sacrifice for a one-unit increase in the output "free book-distribution?" The firm should choose the level of free book-distribution that equates the marginal benefit (expressed in willingness to pay terms) and the marginal cost (amount of profit foregone). Here, we have simplified this decision by looking at benefits and costs of outputs rather than outcomes, but managers should keep in mind that free books are only a means to the desired outcome, promotion of literacy. Free books that people want to read contribute to literacy; free books that will not be read do not.

The firm is deciding how much to sell (and at what price) and how much to give away. The problem conveys the essence of every optimization problem in economics. There is an objective; the two distinct bottom lines become a single objective when the firm agrees on its willingness to trade profits for literacy promotion. There are constraints on what the firm can do (discussed shortly) and there are choice variables under the control of the firm (discussed next).

Used books are not all the same – they vary in condition and contents. The firm is not picking a single price, quantity to sell, and quantity to give away; rather it is picking prices and quantities for each title and book condition. One choice it could make is to charge the same price for all titles and book conditions, but this choice would not be the best way to advance the organization's goals. To simplify in a realistic way, suppose the firm feels that the advantages of charging multiple prices (depending on a book's condition) for the same title are too small to justify much thought. Then, they would choose one price for each title, and would just toss (or give away) those books that are not marketable at the chosen price.

The firm faces several constraints. First, the choices must be financially viable. Either the book sales are sufficiently profitable to enable operations for both free and priced books, or there is some cross-subsidy available to the firm that fully finances losses from books. Second, the choices must be sustainable. Depending on the form of legal incorporation and choice of governance mechanisms, sustainability might or might not be a problem, but there are two challenges here. First, managerial decisions must be acceptable to the current board of directors, who might not be willing to approve of social ventures that lose too much money. Second, managerial decisions must not provoke hostile takeover bids, where people buy a controlling share of stock in order to replace the current board with more profit-minded board members (Steinberg, 2015). Third, used books are, by definition, resalable. Those receiving free books might be tempted to sell them, and while schools in low-income neighborhoods can certainly use profits from resale, doing so would interfere with the literacy mission of the firm. If the paid books are sold at a sufficiently low price, resale of free books would fall, but so would profit. Thus although the firm can solve the resale problem with market prices, it is better off finding some other approach, such as donating them on the condition that they not be resold.

To the extent that the firm has market power in the resale market for particular titles available, it should first pick the quantity of sales that makes MR = MC and charge a price on the demand curve above that point. From that starting point, the firm can remove some low-income school districts from the demand curve and see how that changes decisions and profits from paid books. As each group of low-income school districts is removed from the paid-book demand curve and placed in the free books category, the firm can decide whether the added social benefit is worth the reduced profits. The optimal solution is found when the marginal (in this case, incremental) benefits equal the marginal (incremental) costs. If the firm has no market power in the resale market for some or all books, the calculation is a bit easier. Each time a group of school districts is moved from the paid demand curve to the free books group, the price at which it will sell books is unchanged. There is still a profit/social benefit trade-off, but the firm does not need to know the full market demand curve for the book, just the market price.

A pretty good, if not optimal, solution is to *triage* incoming books by their likely financial versus social returns. For example, children's and teen's books and primary and secondary school educational textbooks might be judged to have greater social impact and low market value, while popular fiction or general interest nonfiction (including this textbook, which is pitched at the graduate and advanced undergraduate level) would have lower social value but higher market value (or so the authors hope). If books are triaged in this way, the former can be given away and the latter can be sold, with profits used to provide additional donations of money or books to literary promotion efforts. If titles can be placed on a scale ranging from maximum social impact (on the left) to maximum resale value (on the right) then the choice of where to draw the line between the two categories is an exercise in thinking at the margin. The line between categories is the book title that is equally valuable to the firm when sold or given away, and everything to the left of that line should be given away.

In this example, there are only two groups – paying customers, and charitable beneficiaries. But nothing in the economics of the situation restricts us to two groups. There could be three – a market-price group, a subsidized-price group, and a free-book group. Or there could be different rates of subsidy for different subgroups. The problem then becomes a more complicated one, with additional trade-offs to consider. For example, if there is a subsidized price group, does it consist of those with the lowest willingness to pay (presumably the neediest) or the highest willingness to pay (but still needing a subsidy) group? The firm can afford to serve more school districts if it chooses the latter, so this is a type of quality/quantity trade-off (Steinberg and Weisbrod, 2005).

SUMMARY

What do we learn from these dozen vignettes? We think the answer is that the real world is more complicated than most textbook treatments. Basic economic principles do apply to each of these scenarios, but the proper application of these concepts requires attention to particular details of organizational form, markets, and available choices. We don't always want to maximize profits, as taught in more traditional economics textbooks, but we do want to maximize something and thinking at the margin applies. Revenue from sales is not the only source of revenue and costs of production are not the only costs, but social managers always want to use opportunity costs for their decisions. Donors are not irrational for giving away some of their money without getting anything tangible in return, although cognitive illusions color their decision making. The rules and payoffs in nonprofit and social enterprise games are different from those of poker, nuclear strategy, and for-profit duopoly but game theory still structures interdependent decision making.

We have taught some tools, ranging from simple to complicated, quick and easy to slow and costly. In practical use, compromises should be made. Instead of taking the time and investing the money for a full-blown cost–benefit analysis, with distributional weights and precise estimates of how every person is affected by a project and precise estimates of the values of nontraded goods for every decision, we suggest a graduated approach that weighs the benefits and costs of more sophisticated analyses. Readers may never do a cost–benefit analysis, but we think they will be better managers for thinking through what is involved here, as this will guide their intuition and judgment in more productive directions.

Readers, please take a look at the vignettes from Chapter 1 that we haven't discussed here. How would you have made managerial decisions for each case before you studied this book? How would you make them now?

When you consider a practical approach to timely decision making, what will you leave out of your analysis? Will thinking at the margin help you decide, even if you don't have all the marginal cost and marginal benefit numbers? Will you incorporate implicit costs that you would have neglected before? Will you consider strategic reactions by other people and organizations to your managerial decisions, and whether there is a strategic counter-reaction you could employ before making your decisions? If so, we have accomplished our main goal and wish you well as you pursue yours.

SELECTED REFERENCES AND CITATIONS

Fidelity Investments (2018). Benefits of the Giving Account. Retrieved from https://www.fidelitycharitable.org/giving-account/giving-account-details.shtml (accessed July 10, 2018).

Hansmann, H. (1990). Why do Universities have Endowments? *The Journal of Legal Studies*, *19(1)*, 3–42.

James, E. (1983). How Nonprofits Grow: A Model. *Journal of Policy Analysis and Management*, *2(3)*, 350–365.

Nelsen, W.C. (1991). Incentive-based Management for Nonprofit Organizations. *Nonprofit Management and Leadership*, *2(1)*, 59–69.

Steinberg, R. (2015). What Should Social Finance Invest In and With Whom? In Nicholls, A., Paton, R., and Emerson, J. (Eds.), *Social Finance* (pp. 64–95). Oxford: Oxford University Press.

Steinberg, R. and Weisbrod, B.A. (2005). Nonprofits with Distributional Objectives: Price Discrimination and Corner Solutions. *Journal of Public Economics*, *89*, 2205–2230.

REVIEW CONCEPTS

Agency Costs: Costs incurred by a principal (a person or organization that asks for the assistance of others) because the agent (helper) might have interests in the task that differ from the principal's interests. Agency costs include the opportunity costs of monitoring, providing incentives, and suffering the consequences of remaining agency costs.

Counterfactual: What would happen if a policy or program is not implemented, a scenario constructed to compare with what will happen.

Cross-subsidization: The use of profits from one activity to subsidize the costs of another activity.

Differencing Tests: Used to determine whether the right amount is spent on fund-raising. It is the ratio of historic changes in donations divided by changes in fund-raising expenditures. Net donations are maximized when the ratio equals one; more should be spent if it is greater than one, and less should be spent if the ratio is less than one. A second differencing test is used to decide whether fund-raising expenditures are divided across campaigns or fund-raising methods in an efficient way.

Donor-advised Fund (DAF): A donor fund set up and managed by a public charity that allows donors to make a charitable contribution that is disbursed by the charity following advice from the donor.

Endowment: In legal use, refers to funds permanently restricted by the donor, especially restrictions that prohibit the recipient from spending the corpus (original donation), endowments allow an organization to spend income derived from the corpus. In popular use, endowment is the sum of legal endowment and quasi-endowment.

Quasi-endowment: Funds set aside by (reversible) action of the organization's board, where the initial board allocation is treated like corpus and not spent, but income derived from the allocation can be spent.

Triage: A system for dividing a set of potential beneficiaries into three categories – those that will survive regardless, those that will die regardless, and those that treatment might help. More generally, a process of prioritizing problems and addressing them in order of importance.

Index